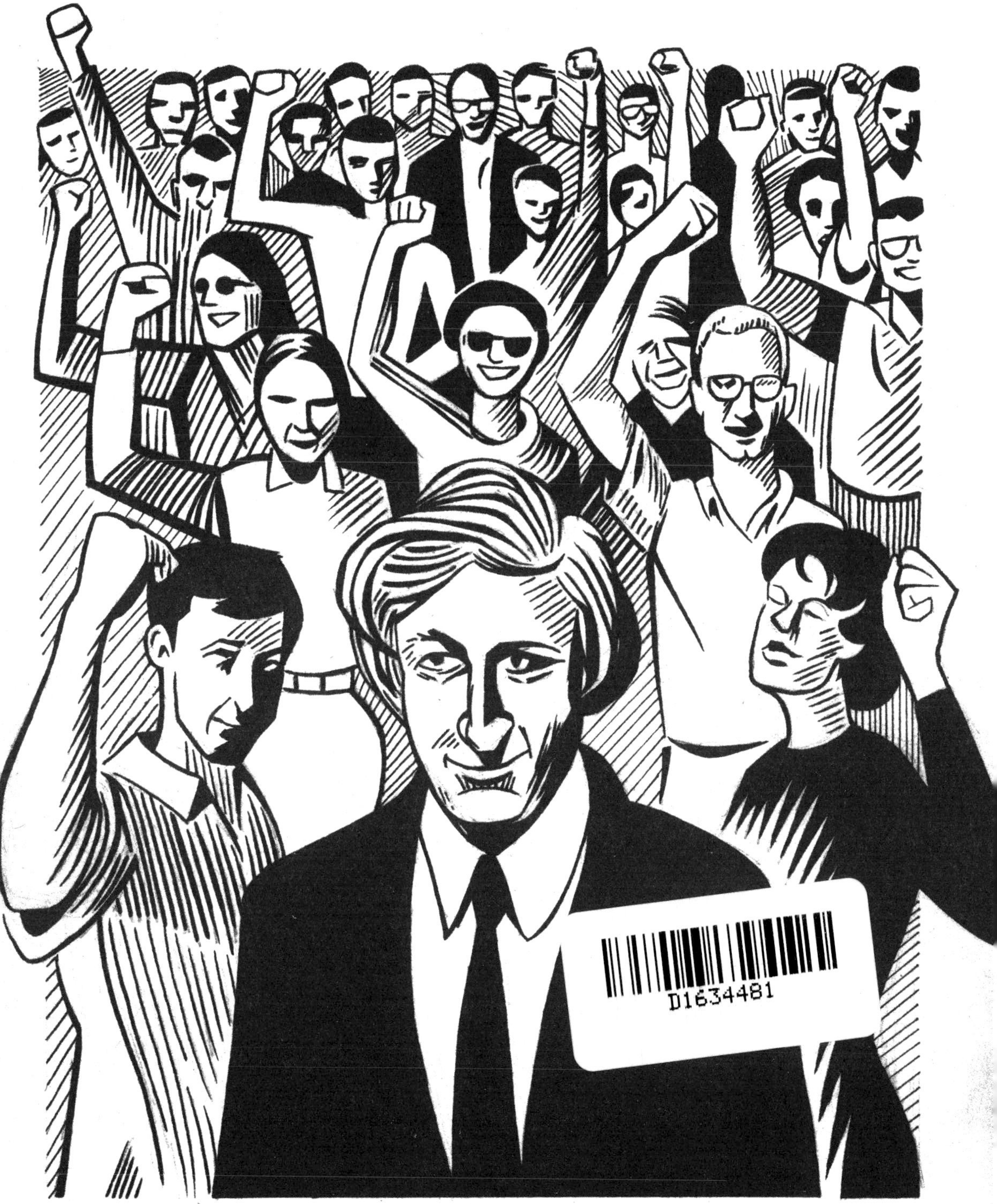

AK PRESS

Len, A Lawyer in History: A Graphic Biography of Radical Attorney Leonard Weinglass

Edited by Paul Buhle and Michael Steven Smith
Illustrated and written by Seth Tobocman

Len, A Lawyer in History:
A Graphic Biography of Radical Attorney Leonard Weinglass

ISBN: 978-1-84935-240-6
E-ISBN: 978-1-84935-241-3
Library of Congress Control Number: 2015959320

AK Press   AK Press
370 Ryan Ave. #100   PO Box 12766
Chico, CA 95973   Edinburgh EH8 9YE
USA   Scotland
www.akpress.org   www.akuk.com
akpress@akpress.org   ak@akedin.demon.co.uk

The above addresses would be delighted to provide you with the latest AK
Press distribution catalog, which features books, pamphlets, zines, and stylish
apparel published and/or distributed by AK Press. Alternatively, visit our
websites for the complete catalog, latest news, and secure ordering.

Cover painting and illustrations by Seth Tobocman
Inked by: Tamara Tornado, Jordan Worley, Jess Wehrle, and Hayley Gold
Graphic Assistant: Hayley Gold
Printed in the USA on acid-free, recycled paper

CONTENTS

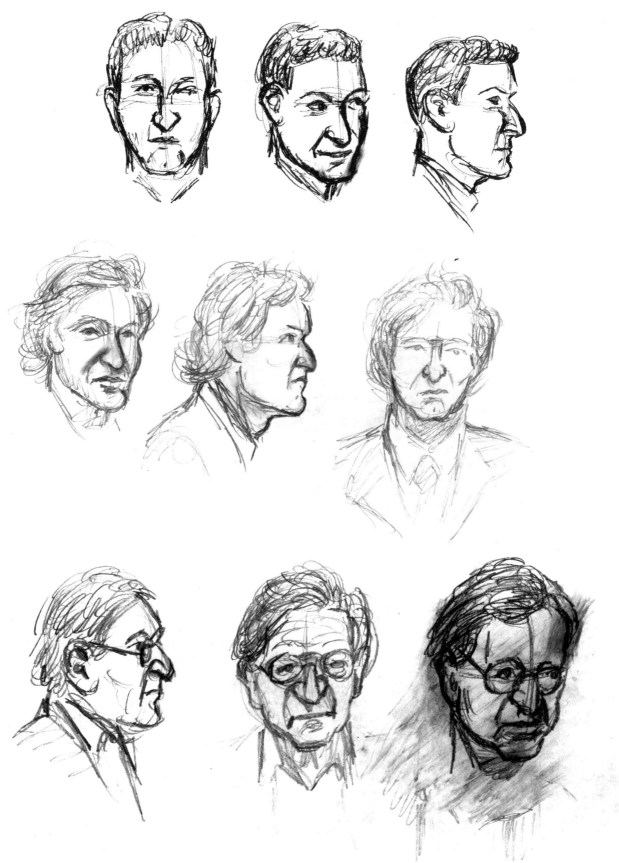

INTRODUCTION

Michael Steven Smith

"Death is not real when one's life work is done well. Even in death, certain men radiate the light of an aurora." —José Martí

Len was not a sixties radical. He was something more unusual: he was a fifties radical. He developed his values, his critical thinking and world view in a time when non-conforming was rare. In 1980, he told a newspaper interviewer in Santa Barbara that "I would classify myself as a radical American. I am anti-capitalist in this sense—I don't believe capitalism is now compatible with democracy." He thought socialism could be, if given a chance. Len argued that socialism was still a young phenomenon on the world scene, that another world, a non-capitalist world, was possible.

He saw his legal work as his contribution to the collective work of the movement. He didn't care a bit about making a fee. "I want to spend my time defending people who have committed their time to progressive change. That's the criteria. Now, that could be people in armed struggle, people in protest politics, people in confrontational politics, people in mass organizations, people in labor." Defending people against "the machinery of the state," as he put it, was his calling. He felt that one may have a fulfilled and satisfying life if one "aligns with the major thrust of forces in the time in which you live."

The third of four children, he grew up in a Jewish community of two-hundred families in Bellville, NJ and attended high school in nearby Kearney, where he was a star on the football team and vice president of his high school class. He played saxophone, was tall and handsome, and sported a fifties pompadour hair style, spending a lot of grooming time behind a closed door and in front of the bathroom mirror. His father jokingly complained that he had raised a girl.

When Len graduated, he wanted to take a trip across the country to California. He got his father to drive him to the highway. His dad sat in his car weeping as Len hoisted his thumb at passing trucks. Soon an eighteen wheeler stopped and Len piled in. He called often from the road, reporting that he was frequently picked up by cars and trucks, that everyone was nice to him, buying him meals and that he was making good time on his trip west.

He didn't take any identification with him. There was a lot of anti-semitism in the US in the early fifties. Len didn't want people seeing his last name was Weinglass and identifying him as a Jew. When he got to California he got work on a truck farm, doing stoop farm labor with Japanese agricultural workers. One night one of them was killed. Len was afraid that without an ID he would be a suspect. He jumped the fence in the middle of the night and got out of there.

He went on to George Washington University in DC for college on a scholarship. Len was an outstanding student and was accepted in 1955 into Yale Law School.

Len went from Yale in 1958 directly into the Air Force. In those days, because of the draft, there was no choice; one had to go into the military. Len was a lawyer in the Judge Advocate General's Corp and rose from second lieutenant to the rank of captain. The Air Force had charged a black airman with some sort of crime. Len was assigned the case and got him acquitted. This infuriated the brass, which was used to exerting its command influence over the results of military trials.

He was discharged from the Air Force in 1961 and went on to set up a one-man law practice in Newark, New Jersey. When interviewed by the *New York Times* for Len's obituary, Len's friend and law colleague Michael Krinsky (Len was of counsel to the firm Rabinowitz, Boudin, Standard, Krinsky & Lieberman of New York, NY) said he first met Len in Newark in 1969. He considered him "a modern day Clarence Darrow".

Krinsky told the reporter that Newark "was a rough place to be. A police department and a city administration that was racist and as terrifying as any in America, and there was Lenny representing civil rights people, political people, ordinary people who got charged with stuff and got beat up by the cops. He did it without fame or fortune, and that's what he kept doing, in one way or another." He did it for fifty-three years, being admitted to the bars in New Jersey, California, and New York.

We all know of Len for his famous legal work in the Chicago Seven case with Abbie Hoffman, Dave Dellinger, and Tom Hayden during the Vietnam War period. We remember his expertise in advocating for death-row inmate Mumia Abu-Jamal. He finally got his friend Kathy Boudin out of prison after twenty-three years. He represented Puerto Rican independentista Juan Segarra for fifteen years. In the Palestine 8 case, where the defendants were charged with aiding the Marxist Popular Front for the Liberation of Palestine, he was part of a team that stopped their deportation. That took twenty years. David Cole, his co-counsel along with Marc Van der Hout, remembers that Len "coined the term 'terrorologist' while cross-examining the government's expert witness on the PLO. He was a joy to work with in the courtroom. Whenever there was a proceeding, our immigration judge, who was Lenny's age, always eagerly wanted to know whether 'Mr. Weinglass' would be appearing."

Len took the tough political cases, the seemingly impossible ones where his clients were charged with heavy crimes like kidnap, espionage, and murder. "He wasn't drawn to making money. He was drawn to defending justice," Daniel Ellsberg said. "He felt in many cases he was representing one person standing against the state. He was on the side of the underdog. He was also very shrewd in his judgment of juries." Len said that a typical phone call he received started out with the caller saying, "'You're the fifth lawyer I've spoken to'. Then I get interested."

The Cuban Five was Len's last major case. He worked on it for years up to the time of his passing, even reading a court submission from his bed in Montefiore Hospital in the Bronx. The case highlighted what Len considered the US government's hypocrisy in its "war against terror."

Len came into the matter at the appellate level after the Five had been convicted by a prejudiced jury in Miami. His client Antonio Guererro and the others were found guilty of conspiracy to commit espionage against the US sometime in the future. They were sent from Cuba to Miami by the government of Cuba to spy, not on the US, but on the counter-revolutionary Cubans in Miami who were launching terrorist activities from Florida directed at persons and property in Cuba, attempting to sabotage the Cuban tourist economy. They gathered information on the Miami-based terrorists, compiling a lengthy dossier on their murderous activities, and turned it over to the FBI. They asked the US government to stop the terrorists, who were targeting the Cuban tourist industry by planting bombs at the Havana airport, on buses, and in an hotel, killing an Italian vacationer. But instead of stopping the terrorists, the US government used the dossier to figure out the identities of the Cuban Five, had them arrested, prosecuted, convicted, and sentenced to long prison terms.

What Len said about the use of the conspiracy charge is illustrative of his precision and clarity of thought.

Conspiracy has always been the charge used by the prosecution in political cases. A conspiracy is an agreement between people to commit a substantive crime. By using the charge of conspiracy, the government is relieved of the requirement that the underlying crime be proven. All the government has to prove to a jury is that there was an agreement to do the crime. The individuals charged with conspiracy are convicted even if the underlying crime was never committed. In the case of the Five, the Miami jury was asked to find that there was an agreement to commit espionage. The government never had to prove that espionage actually happened. It could not have proven that espionage occurred. None of the Five sought or possessed any top secret information or US national defense secrets.

Len had an ironic and wry sense of humor. He had a large one-room cabin atop a high hill overlooking the Rondout reservoir in New York's Catskill Mountains. He lived in a teepee there off and on for several years before designing the cottage. He had a special joy, which he inherited from his mother Clara, for gardening and raising fruit trees. This was an especially difficult pursuit because he had mistakenly planted the trees on the south side of the hill where they got plenty of sun but were vulnerable to a false spring, blooming early, then getting damaged by a frost, which could occur up there as late as June. Nonetheless Len persisted and sometimes got a crop of apples, pears, and plums. The crop would then be eaten by the neighborhood bears. "I grow the fruit," Len complained, "then the bears come and eat it and I go to Gristedes."

He kept his sense of humor even during those terrible final days at Montefiore Hospital. His surgeon operated on him but abandoned his attempt to remove what turned out to be a large spreading malignant tumor, undetected by the pre-op CTscan. When the surgeon saw what it really was, that it was an inoperable tumor, he could do nothing but sew Len back up and tell him the bad news. Len looked up at us from his bed in the recovery room after being informed by the surgeon, and said, simply, "summary judgement." And so it was. He lived but another six weeks, steadily declining, never getting to go home, never giving up, even as several doctors told him "you are in the final stretch."

Len was strong and vigorous up to his last illness. Since his high school days he never lost his interest in football, and closely followed the professional game. He was a Giants fan of course, but sentimentally he liked the Green Bay Packers because they were the only team in the league owned not by billionaires, but by the municipality of Green Bay. While Len was in Montefiore Hospital the Packers made it into the Superbowl against the Pittsburgh Steelers. "Want to bet on the game?" I asked. "How about five bucks." He raised his finger to the sky. "Ten?" I ventured. "No," he whispered, "fifty." So my nephew Ben got us a bookie in Connecticut and we put down fifty bucks apiece. The Packers were favored so we had to give away 3½ points. Len advised that this was a responsible bet. It sure was. The Packers wound up winning in the last quarter by 4 points. I congratulated Len on his sagacity. That win lifted his spirits.

Len was a longtime member of the National Lawyers Guild and served for a time as the co-chair of its international committee. He was the recipient of the Guild's Ernie Goodman Award, named after the extraordinary Detroit socialist lawyer and Guild leader who helped build the auto workers union and later organized the Guild to send its members down south to protect black people during the civil rights movement.

The Dean of Yale Law School, Robert C. Post, wrote Len's sister Elaine to express his sympathy, writing that "Leonard Weinglass lived a full and admirable life in the law and exemplified the spirit of citizenship that lawyers at their very best display. He brought great honor to the legal community and to Yale Law School, which takes pride in all he did and was."

Len was a Jew, but rejected the idea that it was racial ties or bonds of blood that made up the Jewish community, seeing that view as a degenerate philosophy leading to chauvinism and cruelty. He rejected Jewish nationalism, embracing instead an unconditional solidarity with the persecuted and exterminated.

Len was not religious. The emergency room admitting nurse asked him what his religion was so she could fill out the questionnaire. He paused and answered, "Leave it blank." Two weeks later, when he was admitted to the hospital, he again was asked what his religion was. "None," he answered. Religion to Len was superstition. Being part of a sect was too narrow and confining for Len. The Jewish heretic who transcends Jewry belongs to a Jewish tradition. The historian Isaac Deutscher had a phrase for it, "the non-Jewish Jew." Len was in line with the great revolutionaries of modern thought; Spinoza, Heine, Marx, Luxemburg, Trotsky, Freud, and Einstein, whose photo hung in Len's Chelsea loft. These people went beyond the boundaries of Judaism, finding it too narrow, archaic, constricting.

I don't wish to stretch the comparison. Len was not so much a radical thinker as a man of action. But his intellectual understanding—he was well educated and widely read—powered his activity. He had in common with these great thinkers the idea that for knowledge to be real it must be acted upon. As Marx observed, "Hitherto philosophers have only interpreted the world, the point however is to change it."

Like his intellectual predecessors. Len saw reality in a state of flux, as dynamic, not static, and he was aware of the constantly changing and contradictory nature of society. Len was essentially an optimist and shared with the great Jewish revolutionaries an optimistic belief in the solidarity of humankind.

Introduction

Len died the evening of March 23, 2011, as spring was approaching in New York. He had plans to celebrate Passover in April, as usual, with his family in New Jersey. He knew quite a lot about Passover, led his family's observance at the seder every year, and kept up a file on the holiday. He liked the idea that the Jews had the chutzpah to conflate their own flight from slavery with spring and the liberation of nature.

He had plans to tend his fruit trees on the side of the hill next to his Catskill cabin. He would have put in a vegetable garden near his three-block long driveway, which frequently washed out and which he repaired with sysiphean regularity. He would have set out birdseed on the cabin's porch rail, where he would sit in a lounge chair on a platform and watch the songbirds feed.

He loved being out on that porch, high up on a hill, particularly at day's end, seeing the sun go down over the Rondout Reservoir, which supplies some of the drinking water to New York City. Back in 1976 he told a student reporter for UCLA's *Daily Bruin* that leading a committed life was satisfying, fulfilling, and made him happy.

He will be remembered personally as a good, generous, and loyal friend, a gentle and kind person; politically as a great persuasive speaker, an acute analyst of the political scene, and a far-seeing visionary. Professionally, Len Weinglass will live on as one of the great lawyers of his time, joining the legal pantheon of leading twentieth century advocates for justice along with Clarence Darrow, Leonard Boudin, Arthur Kinoy, Ernest Goodman, and William Kunstler.

"Lenny cannot be replaced," wrote his friend Sandra Levinson. "There are no words for the loss we all feel. Do something brave, put yourself out there for someone, fight for someone's dignity, do something to honor this courageous just man."

Leonard Irving Weinglass: Presente.

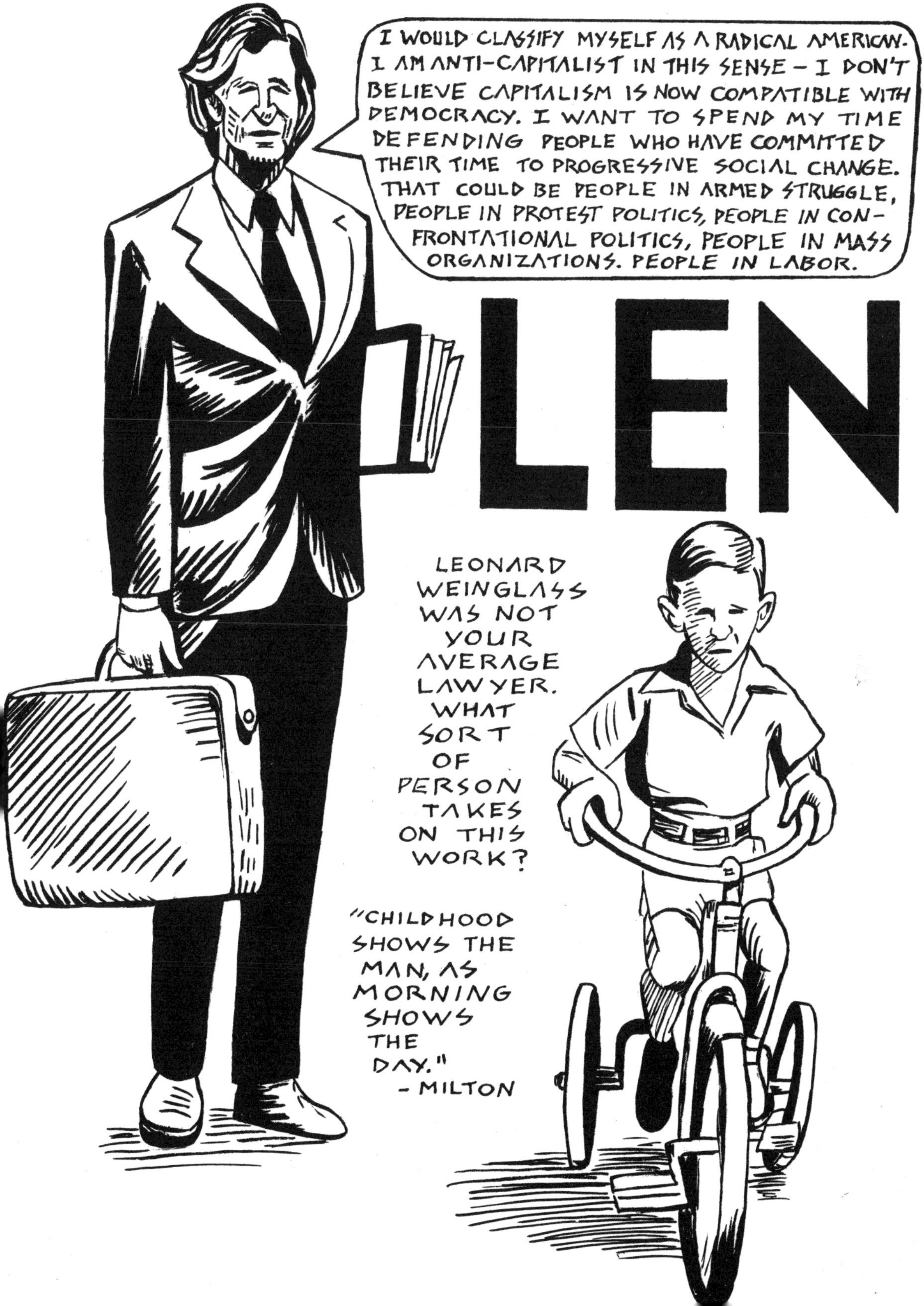
I WOULD CLASSIFY MYSELF AS A RADICAL AMERICAN. I AM ANTI-CAPITALIST IN THIS SENSE – I DON'T BELIEVE CAPITALISM IS NOW COMPATIBLE WITH DEMOCRACY. I WANT TO SPEND MY TIME DEFENDING PEOPLE WHO HAVE COMMITTED THEIR TIME TO PROGRESSIVE SOCIAL CHANGE. THAT COULD BE PEOPLE IN ARMED STRUGGLE, PEOPLE IN PROTEST POLITICS, PEOPLE IN CONFRONTATIONAL POLITICS, PEOPLE IN MASS ORGANIZATIONS. PEOPLE IN LABOR.
LEN
LEONARD WEINGLASS WAS NOT YOUR AVERAGE LAWYER. WHAT SORT OF PERSON TAKES ON THIS WORK?
"CHILDHOOD SHOWS THE MAN, AS MORNING SHOWS THE DAY." - MILTON

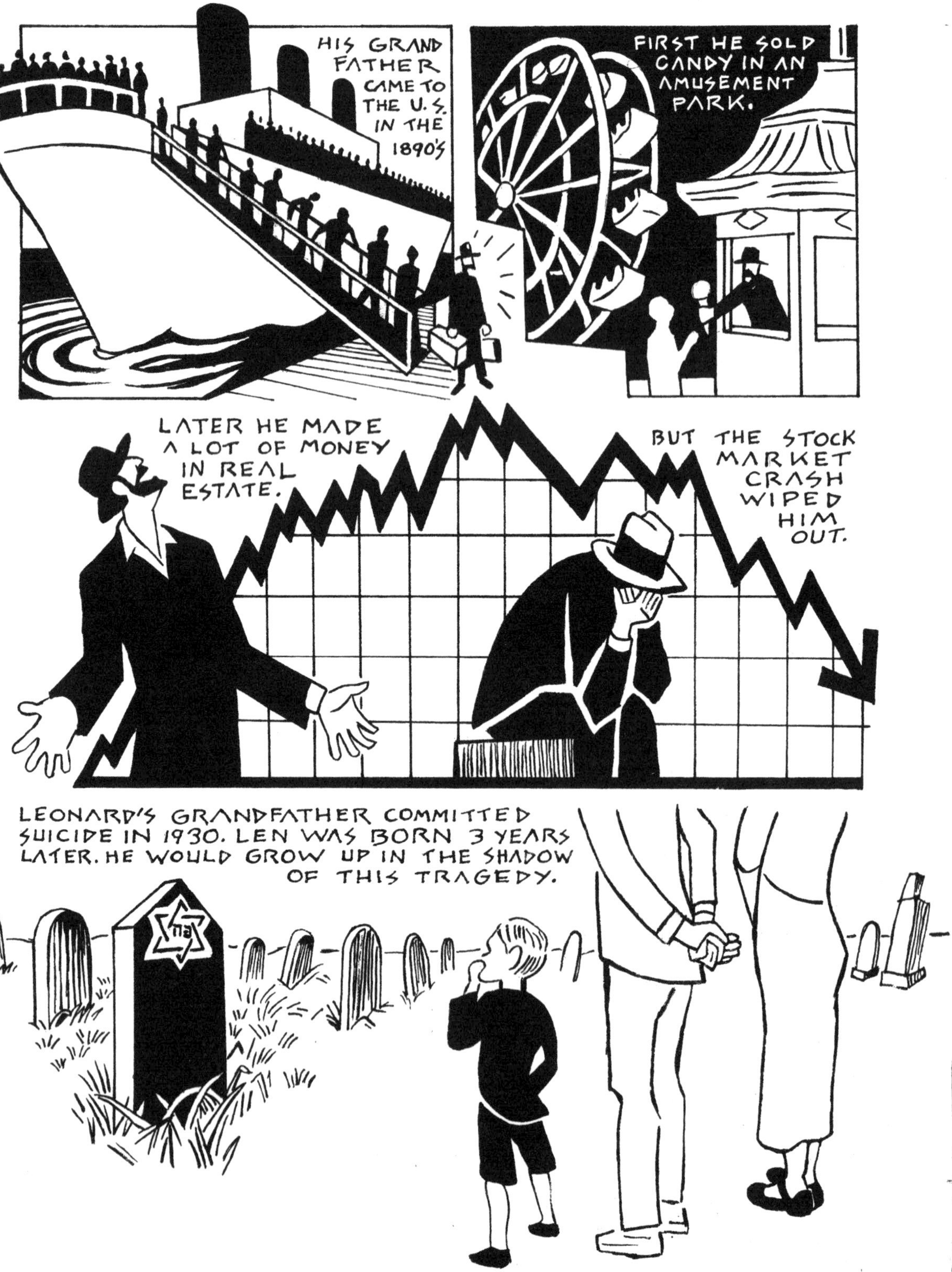
HIS GRAND FATHER CAME TO THE U.S. IN THE 1890'S
FIRST HE SOLD CANDY IN AN AMUSEMENT PARK.
LATER HE MADE A LOT OF MONEY IN REAL ESTATE.
BUT THE STOCK MARKET CRASH WIPED HIM OUT.
LEONARD'S GRANDFATHER COMMITTED SUICIDE IN 1930. LEN WAS BORN 3 YEARS LATER. HE WOULD GROW UP IN THE SHADOW OF THIS TRAGEDY.

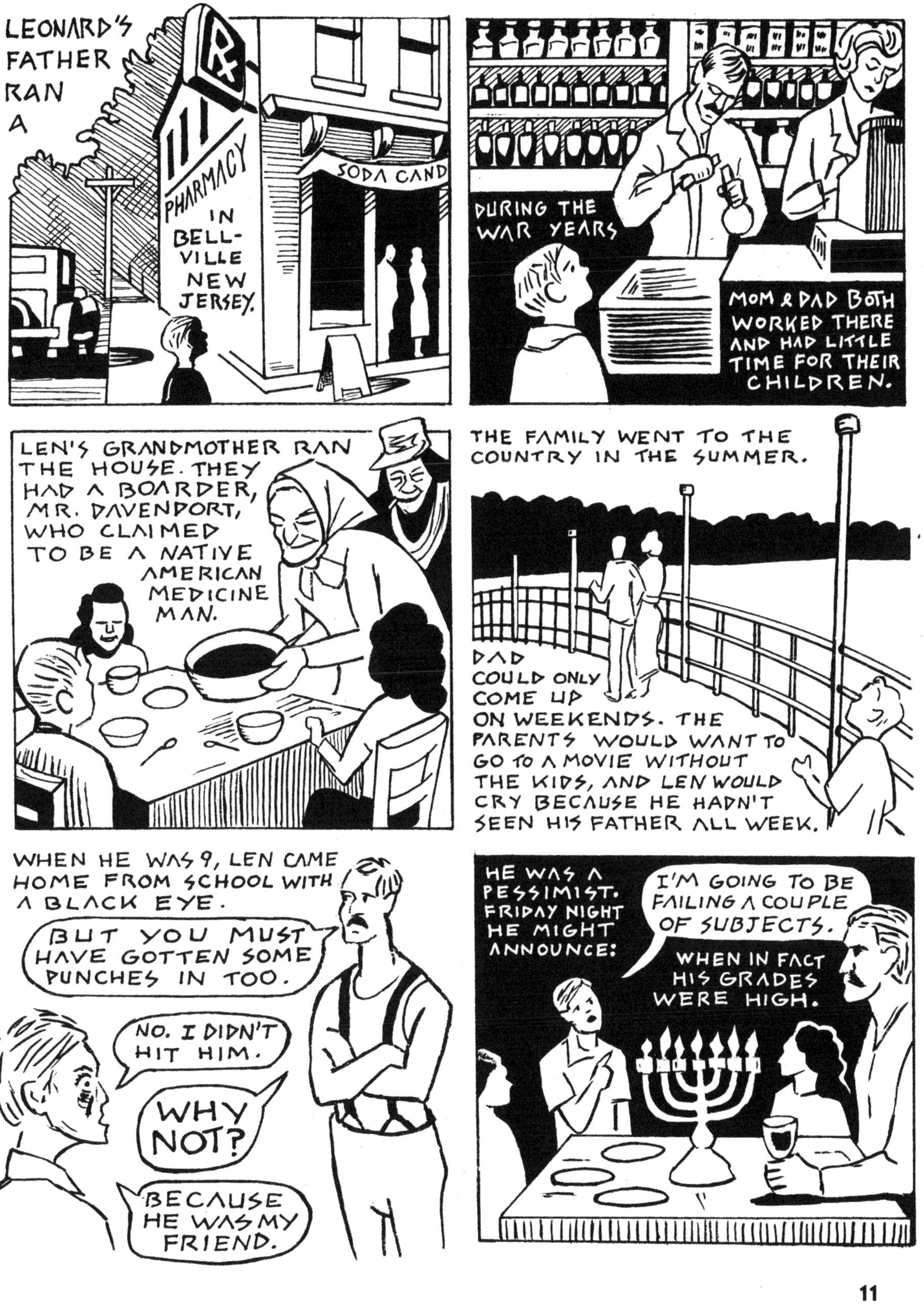
LEONARD'S FATHER RAN A
PHARMACY
IN BELL-VILLE NEW JERSEY.
SODA CAND
DURING THE WAR YEARS
MOM & DAD BOTH WORKED THERE AND HAD LITTLE TIME FOR THEIR CHILDREN.
LEN'S GRANDMOTHER RAN THE HOUSE. THEY HAD A BOARDER, MR. DAVENPORT, WHO CLAIMED TO BE A NATIVE AMERICAN MEDICINE MAN.
THE FAMILY WENT TO THE COUNTRY IN THE SUMMER.
DAD COULD ONLY COME UP ON WEEKENDS. THE PARENTS WOULD WANT TO GO TO A MOVIE WITHOUT THE KIDS, AND LEN WOULD CRY BECAUSE HE HADN'T SEEN HIS FATHER ALL WEEK.
WHEN HE WAS 9, LEN CAME HOME FROM SCHOOL WITH A BLACK EYE.
BUT YOU MUST HAVE GOTTEN SOME PUNCHES IN TOO.
NO. I DIDN'T HIT HIM.
WHY NOT?
BECAUSE HE WAS MY FRIEND.
HE WAS A PESSIMIST. FRIDAY NIGHT HE MIGHT ANNOUNCE:
I'M GOING TO BE FAILING A COUPLE OF SUBJECTS.
WHEN IN FACT HIS GRADES WERE HIGH.

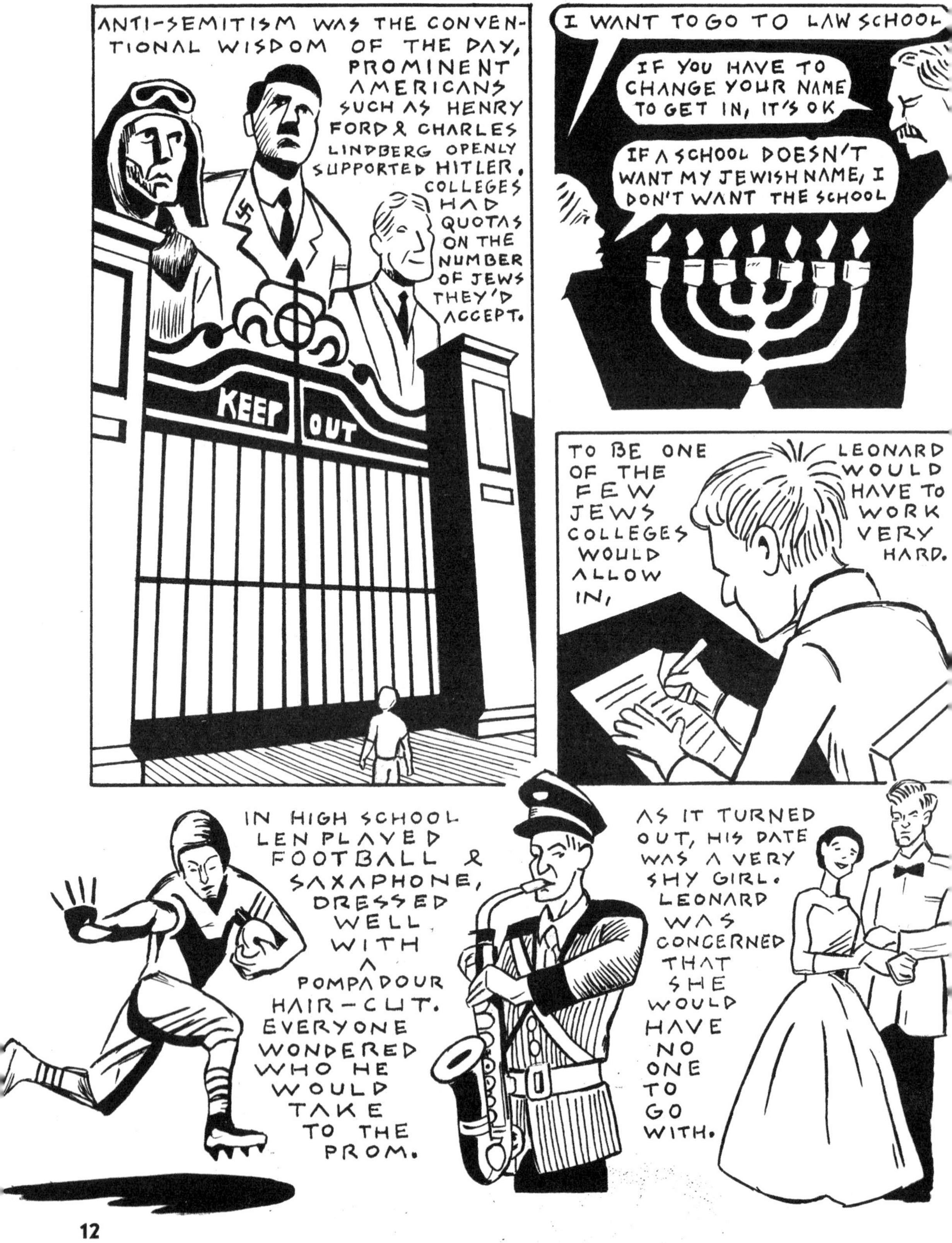

ANTI-SEMITISM WAS THE CONVENTIONAL WISDOM OF THE DAY, PROMINENT AMERICANS SUCH AS HENRY FORD & CHARLES LINDBERG OPENLY SUPPORTED HITLER. COLLEGES HAD QUOTAS ON THE NUMBER OF JEWS THEY'D ACCEPT.
KEEP OUT
I WANT TO GO TO LAW SCHOOL
IF YOU HAVE TO CHANGE YOUR NAME TO GET IN, IT'S OK
IF A SCHOOL DOESN'T WANT MY JEWISH NAME, I DON'T WANT THE SCHOOL
TO BE ONE OF THE FEW JEWS COLLEGES WOULD ALLOW IN,
LEONARD WOULD HAVE TO WORK VERY HARD.
IN HIGH SCHOOL LEN PLAYED FOOTBALL & SAXAPHONE, DRESSED WELL WITH A POMPADOUR HAIR-CUT. EVERYONE WONDERED WHO HE WOULD TAKE TO THE PROM.
AS IT TURNED OUT, HIS DATE WAS A VERY SHY GIRL. LEONARD WAS CONCERNED THAT SHE WOULD HAVE NO ONE TO GO WITH.

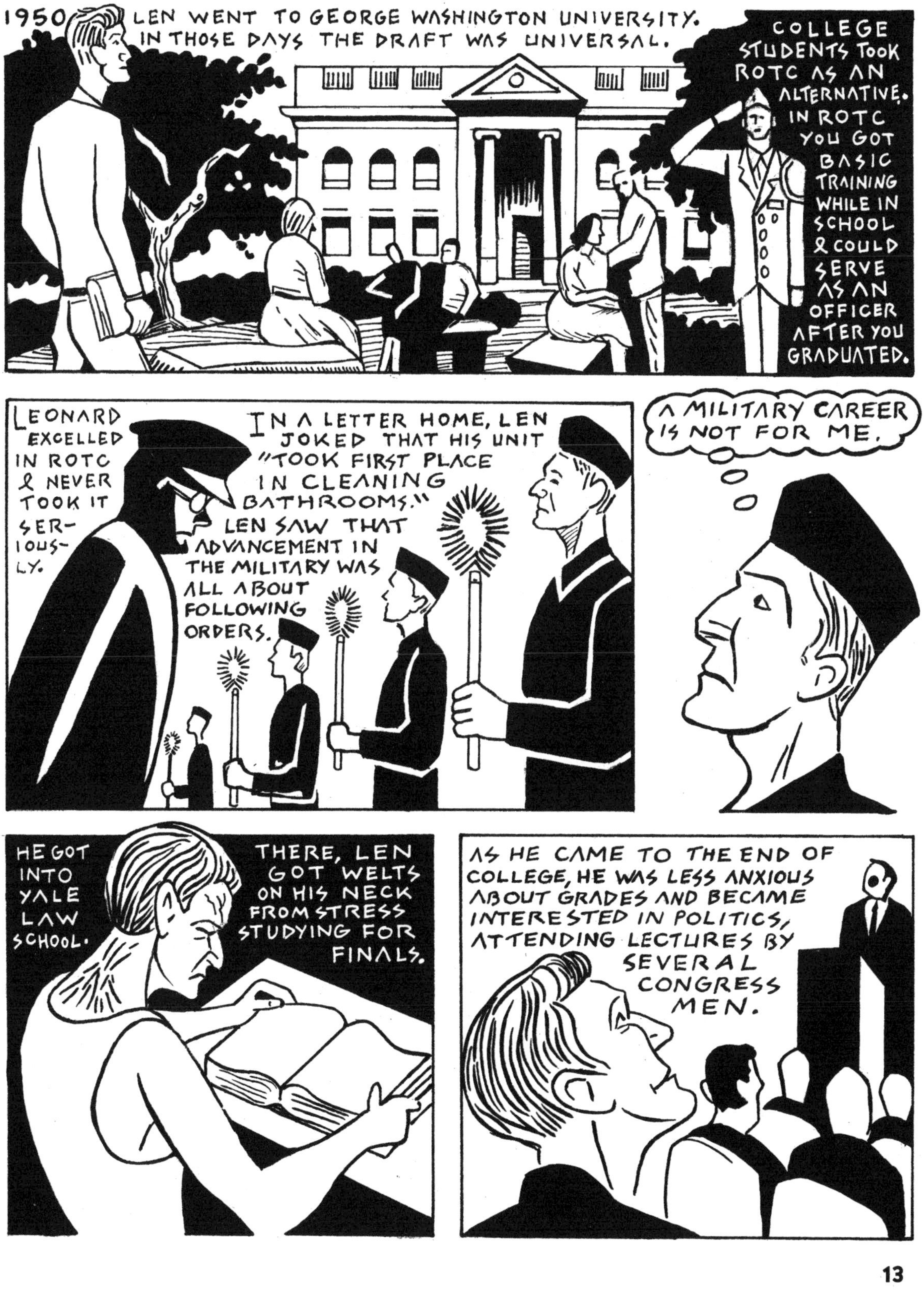
1950
LEN WENT TO GEORGE WASHINGTON UNIVERSITY. IN THOSE DAYS THE DRAFT WAS UNIVERSAL.
COLLEGE STUDENTS TOOK ROTC AS AN ALTERNATIVE. IN ROTC YOU GOT BASIC TRAINING WHILE IN SCHOOL & COULD SERVE AS AN OFFICER AFTER YOU GRADUATED.
LEONARD EXCELLED IN ROTC & NEVER TOOK IT SERIOUSLY.
IN A LETTER HOME, LEN JOKED THAT HIS UNIT "TOOK FIRST PLACE IN CLEANING BATHROOMS."
LEN SAW THAT ADVANCEMENT IN THE MILITARY WAS ALL ABOUT FOLLOWING ORDERS.
A MILITARY CAREER IS NOT FOR ME.
HE GOT INTO YALE LAW SCHOOL.
THERE, LEN GOT WELTS ON HIS NECK FROM STRESS STUDYING FOR FINALS.
AS HE CAME TO THE END OF COLLEGE, HE WAS LESS ANXIOUS ABOUT GRADES AND BECAME INTERESTED IN POLITICS, ATTENDING LECTURES BY SEVERAL CONGRESS MEN.

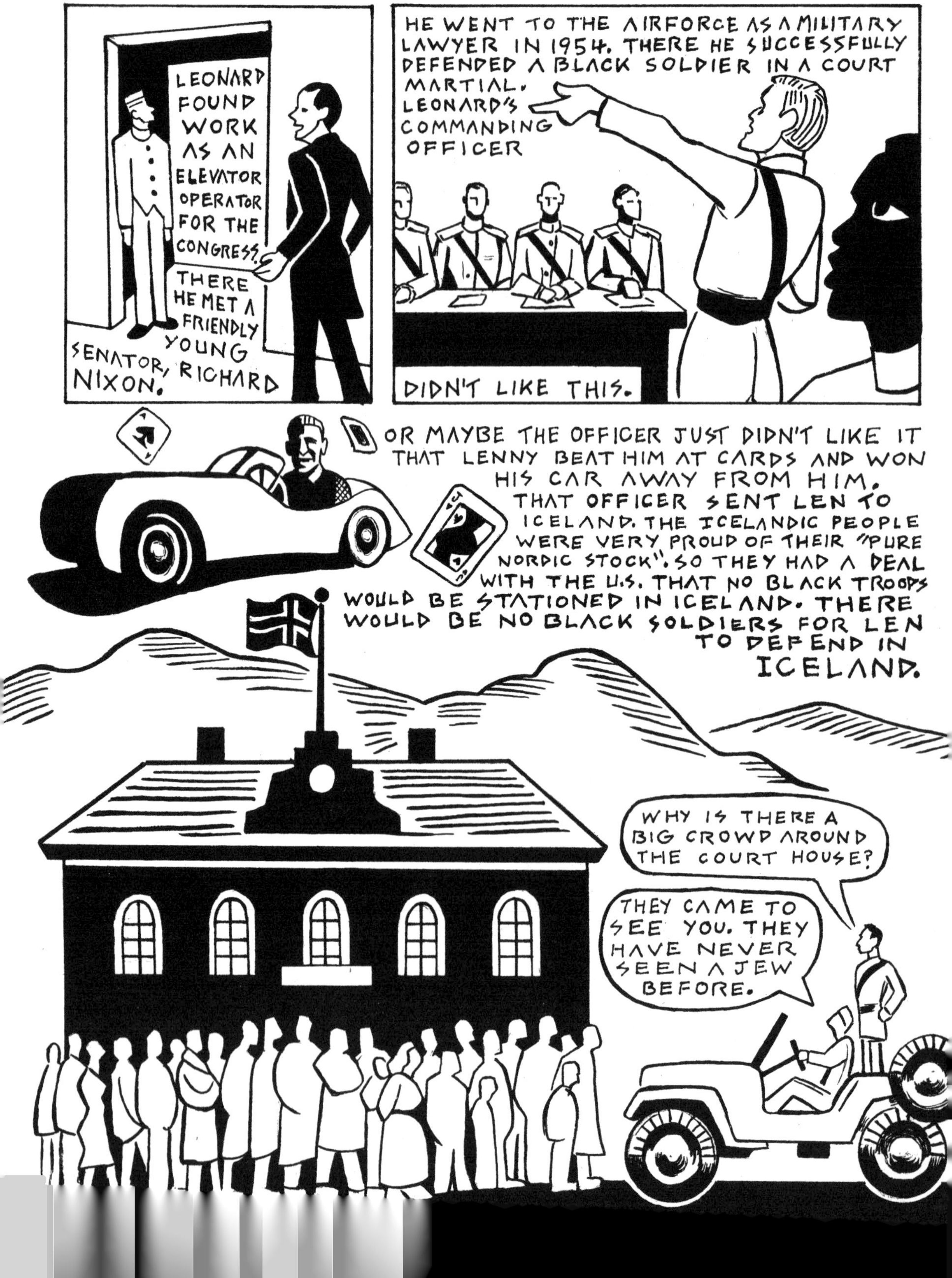

LEONARD FOUND WORK AS AN ELEVATOR OPERATOR FOR THE CONGRESS.
THERE HE MET A FRIENDLY YOUNG SENATOR, RICHARD NIXON.
HE WENT TO THE AIRFORCE AS A MILITARY LAWYER IN 1954. THERE HE SUCCESSFULLY DEFENDED A BLACK SOLDIER IN A COURT MARTIAL.
LEONARD'S COMMANDING OFFICER
DIDN'T LIKE THIS.
OR MAYBE THE OFFICER JUST DIDN'T LIKE IT THAT LENNY BEAT HIM AT CARDS AND WON HIS CAR AWAY FROM HIM.
THAT OFFICER SENT LEN TO ICELAND. THE ICELANDIC PEOPLE WERE VERY PROUD OF THEIR "PURE NORDIC STOCK". SO THEY HAD A DEAL WITH THE U.S. THAT NO BLACK TROOPS WOULD BE STATIONED IN ICELAND. THERE WOULD BE NO BLACK SOLDIERS FOR LEN TO DEFEND IN ICELAND.
WHY IS THERE A BIG CROWD AROUND THE COURT HOUSE?
THEY CAME TO SEE YOU. THEY HAVE NEVER SEEN A JEW BEFORE.

AFTER THE AIR FORCE, HE WORKED AT A BIG NEW JERSEY LAW FIRM, THEN AS AN ASSISTANT TO THE NEW JERSEY ATTORNEY GENERAL.

HE WAS GETTING THESE TOP JOBS BECAUSE EVEN AS A YOUNG MAN, HIS LEGAL SKILLS WERE RESPECTED.

WHEN A RELATIVE CAME TO VISIT, HE TOOK HER TO A COCKTAIL PARTY WITH HIS LEGAL CONTACTS. HE SHOWED HER HOW HE'D THROW HIS DRINK INTO A POTTED PLANT,

IN ORDER TO STAY SOBER WITHOUT OFFENDING HIS CLIENTS.

LEN SOON TIRED OF FANCY LAW JOBS. INSTEAD HE OPENED A SMALL PRIVATE PRACTICE IN A POOR BLACK COMMUNITY IN NEWARK, NEW JERSEY. OPERATING IN OLDTIME JEWISH STYLE, WITH A STREET LEVEL OFFICE THAT WAS ALSO HIS HOME. HIS REAL WORK WOULD BEGIN HERE.

LAWYER 43

15

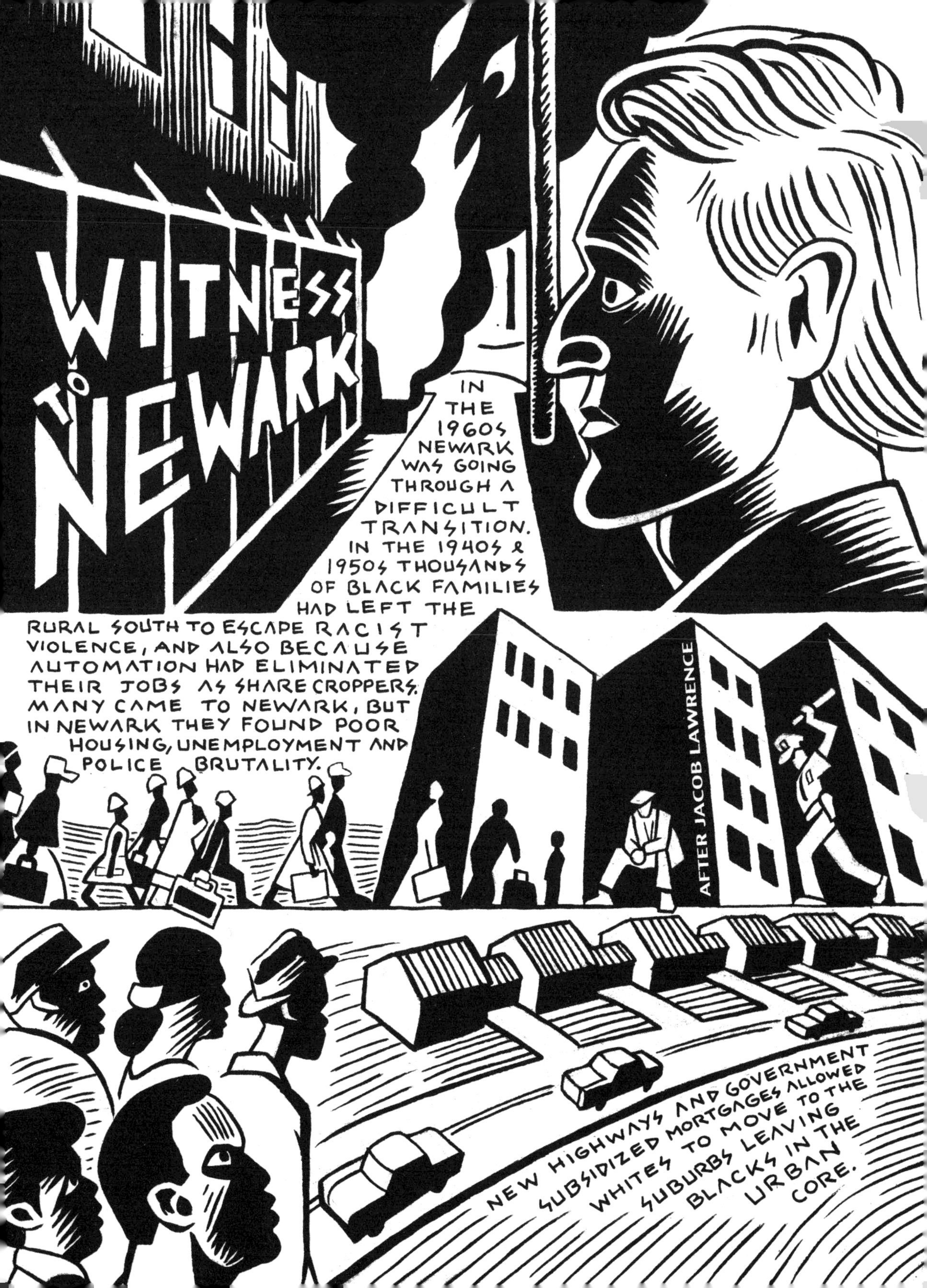
WITNESS TO NEWARK
IN THE 1960S NEWARK WAS GOING THROUGH A DIFFICULT TRANSITION. IN THE 1940S & 1950S THOUSANDS OF BLACK FAMILIES HAD LEFT THE RURAL SOUTH TO ESCAPE RACIST VIOLENCE, AND ALSO BECAUSE AUTOMATION HAD ELIMINATED THEIR JOBS AS SHARECROPPERS. MANY CAME TO NEWARK, BUT IN NEWARK THEY FOUND POOR HOUSING, UNEMPLOYMENT AND POLICE BRUTALITY.
AFTER JACOB LAWRENCE
NEW HIGHWAYS AND GOVERNMENT SUBSIDIZED MORTGAGES ALLOWED WHITES TO MOVE TO THE SUBURBS LEAVING BLACKS IN THE URBAN CORE.

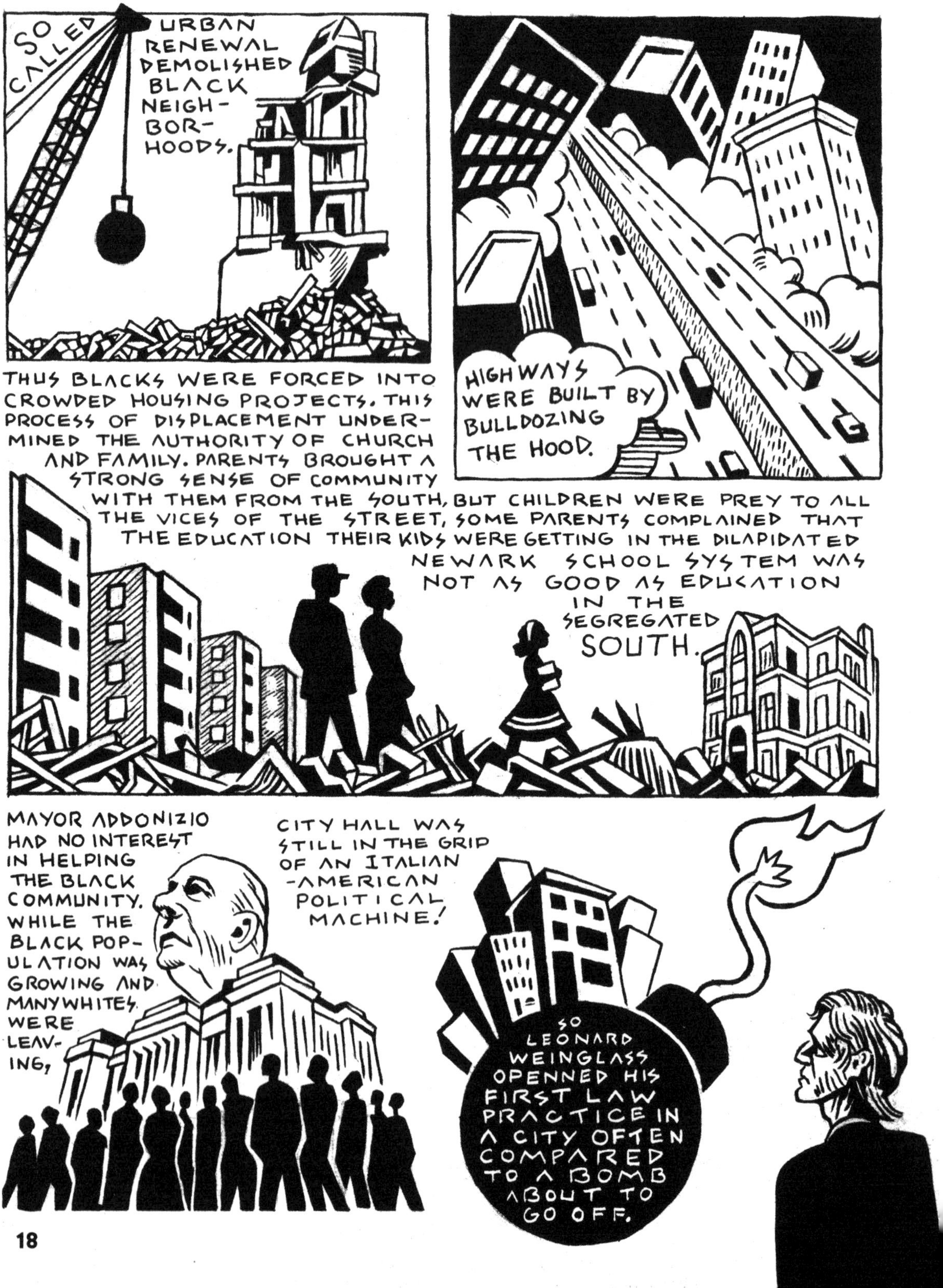
SO CALLED URBAN RENEWAL DEMOLISHED BLACK NEIGH-BOR-HOODS.
THUS BLACKS WERE FORCED INTO CROWDED HOUSING PROJECTS. THIS PROCESS OF DISPLACEMENT UNDER-MINED THE AUTHORITY OF CHURCH AND FAMILY. PARENTS BROUGHT A STRONG SENSE OF COMMUNITY
HIGHWAYS WERE BUILT BY BULLDOZING THE HOOD.
WITH THEM FROM THE SOUTH, BUT CHILDREN WERE PREY TO ALL THE VICES OF THE STREET, SOME PARENTS COMPLAINED THAT THE EDUCATION THEIR KIDS WERE GETTING IN THE DILAPIDATED NEWARK SCHOOL SYSTEM WAS NOT AS GOOD AS EDUCATION IN THE SEGREGATED SOUTH.
MAYOR ADDONIZIO HAD NO INTEREST IN HELPING THE BLACK COMMUNITY. WHILE THE BLACK POP-ULATION WAS GROWING AND MANY WHITES WERE LEAV-ING,
CITY HALL WAS STILL IN THE GRIP OF AN ITALIAN -AMERICAN POLITICAL MACHINE!
SO LEONARD WEINGLASS OPENNED HIS FIRST LAW PRACTICE IN A CITY OFTEN COMPARED TO A BOMB ABOUT TO GO OFF.

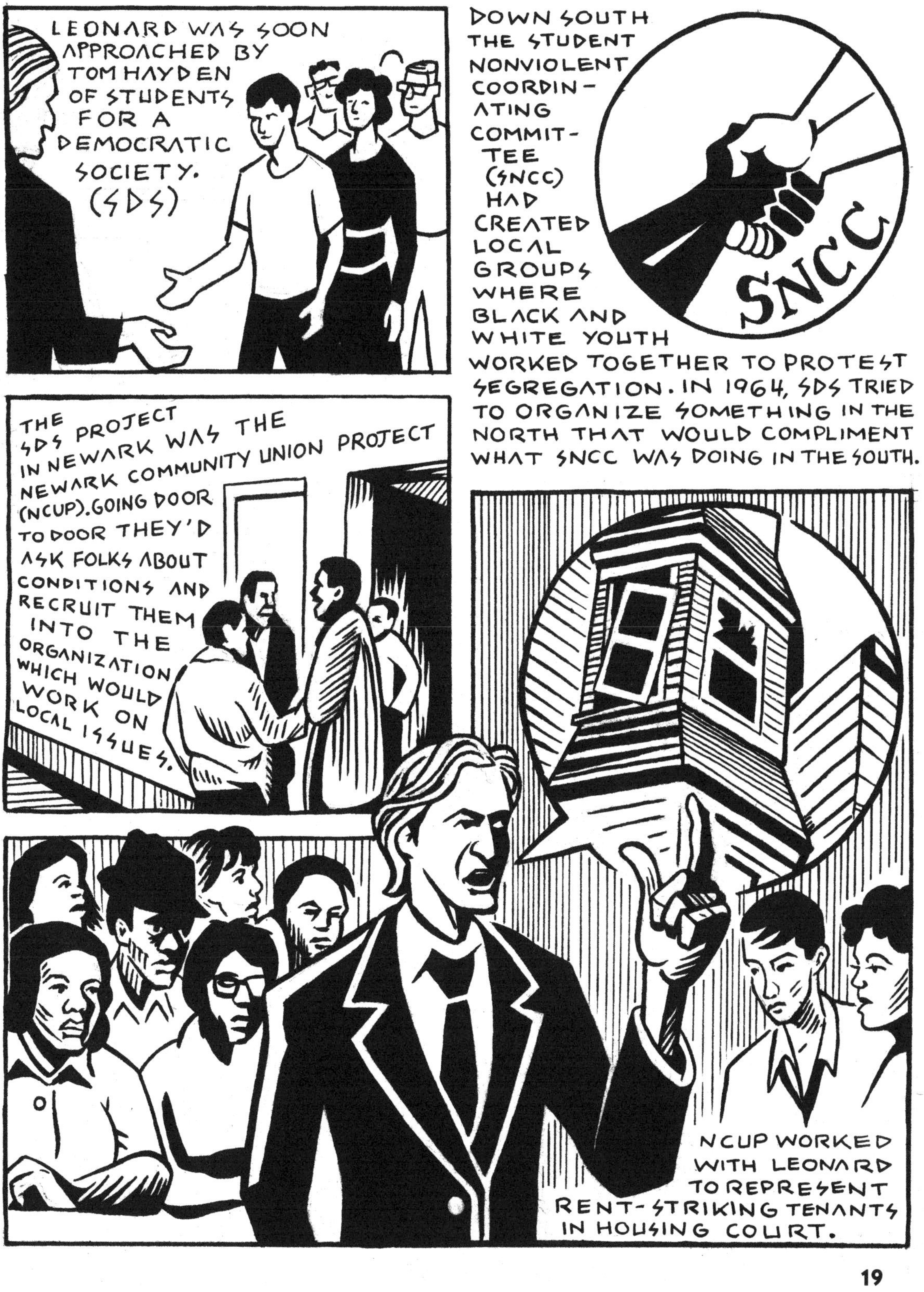
LEONARD WAS SOON APPROACHED BY TOM HAYDEN OF STUDENTS FOR A DEMOCRATIC SOCIETY. (SDS)
DOWN SOUTH THE STUDENT NONVIOLENT COORDINATING COMMITTEE (SNCC) HAD CREATED LOCAL GROUPS WHERE BLACK AND WHITE YOUTH WORKED TOGETHER TO PROTEST SEGREGATION. IN 1964, SDS TRIED TO ORGANIZE SOMETHING IN THE NORTH THAT WOULD COMPLIMENT WHAT SNCC WAS DOING IN THE SOUTH.
SNCC
THE SDS PROJECT IN NEWARK WAS THE NEWARK COMMUNITY UNION PROJECT (NCUP). GOING DOOR TO DOOR THEY'D ASK FOLKS ABOUT CONDITIONS AND RECRUIT THEM INTO THE ORGANIZATION WHICH WOULD WORK ON LOCAL ISSUES.
NCUP WORKED WITH LEONARD TO REPRESENT RENT-STRIKING TENANTS IN HOUSING COURT.

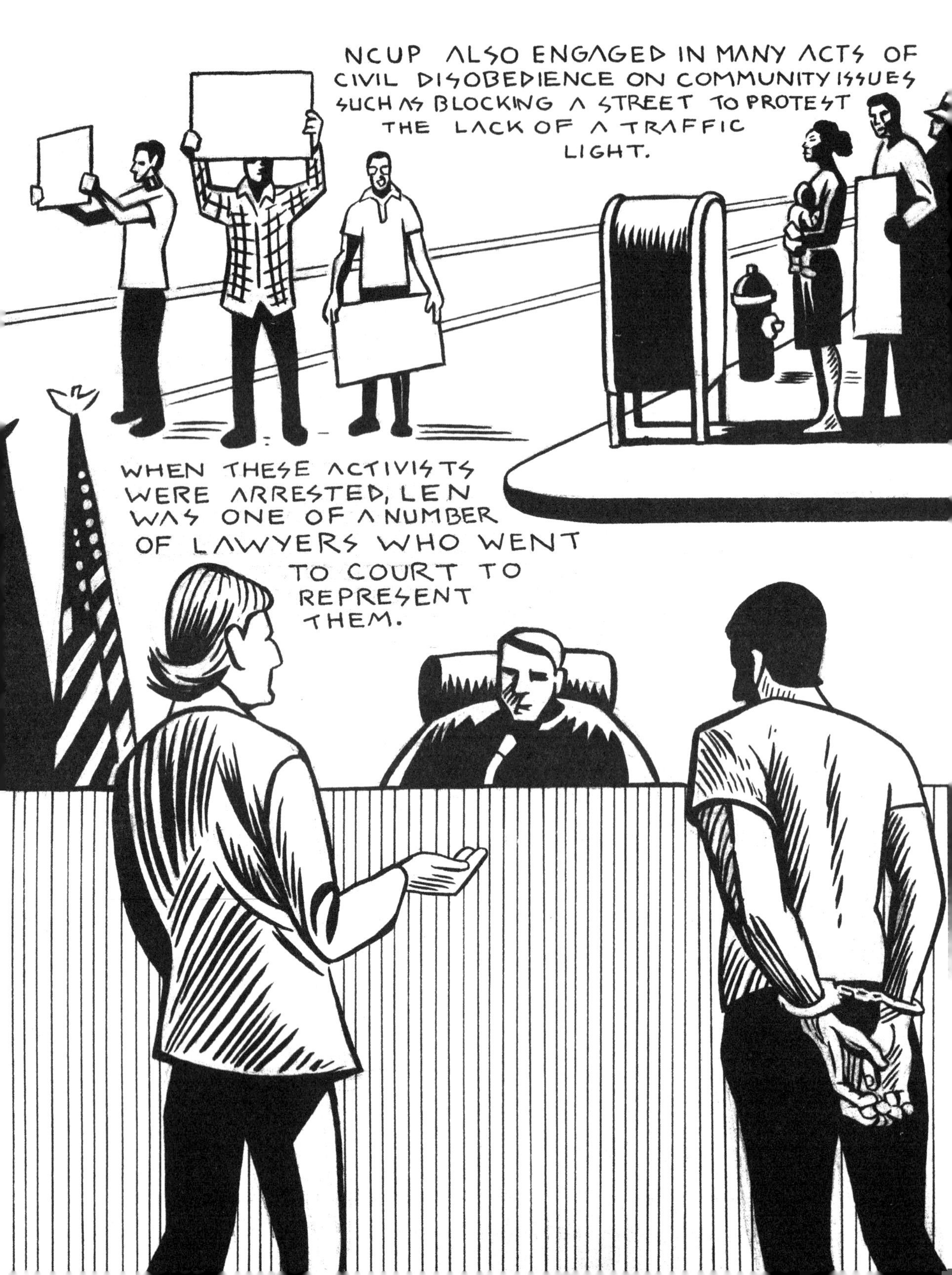
NCUP ALSO ENGAGED IN MANY ACTS OF CIVIL DISOBEDIENCE ON COMMUNITY ISSUES SUCH AS BLOCKING A STREET TO PROTEST THE LACK OF A TRAFFIC LIGHT.
WHEN THESE ACTIVISTS WERE ARRESTED, LEN WAS ONE OF A NUMBER OF LAWYERS WHO WENT TO COURT TO REPRESENT THEM.

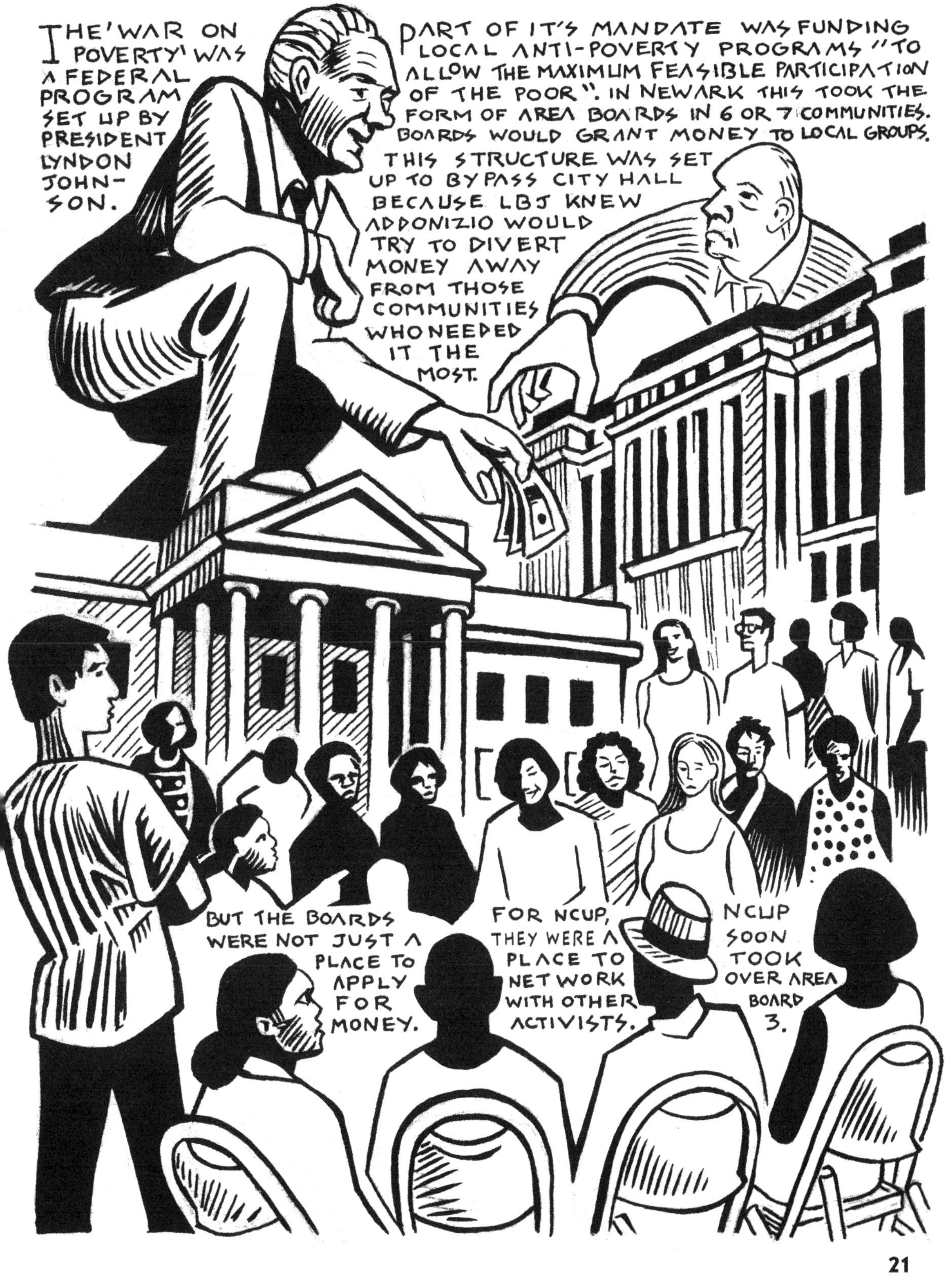
THE 'WAR ON POVERTY' WAS A FEDERAL PROGRAM SET UP BY PRESIDENT LYNDON JOHNSON.
PART OF IT'S MANDATE WAS FUNDING LOCAL ANTI-POVERTY PROGRAMS "TO ALLOW THE MAXIMUM FEASIBLE PARTICIPATION OF THE POOR". IN NEWARK THIS TOOK THE FORM OF AREA BOARDS IN 6 OR 7 COMMUNITIES. BOARDS WOULD GRANT MONEY TO LOCAL GROUPS.
THIS STRUCTURE WAS SET UP TO BYPASS CITY HALL BECAUSE LBJ KNEW ADDONIZIO WOULD TRY TO DIVERT MONEY AWAY FROM THOSE COMMUNITIES WHO NEEDED IT THE MOST.
BUT THE BOARDS WERE NOT JUST A PLACE TO APPLY FOR MONEY.
FOR NCUP, THEY WERE A PLACE TO NETWORK WITH OTHER ACTIVISTS.
NCUP SOON TOOK OVER AREA BOARD 3.

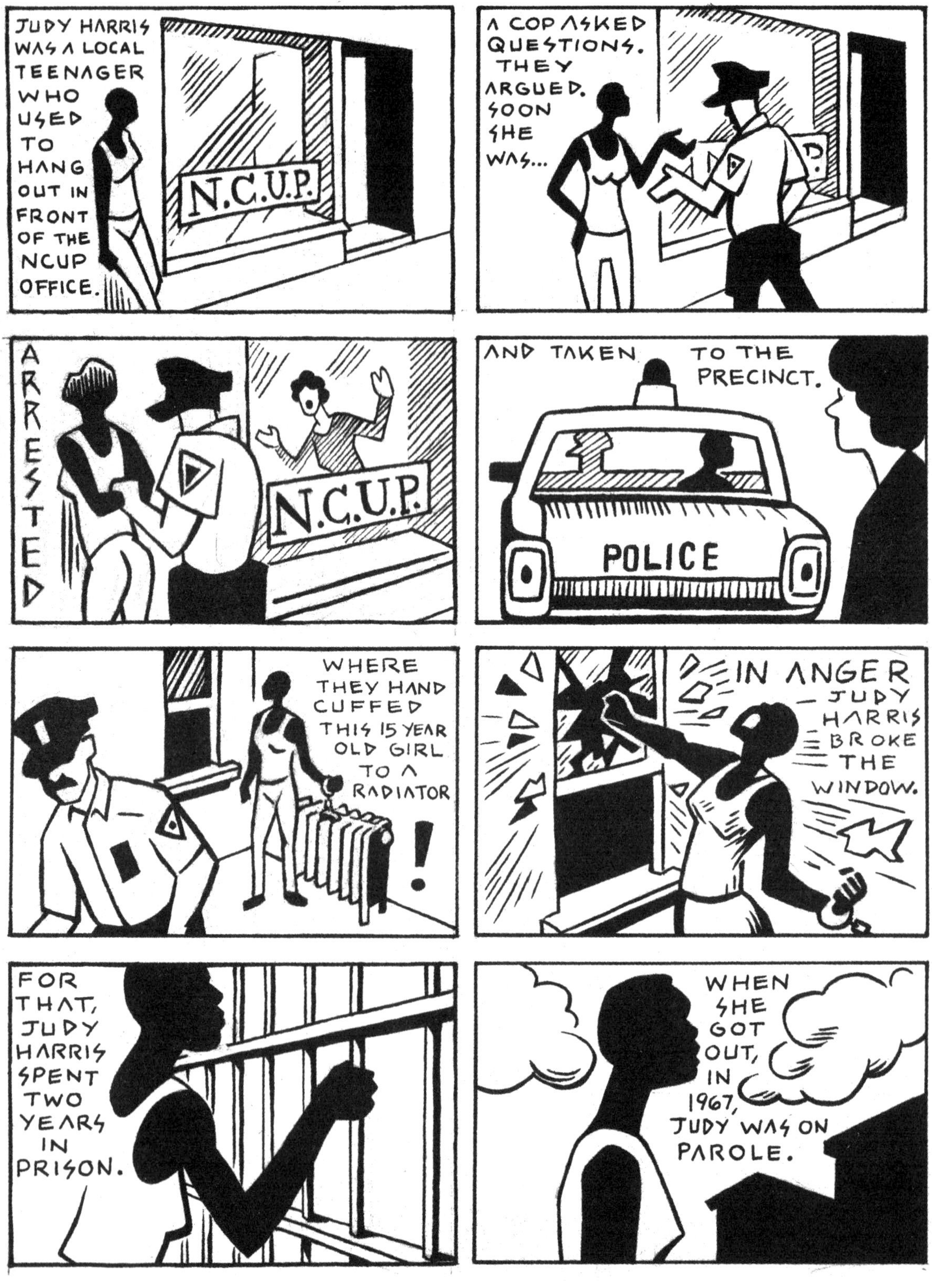
JUDY HARRIS WAS A LOCAL TEENAGER WHO USED TO HANG OUT IN FRONT OF THE NCUP OFFICE.
N.C.U.P.
A COP ASKED QUESTIONS. THEY ARGUED. SOON SHE WAS...
ARRESTED
N.C.U.P.
AND TAKEN TO THE PRECINCT.
POLICE
WHERE THEY HANDCUFFED THIS 15 YEAR OLD GIRL TO A RADIATOR
!
IN ANGER — JUDY HARRIS BROKE THE WINDOW.
FOR THAT, JUDY HARRIS SPENT TWO YEARS IN PRISON.
WHEN SHE GOT OUT, IN 1967, JUDY WAS ON PAROLE.

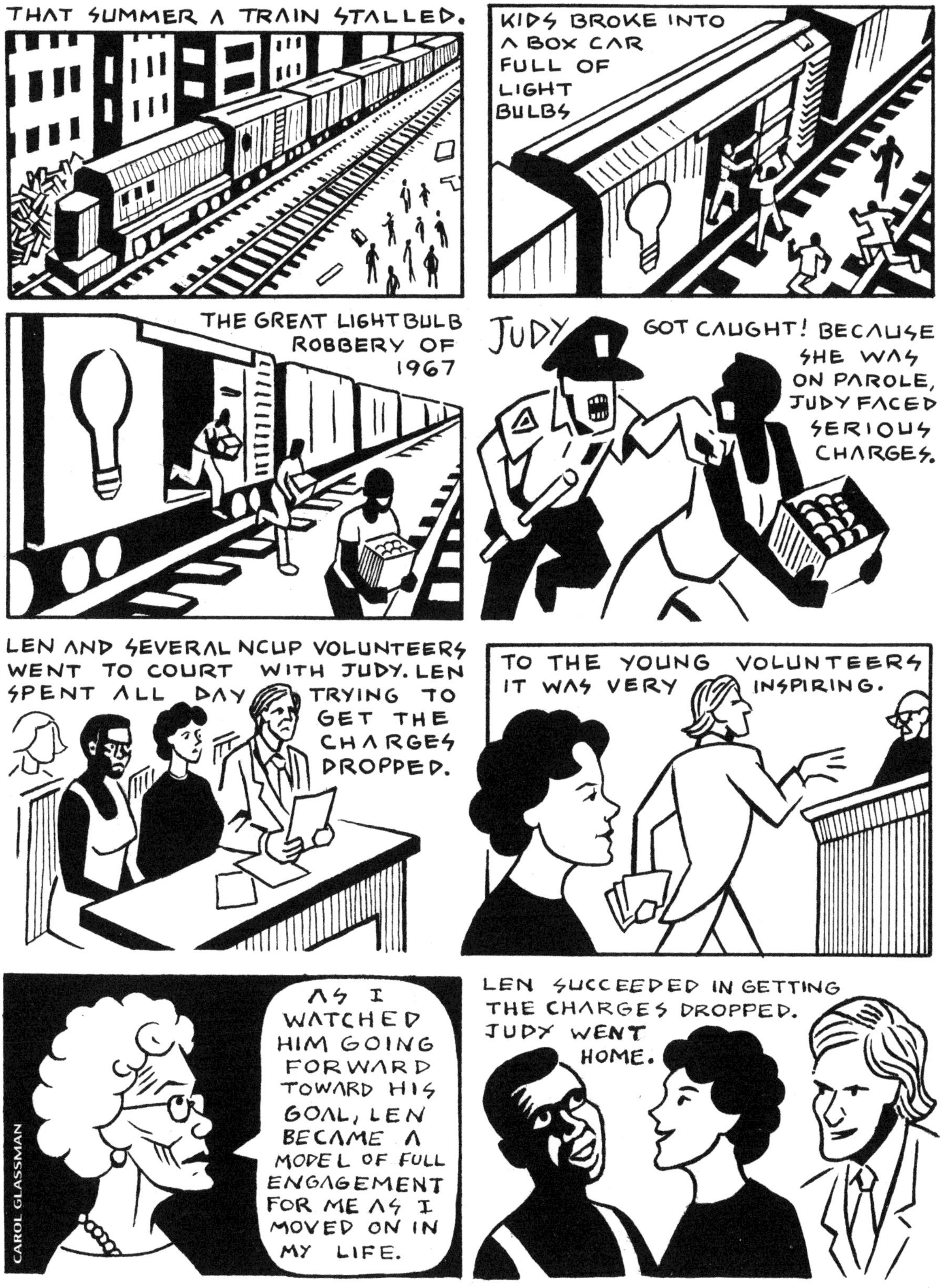

THAT SUMMER A TRAIN STALLED.
KIDS BROKE INTO A BOX CAR FULL OF LIGHT BULBS
THE GREAT LIGHTBULB ROBBERY OF 1967
JUDY
GOT CAUGHT! BECAUSE SHE WAS ON PAROLE, JUDY FACED SERIOUS CHARGES.
LEN AND SEVERAL NCUP VOLUNTEERS WENT TO COURT WITH JUDY. LEN SPENT ALL DAY TRYING TO GET THE CHARGES DROPPED.
TO THE YOUNG VOLUNTEERS IT WAS VERY INSPIRING.
CAROL GLASSMAN
AS I WATCHED HIM GOING FORWARD TOWARD HIS GOAL, LEN BECAME A MODEL OF FULL ENGAGEMENT FOR ME AS I MOVED ON IN MY LIFE.
LEN SUCCEEDED IN GETTING THE CHARGES DROPPED. JUDY WENT HOME.

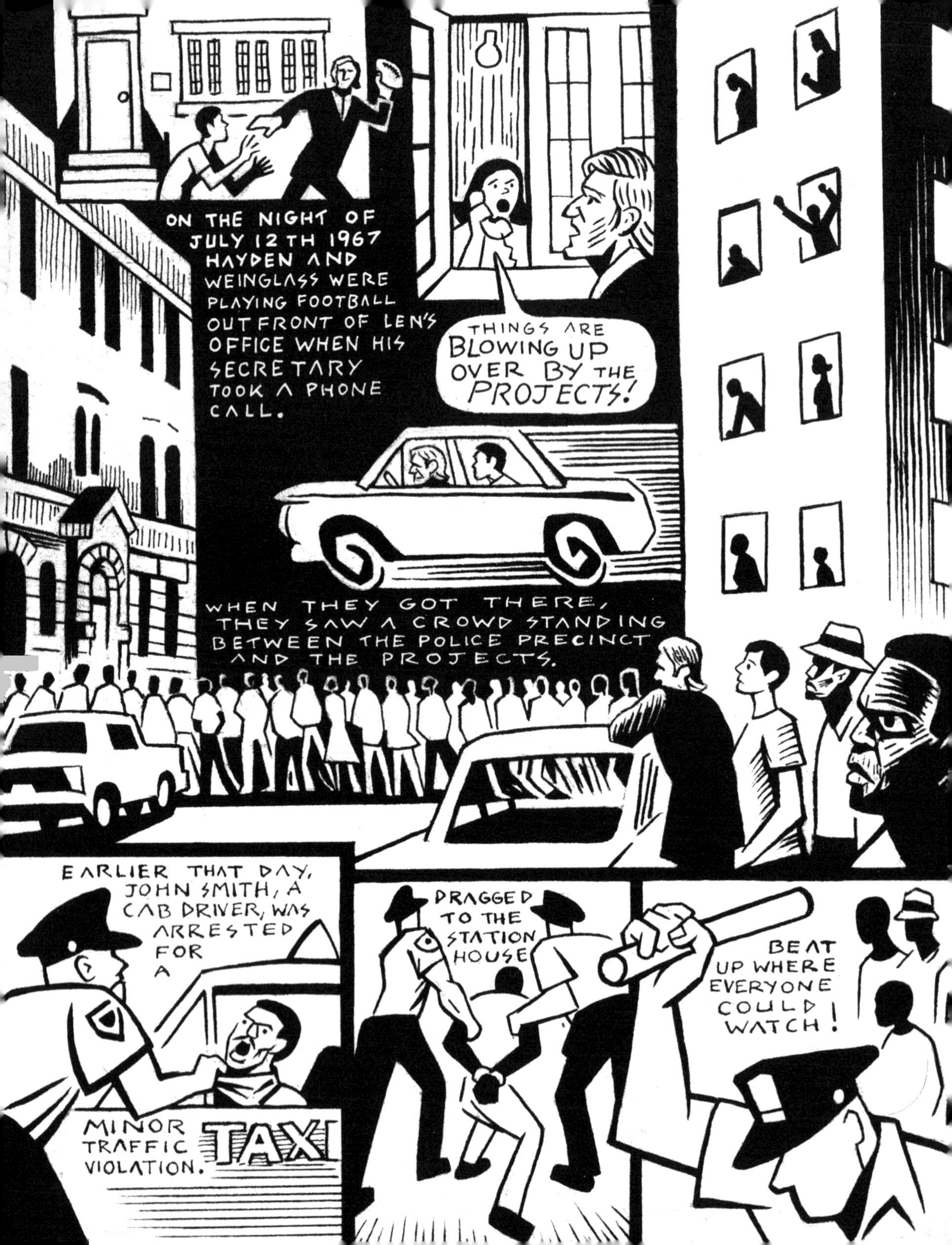

ON THE NIGHT OF JULY 12TH 1967 HAYDEN AND WEINGLASS WERE PLAYING FOOTBALL OUT FRONT OF LEN'S OFFICE WHEN HIS SECRETARY TOOK A PHONE CALL.
THINGS ARE BLOWING UP OVER BY THE PROJECTS!
WHEN THEY GOT THERE, THEY SAW A CROWD STANDING BETWEEN THE POLICE PRECINCT AND THE PROJECTS.
EARLIER THAT DAY, JOHN SMITH, A CAB DRIVER, WAS ARRESTED FOR A
MINOR TRAFFIC VIOLATION.
TAXI
DRAGGED TO THE STATION HOUSE
BEAT UP WHERE EVERYONE COULD WATCH!

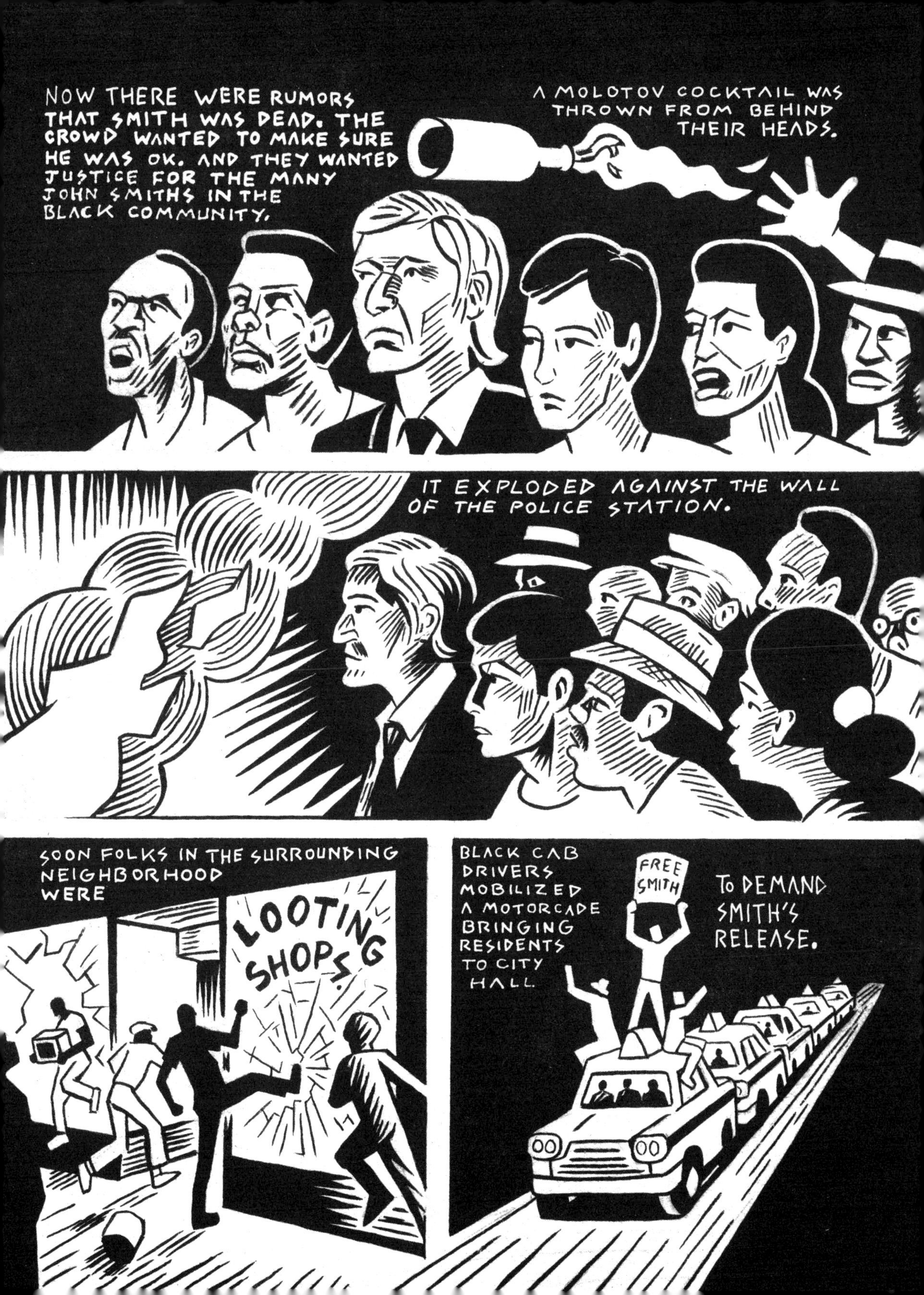
NOW THERE WERE RUMORS THAT SMITH WAS DEAD. THE CROWD WANTED TO MAKE SURE HE WAS OK. AND THEY WANTED JUSTICE FOR THE MANY JOHN SMITHS IN THE BLACK COMMUNITY.
A MOLOTOV COCKTAIL WAS THROWN FROM BEHIND THEIR HEADS.
IT EXPLODED AGAINST THE WALL OF THE POLICE STATION.
SOON FOLKS IN THE SURROUNDING NEIGHBORHOOD WERE
LOOTING SHOPS.
BLACK CAB DRIVERS MOBILIZED A MOTORCADE BRINGING RESIDENTS TO CITY HALL.
FREE SMITH
TO DEMAND SMITH'S RELEASE.

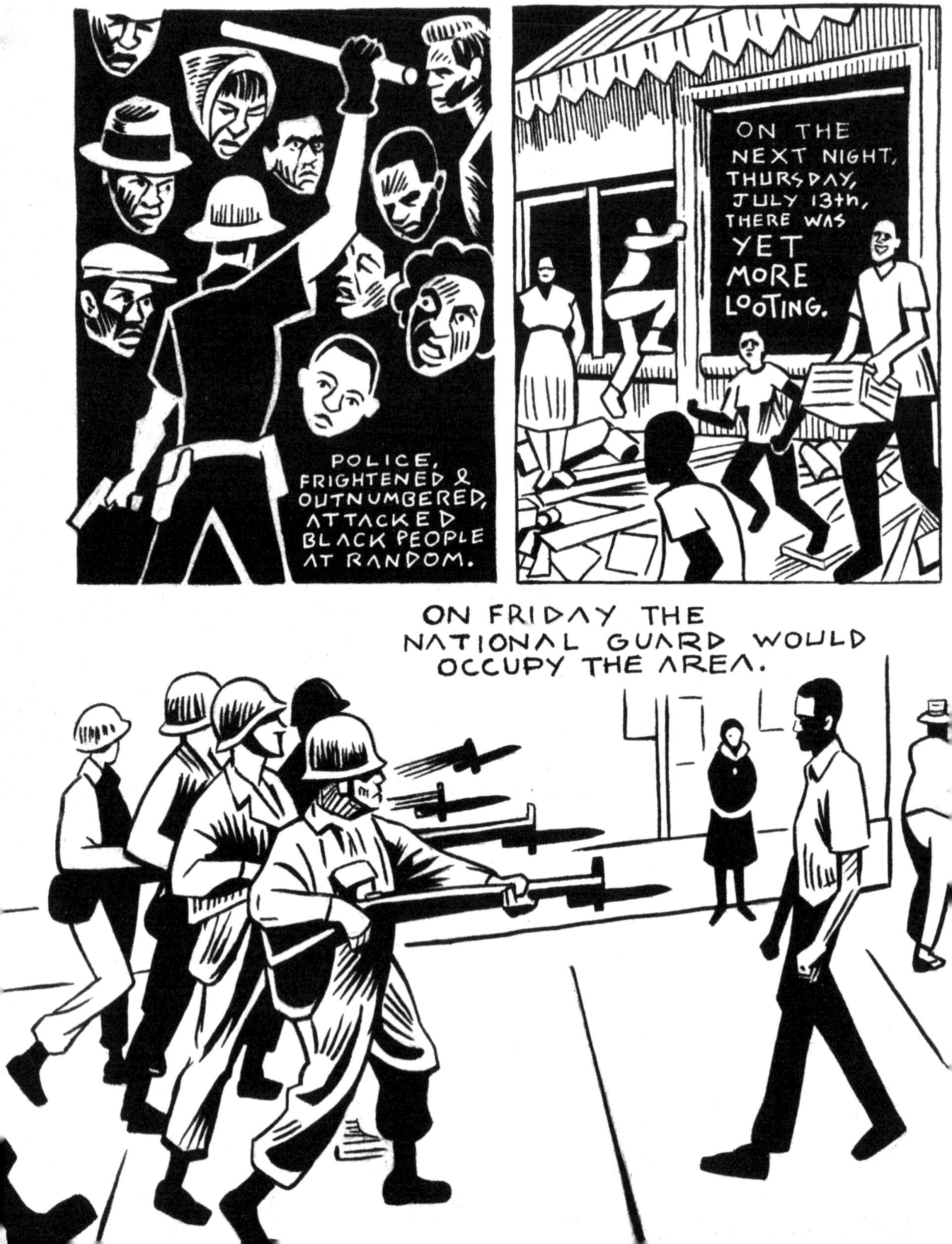
POLICE, FRIGHTENED & OUTNUMBERED, ATTACKED BLACK PEOPLE AT RANDOM.
ON THE NEXT NIGHT, THURSDAY, JULY 13th, THERE WAS YET MORE LOOTING.
ON FRIDAY THE NATIONAL GUARD WOULD OCCUPY THE AREA.

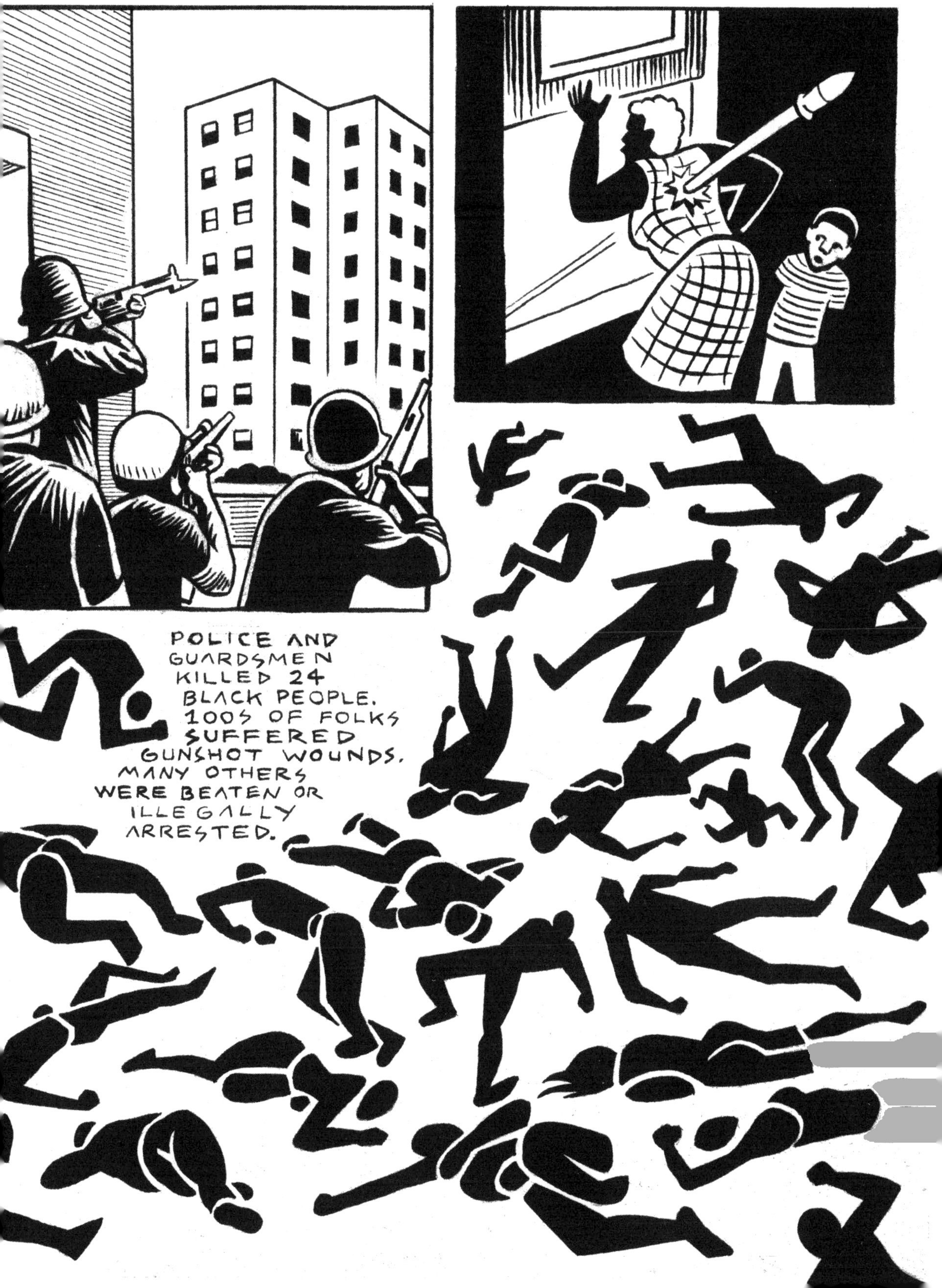
POLICE AND GUARDSMEN KILLED 24 BLACK PEOPLE. 100S OF FOLKS SUFFERED GUNSHOT WOUNDS. MANY OTHERS WERE BEATEN OR ILLEGALLY ARRESTED.

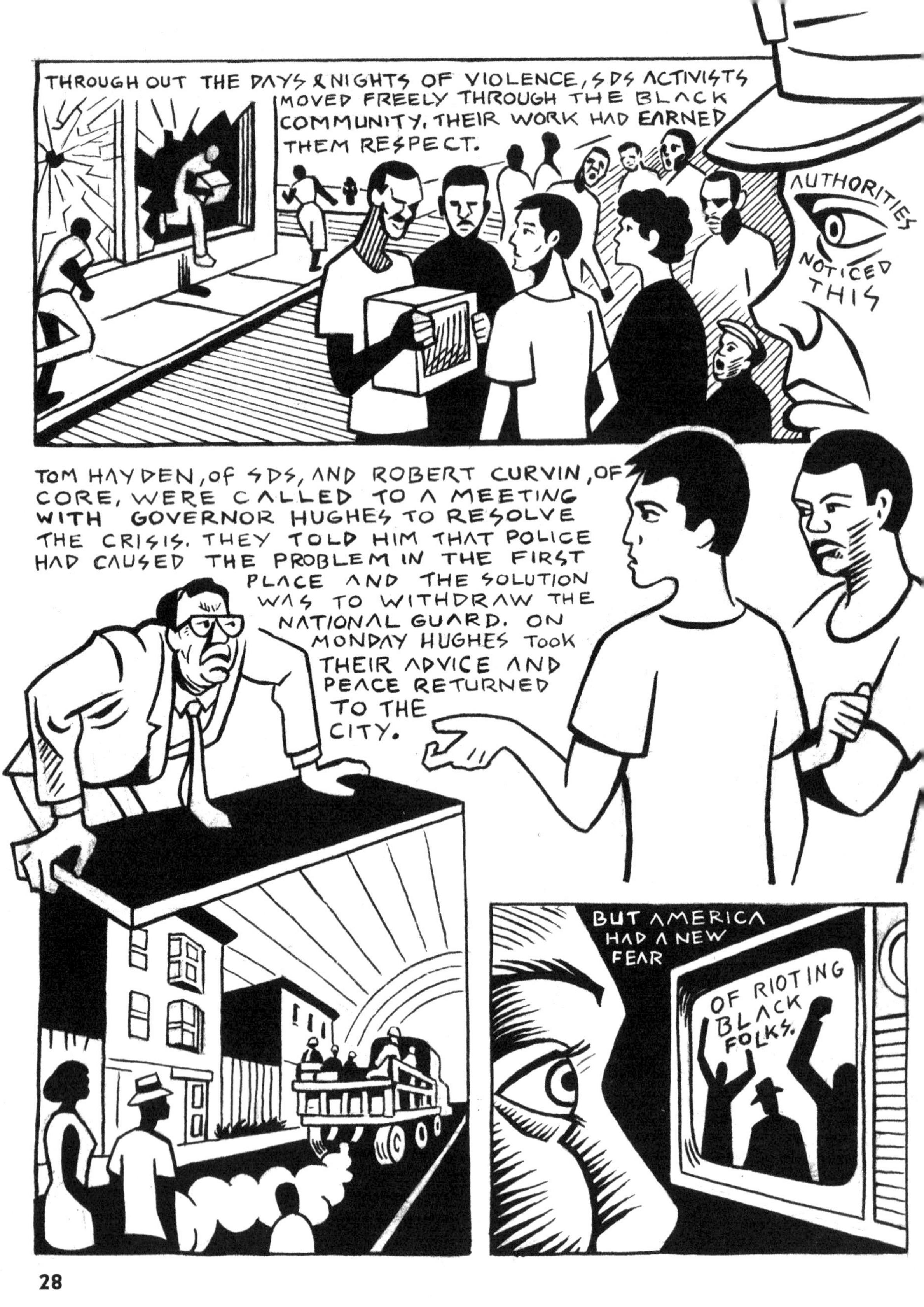
THROUGH OUT THE DAYS & NIGHTS OF VIOLENCE, SDS ACTIVISTS MOVED FREELY THROUGH THE BLACK COMMUNITY. THEIR WORK HAD EARNED THEM RESPECT.
AUTHORITIES NOTICED THIS
TOM HAYDEN, OF SDS, AND ROBERT CURVIN, OF CORE, WERE CALLED TO A MEETING WITH GOVERNOR HUGHES TO RESOLVE THE CRISIS. THEY TOLD HIM THAT POLICE HAD CAUSED THE PROBLEM IN THE FIRST PLACE AND THE SOLUTION WAS TO WITHDRAW THE NATIONAL GUARD. ON MONDAY HUGHES TOOK THEIR ADVICE AND PEACE RETURNED TO THE CITY.
BUT AMERICA HAD A NEW FEAR
OF RIOTING BLACK FOLKS.

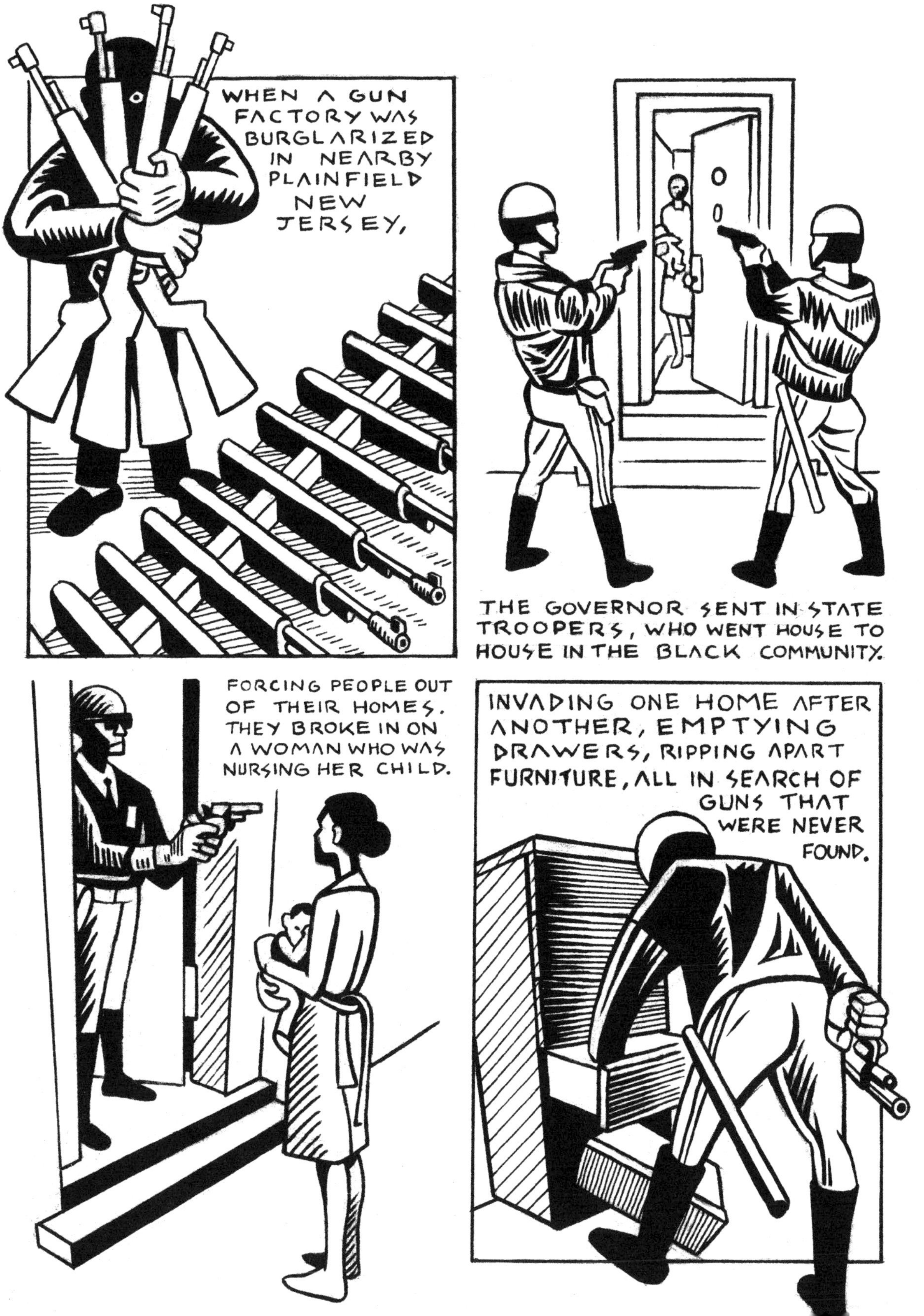
WHEN A GUN FACTORY WAS BURGLARIZED IN NEARBY PLAINFIELD NEW JERSEY,
THE GOVERNOR SENT IN STATE TROOPERS, WHO WENT HOUSE TO HOUSE IN THE BLACK COMMUNITY.
FORCING PEOPLE OUT OF THEIR HOMES. THEY BROKE IN ON A WOMAN WHO WAS NURSING HER CHILD.
INVADING ONE HOME AFTER ANOTHER, EMPTYING DRAWERS, RIPPING APART FURNITURE, ALL IN SEARCH OF GUNS THAT WERE NEVER FOUND.

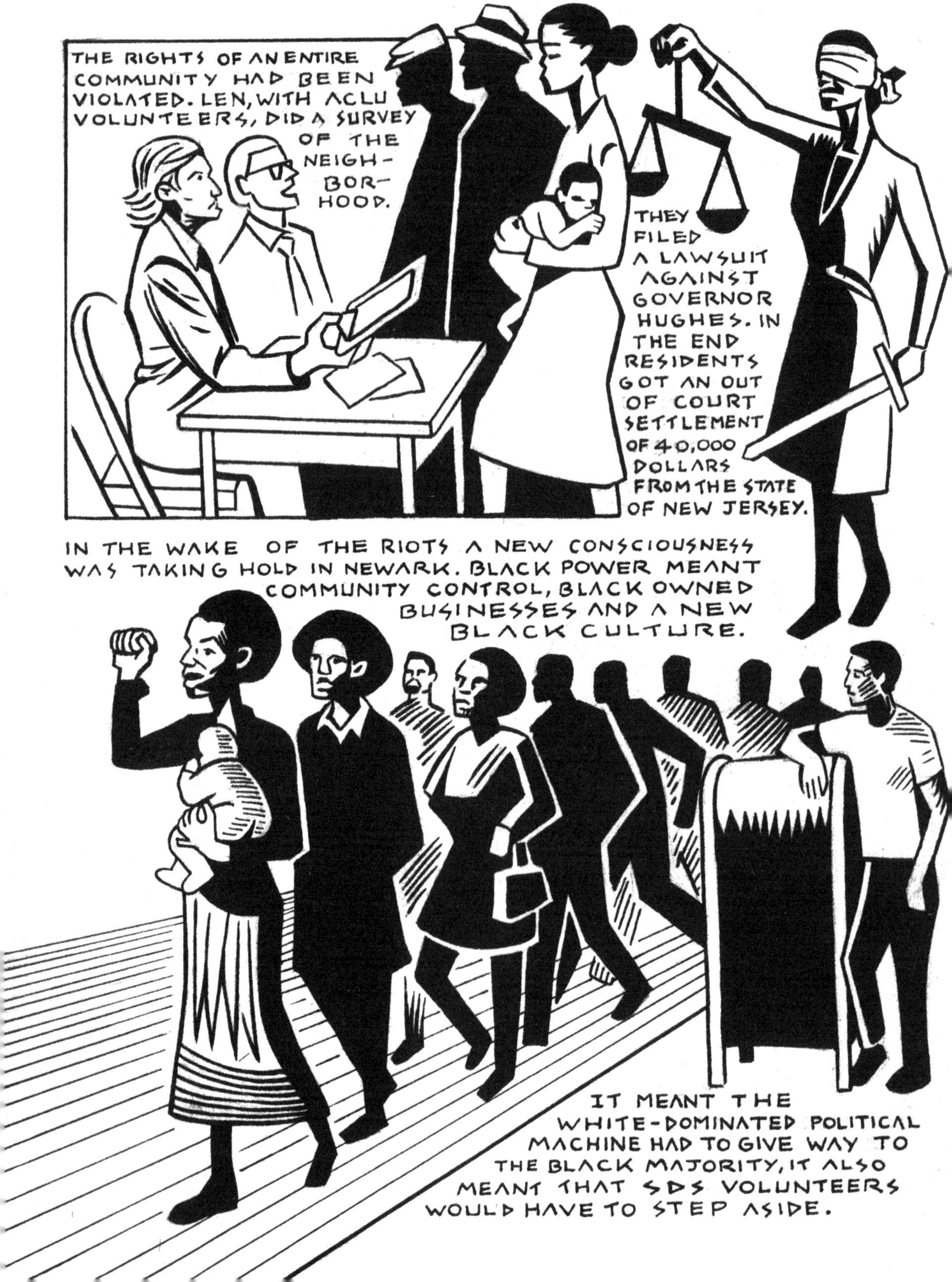
THE RIGHTS OF AN ENTIRE COMMUNITY HAD BEEN VIOLATED. LEN, WITH ACLU VOLUNTEERS, DID A SURVEY OF THE NEIGHBORHOOD.
THEY FILED A LAWSUIT AGAINST GOVERNOR HUGHES. IN THE END RESIDENTS GOT AN OUT OF COURT SETTLEMENT OF 40,000 DOLLARS FROM THE STATE OF NEW JERSEY.
IN THE WAKE OF THE RIOTS A NEW CONSCIOUSNESS WAS TAKING HOLD IN NEWARK. BLACK POWER MEANT COMMUNITY CONTROL, BLACK OWNED BUSINESSES AND A NEW BLACK CULTURE.
IT MEANT THE WHITE-DOMINATED POLITICAL MACHINE HAD TO GIVE WAY TO THE BLACK MAJORITY, IT ALSO MEANT THAT SDS VOLUNTEERS WOULD HAVE TO STEP ASIDE.

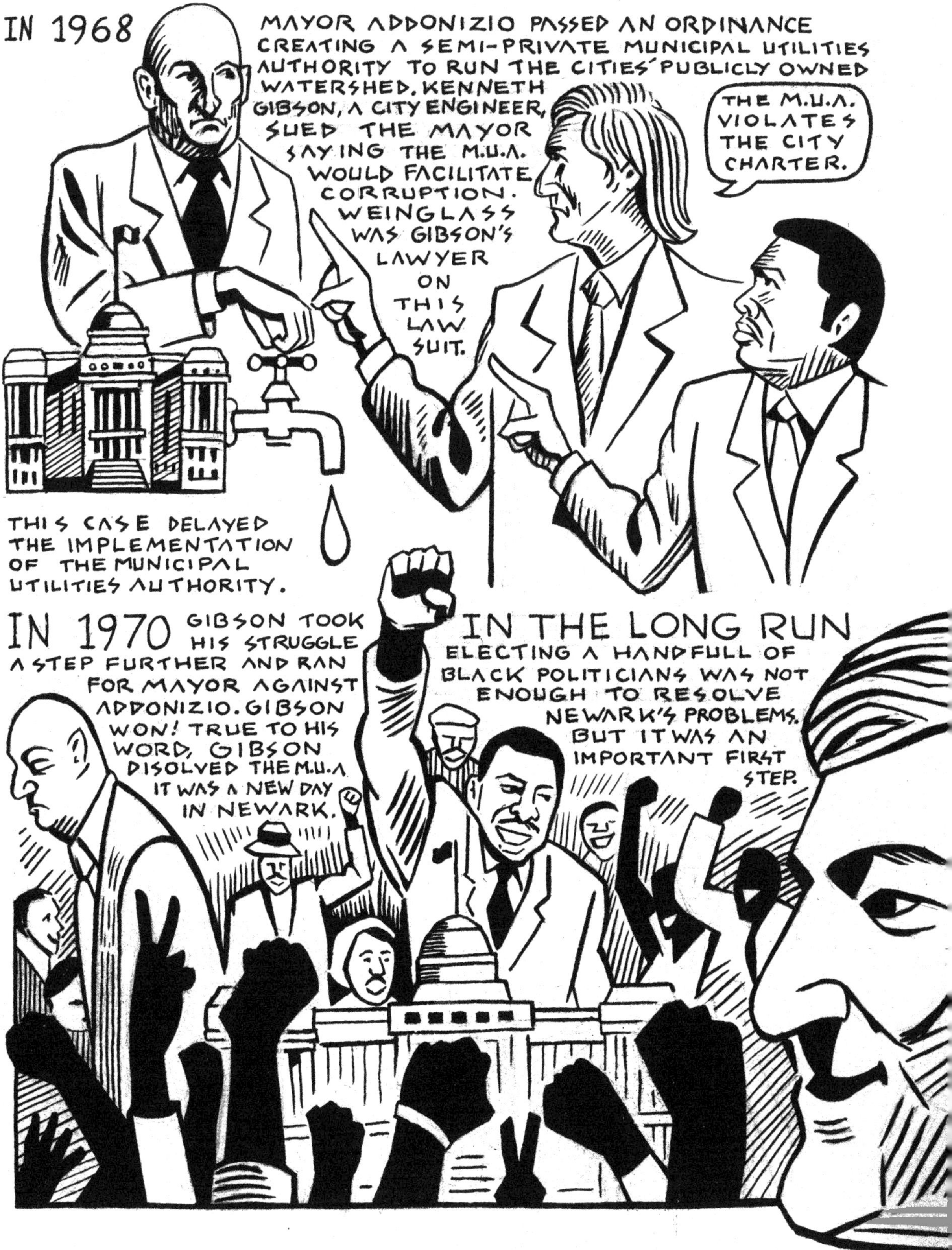
IN 1968
MAYOR ADDONIZIO PASSED AN ORDINANCE CREATING A SEMI-PRIVATE MUNICIPAL UTILITIES AUTHORITY TO RUN THE CITIES' PUBLICLY OWNED WATERSHED. KENNETH GIBSON, A CITY ENGINEER, SUED THE MAYOR SAYING THE M.U.A. WOULD FACILITATE CORRUPTION. WEINGLASS WAS GIBSON'S LAWYER ON THIS LAW SUIT.
THE M.U.A. VIOLATES THE CITY CHARTER.
THIS CASE DELAYED THE IMPLEMENTATION OF THE MUNICIPAL UTILITIES AUTHORITY.
IN 1970 GIBSON TOOK HIS STRUGGLE A STEP FURTHER AND RAN FOR MAYOR AGAINST ADDONIZIO. GIBSON WON! TRUE TO HIS WORD, GIBSON DISOLVED THE M.U.A IT WAS A NEW DAY IN NEWARK.
IN THE LONG RUN
ELECTING A HANDFULL OF BLACK POLITICIANS WAS NOT ENOUGH TO RESOLVE NEWARK'S PROBLEMS. BUT IT WAS AN IMPORTANT FIRST STEP.

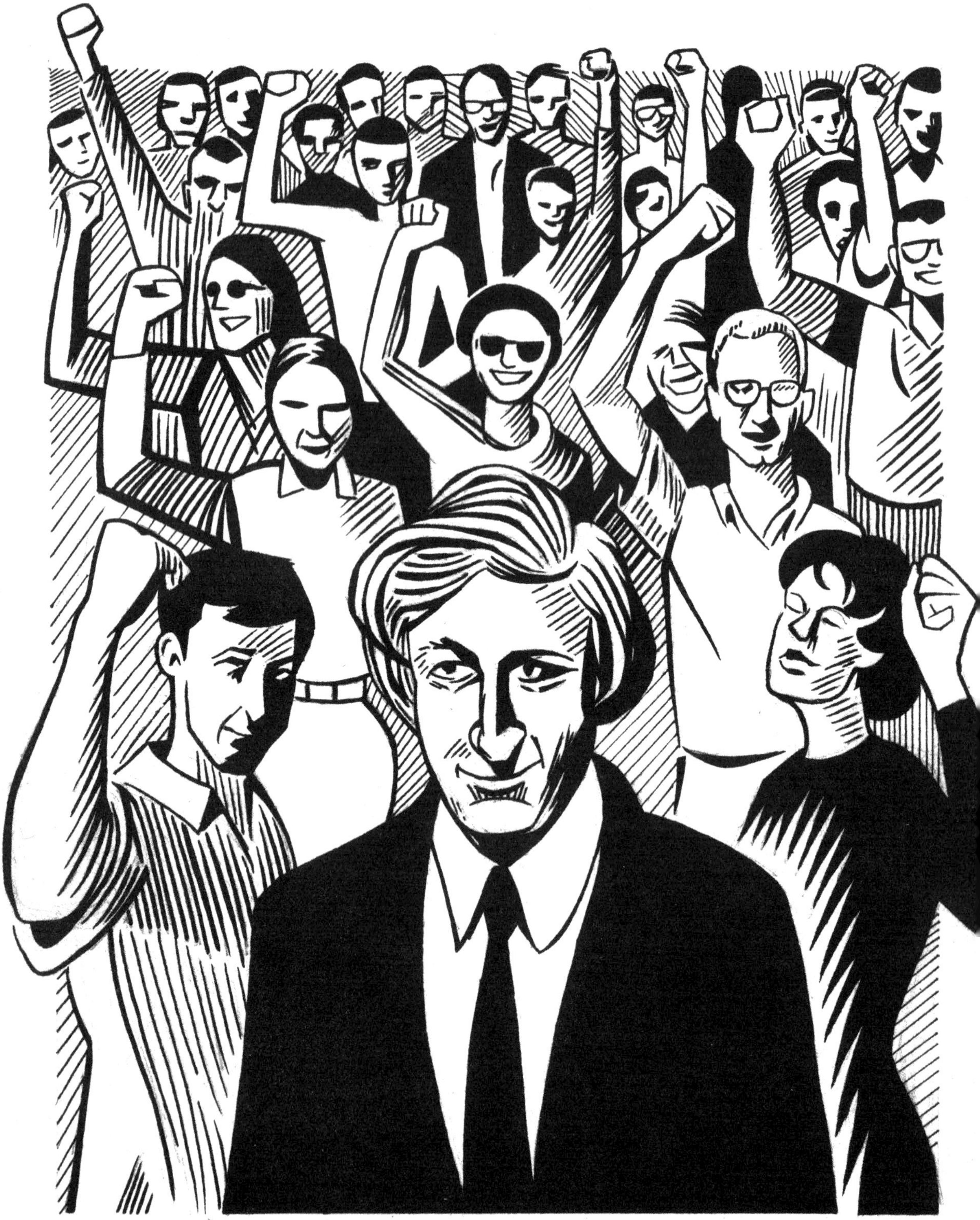

THE SITUATION IN NEWARK AND THE ONGOING VIETNAM WAR RADICALIZED MANY PEOPLE AND LEONARD HAD FOUND HIS CALLING IN LIFE, REPRESENTING THE RADICALS!

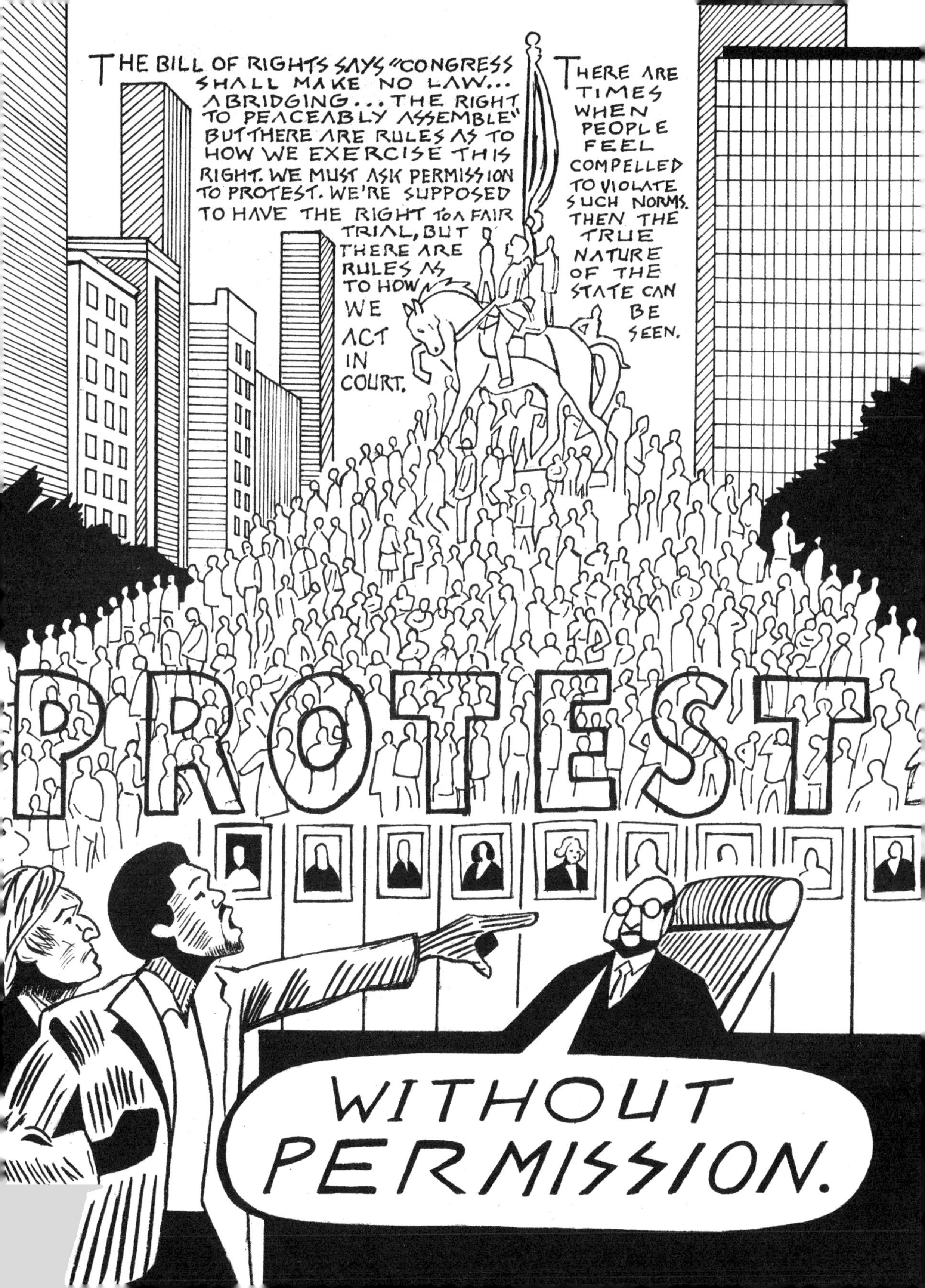
THE BILL OF RIGHTS SAYS "CONGRESS SHALL MAKE NO LAW... ABRIDGING... THE RIGHT TO PEACEABLY ASSEMBLE" BUT THERE ARE RULES AS TO HOW WE EXERCISE THIS RIGHT. WE MUST ASK PERMISSION TO PROTEST. WE'RE SUPPOSED TO HAVE THE RIGHT TO A FAIR TRIAL, BUT THERE ARE RULES AS TO HOW WE ACT IN COURT.
THERE ARE TIMES WHEN PEOPLE FEEL COMPELLED TO VIOLATE SUCH NORMS. THEN THE TRUE NATURE OF THE STATE CAN BE SEEN.
PROTEST
WITHOUT PERMISSION.

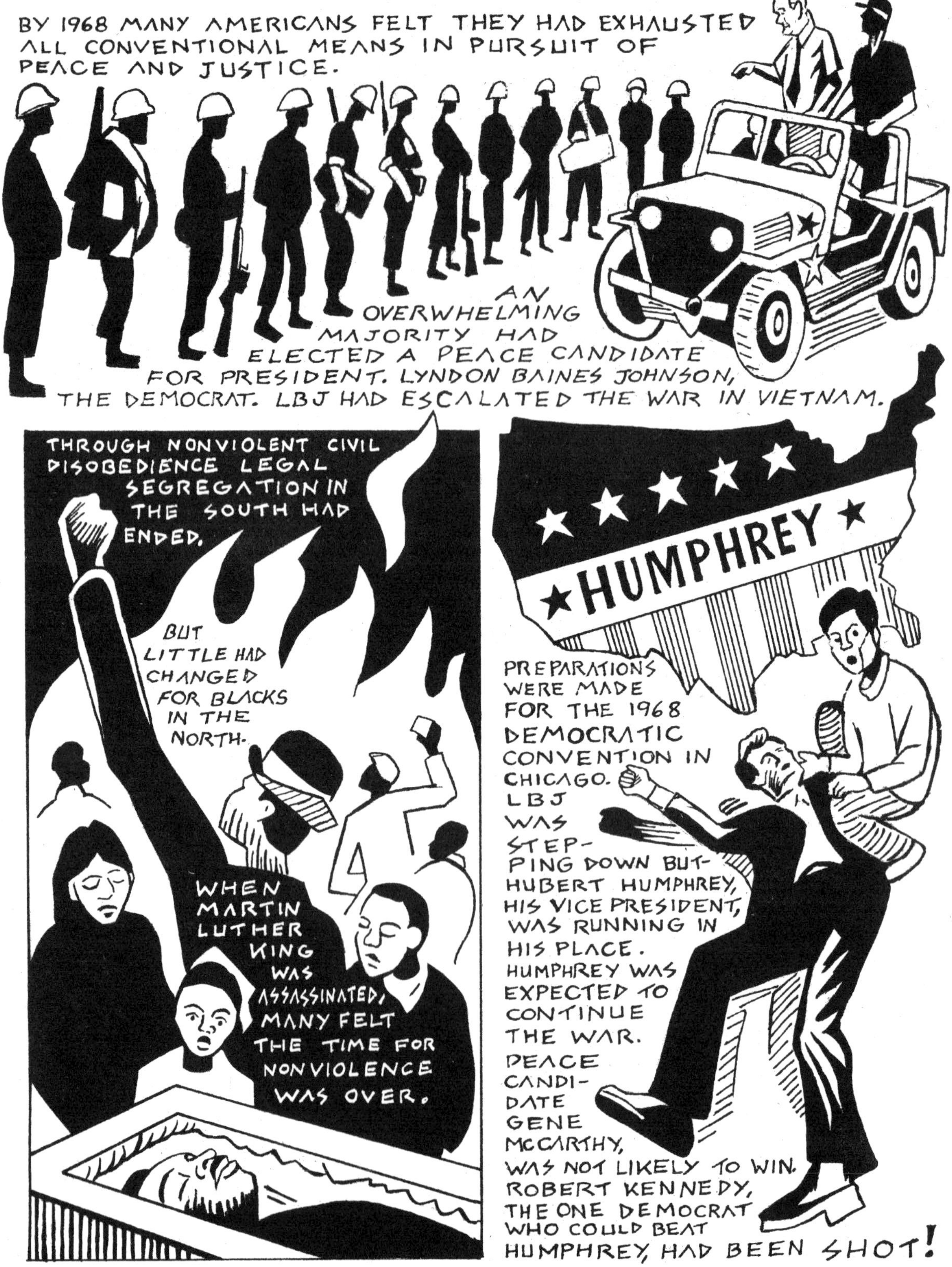

BY 1968 MANY AMERICANS FELT THEY HAD EXHAUSTED ALL CONVENTIONAL MEANS IN PURSUIT OF PEACE AND JUSTICE.
AN OVERWHELMING MAJORITY HAD ELECTED A PEACE CANDIDATE FOR PRESIDENT. LYNDON BAINES JOHNSON, THE DEMOCRAT. LBJ HAD ESCALATED THE WAR IN VIETNAM.
THROUGH NONVIOLENT CIVIL DISOBEDIENCE LEGAL SEGREGATION IN THE SOUTH HAD ENDED.
BUT LITTLE HAD CHANGED FOR BLACKS IN THE NORTH.
WHEN MARTIN LUTHER KING WAS ASSASSINATED, MANY FELT THE TIME FOR NONVIOLENCE WAS OVER.
HUMPHREY
PREPARATIONS WERE MADE FOR THE 1968 DEMOCRATIC CONVENTION IN CHICAGO. LBJ WAS STEP-PING DOWN BUT HUBERT HUMPHREY, HIS VICE PRESIDENT, WAS RUNNING IN HIS PLACE. HUMPHREY WAS EXPECTED TO CONTINUE THE WAR. PEACE CANDI-DATE GENE McCARTHY, WAS NOT LIKELY TO WIN. ROBERT KENNEDY, THE ONE DEMOCRAT WHO COULD BEAT HUMPHREY, HAD BEEN SHOT!

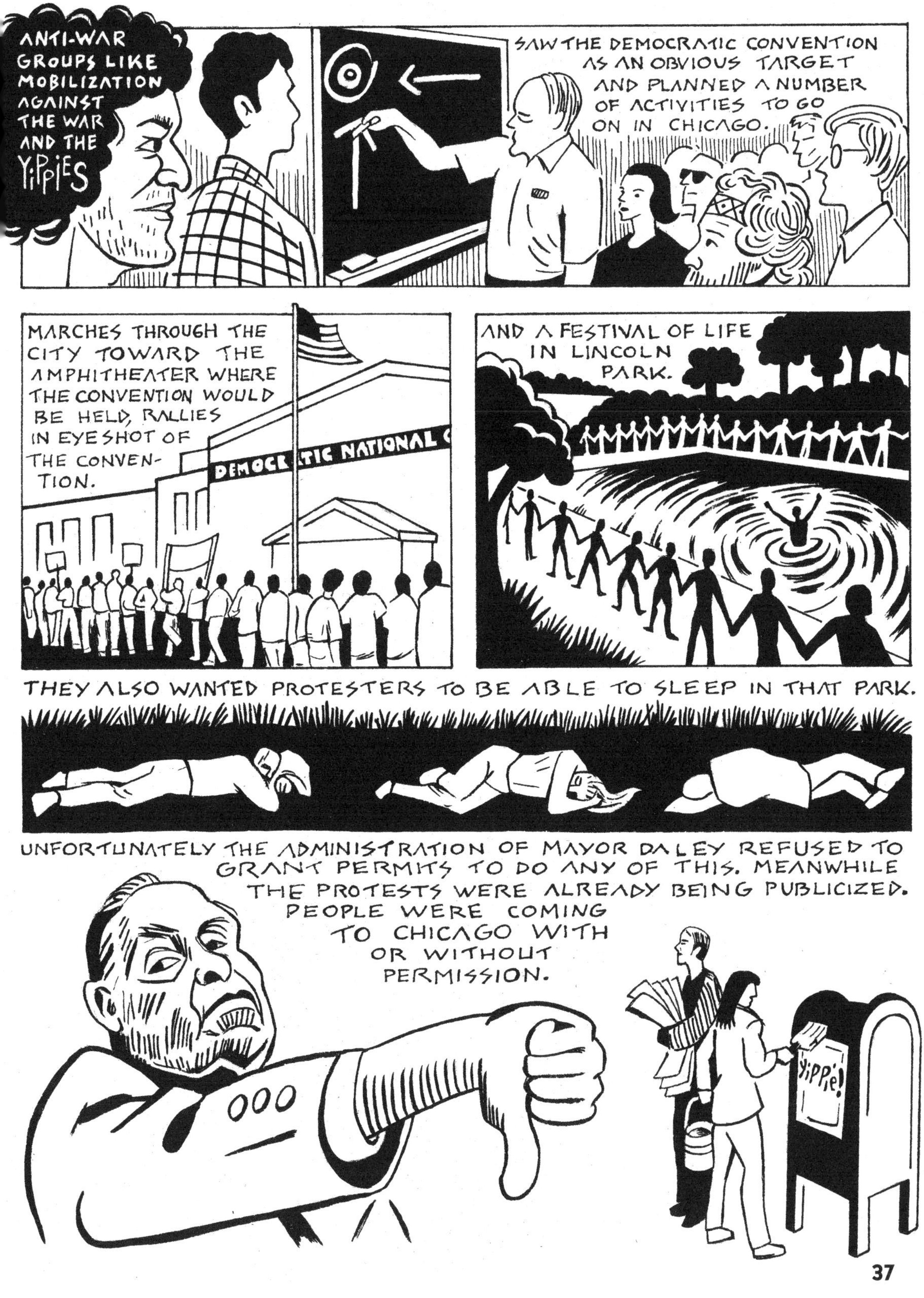
ANTI-WAR GROUPS LIKE MOBILIZATION AGAINST THE WAR AND THE YIPPIES
SAW THE DEMOCRATIC CONVENTION AS AN OBVIOUS TARGET AND PLANNED A NUMBER OF ACTIVITIES TO GO ON IN CHICAGO.
MARCHES THROUGH THE CITY TOWARD THE AMPHITHEATER WHERE THE CONVENTION WOULD BE HELD, RALLIES IN EYESHOT OF THE CONVENTION.
DEMOCRATIC NATIONAL C
AND A FESTIVAL OF LIFE IN LINCOLN PARK.
THEY ALSO WANTED PROTESTERS TO BE ABLE TO SLEEP IN THAT PARK.
UNFORTUNATELY THE ADMINISTRATION OF MAYOR DALEY REFUSED TO GRANT PERMITS TO DO ANY OF THIS. MEANWHILE THE PROTESTS WERE ALREADY BEING PUBLICIZED.
PEOPLE WERE COMING TO CHICAGO WITH OR WITHOUT PERMISSION.
YIPPIE!

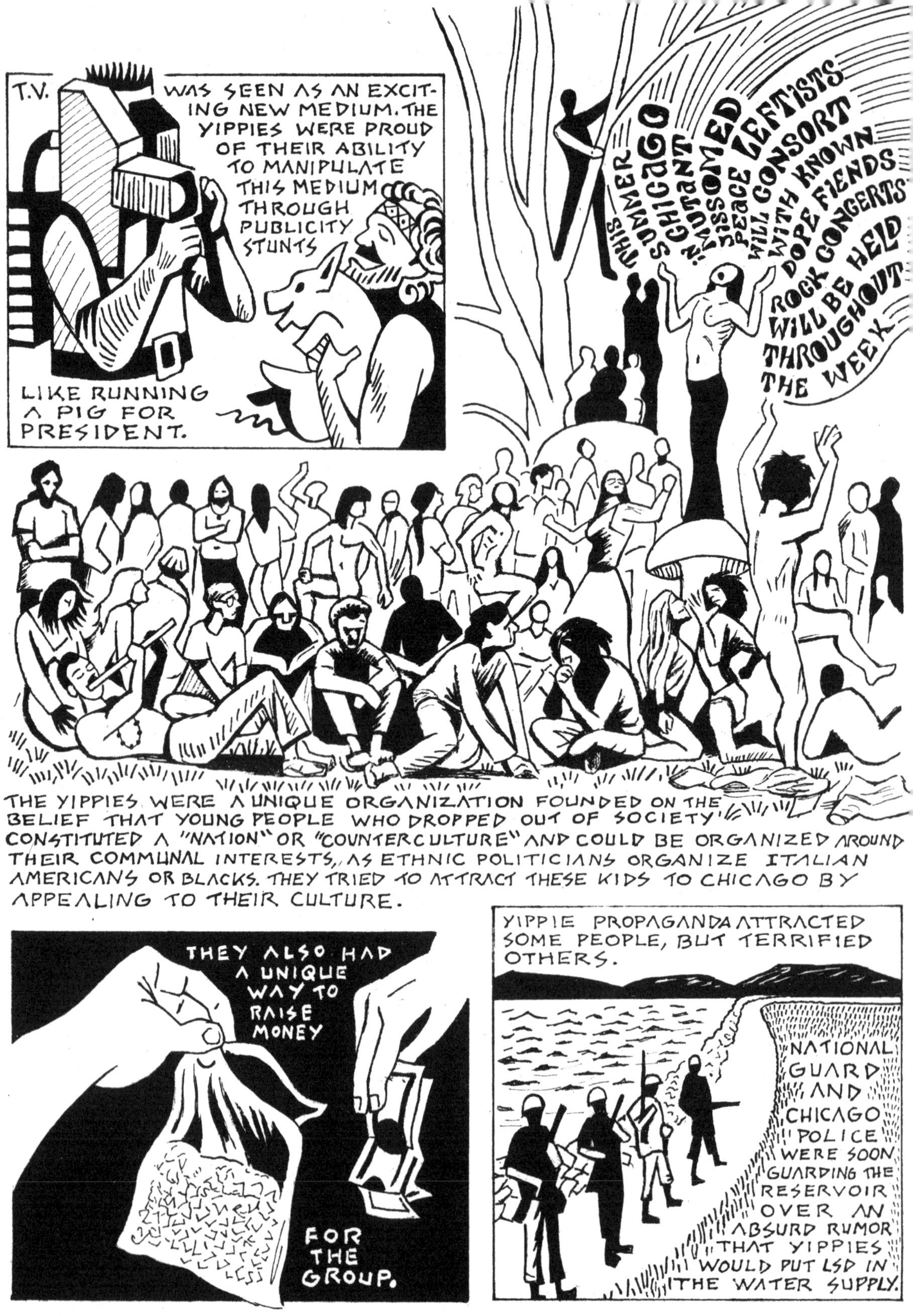
T.V. WAS SEEN AS AN EXCITING NEW MEDIUM. THE YIPPIES WERE PROUD OF THEIR ABILITY TO MANIPULATE THIS MEDIUM THROUGH PUBLICITY STUNTS
LIKE RUNNING A PIG FOR PRESIDENT.
THIS SUMMER SCHICAGO 'N MUTANT JISSOMED PEACE LEFTISTS WILL CONSORT WITH KNOWN DOPE FIENDS ROCK CONCERTS WILL BE HELD THROUGHOUT THE WEEK
THE YIPPIES WERE A UNIQUE ORGANIZATION FOUNDED ON THE BELIEF THAT YOUNG PEOPLE WHO DROPPED OUT OF SOCIETY CONSTITUTED A "NATION" OR "COUNTERCULTURE" AND COULD BE ORGANIZED AROUND THEIR COMMUNAL INTERESTS, AS ETHNIC POLITICIANS ORGANIZE ITALIAN AMERICANS OR BLACKS. THEY TRIED TO ATTRACT THESE KIDS TO CHICAGO BY APPEALING TO THEIR CULTURE.
THEY ALSO HAD A UNIQUE WAY TO RAISE MONEY
FOR THE GROUP.
YIPPIE PROPAGANDA ATTRACTED SOME PEOPLE, BUT TERRIFIED OTHERS.
NATIONAL GUARD AND CHICAGO POLICE WERE SOON GUARDING THE RESERVOIR OVER AN ABSURD RUMOR THAT YIPPIES WOULD PUT LSD IN THE WATER SUPPLY.

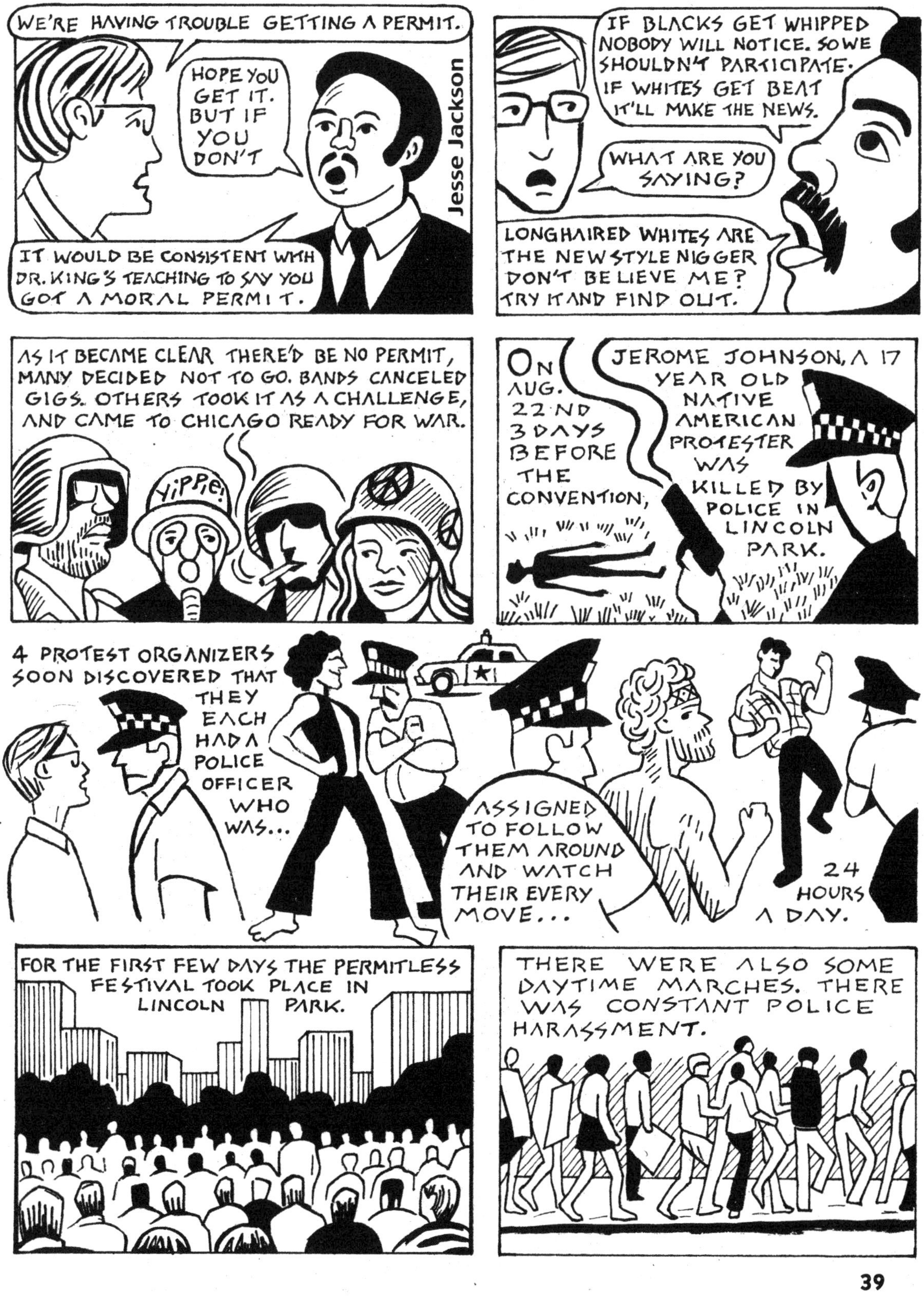
WE'RE HAVING TROUBLE GETTING A PERMIT.
HOPE YOU GET IT. BUT IF YOU DON'T
Jesse Jackson
IT WOULD BE CONSISTENT WITH DR. KING'S TEACHING TO SAY YOU GOT A MORAL PERMIT.
IF BLACKS GET WHIPPED NOBODY WILL NOTICE. SO WE SHOULDN'T PARTICIPATE. IF WHITES GET BEAT IT'LL MAKE THE NEWS.
WHAT ARE YOU SAYING?
LONGHAIRED WHITES ARE THE NEW STYLE NIGGER DON'T BELIEVE ME? TRY IT AND FIND OUT.
AS IT BECAME CLEAR THERE'D BE NO PERMIT, MANY DECIDED NOT TO GO. BANDS CANCELED GIGS. OTHERS TOOK IT AS A CHALLENGE, AND CAME TO CHICAGO READY FOR WAR.
YIPPIE!
ON AUG. 22ND 3 DAYS BEFORE THE CONVENTION,
JEROME JOHNSON, A 17 YEAR OLD NATIVE AMERICAN PROTESTER WAS KILLED BY POLICE IN LINCOLN PARK.
4 PROTEST ORGANIZERS SOON DISCOVERED THAT THEY EACH HAD A POLICE OFFICER WHO WAS...
ASSIGNED TO FOLLOW THEM AROUND AND WATCH THEIR EVERY MOVE...
24 HOURS A DAY.
FOR THE FIRST FEW DAYS THE PERMITLESS FESTIVAL TOOK PLACE IN LINCOLN PARK.
THERE WERE ALSO SOME DAYTIME MARCHES. THERE WAS CONSTANT POLICE HARASSMENT.

AT NIGHT COPS WOULD STORM THE PARK. YIPPIES BUILT BARRICADES AND FOUGHT TO HOLD THE PARK.

IT'S OUR FUCKING PARK!

TEARGAS WAS USED TO PUSH PEOPLE OUT OF THE PARK.

ONCE PEOPLE WERE OUT, THEY FILLED THE AVENUES. AS COPS TRIED TO CLEAR STREETS...

WHENEVER THE PEOPLE DISAGREE WITH THE POLITICAL DECISIONS THAT BEEN MADE UPON THEIR HEADS, THE RACIST POWER STRUCTURE SENDS THEIR GUNS TO FORCE THE PEOPLE TO ACCEPT THOSE POLITICAL DECISIONS. BUT WE ARE HERE AS REVOLUTIONARIES TO LET THEM KNOW WE REFUSE TO ACCEPT THOSE DECISIONS THAT MAINTAIN THE OPPRESSION OF OUR BLACK PEOPLE AND PEOPLE AROUND THE WORLD.

...VIOLENCE FLARED.

FREE

HUE

AUGUST 27TH, BOBBY SEALE FLEW IN FROM CALIFORNIA TO SPEAK IN THE PARK. THIS SPEECH WAS THE ONLY INVOLVEMENT OF THE BLACK PANTHER PARTY.

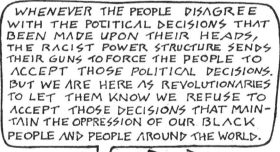

40

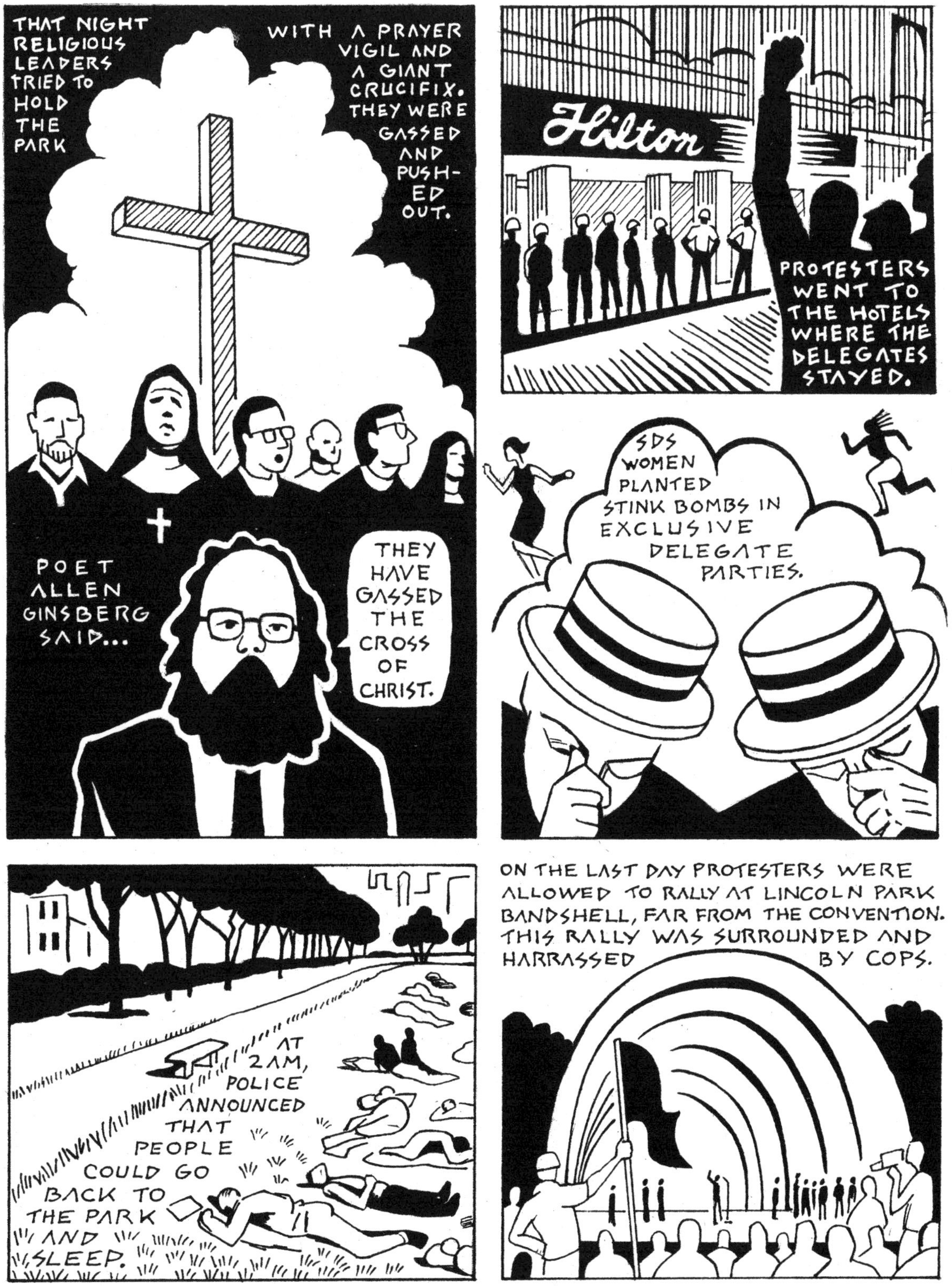
THAT NIGHT RELIGIOUS LEADERS TRIED TO HOLD THE PARK
WITH A PRAYER VIGIL AND A GIANT CRUCIFIX. THEY WERE GASSED AND PUSH-ED OUT.
POET ALLEN GINSBERG SAID...
THEY HAVE GASSED THE CROSS OF CHRIST.
Hilton
PROTESTERS WENT TO THE HOTELS WHERE THE DELEGATES STAYED.
SDS WOMEN PLANTED STINK BOMBS IN EXCLUSIVE DELEGATE PARTIES.
AT 2AM, POLICE ANNOUNCED THAT PEOPLE COULD GO BACK TO THE PARK AND SLEEP.
ON THE LAST DAY PROTESTERS WERE ALLOWED TO RALLY AT LINCOLN PARK BANDSHELL, FAR FROM THE CONVENTION. THIS RALLY WAS SURROUNDED AND HARRASSED BY COPS.

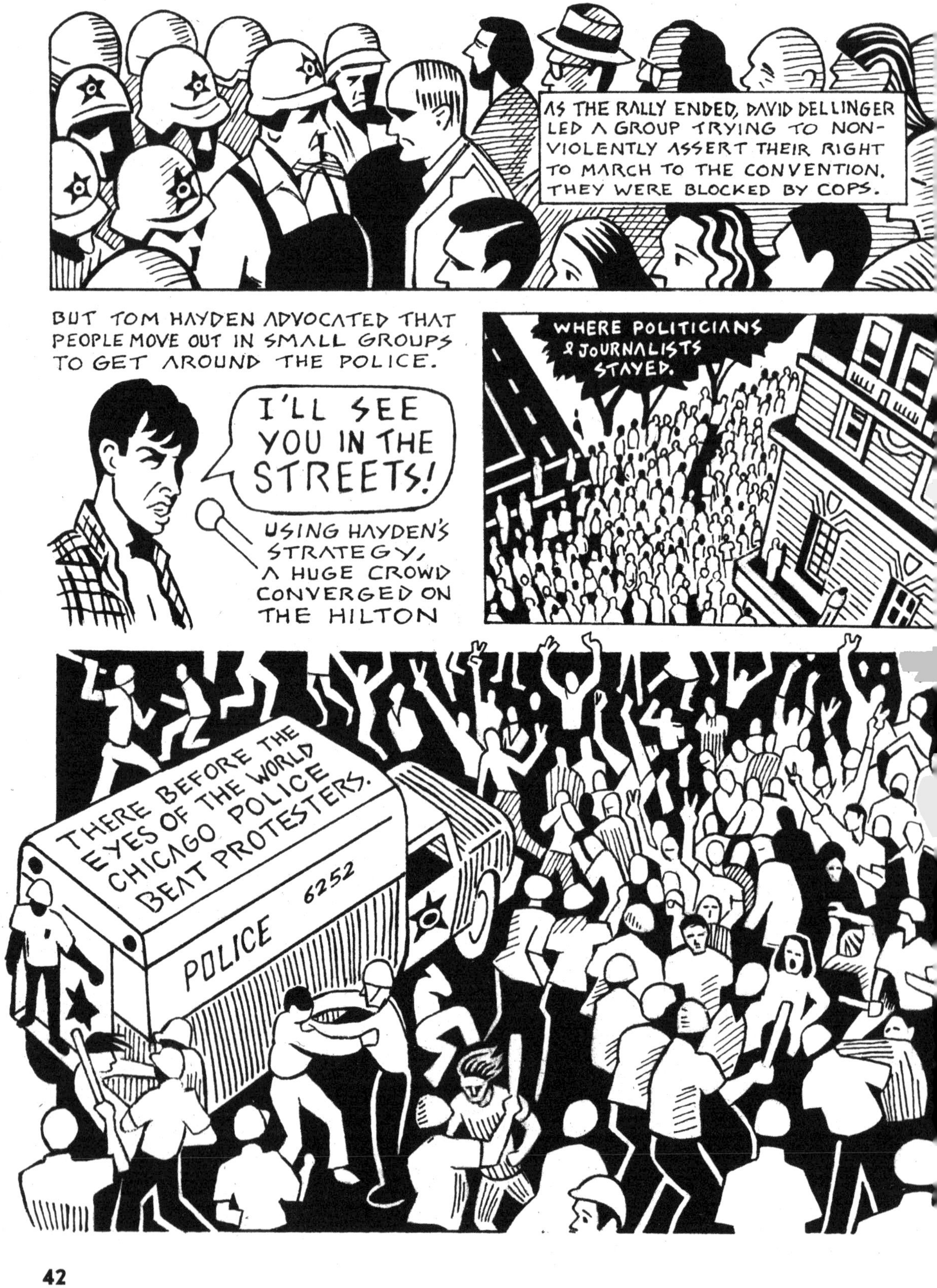
AS THE RALLY ENDED, DAVID DELLINGER LED A GROUP TRYING TO NON-VIOLENTLY ASSERT THEIR RIGHT TO MARCH TO THE CONVENTION. THEY WERE BLOCKED BY COPS.
BUT TOM HAYDEN ADVOCATED THAT PEOPLE MOVE OUT IN SMALL GROUPS TO GET AROUND THE POLICE.
I'LL SEE YOU IN THE STREETS!
USING HAYDEN'S STRATEGY, A HUGE CROWD CONVERGED ON THE HILTON
WHERE POLITICIANS & JOURNALISTS STAYED.
THERE BEFORE THE EYES OF THE WORLD CHICAGO POLICE BEAT PROTESTERS.
6252
POLICE

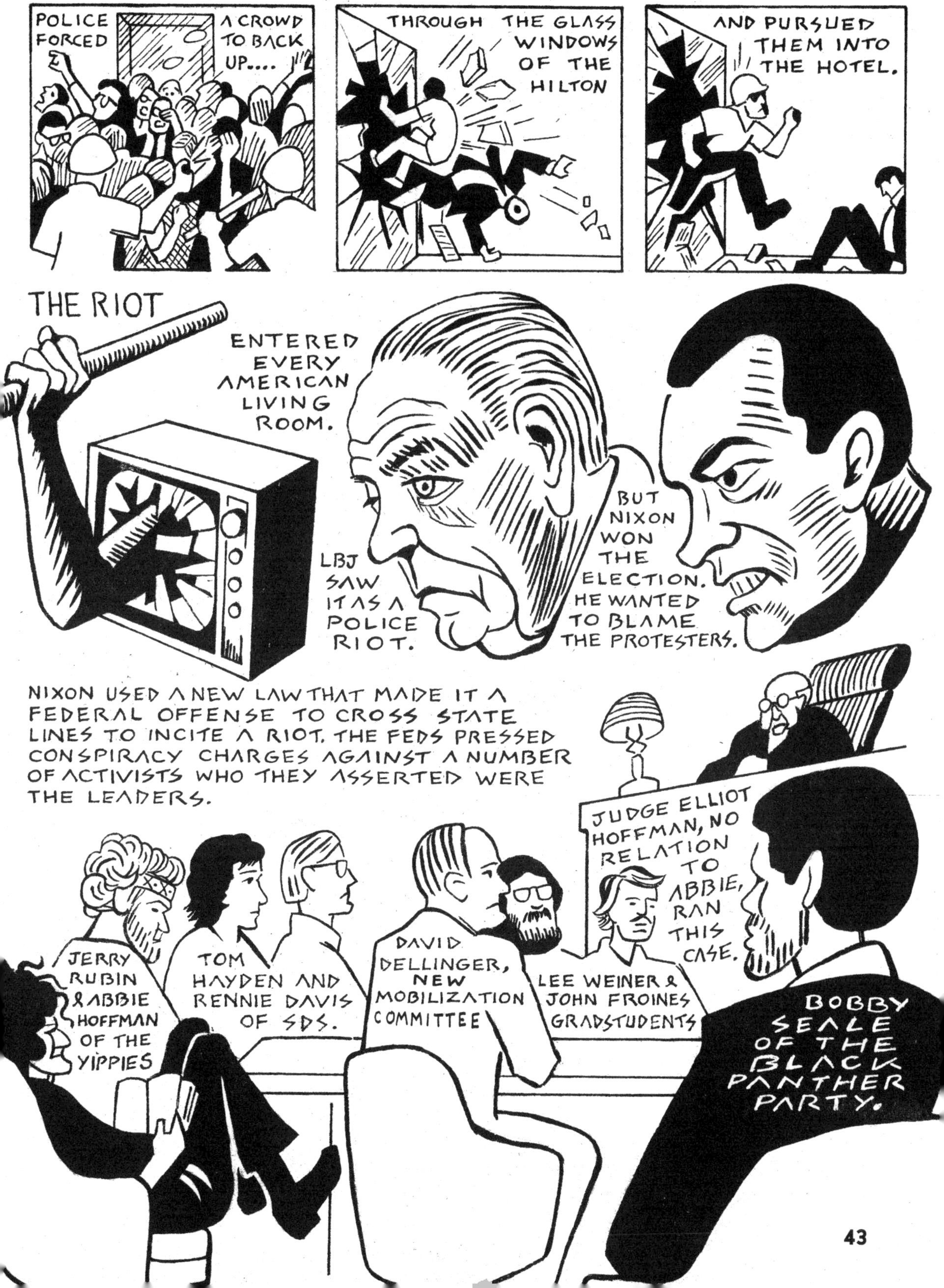
POLICE FORCED
A CROWD TO BACK UP....
THROUGH THE GLASS WINDOWS OF THE HILTON
AND PURSUED THEM INTO THE HOTEL.
THE RIOT
ENTERED EVERY AMERICAN LIVING ROOM.
LBJ SAW IT AS A POLICE RIOT.
BUT NIXON WON THE ELECTION. HE WANTED TO BLAME THE PROTESTERS.
NIXON USED A NEW LAW THAT MADE IT A FEDERAL OFFENSE TO CROSS STATE LINES TO INCITE A RIOT. THE FEDS PRESSED CONSPIRACY CHARGES AGAINST A NUMBER OF ACTIVISTS WHO THEY ASSERTED WERE THE LEADERS.
JUDGE ELLIOT HOFFMAN, NO RELATION TO ABBIE, RAN THIS CASE.
JERRY RUBIN & ABBIE HOFFMAN OF THE YIPPIES
TOM HAYDEN AND RENNIE DAVIS OF SDS.
DAVID DELLINGER, NEW MOBILIZATION COMMITTEE
LEE WEINER & JOHN FROINES GRADSTUDENTS
BOBBY SEALE OF THE BLACK PANTHER PARTY.

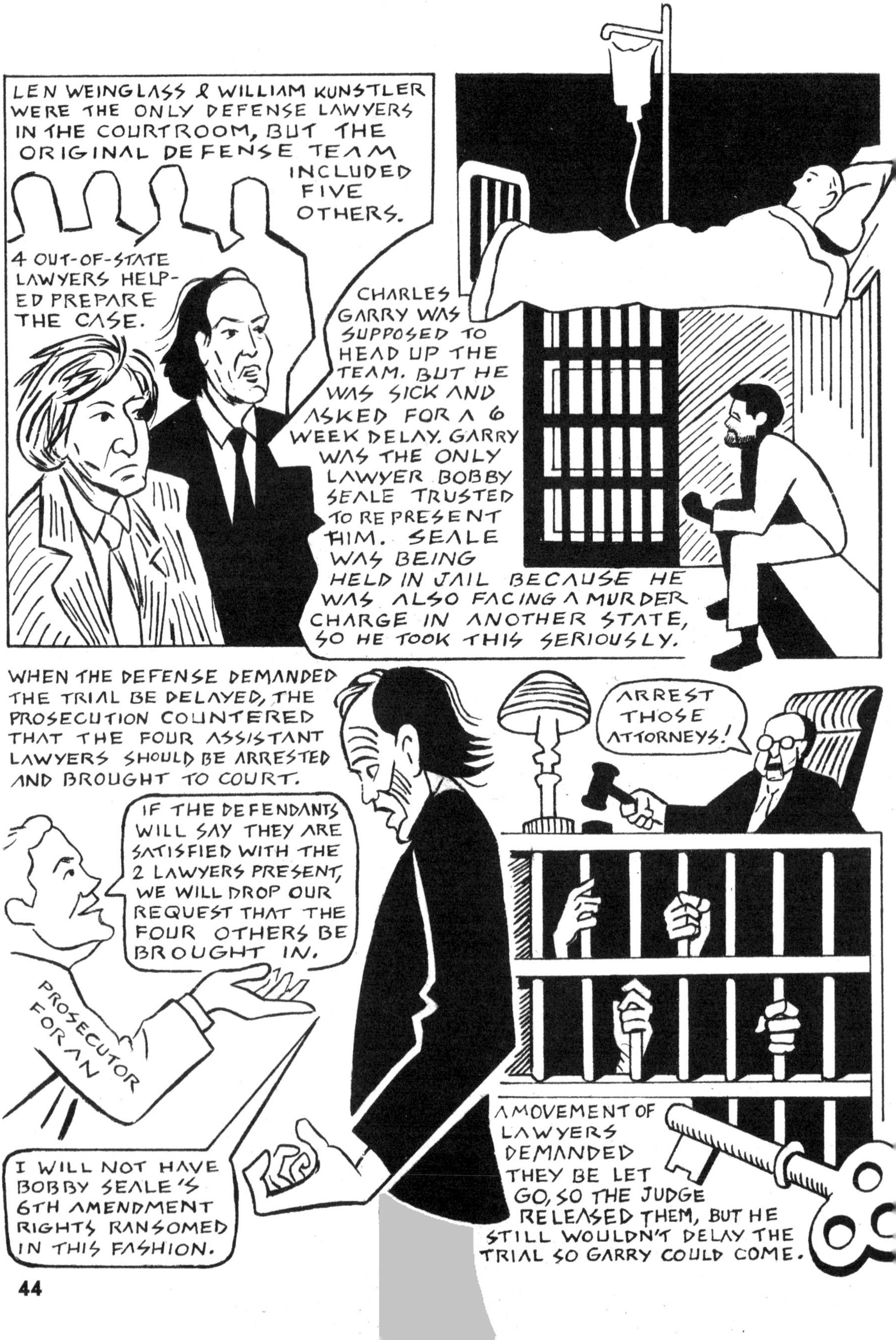
LEN WEINGLASS & WILLIAM KUNSTLER WERE THE ONLY DEFENSE LAWYERS IN THE COURTROOM, BUT THE ORIGINAL DEFENSE TEAM INCLUDED FIVE OTHERS.
4 OUT-OF-STATE LAWYERS HELPED PREPARE THE CASE.
CHARLES GARRY WAS SUPPOSED TO HEAD UP THE TEAM. BUT HE WAS SICK AND ASKED FOR A 6 WEEK DELAY. GARRY WAS THE ONLY LAWYER BOBBY SEALE TRUSTED TO REPRESENT HIM. SEALE WAS BEING HELD IN JAIL BECAUSE HE WAS ALSO FACING A MURDER CHARGE IN ANOTHER STATE, SO HE TOOK THIS SERIOUSLY.
WHEN THE DEFENSE DEMANDED THE TRIAL BE DELAYED, THE PROSECUTION COUNTERED THAT THE FOUR ASSISTANT LAWYERS SHOULD BE ARRESTED AND BROUGHT TO COURT.
ARREST THOSE ATTORNEYS!
IF THE DEFENDANTS WILL SAY THEY ARE SATISFIED WITH THE 2 LAWYERS PRESENT, WE WILL DROP OUR REQUEST THAT THE FOUR OTHERS BE BROUGHT IN.
PROSECUTOR FORAN
I WILL NOT HAVE BOBBY SEALE'S 6TH AMENDMENT RIGHTS RANSOMED IN THIS FASHION.
A MOVEMENT OF LAWYERS DEMANDED THEY BE LET GO, SO THE JUDGE RELEASED THEM, BUT HE STILL WOULDN'T DELAY THE TRIAL SO GARRY COULD COME.

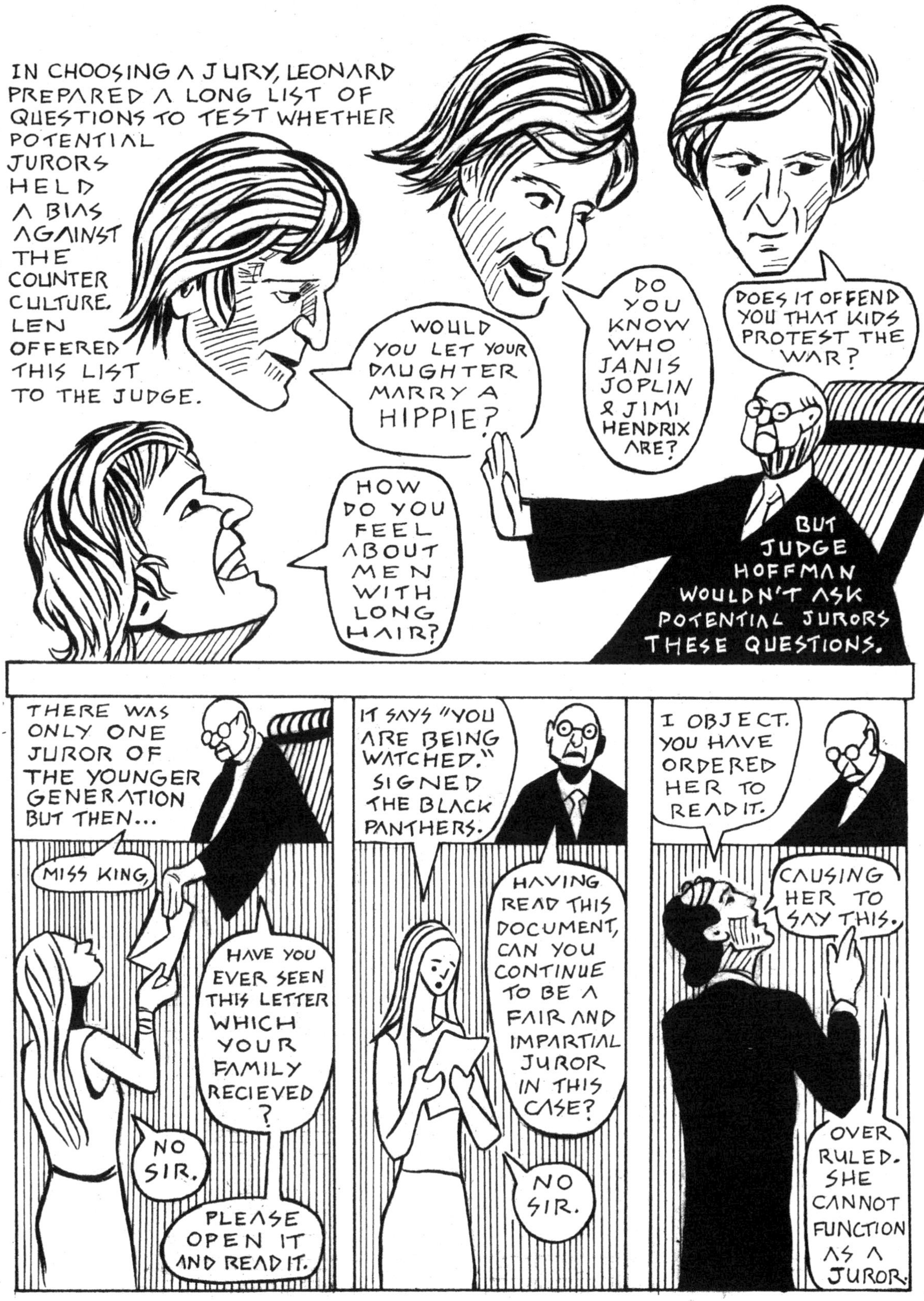
IN CHOOSING A JURY, LEONARD PREPARED A LONG LIST OF QUESTIONS TO TEST WHETHER POTENTIAL JURORS HELD A BIAS AGAINST THE COUNTER CULTURE. LEN OFFERED THIS LIST TO THE JUDGE.
WOULD YOU LET YOUR DAUGHTER MARRY A HIPPIE?
DO YOU KNOW WHO JANIS JOPLIN & JIMI HENDRIX ARE?
DOES IT OFFEND YOU THAT KIDS PROTEST THE WAR?
HOW DO YOU FEEL ABOUT MEN WITH LONG HAIR?
BUT JUDGE HOFFMAN WOULDN'T ASK POTENTIAL JURORS THESE QUESTIONS.
THERE WAS ONLY ONE JUROR OF THE YOUNGER GENERATION BUT THEN...
MISS KING,
HAVE YOU EVER SEEN THIS LETTER WHICH YOUR FAMILY RECIEVED?
NO SIR.
PLEASE OPEN IT AND READ IT.
IT SAYS "YOU ARE BEING WATCHED." SIGNED THE BLACK PANTHERS.
HAVING READ THIS DOCUMENT, CAN YOU CONTINUE TO BE A FAIR AND IMPARTIAL JUROR IN THIS CASE?
NO SIR.
I OBJECT. YOU HAVE ORDERED HER TO READ IT.
CAUSING HER TO SAY THIS.
OVER RULED. SHE CANNOT FUNCTION AS A JUROR.

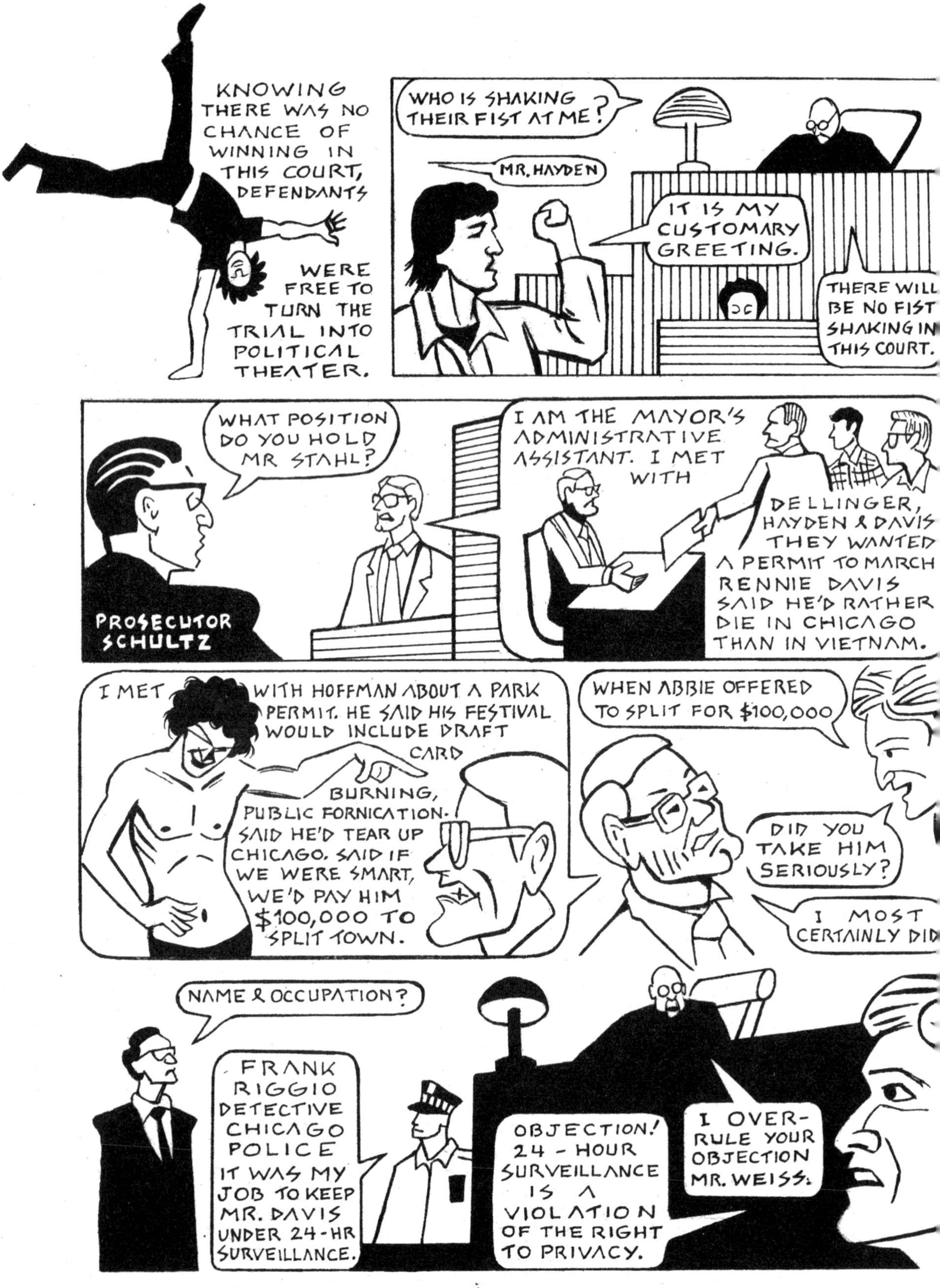
KNOWING THERE WAS NO CHANCE OF WINNING IN THIS COURT, DEFENDANTS
WERE FREE TO TURN THE TRIAL INTO POLITICAL THEATER.
WHO IS SHAKING THEIR FIST AT ME?
MR. HAYDEN
IT IS MY CUSTOMARY GREETING.
THERE WILL BE NO FIST SHAKING IN THIS COURT.
WHAT POSITION DO YOU HOLD MR STAHL?
PROSECUTOR SCHULTZ
I AM THE MAYOR'S ADMINISTRATIVE ASSISTANT. I MET WITH
DELLINGER, HAYDEN & DAVIS THEY WANTED A PERMIT TO MARCH RENNIE DAVIS SAID HE'D RATHER DIE IN CHICAGO THAN IN VIETNAM.
I MET WITH HOFFMAN ABOUT A PARK PERMIT. HE SAID HIS FESTIVAL WOULD INCLUDE DRAFT CARD
BURNING, PUBLIC FORNICATION. SAID HE'D TEAR UP CHICAGO. SAID IF WE WERE SMART, WE'D PAY HIM $100,000 TO SPLIT TOWN.
WHEN ABBIE OFFERED TO SPLIT FOR $100,000
DID YOU TAKE HIM SERIOUSLY?
I MOST CERTAINLY DID
NAME & OCCUPATION?
FRANK RIGGIO DETECTIVE CHICAGO POLICE
IT WAS MY JOB TO KEEP MR. DAVIS UNDER 24-HR SURVEILLANCE.
OBJECTION! 24-HOUR SURVEILLANCE IS A VIOLATION OF THE RIGHT TO PRIVACY.
I OVER-RULE YOUR OBJECTION MR. WEISS.

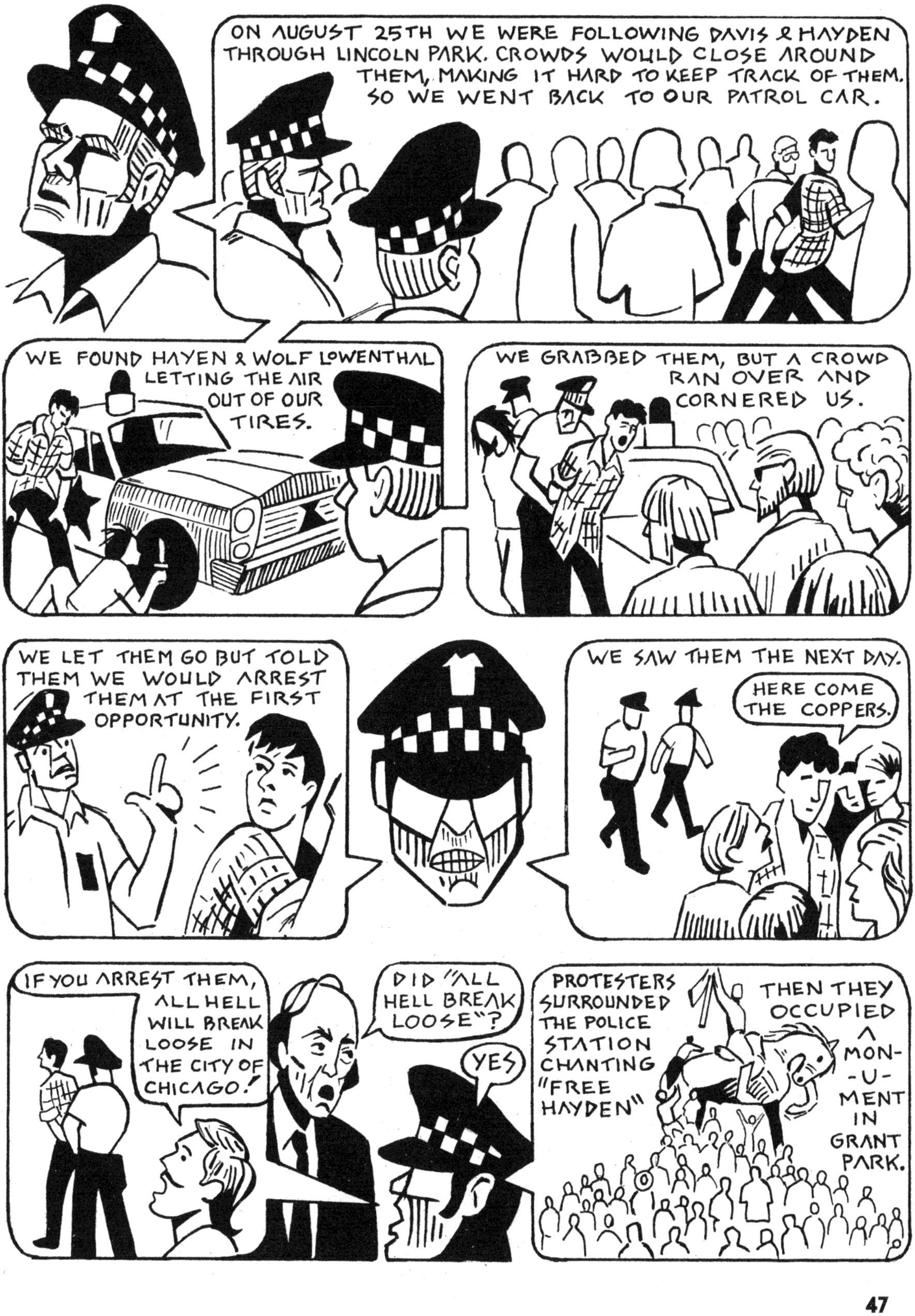
ON AUGUST 25TH WE WERE FOLLOWING DAVIS & HAYDEN THROUGH LINCOLN PARK. CROWDS WOULD CLOSE AROUND THEM, MAKING IT HARD TO KEEP TRACK OF THEM. SO WE WENT BACK TO OUR PATROL CAR.
WE FOUND HAYEN & WOLF LOWENTHAL LETTING THE AIR OUT OF OUR TIRES.
WE GRABBED THEM, BUT A CROWD RAN OVER AND CORNERED US.
WE LET THEM GO BUT TOLD THEM WE WOULD ARREST THEM AT THE FIRST OPPORTUNITY.
WE SAW THEM THE NEXT DAY.
HERE COME THE COPPERS.
IF YOU ARREST THEM, ALL HELL WILL BREAK LOOSE IN THE CITY OF CHICAGO!
DID "ALL HELL BREAK LOOSE"?
YES
PROTESTERS SURROUNDED THE POLICE STATION CHANTING "FREE HAYDEN"
THEN THEY OCCUPIED A MON-U-MENT IN GRANT PARK.

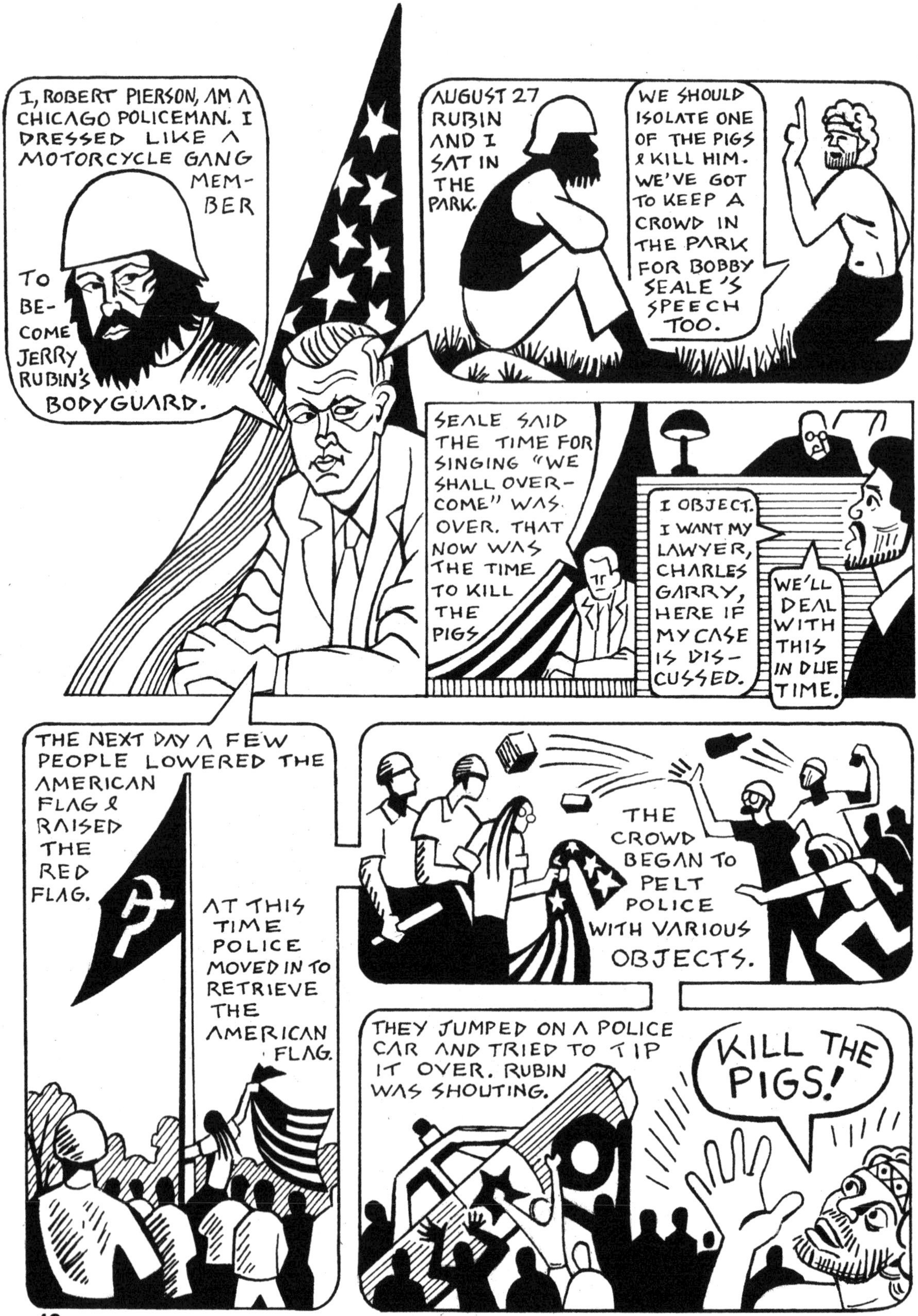
I, ROBERT PIERSON, AM A CHICAGO POLICEMAN. I DRESSED LIKE A MOTORCYCLE GANG MEMBER TO BECOME JERRY RUBIN'S BODYGUARD.
AUGUST 27 RUBIN AND I SAT IN THE PARK.
WE SHOULD ISOLATE ONE OF THE PIGS & KILL HIM. WE'VE GOT TO KEEP A CROWD IN THE PARK FOR BOBBY SEALE'S SPEECH TOO.
SEALE SAID THE TIME FOR SINGING "WE SHALL OVERCOME" WAS OVER. THAT NOW WAS THE TIME TO KILL THE PIGS
I OBJECT. I WANT MY LAWYER, CHARLES GARRY, HERE IF MY CASE IS DISCUSSED.
WE'LL DEAL WITH THIS IN DUE TIME.
THE NEXT DAY A FEW PEOPLE LOWERED THE AMERICAN FLAG & RAISED THE RED FLAG.
AT THIS TIME POLICE MOVED IN TO RETRIEVE THE AMERICAN FLAG.
THE CROWD BEGAN TO PELT POLICE WITH VARIOUS OBJECTS.
THEY JUMPED ON A POLICE CAR AND TRIED TO TIP IT OVER. RUBIN WAS SHOUTING.
KILL THE PIGS!

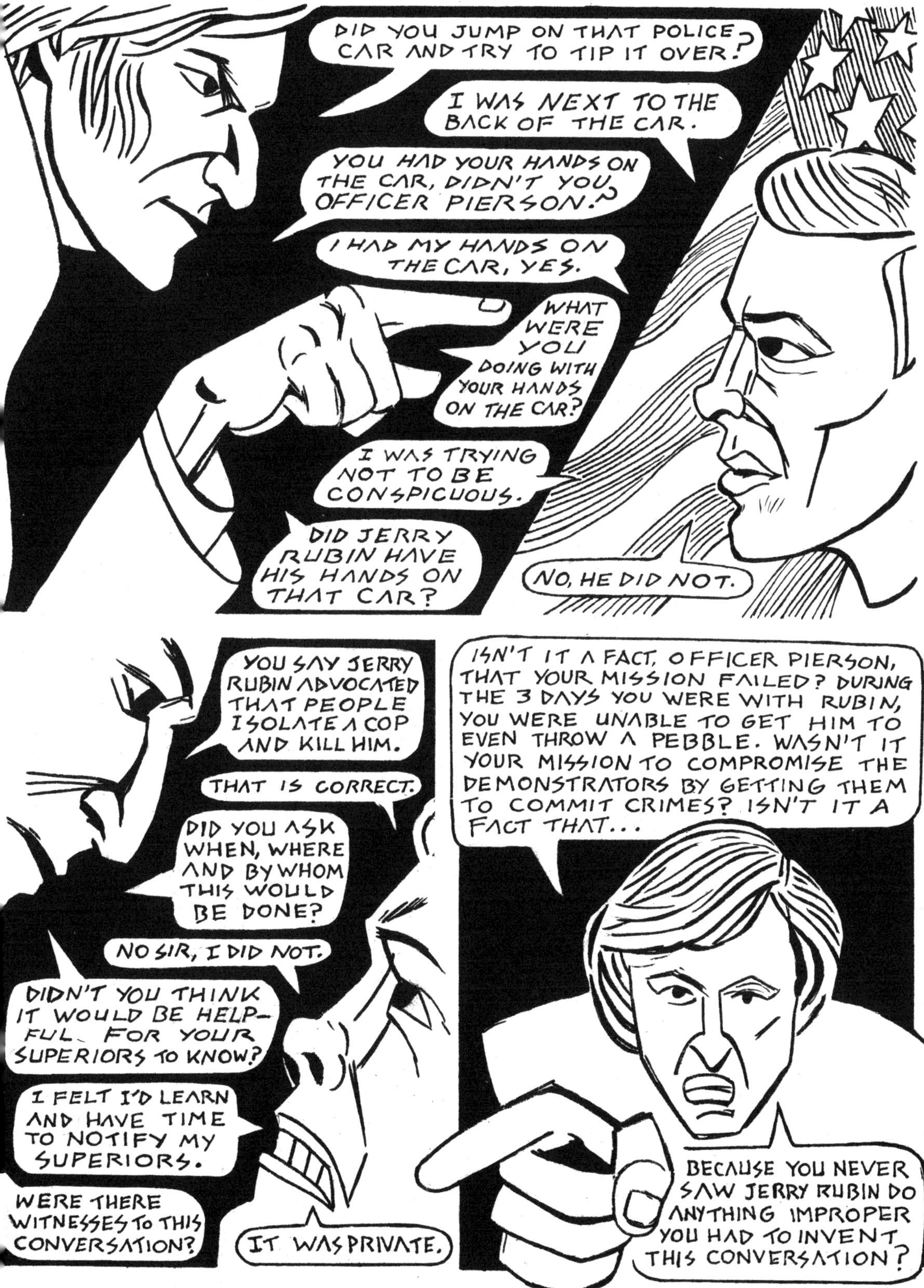
DID YOU JUMP ON THAT POLICE CAR AND TRY TO TIP IT OVER?
I WAS NEXT TO THE BACK OF THE CAR.
YOU HAD YOUR HANDS ON THE CAR, DIDN'T YOU, OFFICER PIERSON?
I HAD MY HANDS ON THE CAR, YES.
WHAT WERE YOU DOING WITH YOUR HANDS ON THE CAR?
I WAS TRYING NOT TO BE CONSPICUOUS.
DID JERRY RUBIN HAVE HIS HANDS ON THAT CAR?
NO, HE DID NOT.
YOU SAY JERRY RUBIN ADVOCATED THAT PEOPLE ISOLATE A COP AND KILL HIM.
THAT IS CORRECT.
DID YOU ASK WHEN, WHERE AND BY WHOM THIS WOULD BE DONE?
NO SIR, I DID NOT.
DIDN'T YOU THINK IT WOULD BE HELPFUL FOR YOUR SUPERIORS TO KNOW?
I FELT I'D LEARN AND HAVE TIME TO NOTIFY MY SUPERIORS.
WERE THERE WITNESSES TO THIS CONVERSATION?
IT WAS PRIVATE.
ISN'T IT A FACT, OFFICER PIERSON, THAT YOUR MISSION FAILED? DURING THE 3 DAYS YOU WERE WITH RUBIN, YOU WERE UNABLE TO GET HIM TO EVEN THROW A PEBBLE. WASN'T IT YOUR MISSION TO COMPROMISE THE DEMONSTRATORS BY GETTING THEM TO COMMIT CRIMES? ISN'T IT A FACT THAT...
BECAUSE YOU NEVER SAW JERRY RUBIN DO ANYTHING IMPROPER YOU HAD TO INVENT THIS CONVERSATION?

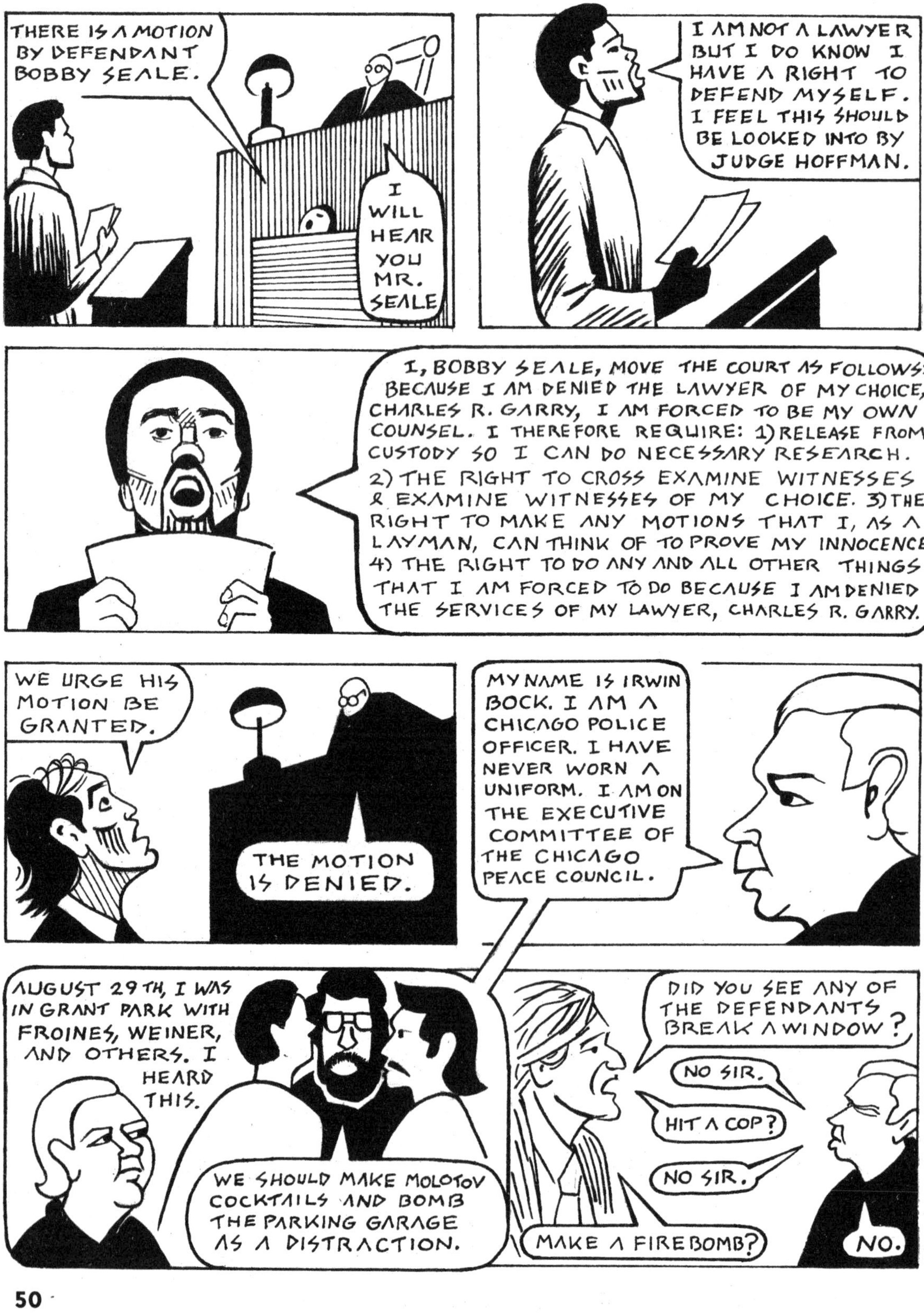
THERE IS A MOTION BY DEFENDANT BOBBY SEALE.
I WILL HEAR YOU MR. SEALE
I AM NOT A LAWYER BUT I DO KNOW I HAVE A RIGHT TO DEFEND MYSELF. I FEEL THIS SHOULD BE LOOKED INTO BY JUDGE HOFFMAN.
I, BOBBY SEALE, MOVE THE COURT AS FOLLOWS: BECAUSE I AM DENIED THE LAWYER OF MY CHOICE, CHARLES R. GARRY, I AM FORCED TO BE MY OWN COUNSEL. I THEREFORE REQUIRE: 1) RELEASE FROM CUSTODY SO I CAN DO NECESSARY RESEARCH. 2) THE RIGHT TO CROSS EXAMINE WITNESSES & EXAMINE WITNESSES OF MY CHOICE. 3) THE RIGHT TO MAKE ANY MOTIONS THAT I, AS A LAYMAN, CAN THINK OF TO PROVE MY INNOCENCE 4) THE RIGHT TO DO ANY AND ALL OTHER THINGS THAT I AM FORCED TO DO BECAUSE I AM DENIED THE SERVICES OF MY LAWYER, CHARLES R. GARRY.
WE URGE HIS MOTION BE GRANTED.
THE MOTION IS DENIED.
MY NAME IS IRWIN BOCK. I AM A CHICAGO POLICE OFFICER. I HAVE NEVER WORN A UNIFORM. I AM ON THE EXECUTIVE COMMITTEE OF THE CHICAGO PEACE COUNCIL.
AUGUST 29TH, I WAS IN GRANT PARK WITH FROINES, WEINER, AND OTHERS. I HEARD THIS.
WE SHOULD MAKE MOLOTOV COCKTAILS AND BOMB THE PARKING GARAGE AS A DISTRACTION.
DID YOU SEE ANY OF THE DEFENDANTS BREAK A WINDOW?
NO SIR.
HIT A COP?
NO SIR.
MAKE A FIREBOMB?
NO.

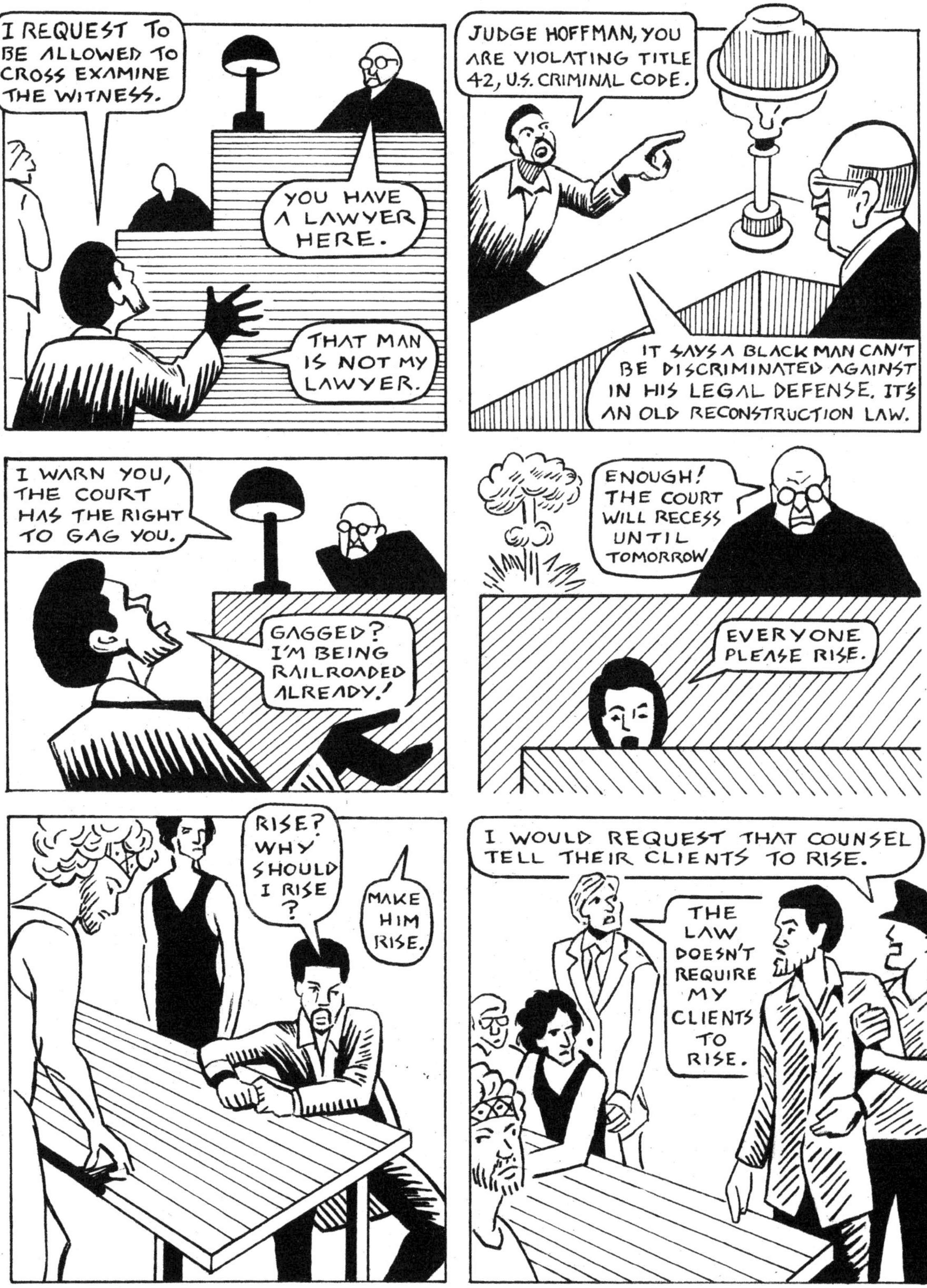
I REQUEST TO BE ALLOWED TO CROSS EXAMINE THE WITNESS.
YOU HAVE A LAWYER HERE.
THAT MAN IS NOT MY LAWYER.
JUDGE HOFFMAN, YOU ARE VIOLATING TITLE 42, U.S. CRIMINAL CODE.
IT SAYS A BLACK MAN CAN'T BE DISCRIMINATED AGAINST IN HIS LEGAL DEFENSE. IT'S AN OLD RECONSTRUCTION LAW.
I WARN YOU, THE COURT HAS THE RIGHT TO GAG YOU.
GAGGED? I'M BEING RAILROADED ALREADY!
ENOUGH! THE COURT WILL RECESS UNTIL TOMORROW
EVERYONE PLEASE RISE.
RISE? WHY SHOULD I RISE?
MAKE HIM RISE.
I WOULD REQUEST THAT COUNSEL TELL THEIR CLIENTS TO RISE.
THE LAW DOESN'T REQUIRE MY CLIENTS TO RISE.

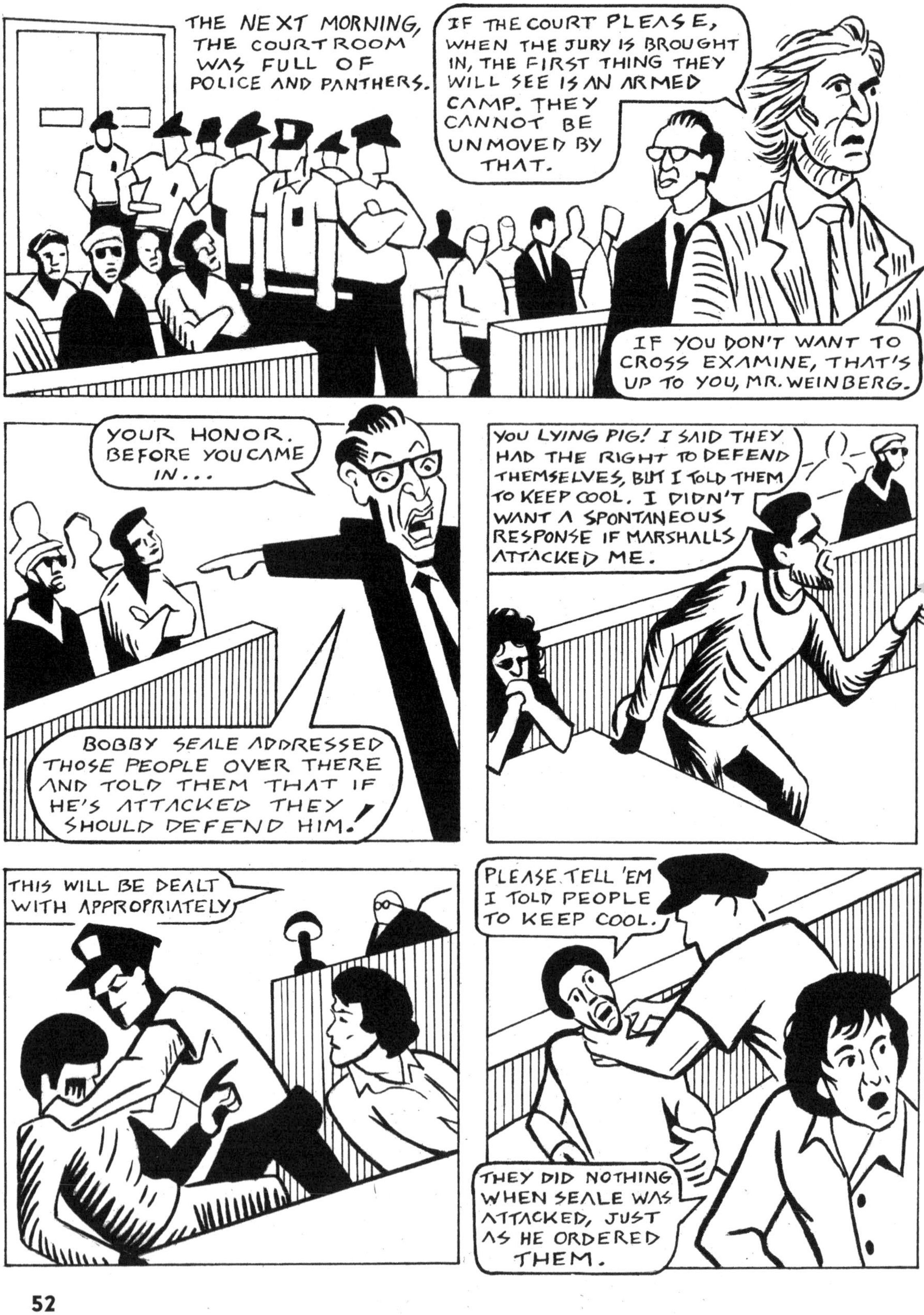
THE NEXT MORNING, THE COURTROOM WAS FULL OF POLICE AND PANTHERS.
IF THE COURT PLEASE, WHEN THE JURY IS BROUGHT IN, THE FIRST THING THEY WILL SEE IS AN ARMED CAMP. THEY CANNOT BE UNMOVED BY THAT.
IF YOU DON'T WANT TO CROSS EXAMINE, THAT'S UP TO YOU, MR. WEINBERG.
YOUR HONOR. BEFORE YOU CAME IN...
BOBBY SEALE ADDRESSED THOSE PEOPLE OVER THERE AND TOLD THEM THAT IF HE'S ATTACKED THEY SHOULD DEFEND HIM!
YOU LYING PIG! I SAID THEY HAD THE RIGHT TO DEFEND THEMSELVES, BUT I TOLD THEM TO KEEP COOL. I DIDN'T WANT A SPONTANEOUS RESPONSE IF MARSHALLS ATTACKED ME.
THIS WILL BE DEALT WITH APPROPRIATELY
PLEASE TELL 'EM I TOLD PEOPLE TO KEEP COOL.
THEY DID NOTHING WHEN SEALE WAS ATTACKED, JUST AS HE ORDERED THEM.

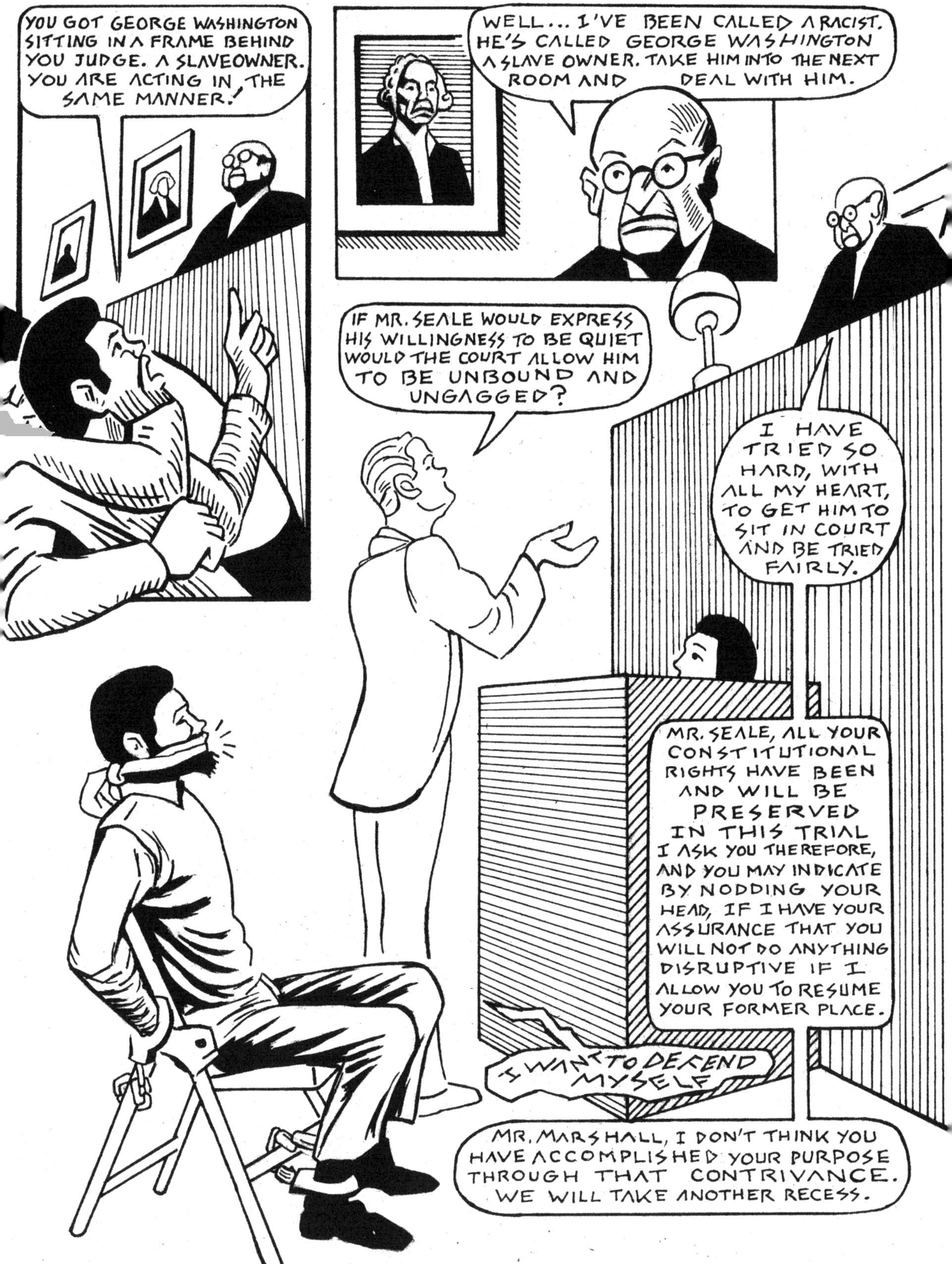
YOU GOT GEORGE WASHINGTON SITTING IN A FRAME BEHIND YOU JUDGE. A SLAVEOWNER. YOU ARE ACTING IN THE SAME MANNER!
WELL... I'VE BEEN CALLED A RACIST. HE'S CALLED GEORGE WASHINGTON A SLAVE OWNER. TAKE HIM INTO THE NEXT ROOM AND DEAL WITH HIM.
IF MR. SEALE WOULD EXPRESS HIS WILLINGNESS TO BE QUIET WOULD THE COURT ALLOW HIM TO BE UNBOUND AND UNGAGGED?
I HAVE TRIED SO HARD, WITH ALL MY HEART, TO GET HIM TO SIT IN COURT AND BE TRIED FAIRLY.
MR. SEALE, ALL YOUR CONSTITUTIONAL RIGHTS HAVE BEEN AND WILL BE PRESERVED IN THIS TRIAL I ASK YOU THEREFORE, AND YOU MAY INDICATE BY NODDING YOUR HEAD, IF I HAVE YOUR ASSURANCE THAT YOU WILL NOT DO ANYTHING DISRUPTIVE IF I ALLOW YOU TO RESUME YOUR FORMER PLACE.
I WANT TO DEFEND MYSELF
MR. MARSHALL, I DON'T THINK YOU HAVE ACCOMPLISHED YOUR PURPOSE THROUGH THAT CONTRIVANCE. WE WILL TAKE ANOTHER RECESS.

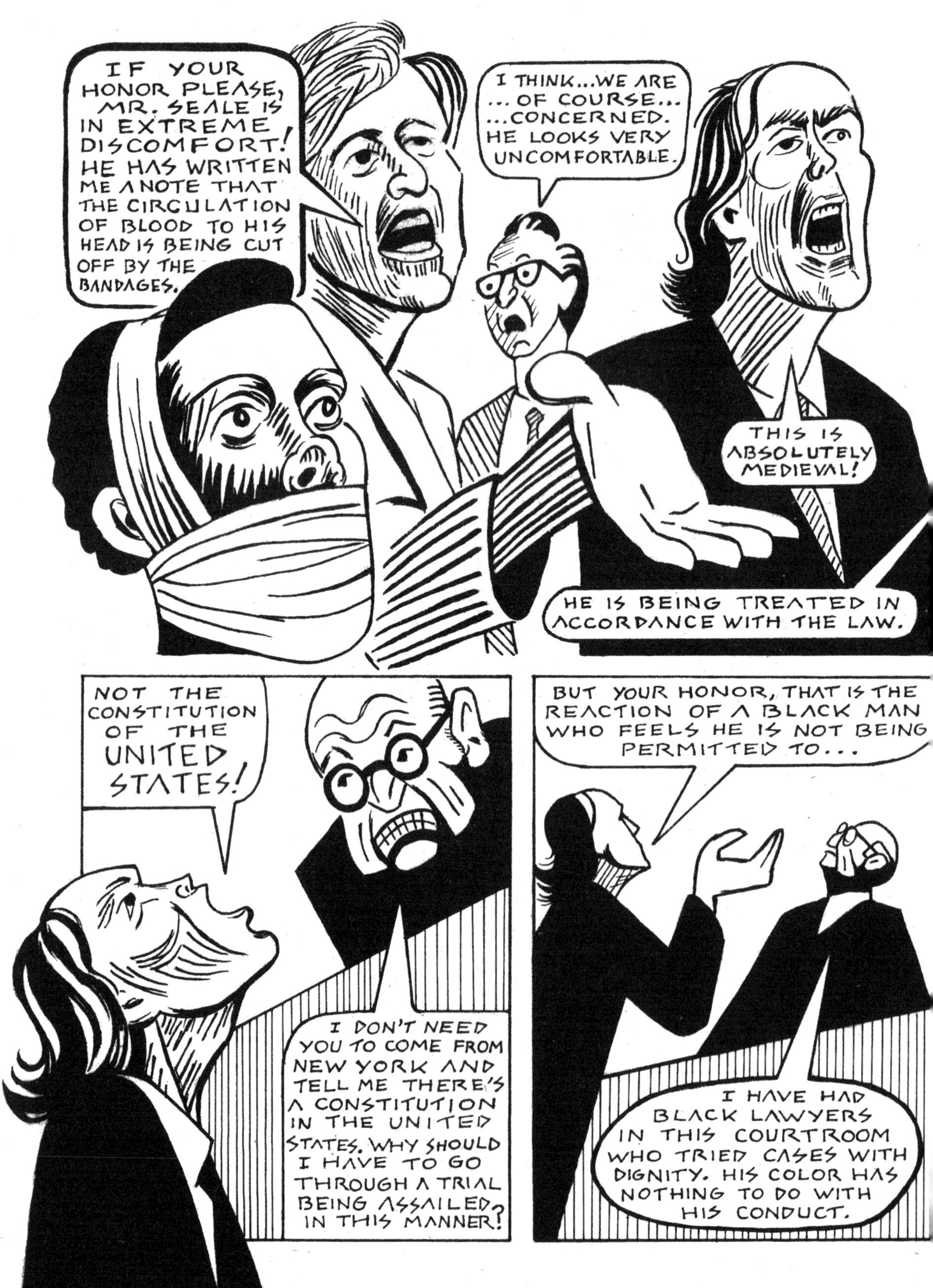
IF YOUR HONOR PLEASE, MR. SEALE IS IN EXTREME DISCOMFORT! HE HAS WRITTEN ME A NOTE THAT THE CIRCULATION OF BLOOD TO HIS HEAD IS BEING CUT OFF BY THE BANDAGES.
I THINK...WE ARE ...OF COURSE... ...CONCERNED. HE LOOKS VERY UNCOMFORTABLE.
THIS IS ABSOLUTELY MEDIEVAL!
HE IS BEING TREATED IN ACCORDANCE WITH THE LAW.
NOT THE CONSTITUTION OF THE UNITED STATES!
I DON'T NEED YOU TO COME FROM NEW YORK AND TELL ME THERE'S A CONSTITUTION IN THE UNITED STATES. WHY SHOULD I HAVE TO GO THROUGH A TRIAL BEING ASSAILED IN THIS MANNER?
BUT YOUR HONOR, THAT IS THE REACTION OF A BLACK MAN WHO FEELS HE IS NOT BEING PERMITTED TO...
I HAVE HAD BLACK LAWYERS IN THIS COURTROOM WHO TRIED CASES WITH DIGNITY. HIS COLOR HAS NOTHING TO DO WITH HIS CONDUCT.

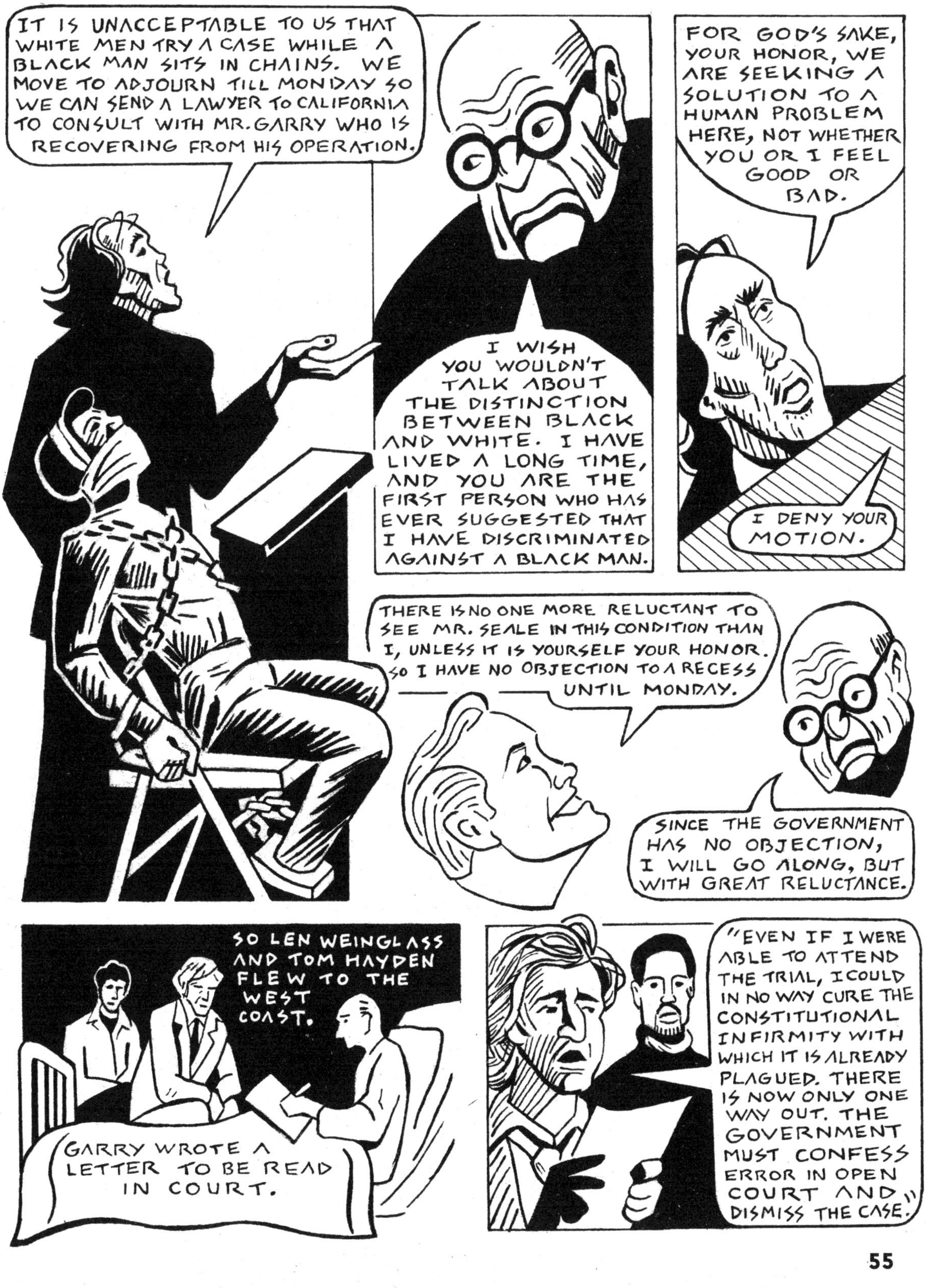
IT IS UNACCEPTABLE TO US THAT WHITE MEN TRY A CASE WHILE A BLACK MAN SITS IN CHAINS. WE MOVE TO ADJOURN TILL MONDAY SO WE CAN SEND A LAWYER TO CALIFORNIA TO CONSULT WITH MR. GARRY WHO IS RECOVERING FROM HIS OPERATION.
I WISH YOU WOULDN'T TALK ABOUT THE DISTINCTION BETWEEN BLACK AND WHITE. I HAVE LIVED A LONG TIME, AND YOU ARE THE FIRST PERSON WHO HAS EVER SUGGESTED THAT I HAVE DISCRIMINATED AGAINST A BLACK MAN.
FOR GOD'S SAKE, YOUR HONOR, WE ARE SEEKING A SOLUTION TO A HUMAN PROBLEM HERE, NOT WHETHER YOU OR I FEEL GOOD OR BAD.
I DENY YOUR MOTION.
THERE IS NO ONE MORE RELUCTANT TO SEE MR. SEALE IN THIS CONDITION THAN I, UNLESS IT IS YOURSELF YOUR HONOR. SO I HAVE NO OBJECTION TO A RECESS UNTIL MONDAY.
SINCE THE GOVERNMENT HAS NO OBJECTION, I WILL GO ALONG, BUT WITH GREAT RELUCTANCE.
SO LEN WEINGLASS AND TOM HAYDEN FLEW TO THE WEST COAST.
GARRY WROTE A LETTER TO BE READ IN COURT.
"EVEN IF I WERE ABLE TO ATTEND THE TRIAL, I COULD IN NO WAY CURE THE CONSTITUTIONAL INFIRMITY WITH WHICH IT IS ALREADY PLAGUED. THERE IS NOW ONLY ONE WAY OUT. THE GOVERNMENT MUST CONFESS ERROR IN OPEN COURT AND DISMISS THE CASE."

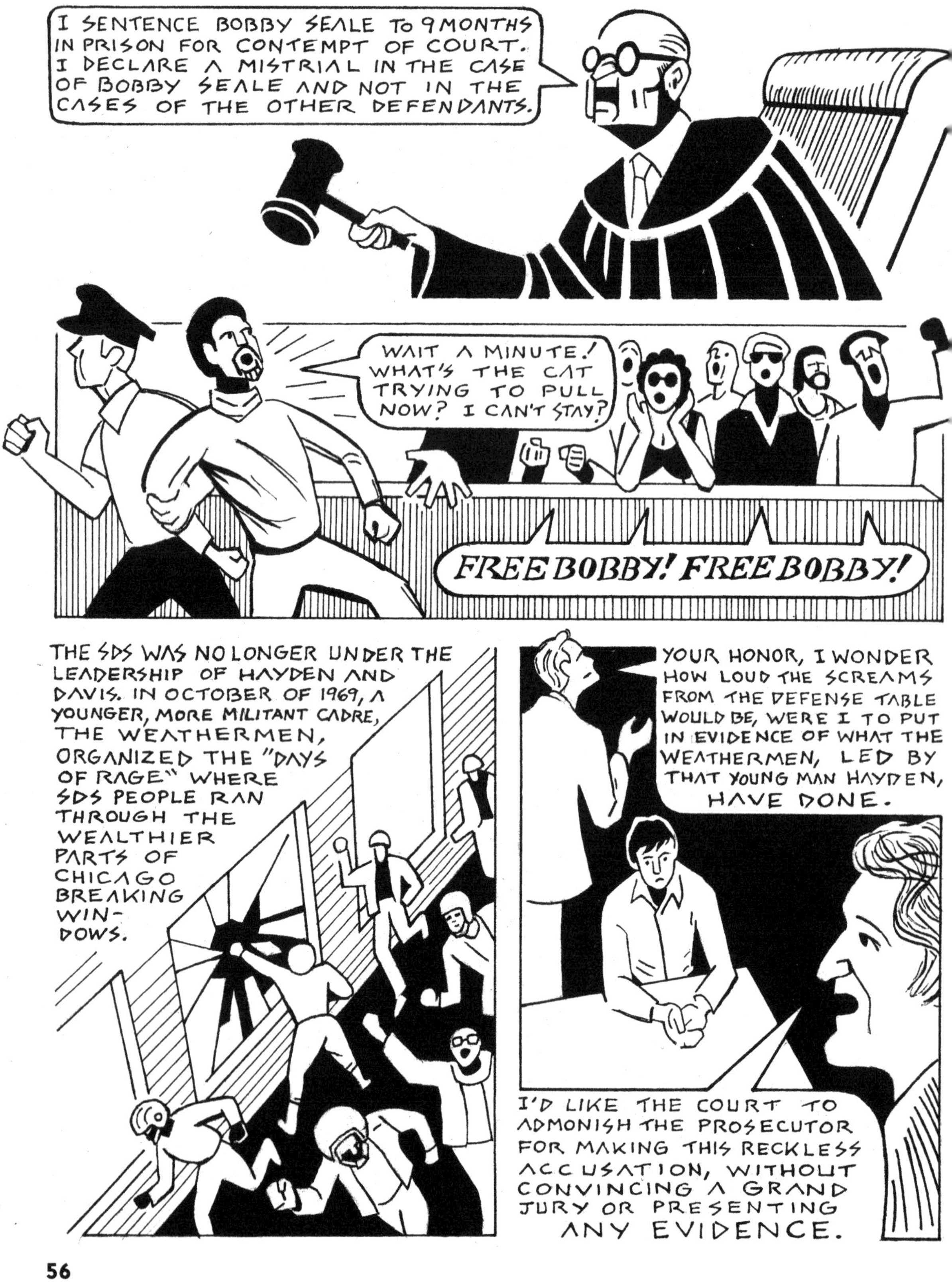
I SENTENCE BOBBY SEALE TO 9 MONTHS IN PRISON FOR CONTEMPT OF COURT. I DECLARE A MISTRIAL IN THE CASE OF BOBBY SEALE AND NOT IN THE CASES OF THE OTHER DEFENDANTS.
WAIT A MINUTE! WHAT'S THE CAT TRYING TO PULL NOW? I CAN'T STAY?
FREE BOBBY! FREE BOBBY!
THE SDS WAS NO LONGER UNDER THE LEADERSHIP OF HAYDEN AND DAVIS. IN OCTOBER OF 1969, A YOUNGER, MORE MILITANT CADRE, THE WEATHERMEN, ORGANIZED THE "DAYS OF RAGE" WHERE SDS PEOPLE RAN THROUGH THE WEALTHIER PARTS OF CHICAGO BREAKING WIN-DOWS.
YOUR HONOR, I WONDER HOW LOUD THE SCREAMS FROM THE DEFENSE TABLE WOULD BE, WERE I TO PUT IN EVIDENCE OF WHAT THE WEATHERMEN, LED BY THAT YOUNG MAN HAYDEN, HAVE DONE.
I'D LIKE THE COURT TO ADMONISH THE PROSECUTOR FOR MAKING THIS RECKLESS ACCUSATION, WITHOUT CONVINCING A GRAND JURY OR PRESENTING ANY EVIDENCE.

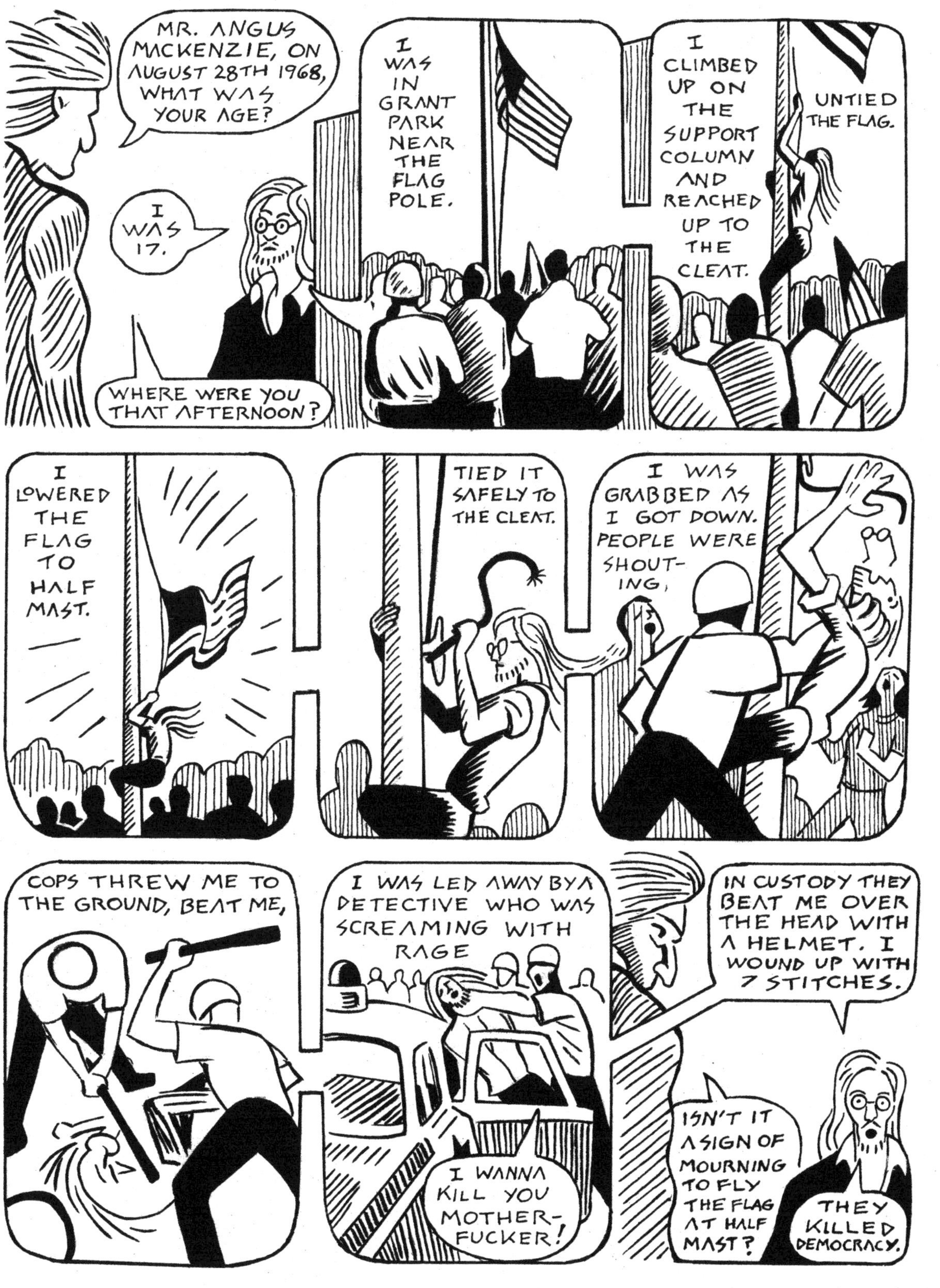

MR. ANGUS MACKENZIE, ON AUGUST 28TH 1968, WHAT WAS YOUR AGE?
I WAS 17.
WHERE WERE YOU THAT AFTERNOON?
I WAS IN GRANT PARK NEAR THE FLAG POLE.
I CLIMBED UP ON THE SUPPORT COLUMN AND REACHED UP TO THE CLEAT.
UNTIED THE FLAG.
I LOWERED THE FLAG TO HALF MAST.
TIED IT SAFELY TO THE CLEAT.
I WAS GRABBED AS I GOT DOWN. PEOPLE WERE SHOUTING,
COPS THREW ME TO THE GROUND, BEAT ME,
I WAS LED AWAY BY A DETECTIVE WHO WAS SCREAMING WITH RAGE
I WANNA KILL YOU MOTHER-FUCKER!
IN CUSTODY THEY BEAT ME OVER THE HEAD WITH A HELMET. I WOUND UP WITH 7 STITCHES.
ISN'T IT A SIGN OF MOURNING TO FLY THE FLAG AT HALF MAST?
THEY KILLED DEMOCRACY.

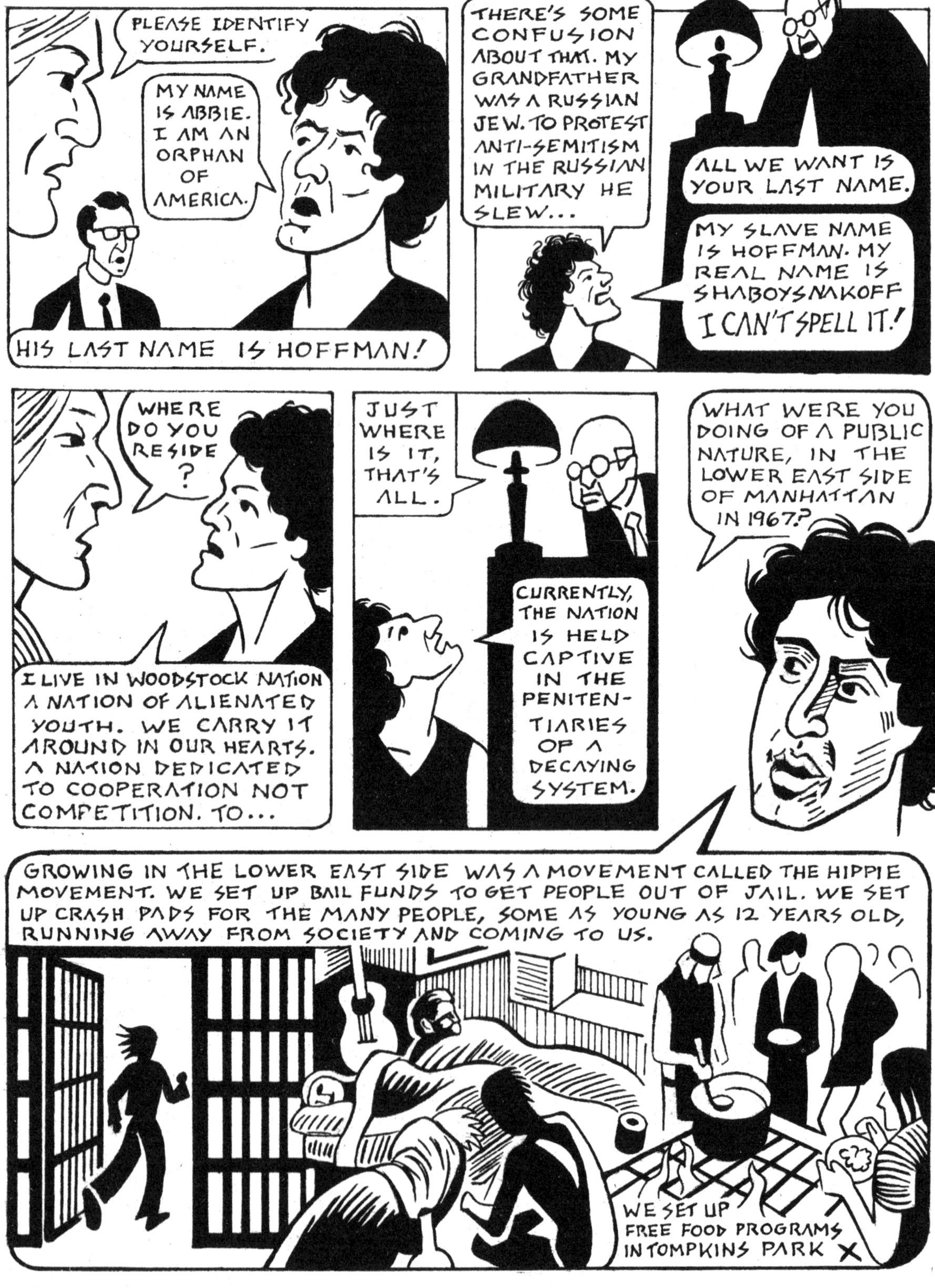
PLEASE IDENTIFY YOURSELF.
MY NAME IS ABBIE. I AM AN ORPHAN OF AMERICA.
HIS LAST NAME IS HOFFMAN!
THERE'S SOME CONFUSION ABOUT THAT. MY GRANDFATHER WAS A RUSSIAN JEW. TO PROTEST ANTI-SEMITISM IN THE RUSSIAN MILITARY HE SLEW...
ALL WE WANT IS YOUR LAST NAME.
MY SLAVE NAME IS HOFFMAN. MY REAL NAME IS SHABOYSNAKOFF I CAN'T SPELL IT!
WHERE DO YOU RESIDE?
I LIVE IN WOODSTOCK NATION A NATION OF ALIENATED YOUTH. WE CARRY IT AROUND IN OUR HEARTS. A NATION DEDICATED TO COOPERATION NOT COMPETITION. TO...
JUST WHERE IS IT, THAT'S ALL.
CURRENTLY, THE NATION IS HELD CAPTIVE IN THE PENITEN-TIARIES OF A DECAYING SYSTEM.
WHAT WERE YOU DOING OF A PUBLIC NATURE, IN THE LOWER EAST SIDE OF MANHATTAN IN 1967?
GROWING IN THE LOWER EAST SIDE WAS A MOVEMENT CALLED THE HIPPIE MOVEMENT. WE SET UP BAIL FUNDS TO GET PEOPLE OUT OF JAIL. WE SET UP CRASH PADS FOR THE MANY PEOPLE, SOME AS YOUNG AS 12 YEARS OLD, RUNNING AWAY FROM SOCIETY AND COMING TO US.
WE SET UP FREE FOOD PROGRAMS IN TOMPKINS PARK

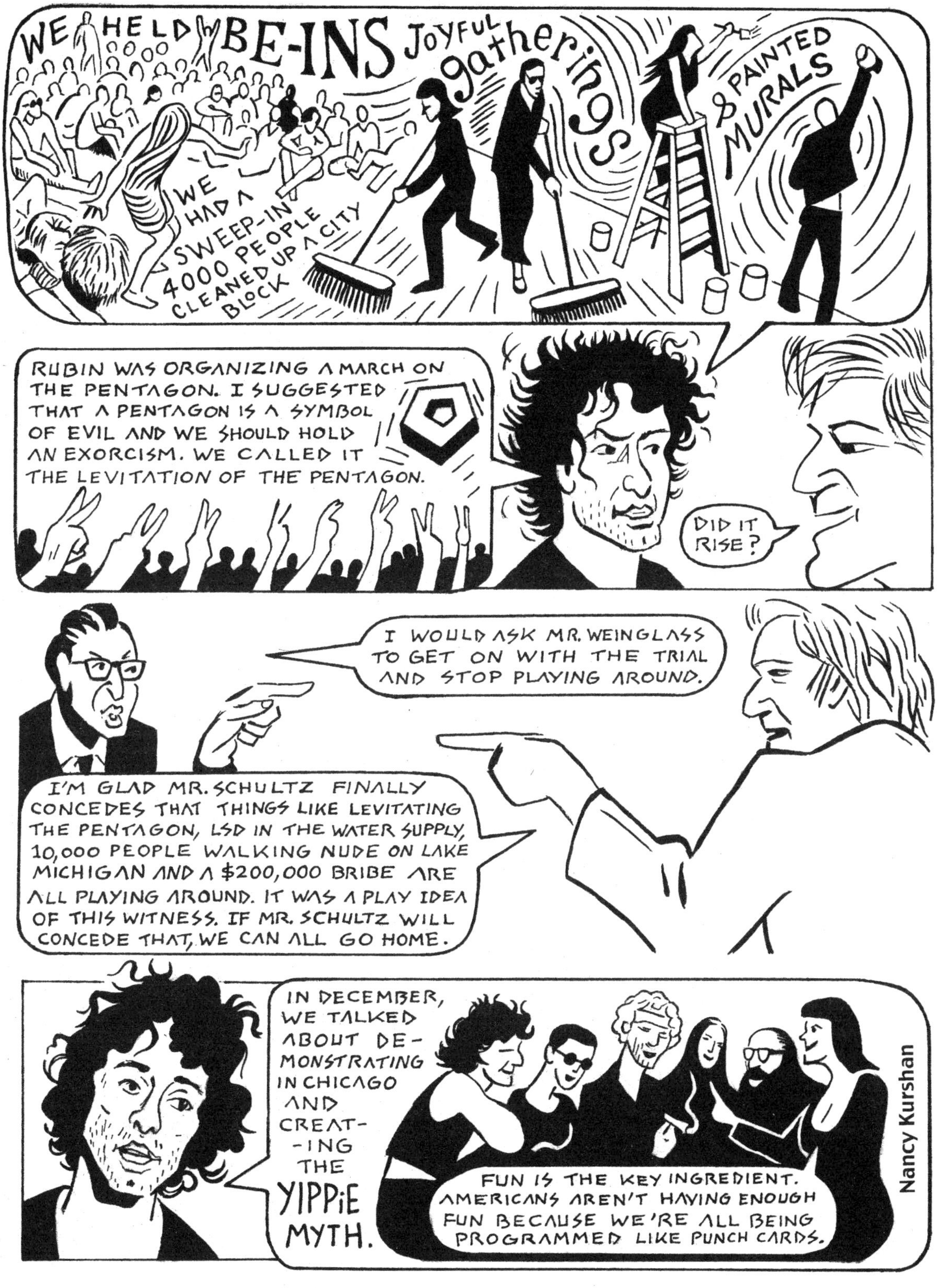
WE HELD BE-INS JOYFUL gatherings & PAINTED MURALS
WE HAD A SWEEP-IN 4000 PEOPLE CLEANED UP A CITY BLOCK
RUBIN WAS ORGANIZING A MARCH ON THE PENTAGON. I SUGGESTED THAT A PENTAGON IS A SYMBOL OF EVIL AND WE SHOULD HOLD AN EXORCISM. WE CALLED IT THE LEVITATION OF THE PENTAGON.
DID IT RISE?
I WOULD ASK MR. WEINGLASS TO GET ON WITH THE TRIAL AND STOP PLAYING AROUND.
I'M GLAD MR. SCHULTZ FINALLY CONCEDES THAT THINGS LIKE LEVITATING THE PENTAGON, LSD IN THE WATER SUPPLY, 10,000 PEOPLE WALKING NUDE ON LAKE MICHIGAN AND A $200,000 BRIBE ARE ALL PLAYING AROUND. IT WAS A PLAY IDEA OF THIS WITNESS. IF MR. SCHULTZ WILL CONCEDE THAT, WE CAN ALL GO HOME.
IN DECEMBER, WE TALKED ABOUT DE-MONSTRATING IN CHICAGO AND CREAT-ING THE YIPPIE MYTH.
FUN IS THE KEY INGREDIENT. AMERICANS AREN'T HAVING ENOUGH FUN BECAUSE WE'RE ALL BEING PROGRAMMED LIKE PUNCH CARDS.
Nancy Kurshan

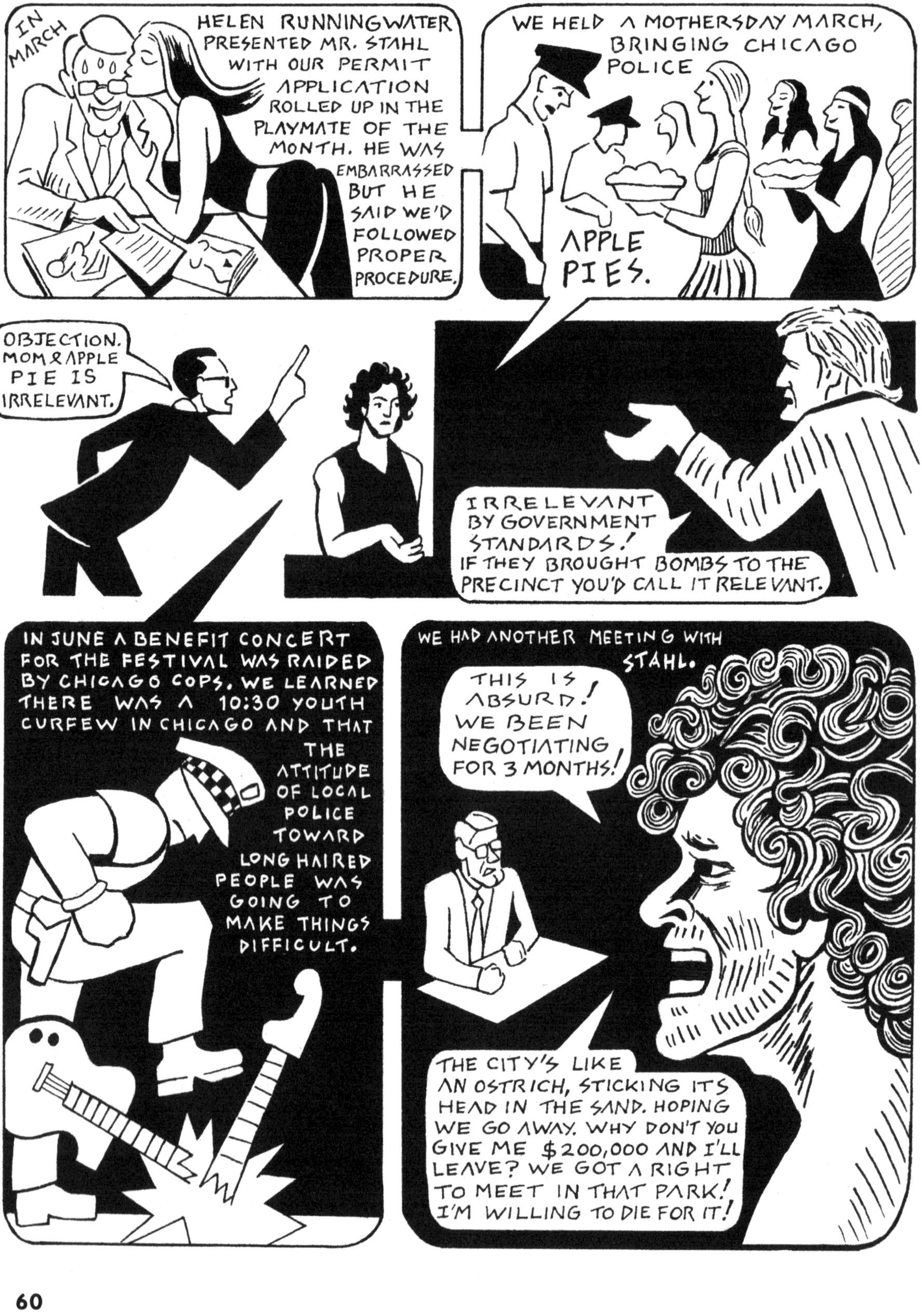
IN MARCH
HELEN RUNNINGWATER PRESENTED MR. STAHL WITH OUR PERMIT APPLICATION ROLLED UP IN THE PLAYMATE OF THE MONTH. HE WAS EMBARRASSED BUT HE SAID WE'D FOLLOWED PROPER PROCEDURE.
WE HELD A MOTHERSDAY MARCH, BRINGING CHICAGO POLICE
APPLE PIES.
OBJECTION. MOM & APPLE PIE IS IRRELEVANT.
IRRELEVANT BY GOVERNMENT STANDARDS! IF THEY BROUGHT BOMBS TO THE PRECINCT YOU'D CALL IT RELEVANT.
IN JUNE A BENEFIT CONCERT FOR THE FESTIVAL WAS RAIDED BY CHICAGO COPS. WE LEARNED THERE WAS A 10:30 YOUTH CURFEW IN CHICAGO AND THAT THE ATTITUDE OF LOCAL POLICE TOWARD LONG HAIRED PEOPLE WAS GOING TO MAKE THINGS DIFFICULT.
WE HAD ANOTHER MEETING WITH STAHL.
THIS IS ABSURD! WE BEEN NEGOTIATING FOR 3 MONTHS!
THE CITY'S LIKE AN OSTRICH, STICKING ITS HEAD IN THE SAND. HOPING WE GO AWAY. WHY DON'T YOU GIVE ME $200,000 AND I'LL LEAVE? WE GOT A RIGHT TO MEET IN THAT PARK! I'M WILLING TO DIE FOR IT!

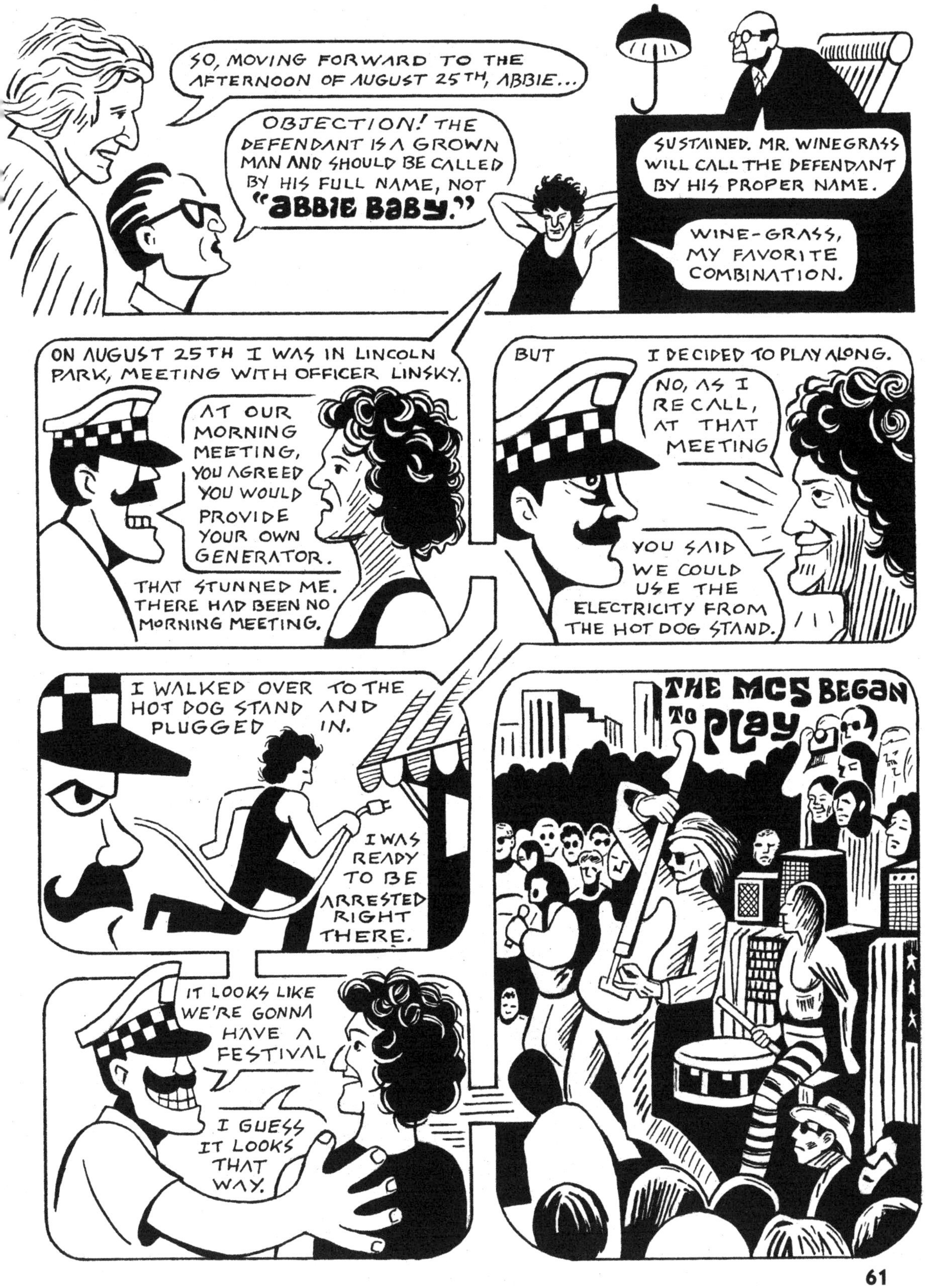
SO, MOVING FORWARD TO THE AFTERNOON OF AUGUST 25TH, ABBIE...
OBJECTION! THE DEFENDANT IS A GROWN MAN AND SHOULD BE CALLED BY HIS FULL NAME, NOT "ABBIE BABY."
SUSTAINED. MR. WINEGRASS WILL CALL THE DEFENDANT BY HIS PROPER NAME.
WINE-GRASS, MY FAVORITE COMBINATION.
ON AUGUST 25TH I WAS IN LINCOLN PARK, MEETING WITH OFFICER LINSKY.
AT OUR MORNING MEETING, YOU AGREED YOU WOULD PROVIDE YOUR OWN GENERATOR.
THAT STUNNED ME. THERE HAD BEEN NO MORNING MEETING.
BUT I DECIDED TO PLAY ALONG.
NO, AS I RECALL, AT THAT MEETING
YOU SAID WE COULD USE THE ELECTRICITY FROM THE HOT DOG STAND.
I WALKED OVER TO THE HOT DOG STAND AND PLUGGED IN.
I WAS READY TO BE ARRESTED RIGHT THERE.
THE MC5 BEGAN TO PLAY
IT LOOKS LIKE WE'RE GONNA HAVE A FESTIVAL
I GUESS IT LOOKS THAT WAY.

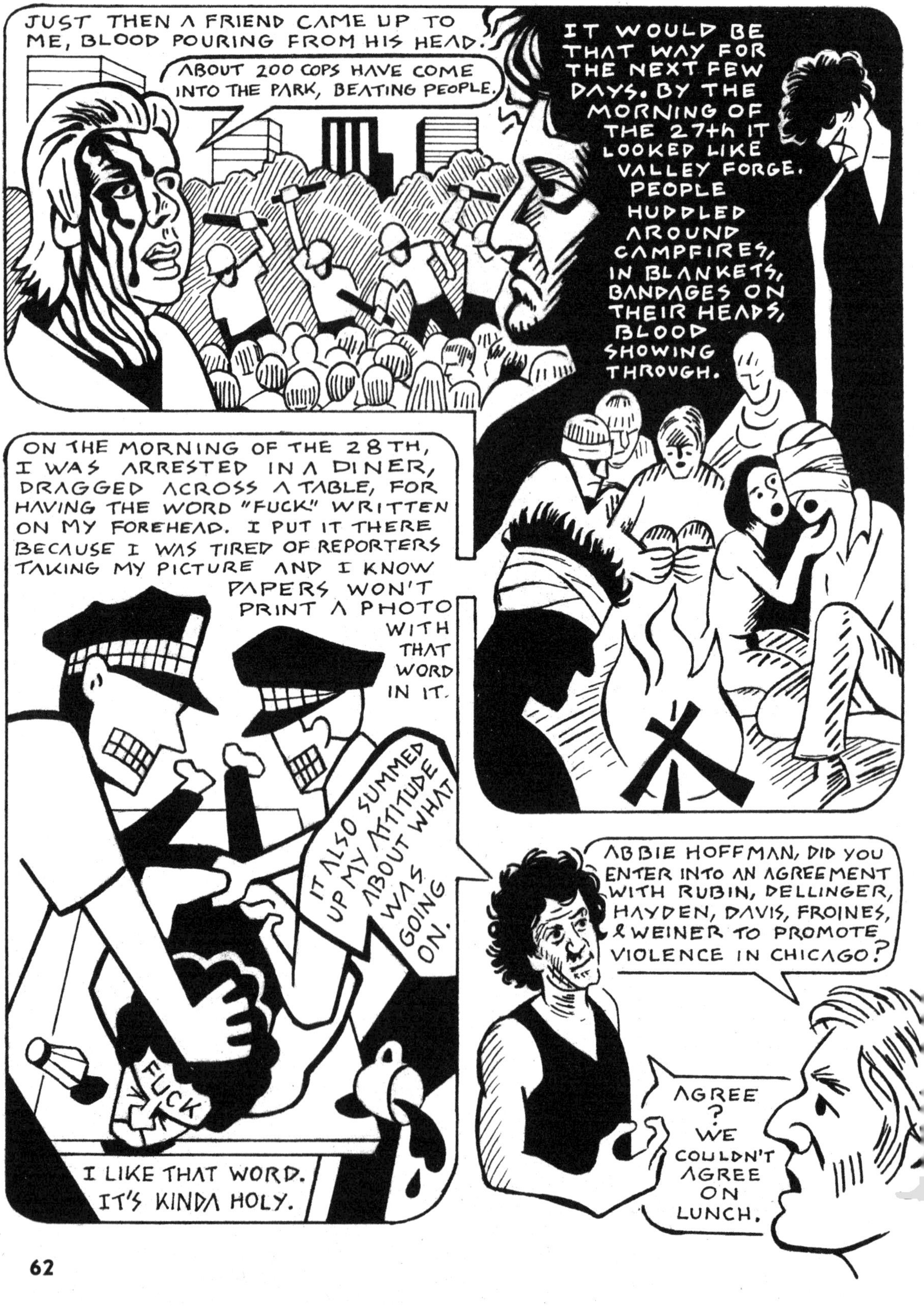

JUST THEN A FRIEND CAME UP TO ME, BLOOD POURING FROM HIS HEAD.
ABOUT 200 COPS HAVE COME INTO THE PARK, BEATING PEOPLE.
IT WOULD BE THAT WAY FOR THE NEXT FEW DAYS. BY THE MORNING OF THE 27th IT LOOKED LIKE VALLEY FORGE. PEOPLE HUDDLED AROUND CAMPFIRES, IN BLANKETS, BANDAGES ON THEIR HEADS, BLOOD SHOWING THROUGH.
ON THE MORNING OF THE 28TH, I WAS ARRESTED IN A DINER, DRAGGED ACROSS A TABLE, FOR HAVING THE WORD "FUCK" WRITTEN ON MY FOREHEAD. I PUT IT THERE BECAUSE I WAS TIRED OF REPORTERS TAKING MY PICTURE AND I KNOW PAPERS WON'T PRINT A PHOTO WITH THAT WORD IN IT.
IT ALSO SUMMED UP MY ATTITUDE ABOUT WHAT WAS GOING ON.
FUCK
I LIKE THAT WORD. IT'S KINDA HOLY.
ABBIE HOFFMAN, DID YOU ENTER INTO AN AGREEMENT WITH RUBIN, DELLINGER, HAYDEN, DAVIS, FROINES, & WEINER TO PROMOTE VIOLENCE IN CHICAGO?
AGREE? WE COULDN'T AGREE ON LUNCH.

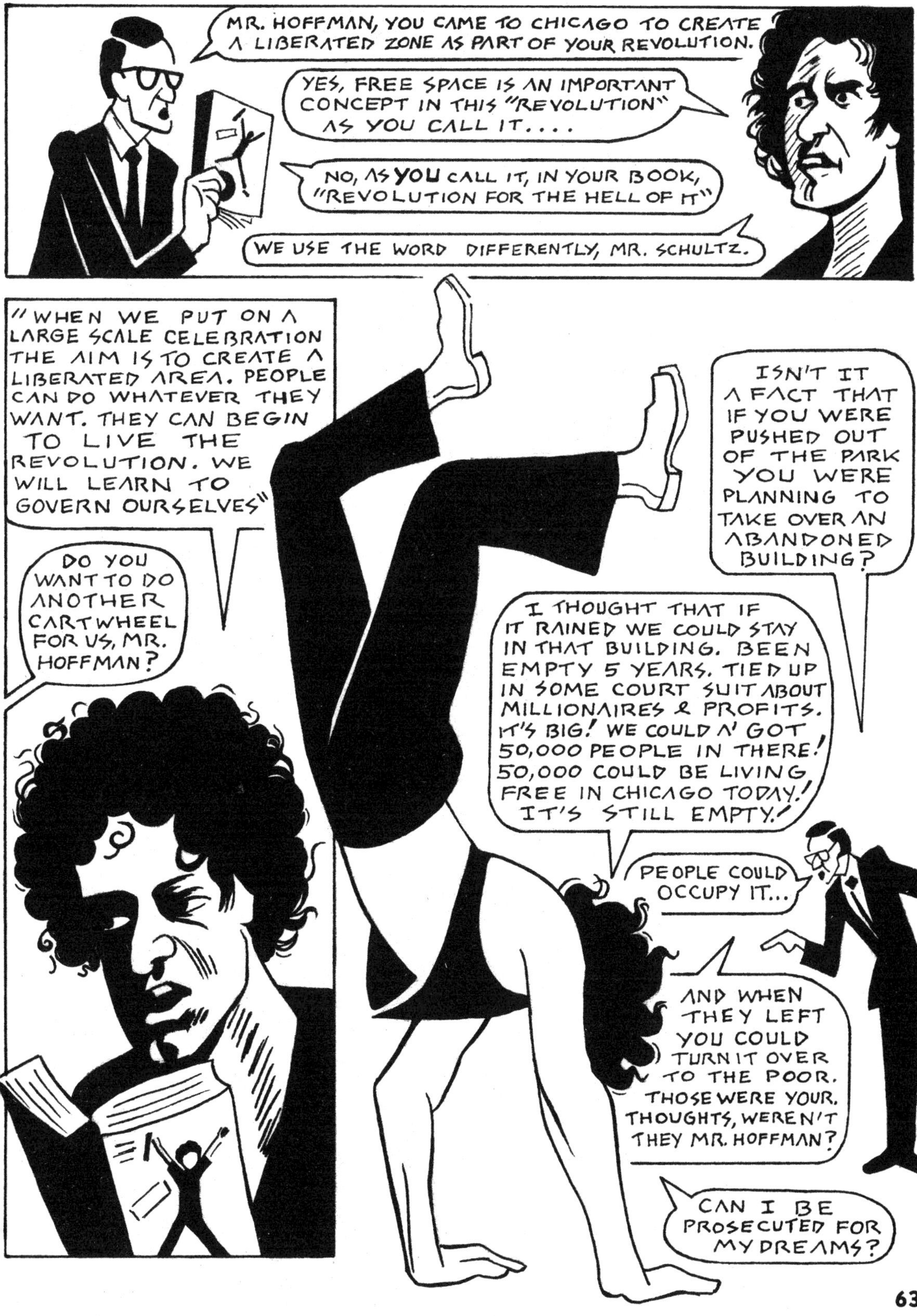
MR. HOFFMAN, YOU CAME TO CHICAGO TO CREATE A LIBERATED ZONE AS PART OF YOUR REVOLUTION.
YES, FREE SPACE IS AN IMPORTANT CONCEPT IN THIS "REVOLUTION" AS YOU CALL IT....
NO, AS YOU CALL IT, IN YOUR BOOK, "REVOLUTION FOR THE HELL OF IT"
WE USE THE WORD DIFFERENTLY, MR. SCHULTZ.
"WHEN WE PUT ON A LARGE SCALE CELEBRATION THE AIM IS TO CREATE A LIBERATED AREA. PEOPLE CAN DO WHATEVER THEY WANT. THEY CAN BEGIN TO LIVE THE REVOLUTION. WE WILL LEARN TO GOVERN OURSELVES"
DO YOU WANT TO DO ANOTHER CARTWHEEL FOR US, MR. HOFFMAN?
ISN'T IT A FACT THAT IF YOU WERE PUSHED OUT OF THE PARK YOU WERE PLANNING TO TAKE OVER AN ABANDONED BUILDING?
I THOUGHT THAT IF IT RAINED WE COULD STAY IN THAT BUILDING. BEEN EMPTY 5 YEARS. TIED UP IN SOME COURT SUIT ABOUT MILLIONAIRES & PROFITS. IT'S BIG! WE COULD A' GOT 50,000 PEOPLE IN THERE! 50,000 COULD BE LIVING FREE IN CHICAGO TODAY! IT'S STILL EMPTY!
PEOPLE COULD OCCUPY IT...
AND WHEN THEY LEFT YOU COULD TURN IT OVER TO THE POOR. THOSE WERE YOUR THOUGHTS, WEREN'T THEY MR. HOFFMAN?
CAN I BE PROSECUTED FOR MY DREAMS?

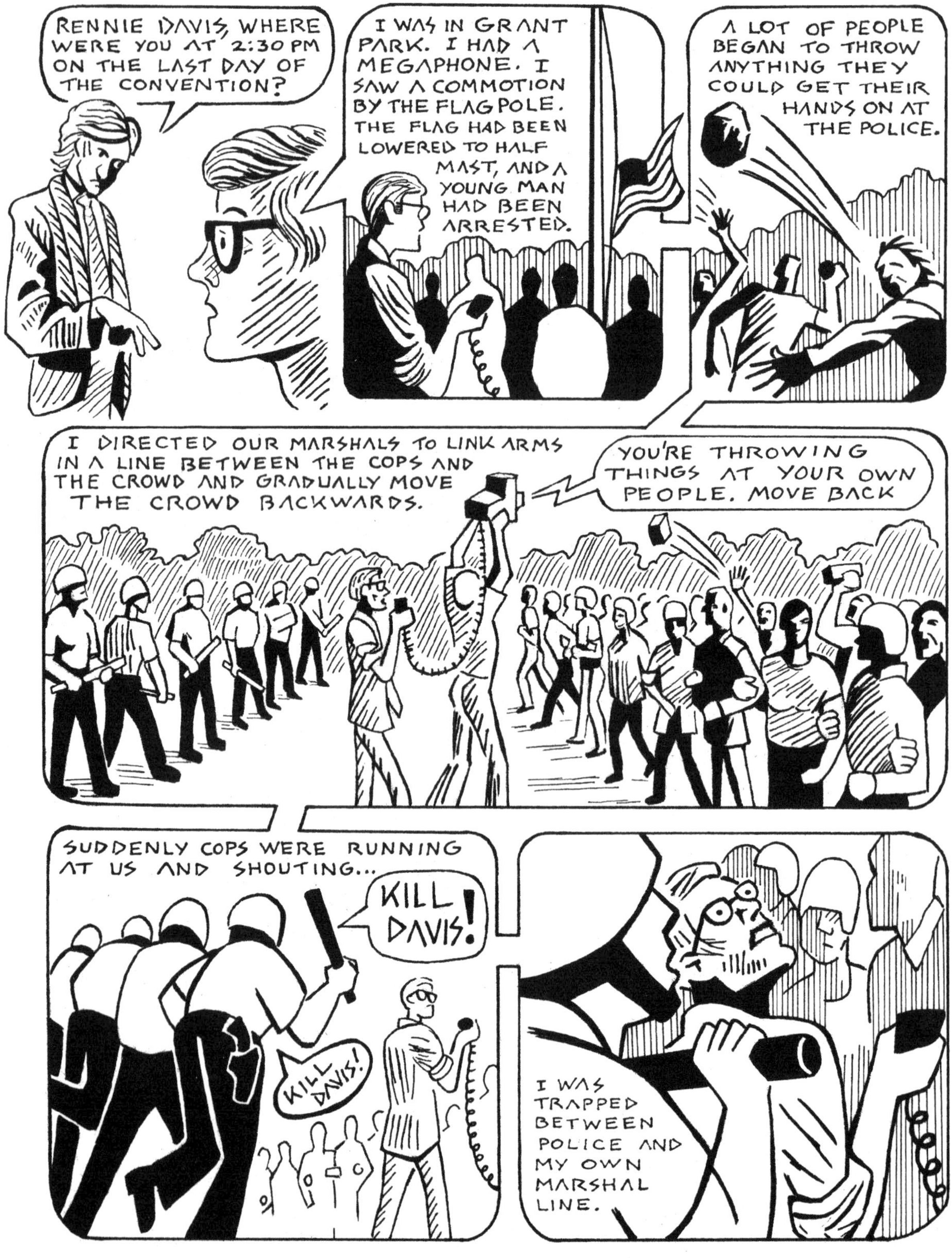
RENNIE DAVIS, WHERE WERE YOU AT 2:30 PM ON THE LAST DAY OF THE CONVENTION?
I WAS IN GRANT PARK. I HAD A MEGAPHONE. I SAW A COMMOTION BY THE FLAGPOLE. THE FLAG HAD BEEN LOWERED TO HALF MAST, AND A YOUNG MAN HAD BEEN ARRESTED.
A LOT OF PEOPLE BEGAN TO THROW ANYTHING THEY COULD GET THEIR HANDS ON AT THE POLICE.
I DIRECTED OUR MARSHALS TO LINK ARMS IN A LINE BETWEEN THE COPS AND THE CROWD AND GRADUALLY MOVE THE CROWD BACKWARDS.
YOU'RE THROWING THINGS AT YOUR OWN PEOPLE. MOVE BACK
SUDDENLY COPS WERE RUNNING AT US AND SHOUTING...
KILL DAVIS!
KILL DAVIS!
I WAS TRAPPED BETWEEN POLICE AND MY OWN MARSHAL LINE.

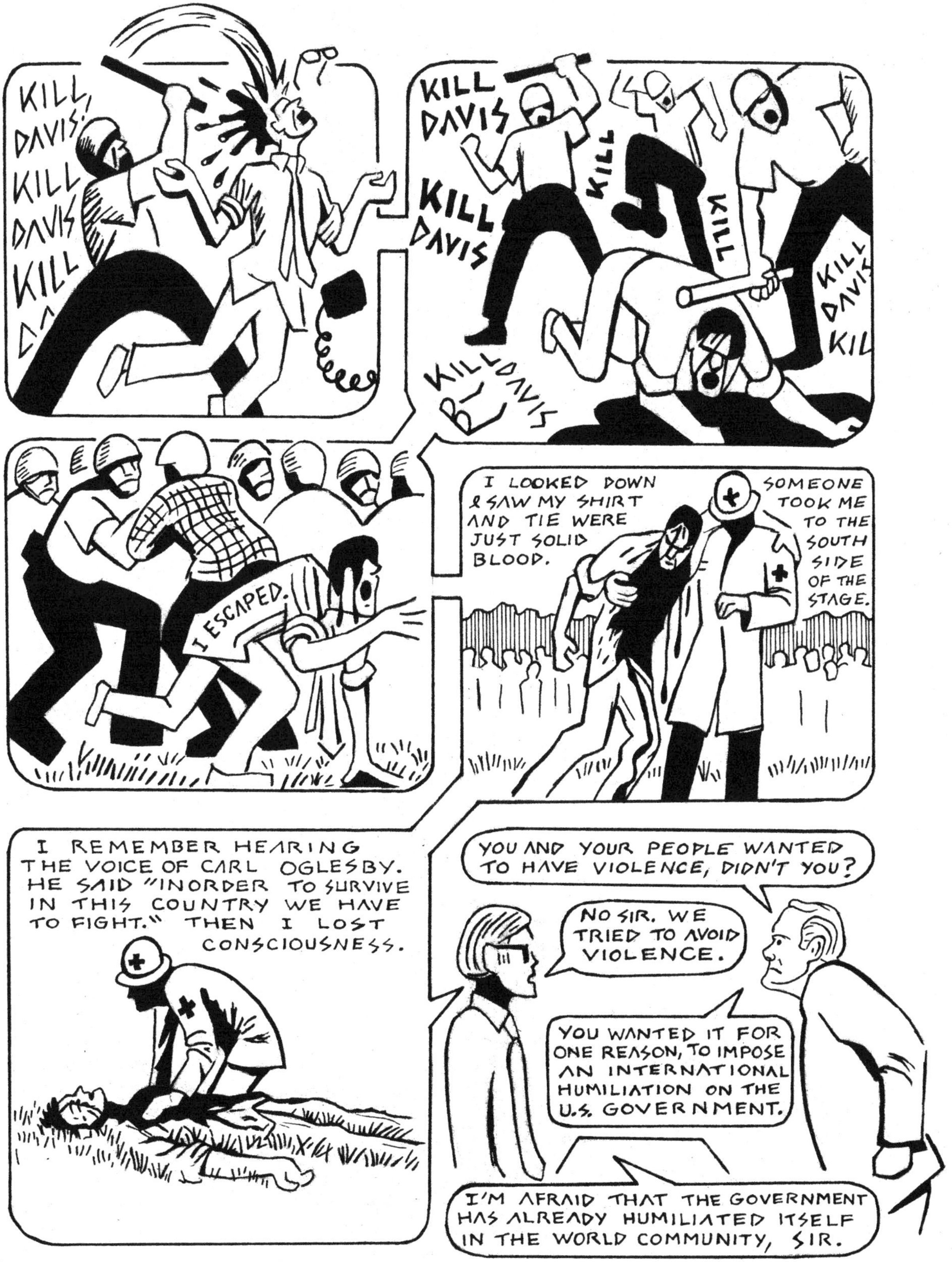
KILL DAVIS! KILL DAVIS KILL
KILL DAVIS
KILL DAVIS
KILL
KILL
KILL DAVIS KIL
KILL DAVIS
I ESCAPED.
I LOOKED DOWN & SAW MY SHIRT AND TIE WERE JUST SOLID BLOOD.
SOMEONE TOOK ME TO THE SOUTH SIDE OF THE STAGE.
I REMEMBER HEARING THE VOICE OF CARL OGLESBY. HE SAID "INORDER TO SURVIVE IN THIS COUNTRY WE HAVE TO FIGHT." THEN I LOST CONSCIOUSNESS.
YOU AND YOUR PEOPLE WANTED TO HAVE VIOLENCE, DIDN'T YOU?
NO SIR. WE TRIED TO AVOID VIOLENCE.
YOU WANTED IT FOR ONE REASON, TO IMPOSE AN INTERNATIONAL HUMILIATION ON THE U.S. GOVERNMENT.
I'M AFRAID THAT THE GOVERNMENT HAS ALREADY HUMILIATED ITSELF IN THE WORLD COMMUNITY, SIR.

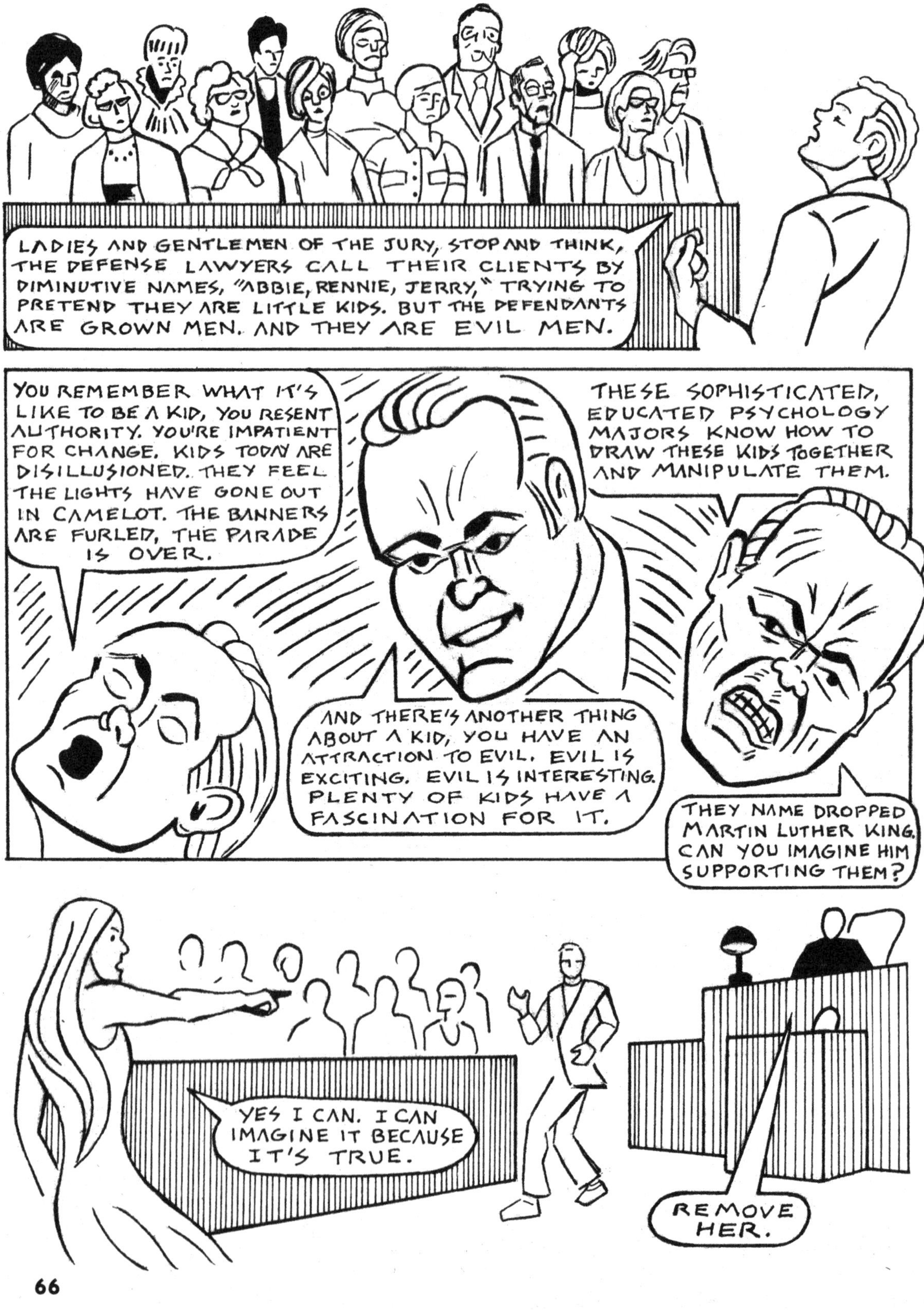
LADIES AND GENTLEMEN OF THE JURY, STOP AND THINK, THE DEFENSE LAWYERS CALL THEIR CLIENTS BY DIMINUTIVE NAMES, "ABBIE, RENNIE, JERRY," TRYING TO PRETEND THEY ARE LITTLE KIDS. BUT THE DEFENDANTS ARE GROWN MEN. AND THEY ARE EVIL MEN.
YOU REMEMBER WHAT IT'S LIKE TO BE A KID, YOU RESENT AUTHORITY. YOU'RE IMPATIENT FOR CHANGE. KIDS TODAY ARE DISILLUSIONED. THEY FEEL THE LIGHTS HAVE GONE OUT IN CAMELOT. THE BANNERS ARE FURLED, THE PARADE IS OVER.
AND THERE'S ANOTHER THING ABOUT A KID, YOU HAVE AN ATTRACTION TO EVIL. EVIL IS EXCITING. EVIL IS INTERESTING. PLENTY OF KIDS HAVE A FASCINATION FOR IT.
THESE SOPHISTICATED, EDUCATED PSYCHOLOGY MAJORS KNOW HOW TO DRAW THESE KIDS TOGETHER AND MANIPULATE THEM.
THEY NAME DROPPED MARTIN LUTHER KING. CAN YOU IMAGINE HIM SUPPORTING THEM?
YES I CAN. I CAN IMAGINE IT BECAUSE IT'S TRUE.
REMOVE HER.

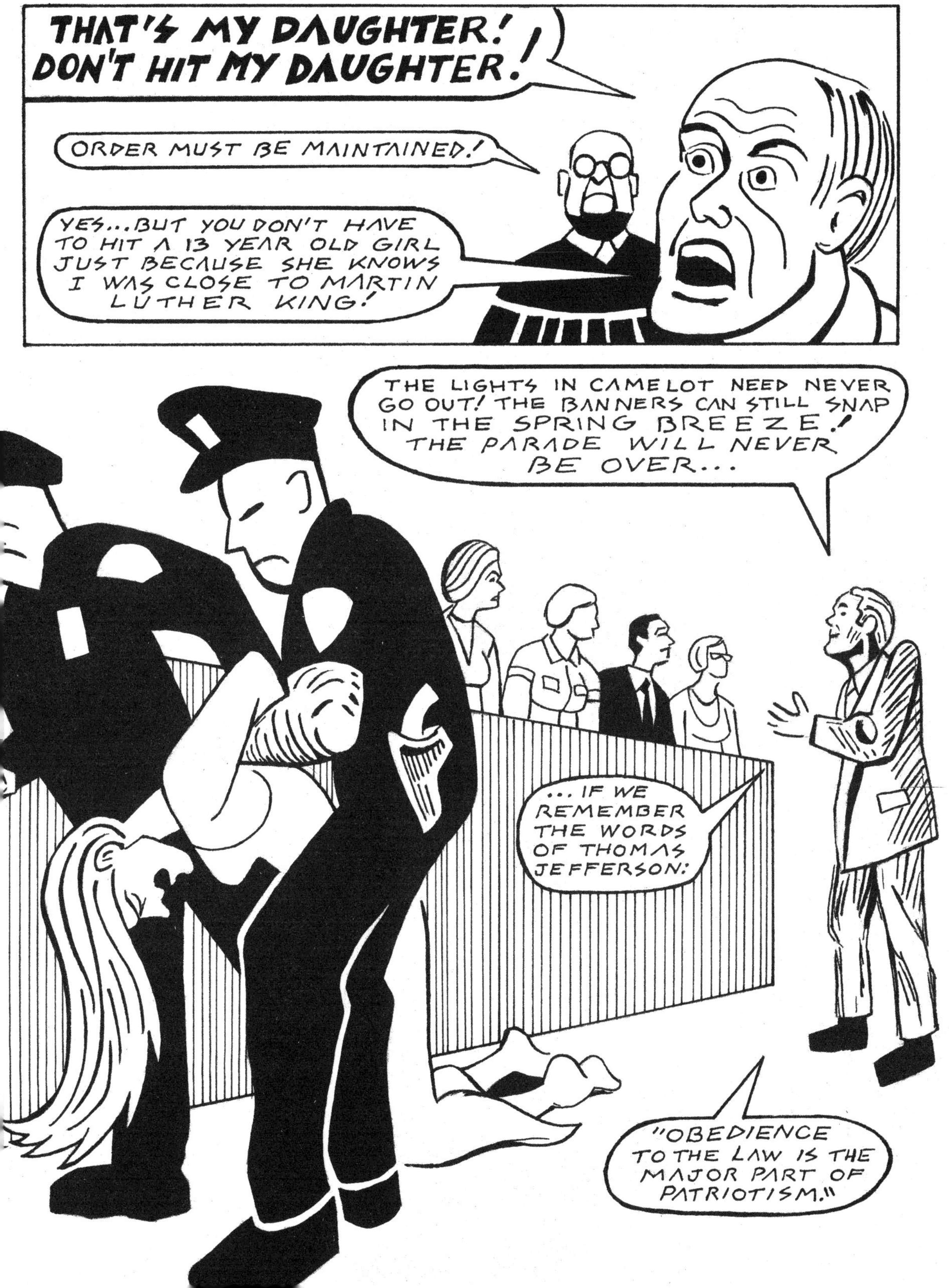
THAT'S MY DAUGHTER! DON'T HIT MY DAUGHTER!
ORDER MUST BE MAINTAINED!
YES...BUT YOU DON'T HAVE TO HIT A 13 YEAR OLD GIRL JUST BECAUSE SHE KNOWS I WAS CLOSE TO MARTIN LUTHER KING!
THE LIGHTS IN CAMELOT NEED NEVER GO OUT! THE BANNERS CAN STILL SNAP IN THE SPRING BREEZE! THE PARADE WILL NEVER BE OVER...
...IF WE REMEMBER THE WORDS OF THOMAS JEFFERSON:
"OBEDIENCE TO THE LAW IS THE MAJOR PART OF PATRIOTISM."

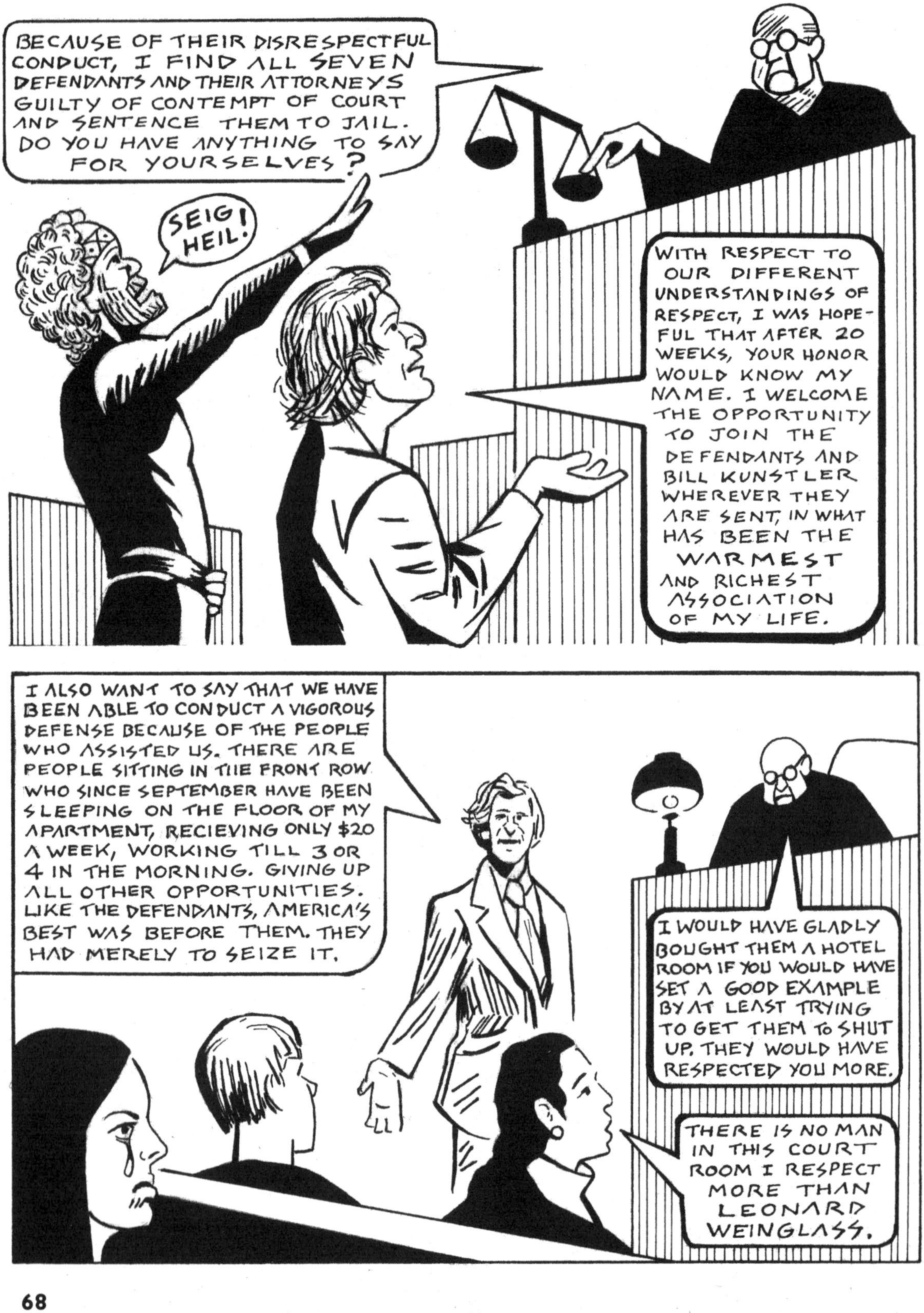
BECAUSE OF THEIR DISRESPECTFUL CONDUCT, I FIND ALL SEVEN DEFENDANTS AND THEIR ATTORNEYS GUILTY OF CONTEMPT OF COURT AND SENTENCE THEM TO JAIL. DO YOU HAVE ANYTHING TO SAY FOR YOURSELVES?
SEIG HEIL!
WITH RESPECT TO OUR DIFFERENT UNDERSTANDINGS OF RESPECT, I WAS HOPEFUL THAT AFTER 20 WEEKS, YOUR HONOR WOULD KNOW MY NAME. I WELCOME THE OPPORTUNITY TO JOIN THE DEFENDANTS AND BILL KUNSTLER WHEREVER THEY ARE SENT, IN WHAT HAS BEEN THE WARMEST AND RICHEST ASSOCIATION OF MY LIFE.
I ALSO WANT TO SAY THAT WE HAVE BEEN ABLE TO CONDUCT A VIGOROUS DEFENSE BECAUSE OF THE PEOPLE WHO ASSISTED US. THERE ARE PEOPLE SITTING IN THE FRONT ROW WHO SINCE SEPTEMBER HAVE BEEN SLEEPING ON THE FLOOR OF MY APARTMENT, RECIEVING ONLY $20 A WEEK, WORKING TILL 3 OR 4 IN THE MORNING. GIVING UP ALL OTHER OPPORTUNITIES. LIKE THE DEFENDANTS, AMERICA'S BEST WAS BEFORE THEM. THEY HAD MERELY TO SEIZE IT.
I WOULD HAVE GLADLY BOUGHT THEM A HOTEL ROOM IF YOU WOULD HAVE SET A GOOD EXAMPLE BY AT LEAST TRYING TO GET THEM TO SHUT UP. THEY WOULD HAVE RESPECTED YOU MORE.
THERE IS NO MAN IN THIS COURT ROOM I RESPECT MORE THAN LEONARD WEINGLASS.

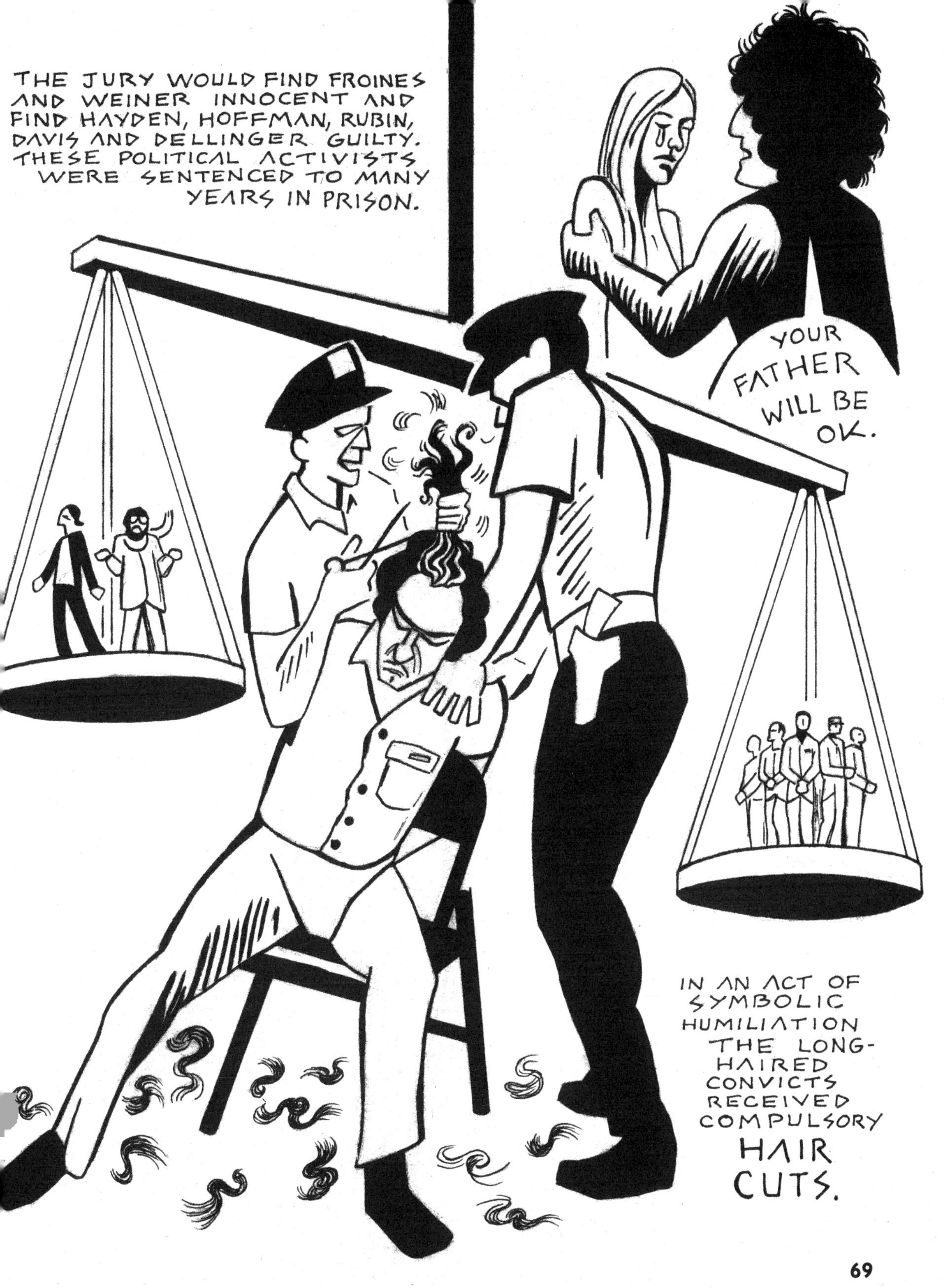
THE JURY WOULD FIND FROINES AND WEINER INNOCENT AND FIND HAYDEN, HOFFMAN, RUBIN, DAVIS AND DELLINGER GUILTY. THESE POLITICAL ACTIVISTS WERE SENTENCED TO MANY YEARS IN PRISON.
YOUR FATHER WILL BE OK.
IN AN ACT OF SYMBOLIC HUMILIATION THE LONG-HAIRED CONVICTS RECEIVED COMPULSORY HAIR CUTS.

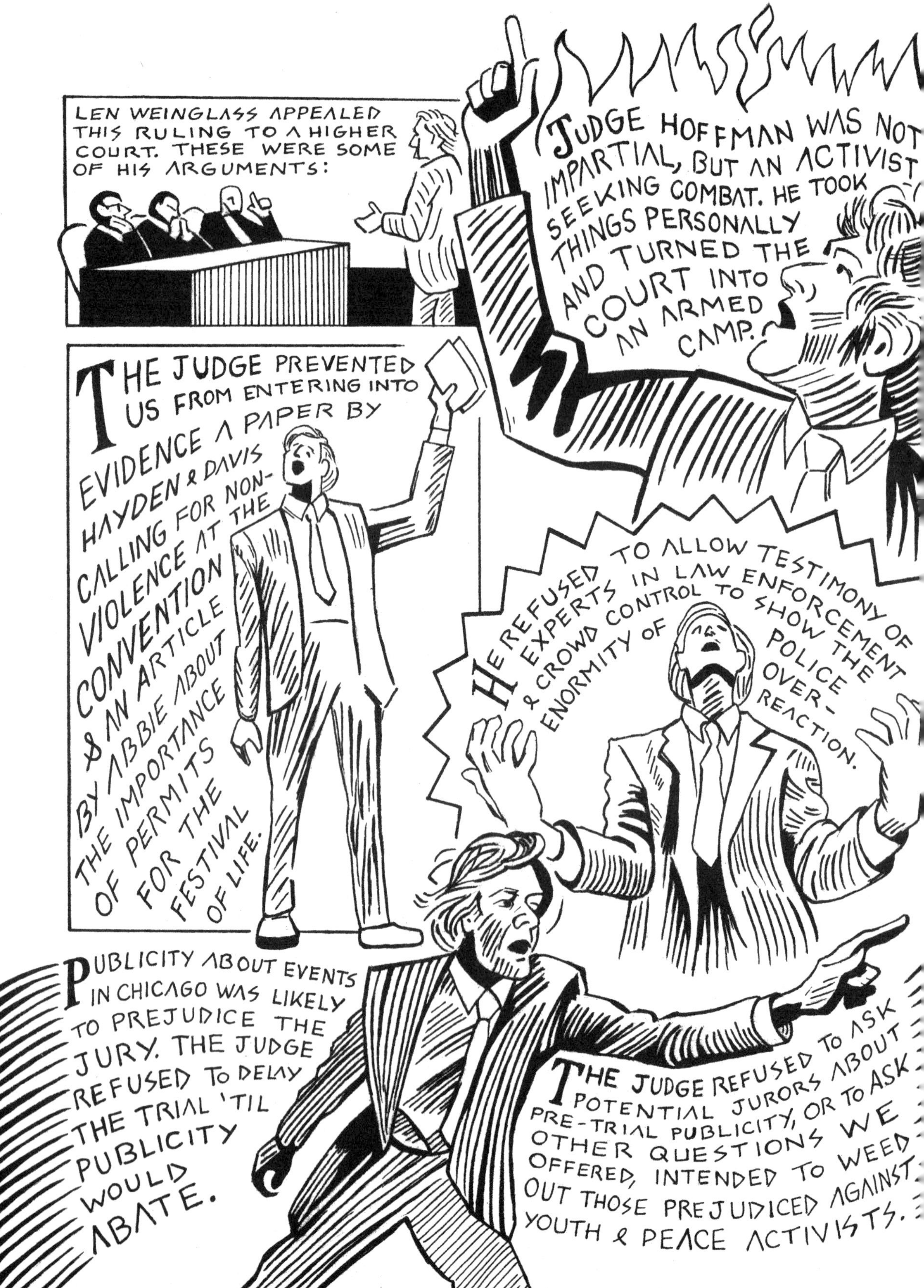

LEN WEINGLASS APPEALED THIS RULING TO A HIGHER COURT. THESE WERE SOME OF HIS ARGUMENTS:
JUDGE HOFFMAN WAS NOT IMPARTIAL, BUT AN ACTIVIST SEEKING COMBAT. HE TOOK THINGS PERSONALLY AND TURNED THE COURT INTO AN ARMED CAMP.
THE JUDGE PREVENTED US FROM ENTERING INTO EVIDENCE A PAPER BY HAYDEN & DAVIS CALLING FOR NON-VIOLENCE AT THE CONVENTION & AN ARTICLE BY ABBIE ABOUT THE IMPORTANCE OF PERMITS FOR THE FESTIVAL OF LIFE.
HE REFUSED TO ALLOW TESTIMONY OF EXPERTS IN LAW ENFORCEMENT OF & CROWD CONTROL TO SHOW THE ENORMITY OF POLICE OVER-REACTION.
PUBLICITY ABOUT EVENTS IN CHICAGO WAS LIKELY TO PREJUDICE THE JURY. THE JUDGE REFUSED TO DELAY THE TRIAL 'TIL PUBLICITY WOULD ABATE.
THE JUDGE REFUSED TO ASK POTENTIAL JURORS ABOUT PRE-TRIAL PUBLICITY, OR TO ASK OTHER QUESTIONS WE OFFERED, INTENDED TO WEED OUT THOSE PREJUDICED AGAINST YOUTH & PEACE ACTIVISTS.

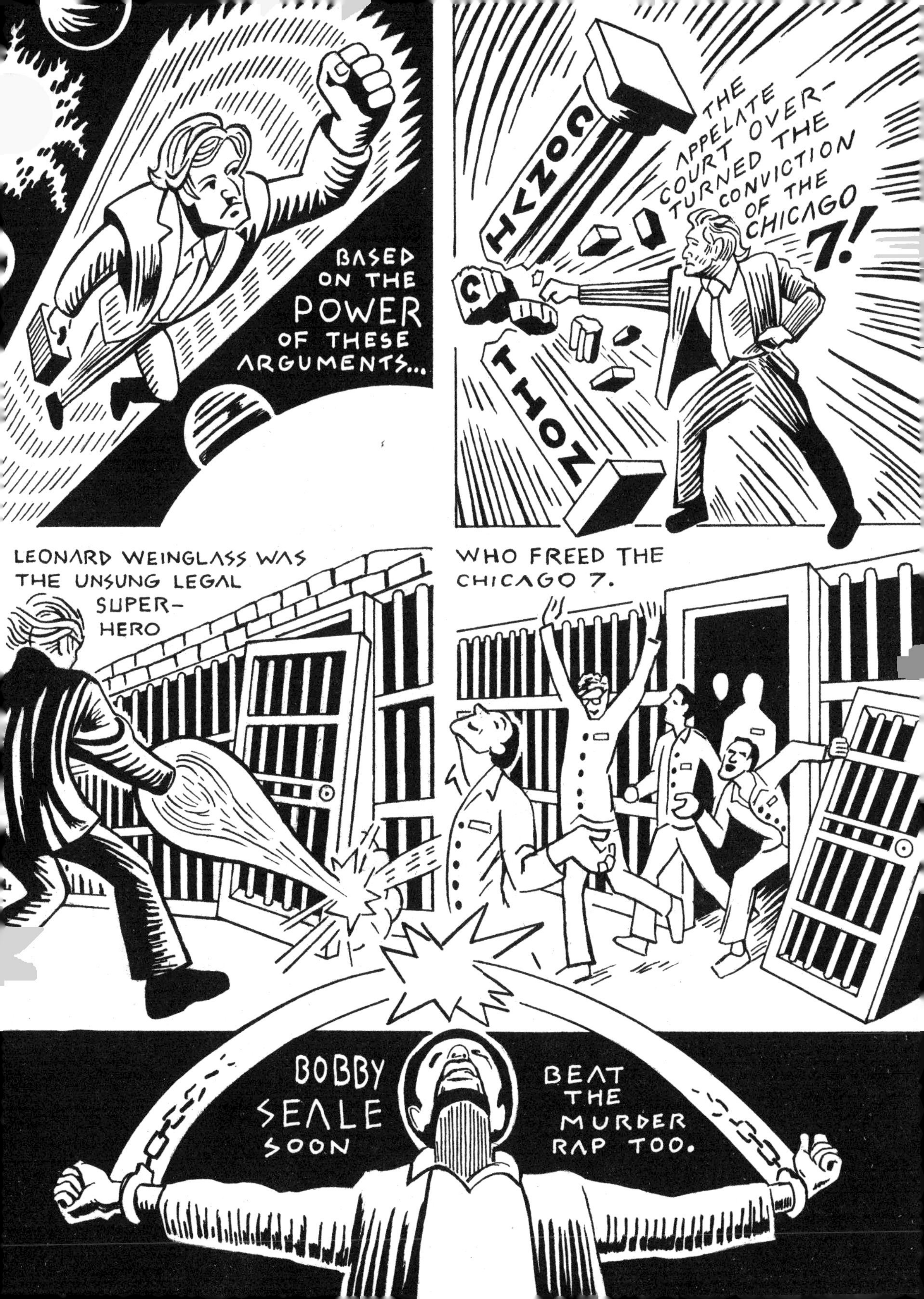
BASED ON THE POWER OF THESE ARGUMENTS...
THE APPELATE COURT OVER-TURNED THE CONVICTION OF THE CHICAGO 7!
LEONARD WEINGLASS WAS THE UNSUNG LEGAL SUPER-HERO
WHO FREED THE CHICAGO 7.
BOBBY SEALE SOON
BEAT THE MURDER RAP TOO.

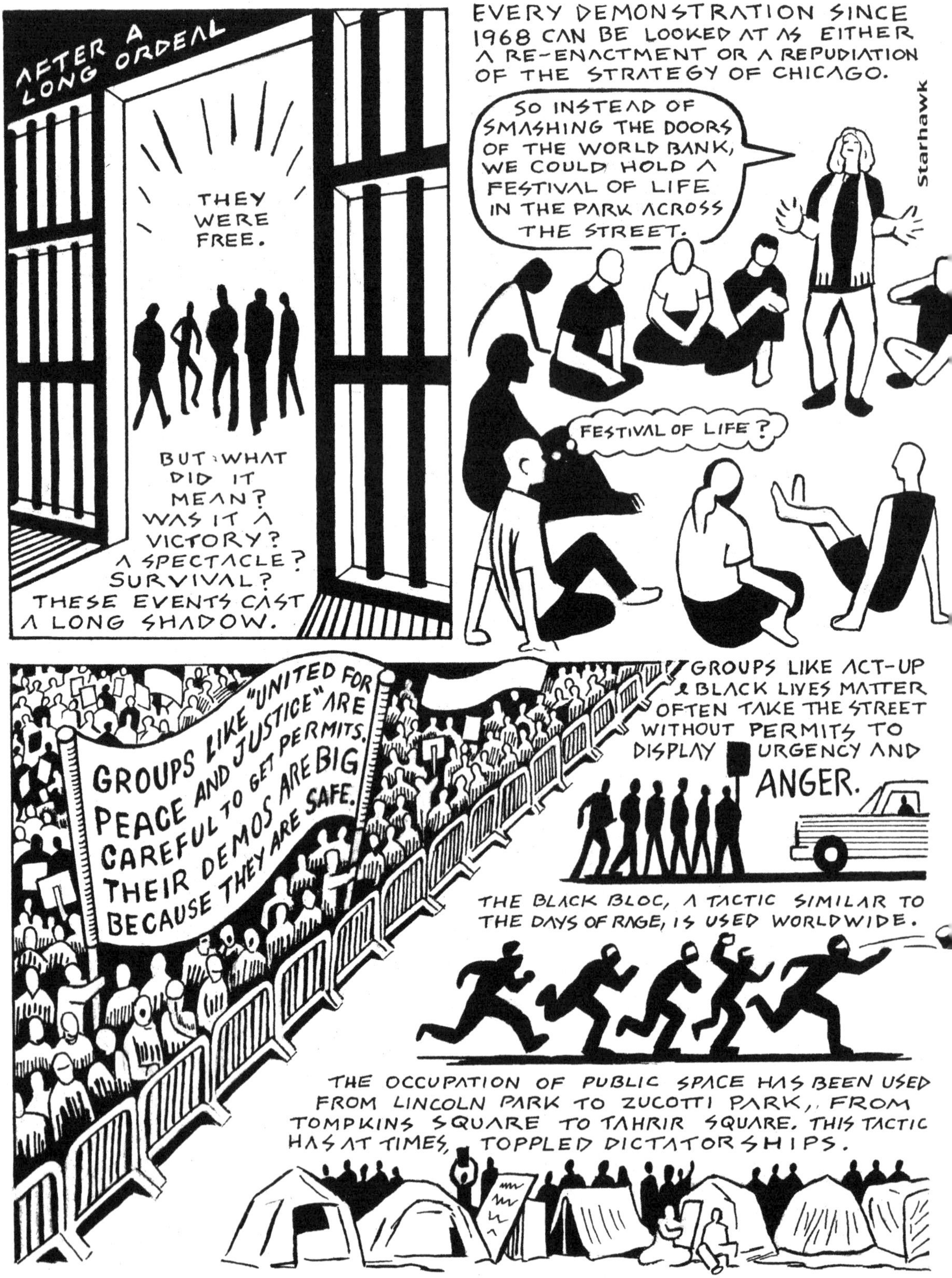
AFTER A LONG ORDEAL
THEY WERE FREE.
BUT WHAT DID IT MEAN? WAS IT A VICTORY? A SPECTACLE? SURVIVAL? THESE EVENTS CAST A LONG SHADOW.
EVERY DEMONSTRATION SINCE 1968 CAN BE LOOKED AT AS EITHER A RE-ENACTMENT OR A REPUDIATION OF THE STRATEGY OF CHICAGO.
Starhawk
SO INSTEAD OF SMASHING THE DOORS OF THE WORLD BANK, WE COULD HOLD A FESTIVAL OF LIFE IN THE PARK ACROSS THE STREET.
FESTIVAL OF LIFE?
GROUPS LIKE "UNITED FOR PEACE AND JUSTICE" ARE CAREFUL TO GET PERMITS. THEIR DEMOS ARE BIG BECAUSE THEY ARE SAFE.
GROUPS LIKE ACT-UP & BLACK LIVES MATTER OFTEN TAKE THE STREET WITHOUT PERMITS TO DISPLAY URGENCY AND ANGER.
THE BLACK BLOC, A TACTIC SIMILAR TO THE DAYS OF RAGE, IS USED WORLDWIDE.
THE OCCUPATION OF PUBLIC SPACE HAS BEEN USED FROM LINCOLN PARK TO ZUCOTTI PARK, FROM TOMPKINS SQUARE TO TAHRIR SQUARE. THIS TACTIC HAS AT TIMES, TOPPLED DICTATORSHIPS.

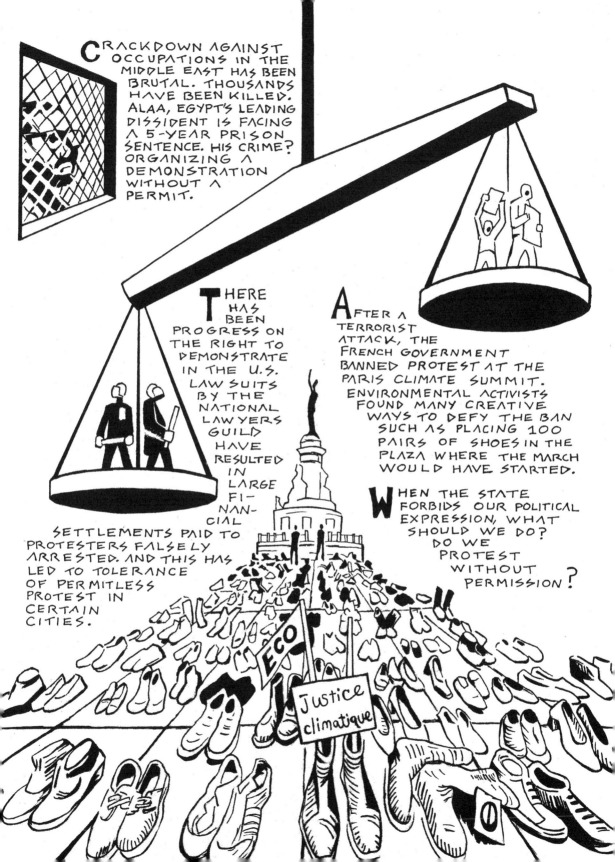

CRACKDOWN AGAINST OCCUPATIONS IN THE MIDDLE EAST HAS BEEN BRUTAL. THOUSANDS HAVE BEEN KILLED. ALAA, EGYPT'S LEADING DISSIDENT IS FACING A 5-YEAR PRISON SENTENCE. HIS CRIME? ORGANIZING A DEMONSTRATION WITHOUT A PERMIT.

THERE HAS BEEN PROGRESS ON THE RIGHT TO DEMONSTRATE IN THE U.S. LAWSUITS BY THE NATIONAL LAWYERS GUILD HAVE RESULTED IN LARGE FINANCIAL SETTLEMENTS PAID TO PROTESTERS FALSELY ARRESTED. AND THIS HAS LED TO TOLERANCE OF PERMITLESS PROTEST IN CERTAIN CITIES.

AFTER A TERRORIST ATTACK, THE FRENCH GOVERNMENT BANNED PROTEST AT THE PARIS CLIMATE SUMMIT. ENVIRONMENTAL ACTIVISTS FOUND MANY CREATIVE WAYS TO DEFY THE BAN SUCH AS PLACING 100 PAIRS OF SHOES IN THE PLAZA WHERE THE MARCH WOULD HAVE STARTED.

WHEN THE STATE FORBIDS OUR POLITICAL EXPRESSION, WHAT SHOULD WE DO? DO WE PROTEST WITHOUT PERMISSION?

ECO

Justice climatique

TRUTH OR TREASON
THE PENTAGON PAPERS CASE

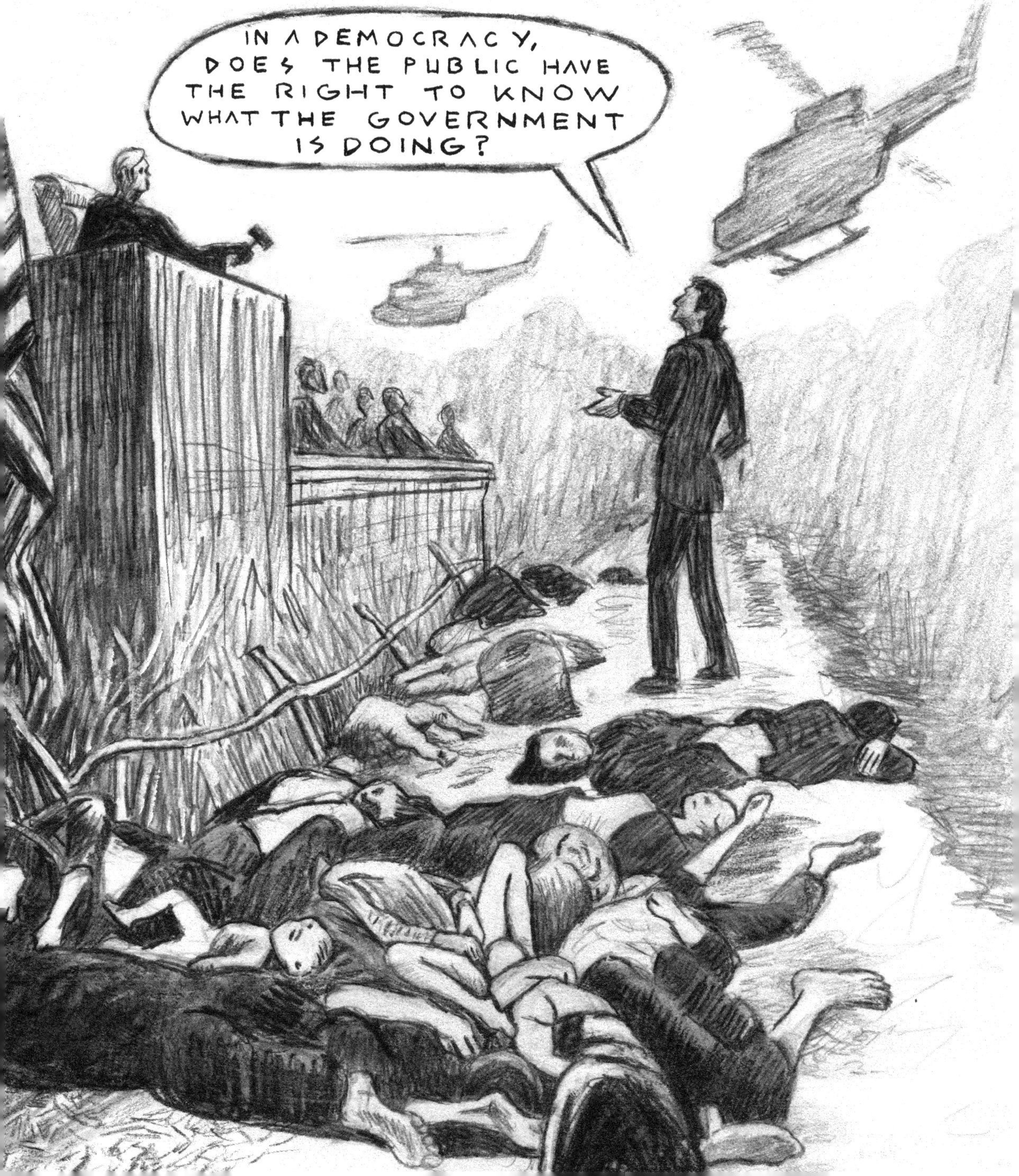
IN A DEMOCRACY, DOES THE PUBLIC HAVE THE RIGHT TO KNOW WHAT THE GOVERNMENT IS DOING?

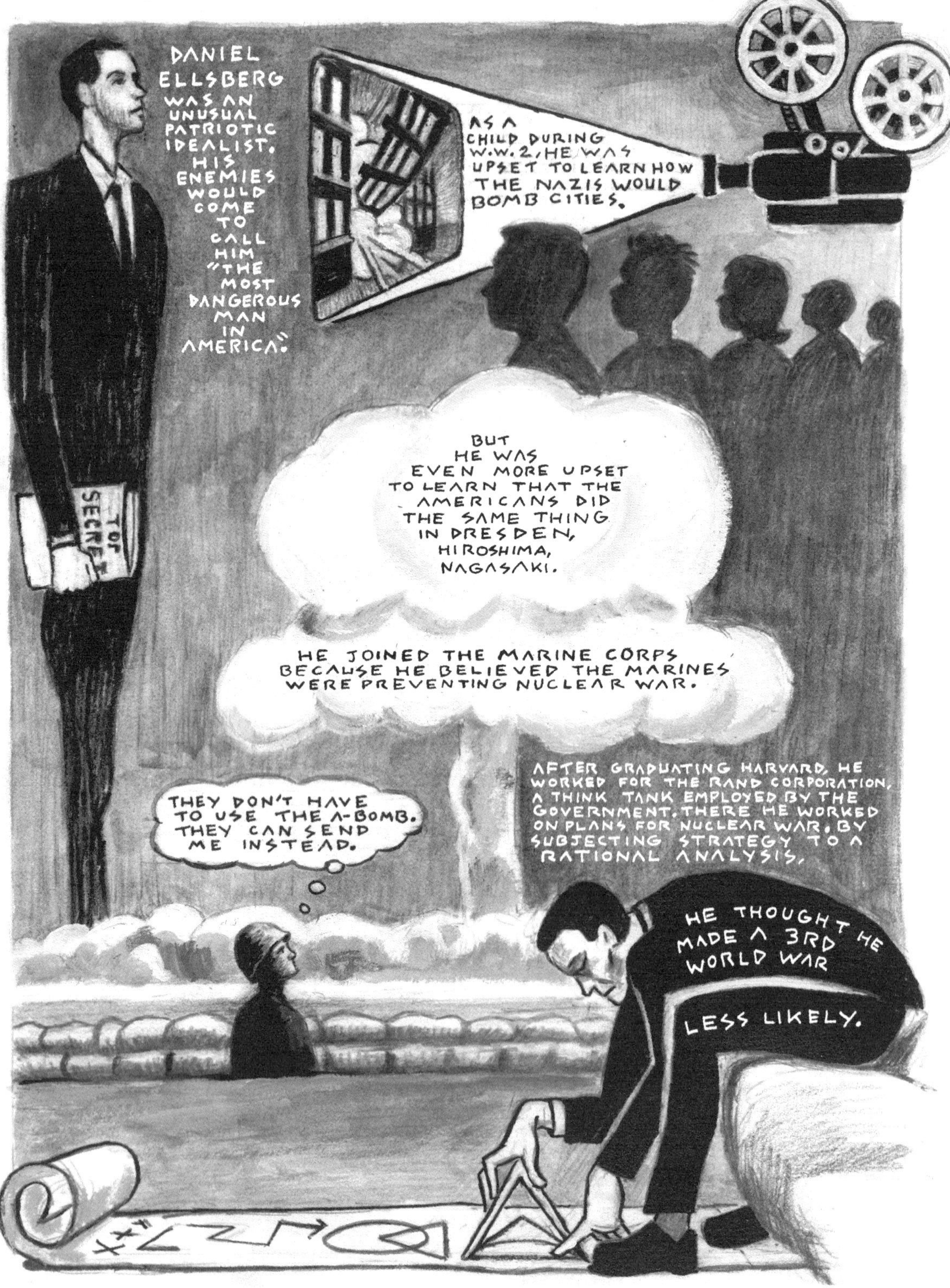
DANIEL ELLSBERG WAS AN UNUSUAL PATRIOTIC IDEALIST. HIS ENEMIES WOULD COME TO CALL HIM "THE MOST DANGEROUS MAN IN AMERICA."
TOP SECRET
AS A CHILD DURING W.W. 2, HE WAS UPSET TO LEARN HOW THE NAZIS WOULD BOMB CITIES.
BUT HE WAS EVEN MORE UPSET TO LEARN THAT THE AMERICANS DID THE SAME THING IN DRESDEN, HIROSHIMA, NAGASAKI.
HE JOINED THE MARINE CORPS BECAUSE HE BELIEVED THE MARINES WERE PREVENTING NUCLEAR WAR.
THEY DON'T HAVE TO USE THE A-BOMB. THEY CAN SEND ME INSTEAD.
AFTER GRADUATING HARVARD, HE WORKED FOR THE RAND CORPORATION, A THINK TANK EMPLOYED BY THE GOVERNMENT. THERE HE WORKED ON PLANS FOR NUCLEAR WAR. BY SUBJECTING STRATEGY TO A RATIONAL ANALYSIS,
HE THOUGHT HE MADE A 3RD WORLD WAR
LESS LIKELY.

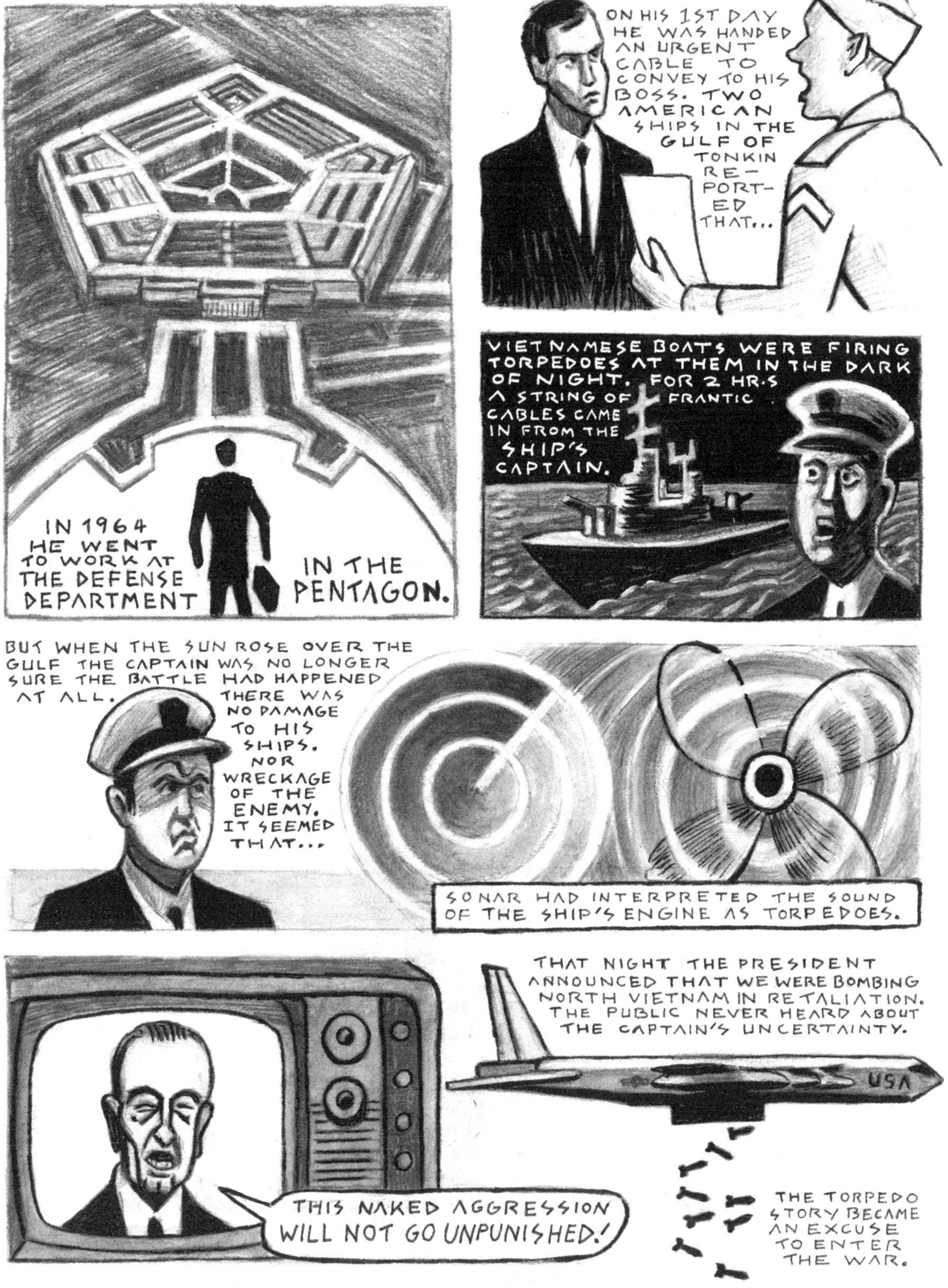
IN 1964 HE WENT TO WORK AT THE DEFENSE DEPARTMENT
IN THE PENTAGON.
ON HIS 1ST DAY HE WAS HANDED AN URGENT CABLE TO CONVEY TO HIS BOSS. TWO AMERICAN SHIPS IN THE GULF OF TONKIN RE-PORT-ED THAT...
VIETNAMESE BOATS WERE FIRING TORPEDOES AT THEM IN THE DARK OF NIGHT. FOR 2 HR.S A STRING OF FRANTIC CABLES CAME IN FROM THE SHIP'S CAPTAIN.
BUT WHEN THE SUN ROSE OVER THE GULF THE CAPTAIN WAS NO LONGER SURE THE BATTLE HAD HAPPENED AT ALL.
THERE WAS NO DAMAGE TO HIS SHIPS. NOR WRECKAGE OF THE ENEMY. IT SEEMED THAT...
SONAR HAD INTERPRETED THE SOUND OF THE SHIP'S ENGINE AS TORPEDOES.
THIS NAKED AGGRESSION WILL NOT GO UNPUNISHED!
THAT NIGHT THE PRESIDENT ANNOUNCED THAT WE WERE BOMBING NORTH VIETNAM IN RETALIATION. THE PUBLIC NEVER HEARD ABOUT THE CAPTAIN'S UNCERTAINTY.
USA
THE TORPEDO STORY BECAME AN EXCUSE TO ENTER THE WAR.

ELLSBERG'S JOB WAS TO READ TONS OF SECRET DOCUMENTS & SUMMARIZE THEM FOR HIGHER-UPS.

TOP SECRET

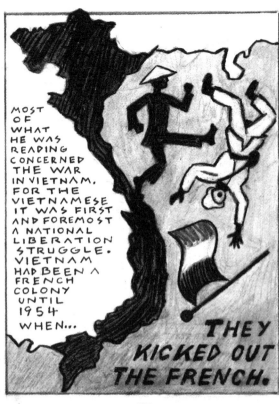

MOST OF WHAT HE WAS READING CONCERNED THE WAR IN VIETNAM. FOR THE VIETNAMESE IT WAS FIRST AND FOREMOST A NATIONAL LIBERATION STRUGGLE. VIETNAM HAD BEEN A FRENCH COLONY UNTIL 1954 WHEN...

THEY KICKED OUT THE FRENCH.

THERE WERE SUPPOSED TO BE ELECTIONS TO UNIFY THE COUNTRY.

HO CHI-MINH, WHO WAS A NATIONAL HERO FOR HAVING LED THE FIGHT AGAINST THE FRENCH, WAS LIKELY TO HAVE WON.

THE U.S.A. WANTED TO KEEP VIETNAM FROM BEING TRULY INDEPENDENT BECAUSE VIETNAM WAS RICH IN RUBBER, TUNGSTEN, TIN AND RICE.

SO THE U.S. PREVENTED THAT VIETNAMESE ELECTION.

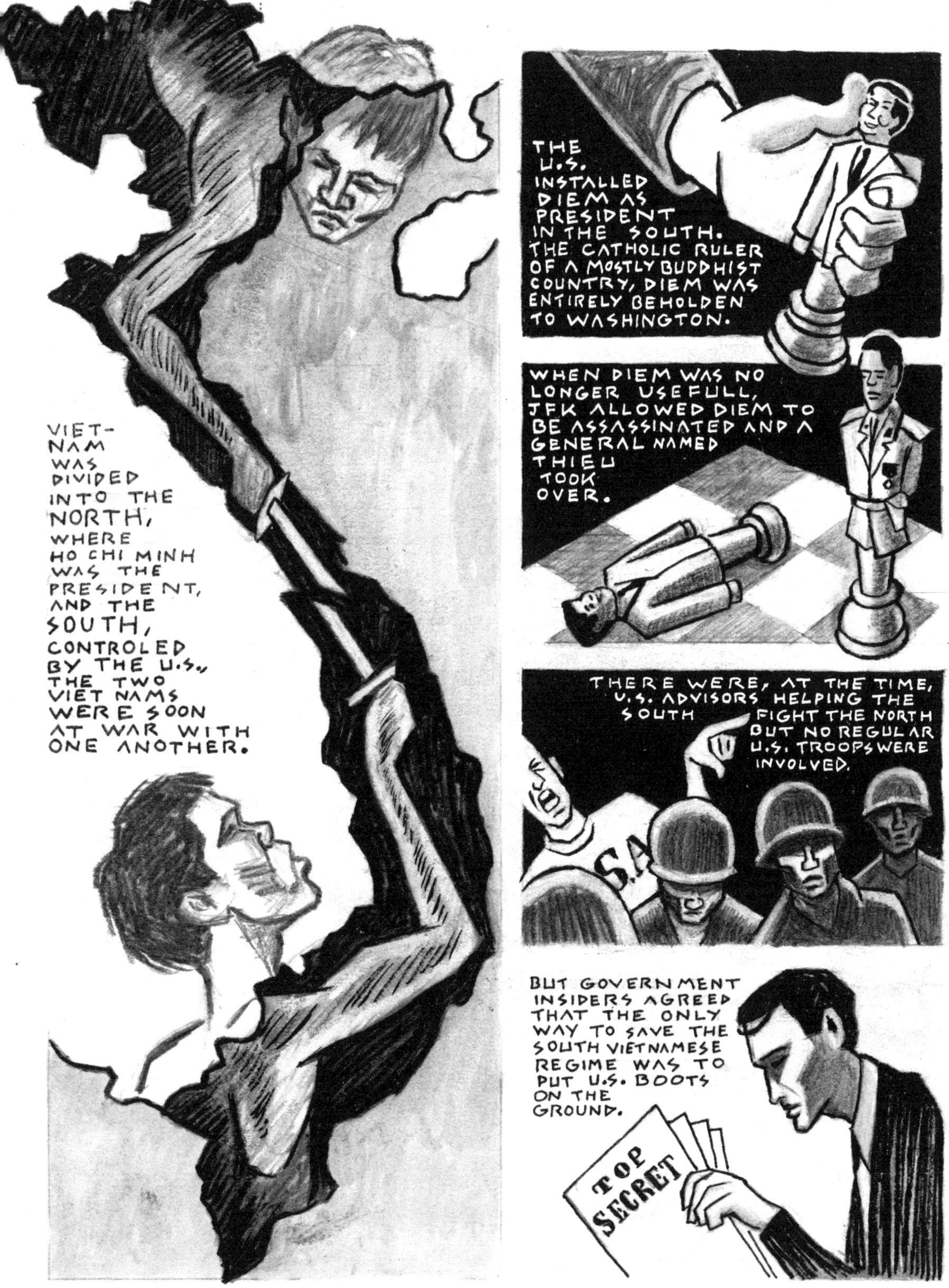
VIET-NAM WAS DIVIDED INTO THE NORTH, WHERE HO CHI MINH WAS THE PRESIDENT, AND THE SOUTH, CONTROLED BY THE U.S., THE TWO VIET NAMS WERE SOON AT WAR WITH ONE ANOTHER.
THE U.S. INSTALLED DIEM AS PRESIDENT IN THE SOUTH. THE CATHOLIC RULER OF A MOSTLY BUDDHIST COUNTRY, DIEM WAS ENTIRELY BEHOLDEN TO WASHINGTON.
WHEN DIEM WAS NO LONGER USEFULL, JFK ALLOWED DIEM TO BE ASSASSINATED AND A GENERAL NAMED THIEU TOOK OVER.
THERE WERE, AT THE TIME, U.S. ADVISORS HELPING THE SOUTH FIGHT THE NORTH BUT NO REGULAR U.S. TROOPS WERE INVOLVED.
S.A
BUT GOVERNMENT INSIDERS AGREED THAT THE ONLY WAY TO SAVE THE SOUTH VIETNAMESE REGIME WAS TO PUT U.S. BOOTS ON THE GROUND.
TOP SECRET

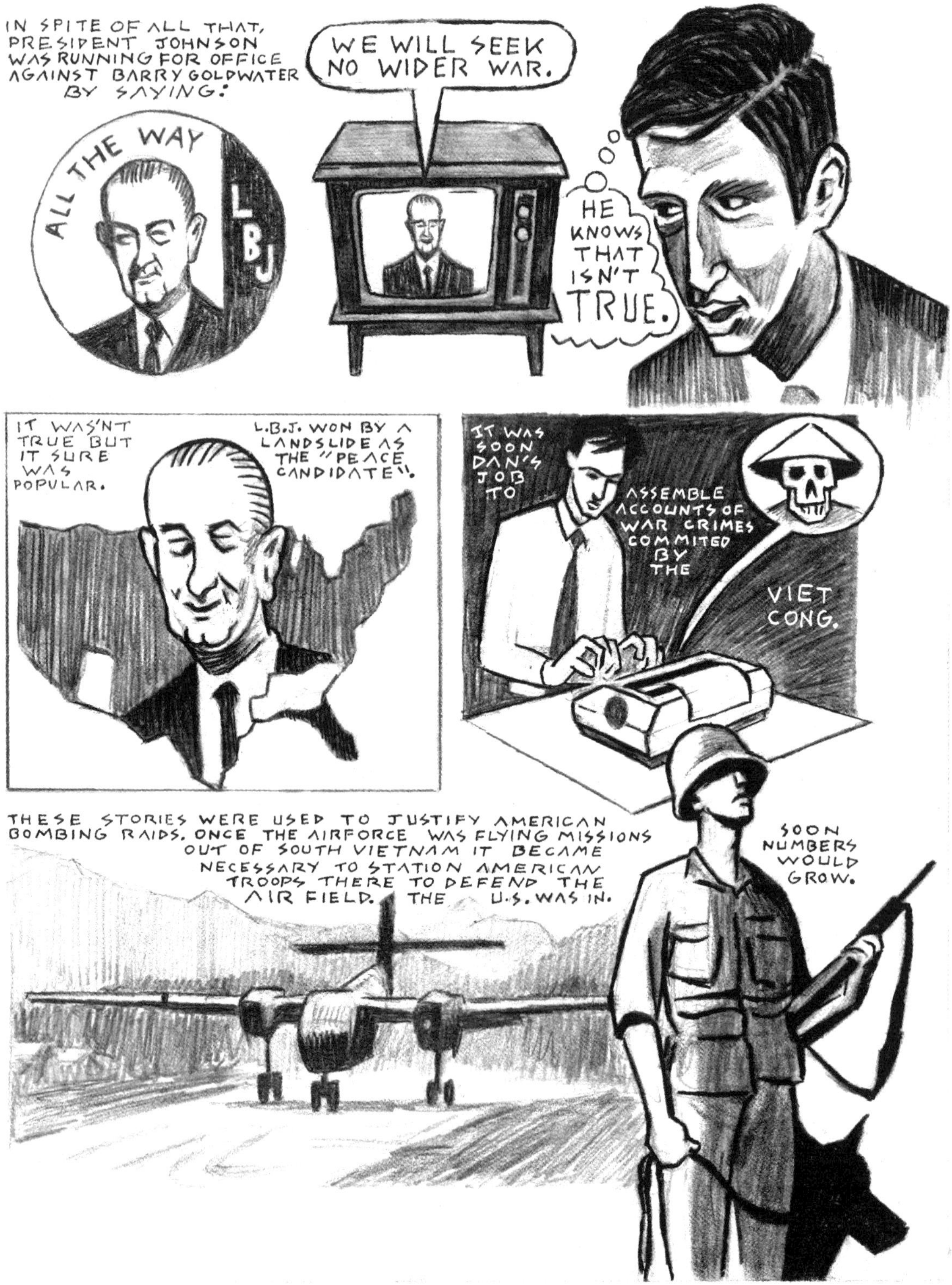
IN SPITE OF ALL THAT, PRESIDENT JOHNSON WAS RUNNING FOR OFFICE AGAINST BARRY GOLDWATER BY SAYING:
WE WILL SEEK NO WIDER WAR.
ALL THE WAY
LBJ
HE KNOWS THAT ISN'T TRUE.
IT WAS'NT TRUE BUT IT SURE WAS POPULAR.
L.B.J. WON BY A LANDSLIDE AS THE "PEACE CANDIDATE".
IT WAS SOON DAN'S JOB TO
ASSEMBLE ACCOUNTS OF WAR CRIMES COMMITED BY THE
VIET CONG.
THESE STORIES WERE USED TO JUSTIFY AMERICAN BOMBING RAIDS. ONCE THE AIRFORCE WAS FLYING MISSIONS OUT OF SOUTH VIETNAM IT BECAME NECESSARY TO STATION AMERICAN TROOPS THERE TO DEFEND THE AIR FIELD. THE U.S. WAS IN.
SOON NUMBERS WOULD GROW.

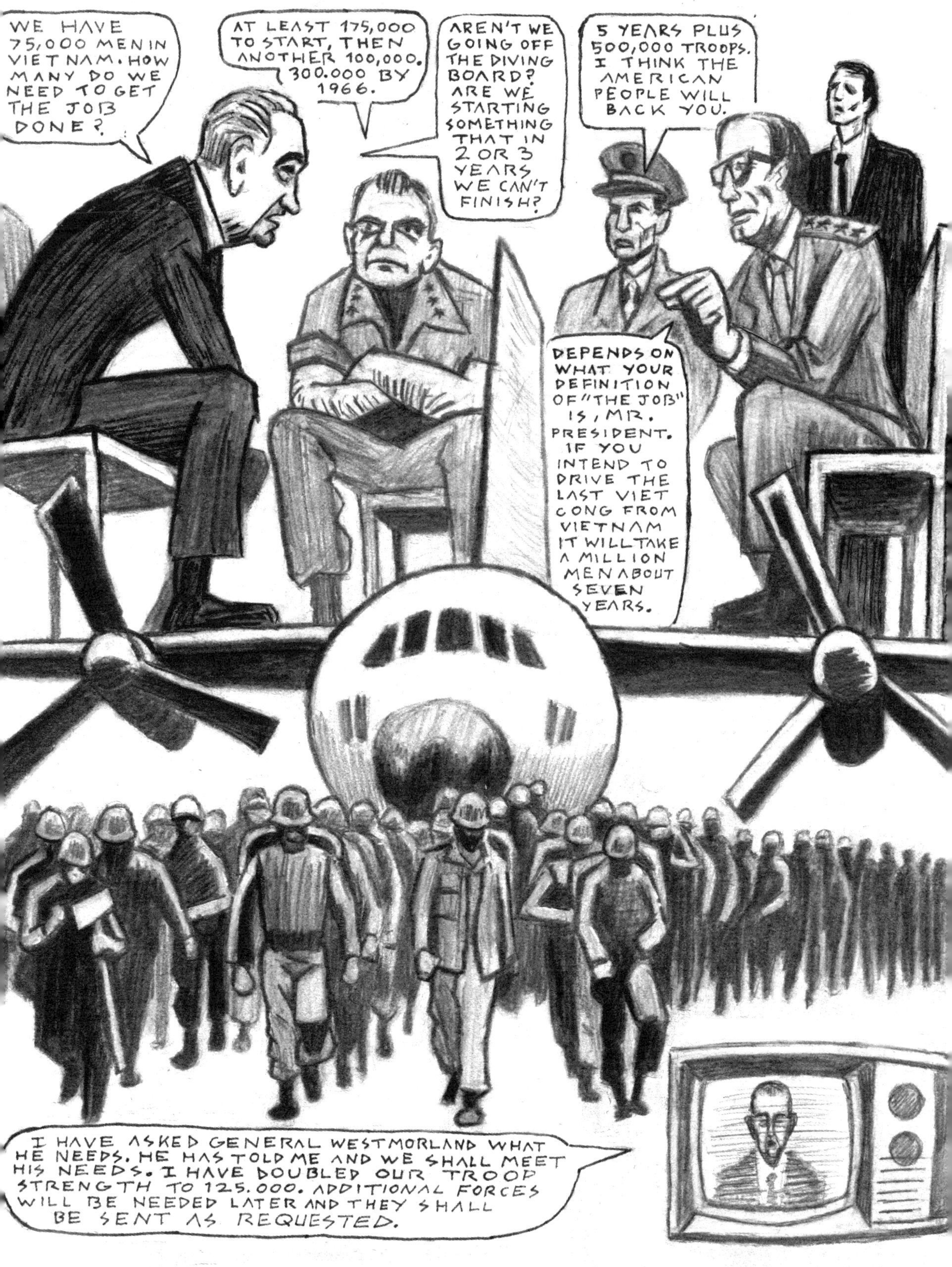
WE HAVE 75,000 MEN IN VIETNAM. HOW MANY DO WE NEED TO GET THE JOB DONE?
AT LEAST 175,000 TO START, THEN ANOTHER 100,000. 300.000 BY 1966.
AREN'T WE GOING OFF THE DIVING BOARD? ARE WE STARTING SOMETHING THAT IN 2 OR 3 YEARS WE CAN'T FINISH?
5 YEARS PLUS 500,000 TROOPS. I THINK THE AMERICAN PEOPLE WILL BACK YOU.
DEPENDS ON WHAT YOUR DEFINITION OF "THE JOB" IS, MR. PRESIDENT. IF YOU INTEND TO DRIVE THE LAST VIET CONG FROM VIETNAM IT WILL TAKE A MILLION MEN ABOUT SEVEN YEARS.
I HAVE ASKED GENERAL WESTMORLAND WHAT HE NEEDS. HE HAS TOLD ME AND WE SHALL MEET HIS NEEDS. I HAVE DOUBLED OUR TROOP STRENGTH TO 125.000. ADDITIONAL FORCES WILL BE NEEDED LATER AND THEY SHALL BE SENT AS REQUESTED.

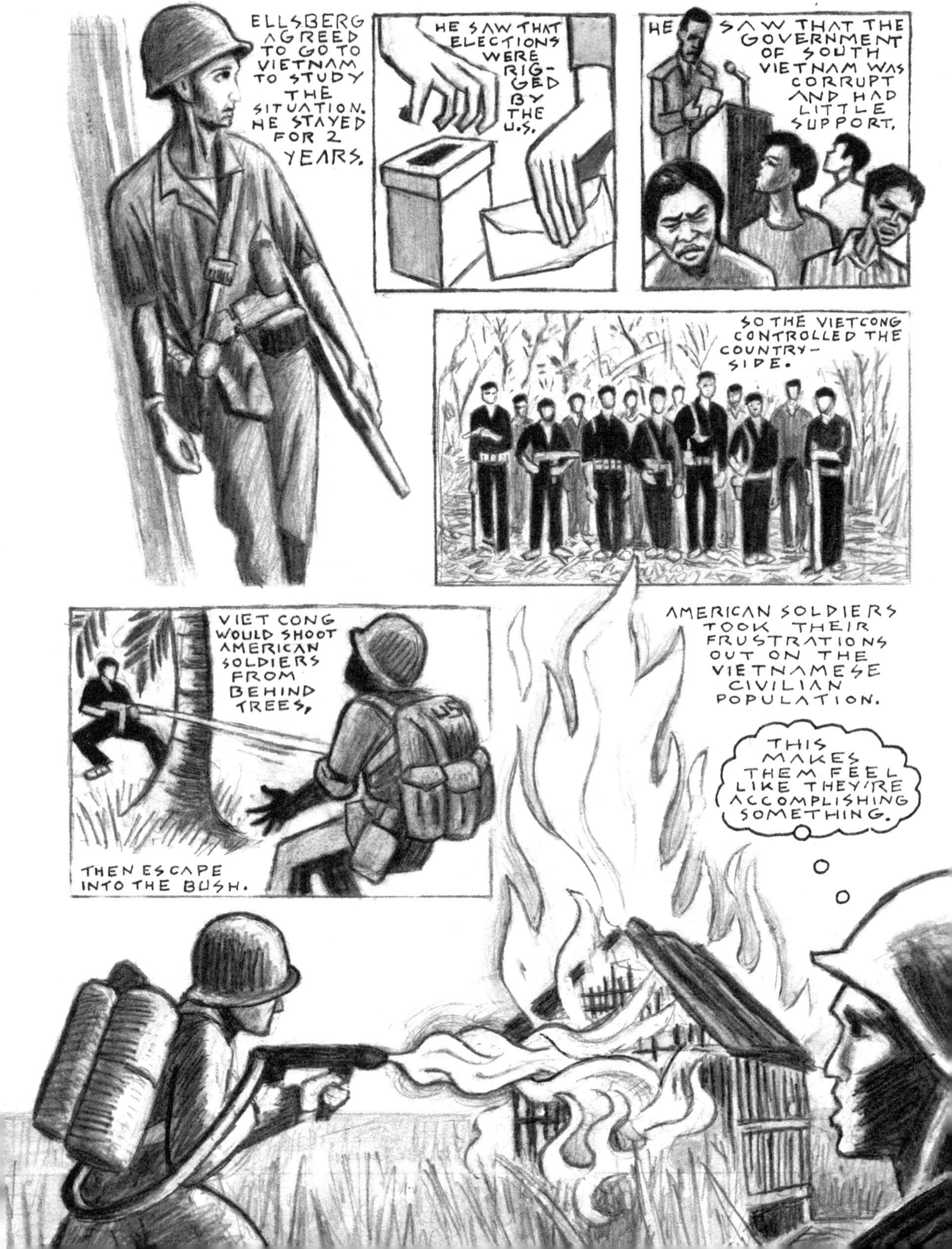
ELLSBERG AGREED TO GO TO VIETNAM TO STUDY THE SITUATION. HE STAYED FOR 2 YEARS.
HE SAW THAT ELECTIONS WERE RIG-GED BY THE U.S.
HE SAW THAT THE GOVERNMENT OF SOUTH VIETNAM WAS CORRUPT AND HAD LITTLE SUPPORT.
SO THE VIETCONG CONTROLLED THE COUNTRY-SIDE.
VIET CONG WOULD SHOOT AMERICAN SOLDIERS FROM BEHIND TREES,
THEN ESCAPE INTO THE BUSH.
AMERICAN SOLDIERS TOOK THEIR FRUSTRATIONS OUT ON THE VIETNAMESE CIVILIAN POPULATION.
THIS MAKES THEM FEEL LIKE THEY'RE ACCOMPLISHING SOMETHING.

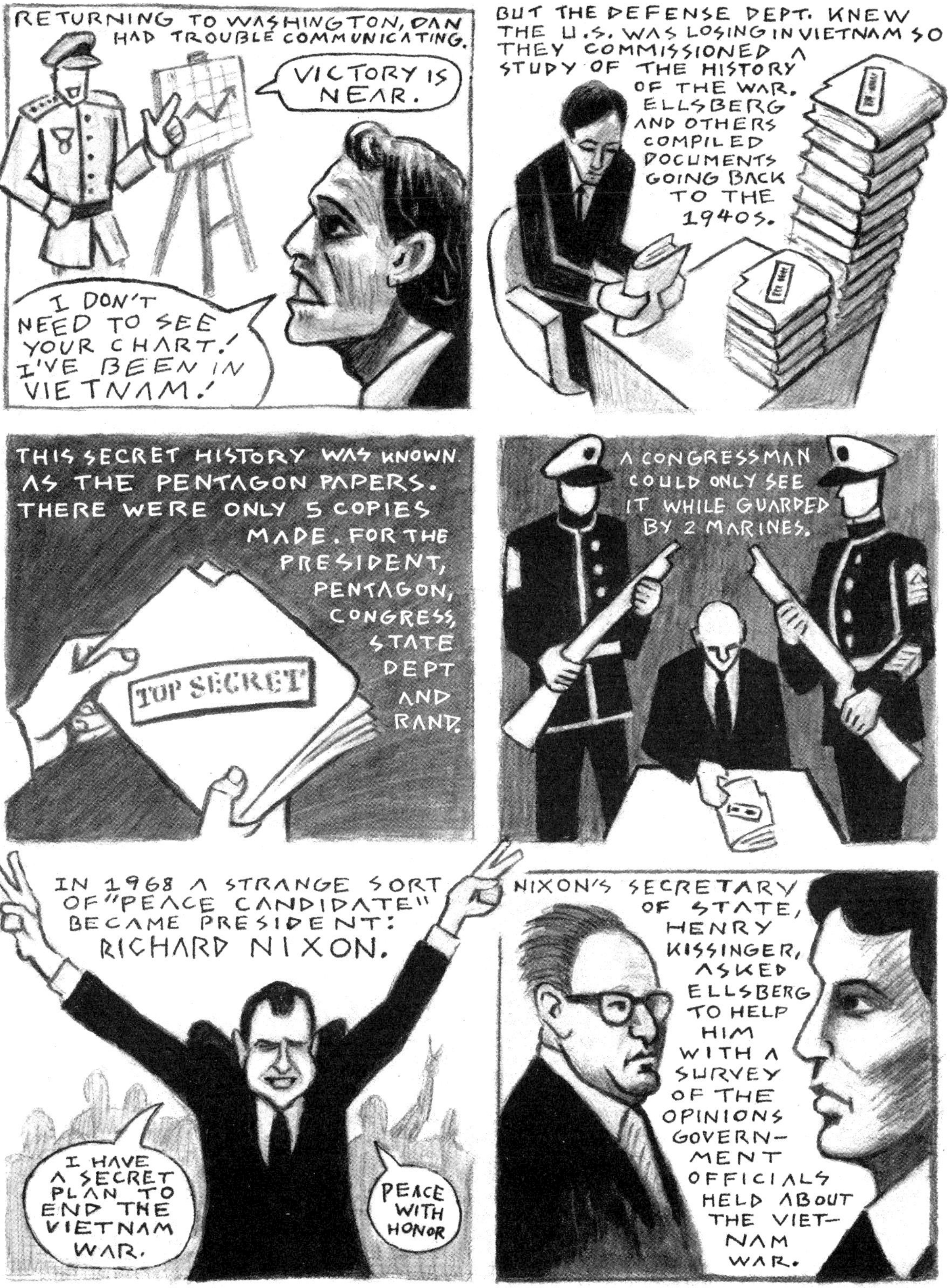
RETURNING TO WASHINGTON, DAN HAD TROUBLE COMMUNICATING.
VICTORY IS NEAR.
I DON'T NEED TO SEE YOUR CHART! I'VE BEEN IN VIETNAM!
BUT THE DEFENSE DEPT. KNEW THE U.S. WAS LOSING IN VIETNAM SO THEY COMMISSIONED A STUDY OF THE HISTORY OF THE WAR. ELLSBERG AND OTHERS COMPILED DOCUMENTS GOING BACK TO THE 1940S.
THIS SECRET HISTORY WAS KNOWN AS THE PENTAGON PAPERS. THERE WERE ONLY 5 COPIES MADE. FOR THE PRESIDENT, PENTAGON, CONGRESS, STATE DEPT AND RAND.
TOP SECRET
A CONGRESSMAN COULD ONLY SEE IT WHILE GUARDED BY 2 MARINES.
IN 1968 A STRANGE SORT OF "PEACE CANDIDATE" BECAME PRESIDENT: RICHARD NIXON.
I HAVE A SECRET PLAN TO END THE VIETNAM WAR.
PEACE WITH HONOR
NIXON'S SECRETARY OF STATE, HENRY KISSINGER, ASKED ELLSBERG TO HELP HIM WITH A SURVEY OF THE OPINIONS GOVERNMENT OFFICIALS HELD ABOUT THE VIETNAM WAR.

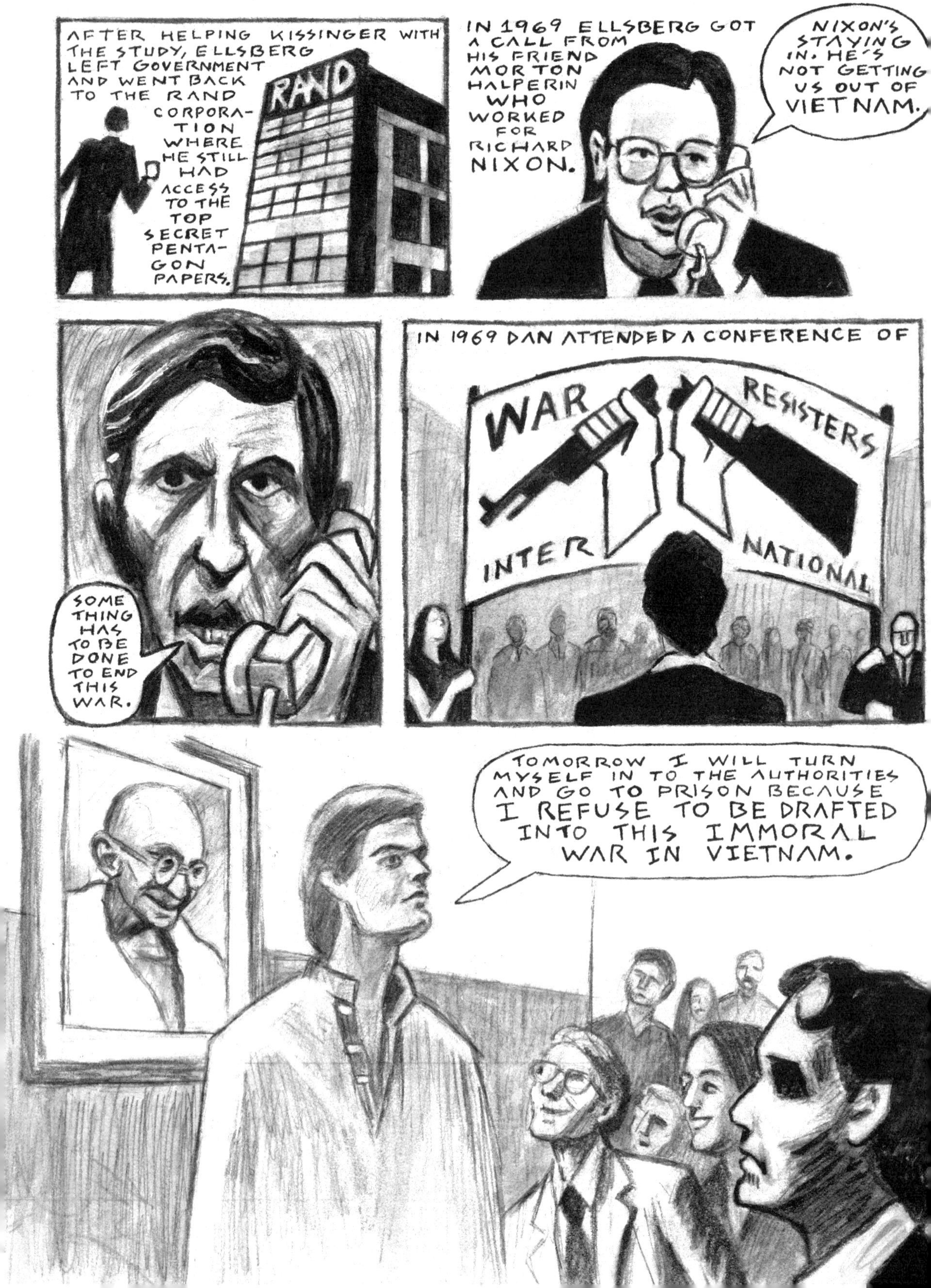
AFTER HELPING KISSINGER WITH THE STUDY, ELLSBERG LEFT GOVERNMENT AND WENT BACK TO THE RAND CORPORATION WHERE HE STILL HAD ACCESS TO THE TOP SECRET PENTAGON PAPERS.
RAND
IN 1969 ELLSBERG GOT A CALL FROM HIS FRIEND MORTON HALPERIN WHO WORKED FOR RICHARD NIXON.
NIXON'S STAYING IN. HE'S NOT GETTING US OUT OF VIETNAM.
SOMETHING HAS TO BE DONE TO END THIS WAR.
IN 1969 DAN ATTENDED A CONFERENCE OF
WAR RESISTERS INTERNATIONAL
TOMORROW I WILL TURN MYSELF IN TO THE AUTHORITIES AND GO TO PRISON BECAUSE I REFUSE TO BE DRAFTED INTO THIS IMMORAL WAR IN VIETNAM.

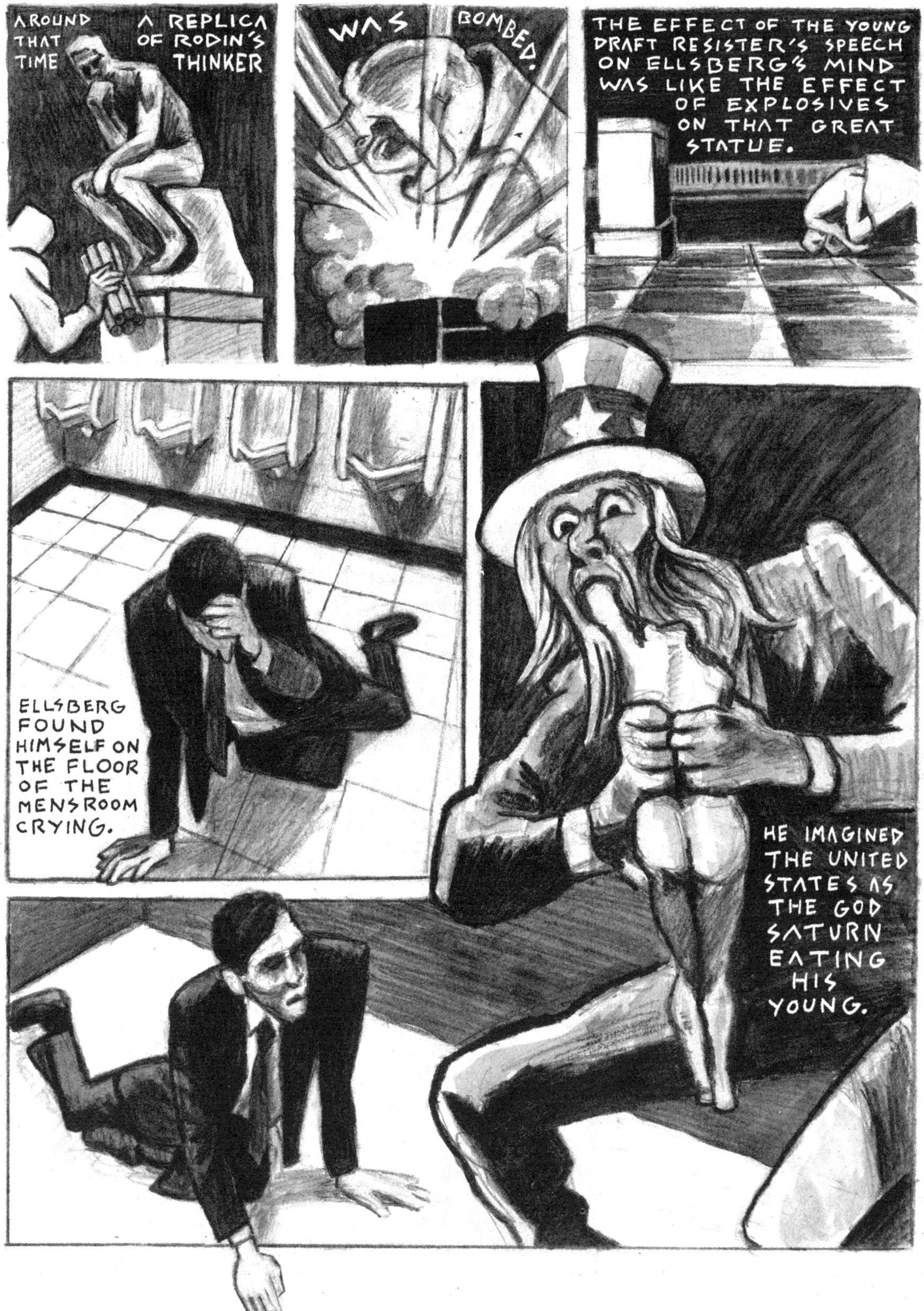
AROUND THAT TIME
A REPLICA OF RODIN'S THINKER
WAS
BOMBED.
THE EFFECT OF THE YOUNG DRAFT RESISTER'S SPEECH ON ELLSBERG'S MIND WAS LIKE THE EFFECT OF EXPLOSIVES ON THAT GREAT STATUE.
ELLSBERG FOUND HIMSELF ON THE FLOOR OF THE MENSROOM CRYING.
HE IMAGINED THE UNITED STATES AS THE GOD SATURN EATING HIS YOUNG.

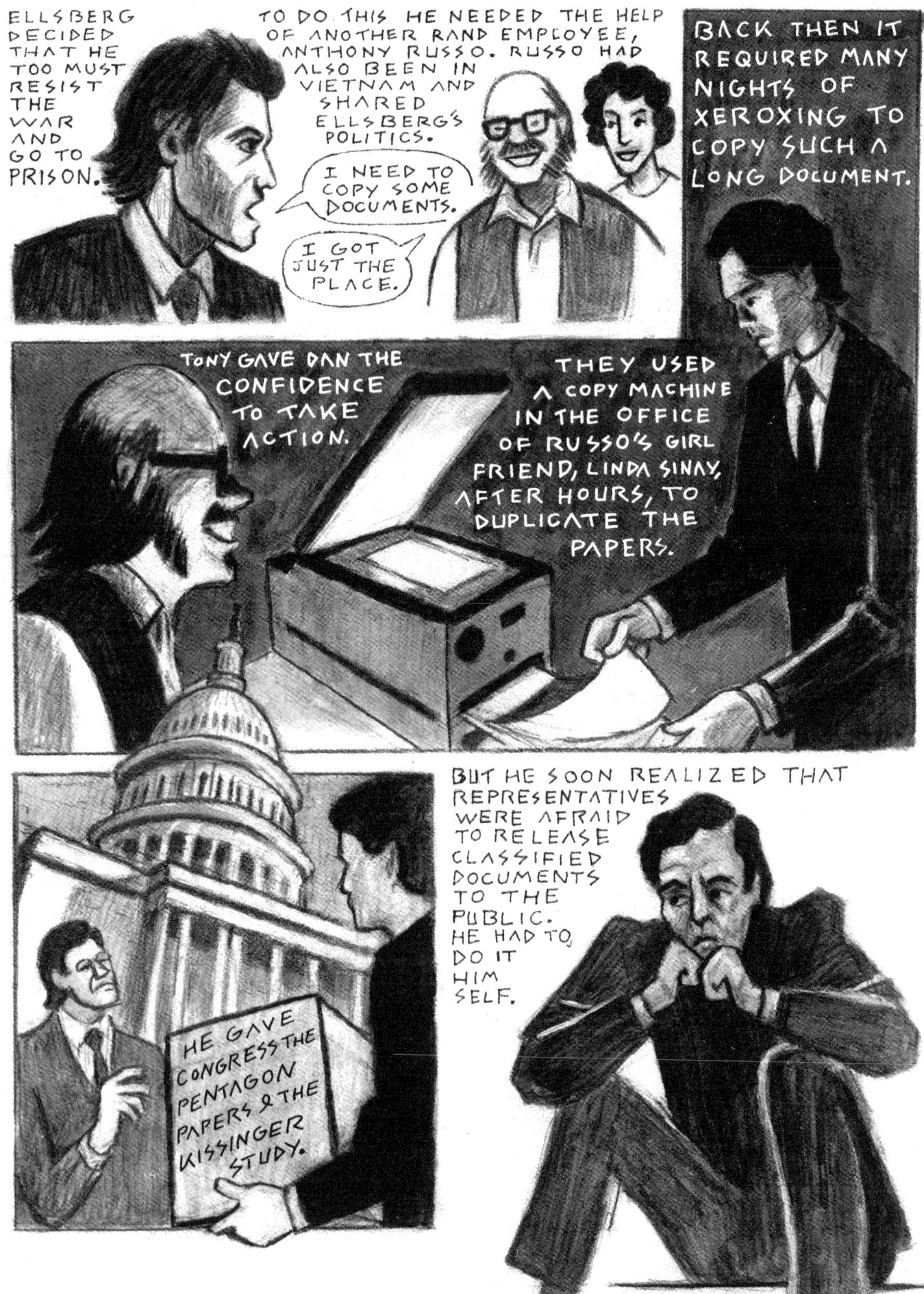

ELLSBERG DECIDED THAT HE TOO MUST RESIST THE WAR AND GO TO PRISON.
TO DO THIS HE NEEDED THE HELP OF ANOTHER RAND EMPLOYEE, ANTHONY RUSSO. RUSSO HAD ALSO BEEN IN VIETNAM AND SHARED ELLSBERG'S POLITICS.
I NEED TO COPY SOME DOCUMENTS.
I GOT JUST THE PLACE.
BACK THEN IT REQUIRED MANY NIGHTS OF XEROXING TO COPY SUCH A LONG DOCUMENT.
TONY GAVE DAN THE CONFIDENCE TO TAKE ACTION.
THEY USED A COPY MACHINE IN THE OFFICE OF RUSSO'S GIRL FRIEND, LINDA SINAY, AFTER HOURS, TO DUPLICATE THE PAPERS.
HE GAVE CONGRESS THE PENTAGON PAPERS & THE KISSINGER STUDY.
BUT HE SOON REALIZED THAT REPRESENTATIVES WERE AFRAID TO RELEASE CLASSIFIED DOCUMENTS TO THE PUBLIC. HE HAD TO DO IT HIM SELF.

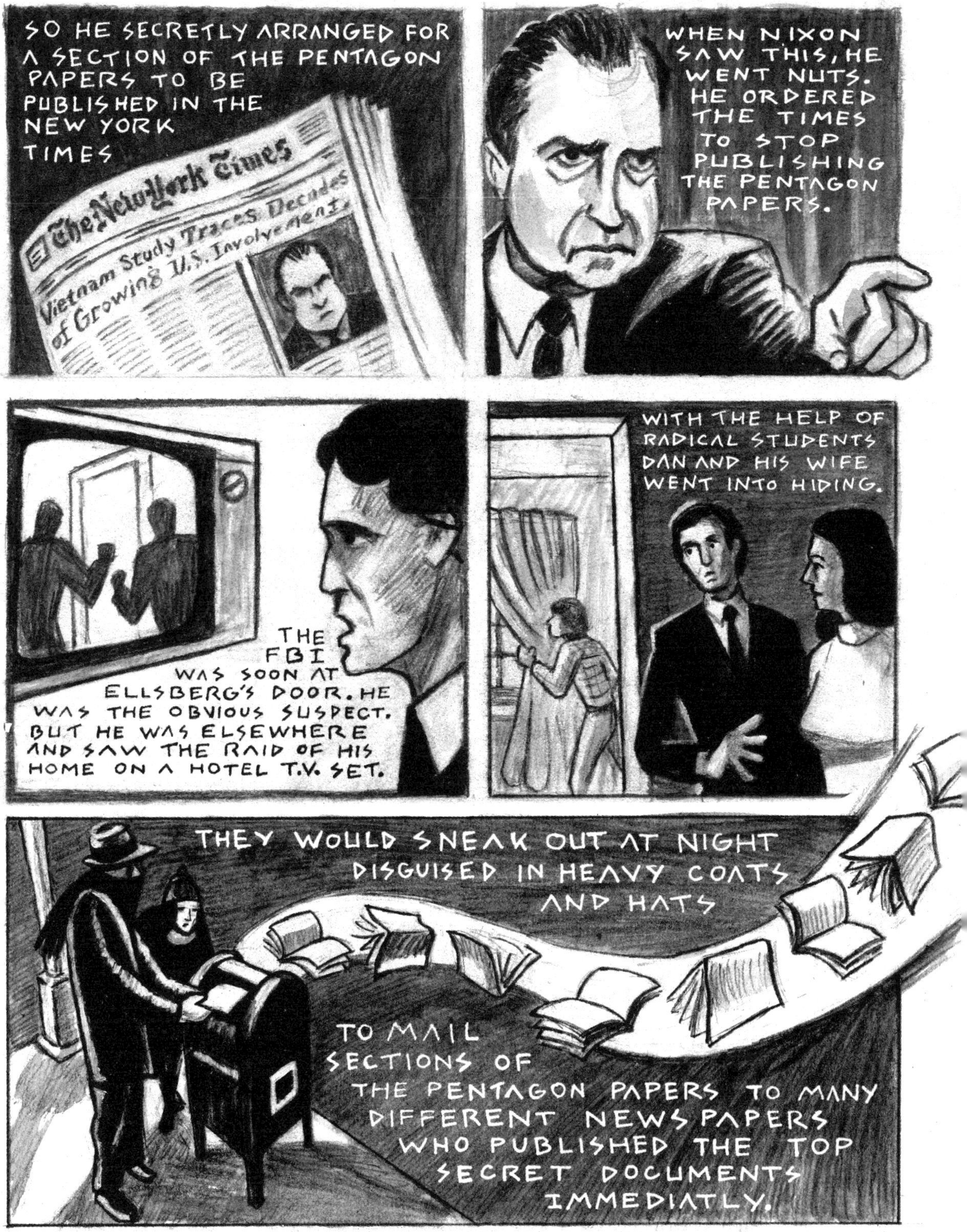
SO HE SECRETLY ARRANGED FOR A SECTION OF THE PENTAGON PAPERS TO BE PUBLISHED IN THE NEW YORK TIMES
The New York Times
Vietnam Study Traces Decades of Growing U.S. Involvement
WHEN NIXON SAW THIS, HE WENT NUTS. HE ORDERED THE TIMES TO STOP PUBLISHING THE PENTAGON PAPERS.
THE FBI WAS SOON AT ELLSBERG'S DOOR. HE WAS THE OBVIOUS SUSPECT. BUT HE WAS ELSEWHERE AND SAW THE RAID OF HIS HOME ON A HOTEL T.V. SET.
WITH THE HELP OF RADICAL STUDENTS DAN AND HIS WIFE WENT INTO HIDING.
THEY WOULD SNEAK OUT AT NIGHT DISGUISED IN HEAVY COATS AND HATS
TO MAIL SECTIONS OF THE PENTAGON PAPERS TO MANY DIFFERENT NEWSPAPERS WHO PUBLISHED THE TOP SECRET DOCUMENTS IMMEDIATLY.

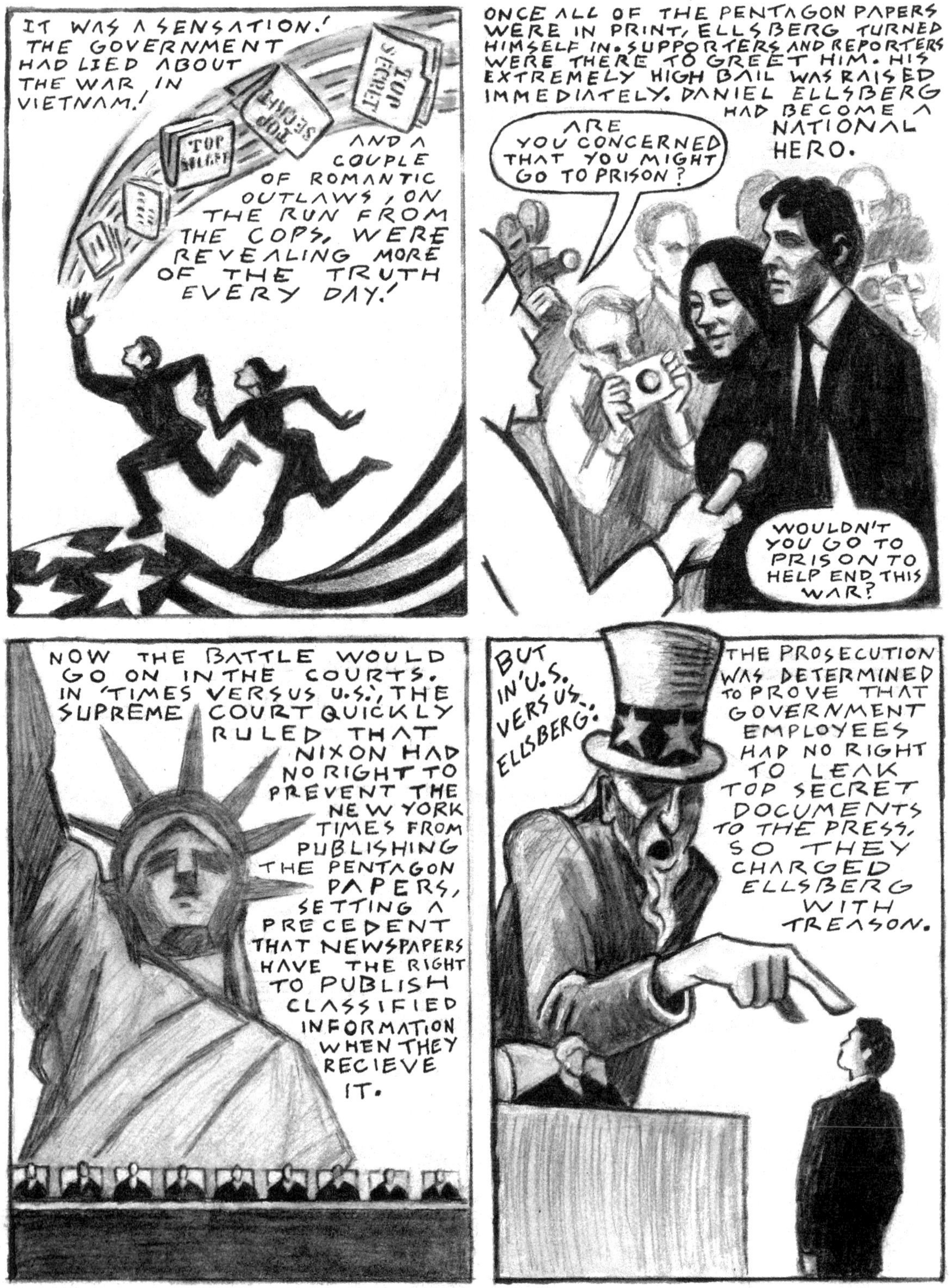
IT WAS A SENSATION! THE GOVERNMENT HAD LIED ABOUT THE WAR IN VIETNAM!
TOP SECRET
AND A COUPLE OF ROMANTIC OUTLAWS, ON THE RUN FROM THE COPS, WERE REVEALING MORE OF THE TRUTH EVERY DAY!
ONCE ALL OF THE PENTAGON PAPERS WERE IN PRINT, ELLSBERG TURNED HIMSELF IN. SUPPORTERS AND REPORTERS WERE THERE TO GREET HIM. HIS EXTREMELY HIGH BAIL WAS RAISED IMMEDIATELY. DANIEL ELLSBERG HAD BECOME A NATIONAL HERO.
ARE YOU CONCERNED THAT YOU MIGHT GO TO PRISON?
WOULDN'T YOU GO TO PRISON TO HELP END THIS WAR?
NOW THE BATTLE WOULD GO ON IN THE COURTS. IN 'TIMES VERSUS U.S.', THE SUPREME COURT QUICKLY RULED THAT NIXON HAD NO RIGHT TO PREVENT THE NEW YORK TIMES FROM PUBLISHING THE PENTAGON PAPERS, SETTING A PRECEDENT THAT NEWSPAPERS HAVE THE RIGHT TO PUBLISH CLASSIFIED INFORMATION WHEN THEY RECIEVE IT.
BUT IN 'U.S. VERSUS ELLSBERG',
THE PROSECUTION WAS DETERMINED TO PROVE THAT GOVERNMENT EMPLOYEES HAD NO RIGHT TO LEAK TOP SECRET DOCUMENTS TO THE PRESS, SO THEY CHARGED ELLSBERG WITH TREASON.

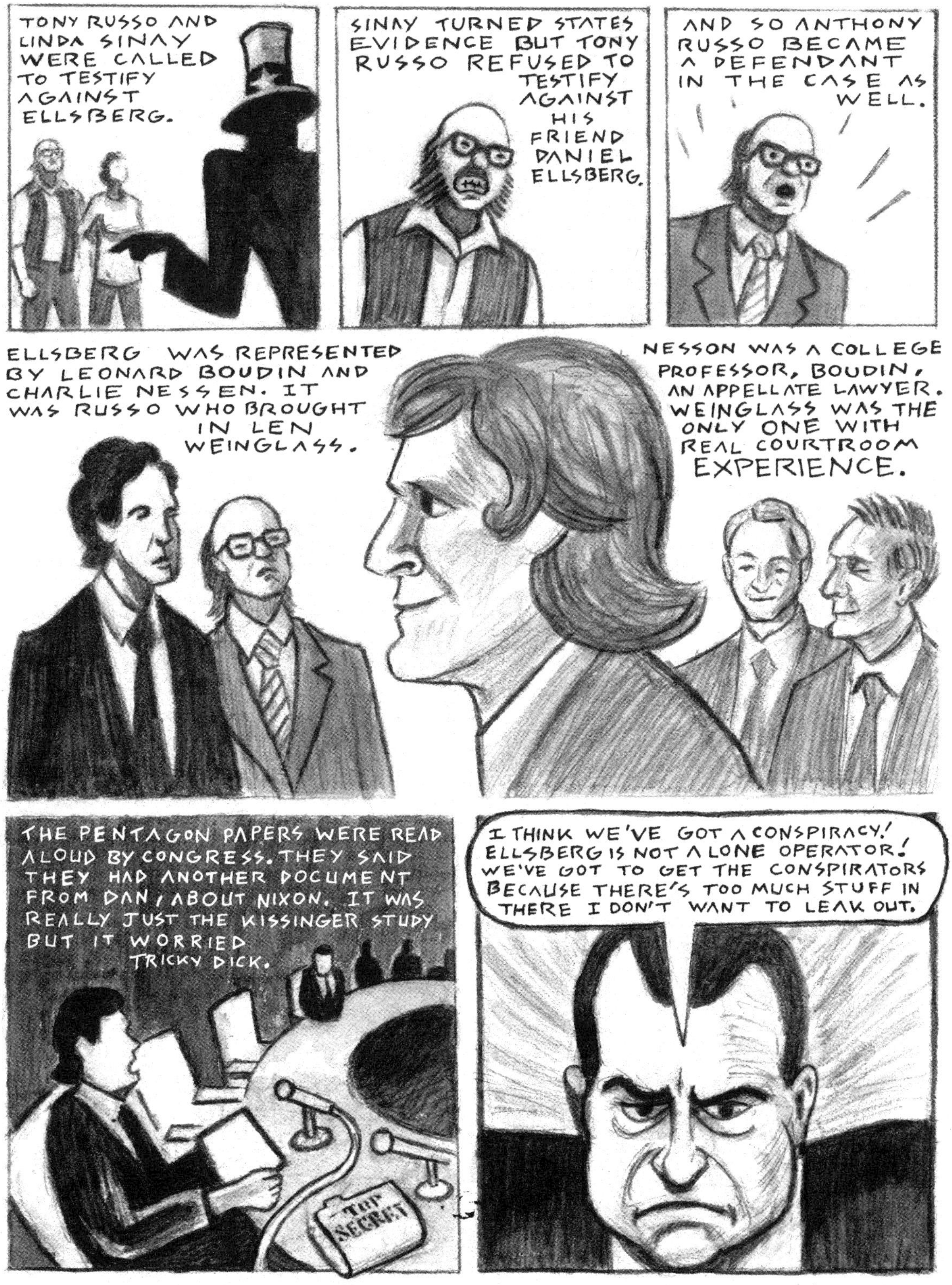
TONY RUSSO AND LINDA SINAY WERE CALLED TO TESTIFY AGAINST ELLSBERG.
SINAY TURNED STATES EVIDENCE BUT TONY RUSSO REFUSED TO TESTIFY AGAINST HIS FRIEND DANIEL ELLSBERG.
AND SO ANTHONY RUSSO BECAME A DEFENDANT IN THE CASE AS WELL.
ELLSBERG WAS REPRESENTED BY LEONARD BOUDIN AND CHARLIE NESSEN. IT WAS RUSSO WHO BROUGHT IN LEN WEINGLASS.
NESSON WAS A COLLEGE PROFESSOR, BOUDIN, AN APPELLATE LAWYER. WEINGLASS WAS THE ONLY ONE WITH REAL COURTROOM EXPERIENCE.
THE PENTAGON PAPERS WERE READ ALOUD BY CONGRESS. THEY SAID THEY HAD ANOTHER DOCUMENT FROM DAN, ABOUT NIXON. IT WAS REALLY JUST THE KISSINGER STUDY BUT IT WORRIED TRICKY DICK.
TOP SECRET
I THINK WE'VE GOT A CONSPIRACY! ELLSBERG IS NOT A LONE OPERATOR! WE'VE GOT TO GET THE CONSPIRATORS BECAUSE THERE'S TOO MUCH STUFF IN THERE I DON'T WANT TO LEAK OUT.

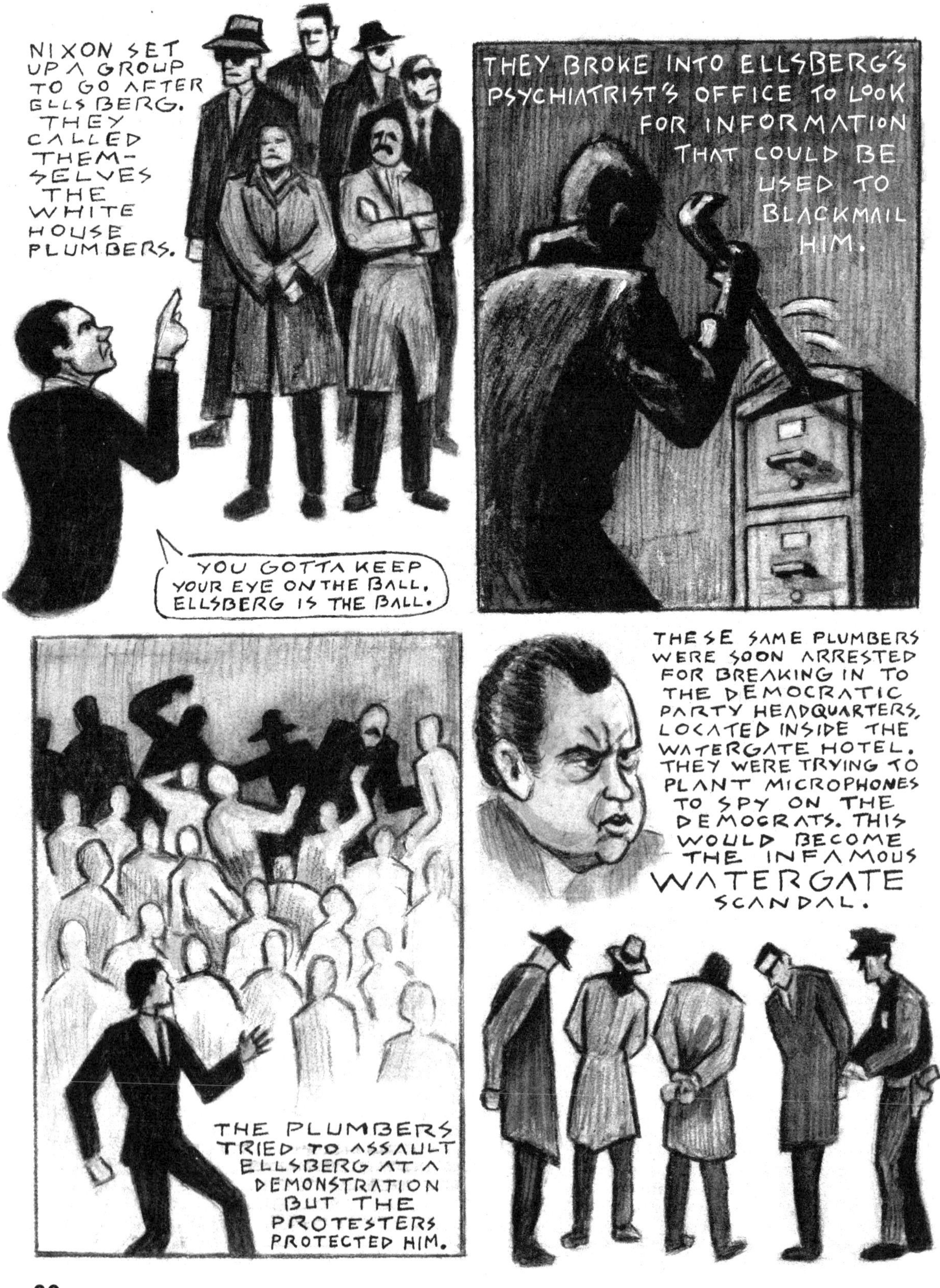
NIXON SET UP A GROUP TO GO AFTER ELLSBERG. THEY CALLED THEMSELVES THE WHITE HOUSE PLUMBERS.
YOU GOTTA KEEP YOUR EYE ON THE BALL. ELLSBERG IS THE BALL.
THEY BROKE INTO ELLSBERG'S PSYCHIATRIST'S OFFICE TO LOOK FOR INFORMATION THAT COULD BE USED TO BLACKMAIL HIM.
THE PLUMBERS TRIED TO ASSAULT ELLSBERG AT A DEMONSTRATION BUT THE PROTESTERS PROTECTED HIM.
THESE SAME PLUMBERS WERE SOON ARRESTED FOR BREAKING IN TO THE DEMOCRATIC PARTY HEADQUARTERS, LOCATED INSIDE THE WATERGATE HOTEL. THEY WERE TRYING TO PLANT MICROPHONES TO SPY ON THE DEMOCRATS. THIS WOULD BECOME THE INFAMOUS WATERGATE SCANDAL.

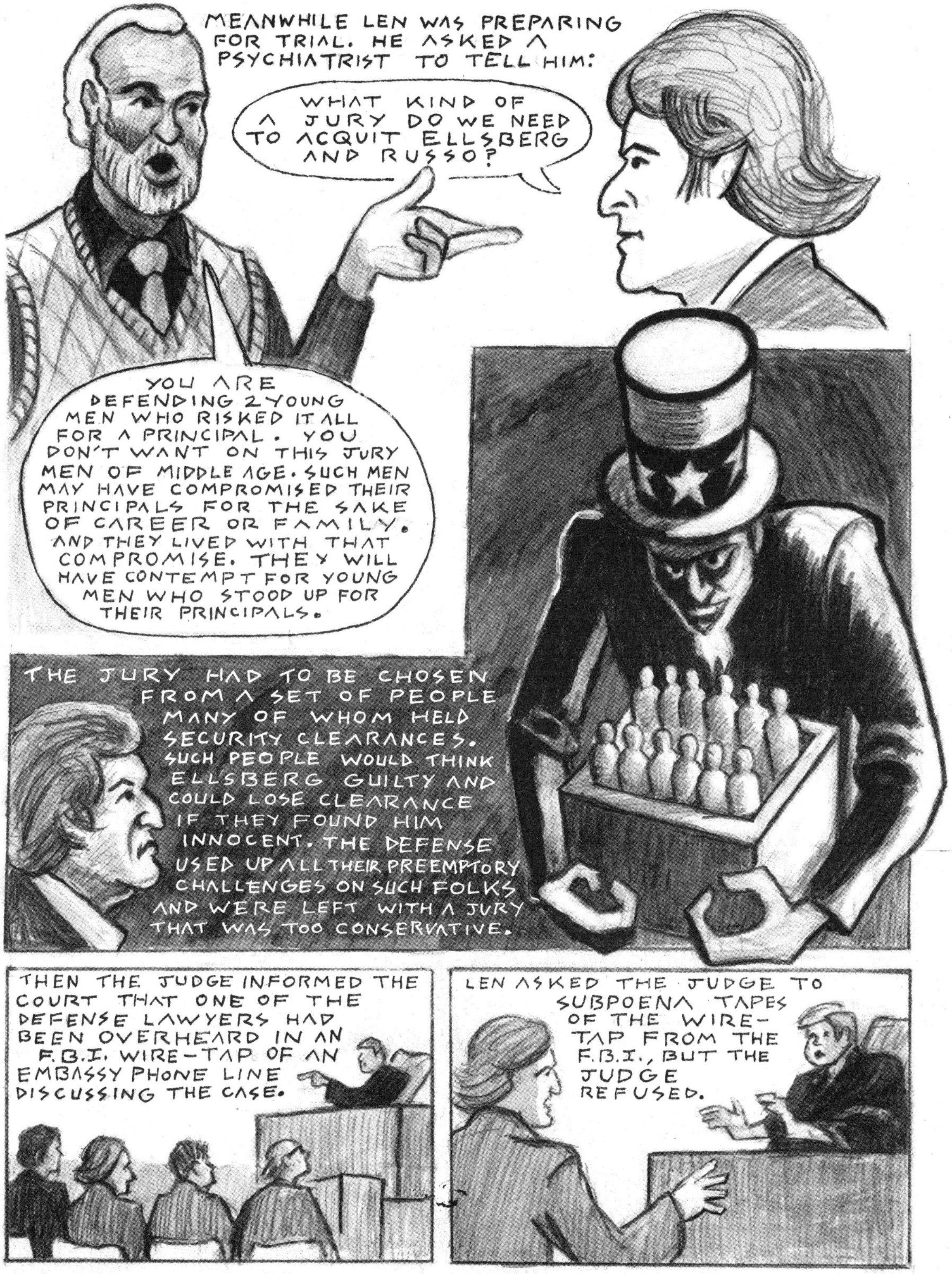
MEANWHILE LEN WAS PREPARING FOR TRIAL. HE ASKED A PSYCHIATRIST TO TELL HIM:
WHAT KIND OF A JURY DO WE NEED TO ACQUIT ELLSBERG AND RUSSO?
YOU ARE DEFENDING 2 YOUNG MEN WHO RISKED IT ALL FOR A PRINCIPAL. YOU DON'T WANT ON THIS JURY MEN OF MIDDLE AGE. SUCH MEN MAY HAVE COMPROMISED THEIR PRINCIPALS FOR THE SAKE OF CAREER OR FAMILY. AND THEY LIVED WITH THAT COMPROMISE. THEY WILL HAVE CONTEMPT FOR YOUNG MEN WHO STOOD UP FOR THEIR PRINCIPALS.
THE JURY HAD TO BE CHOSEN FROM A SET OF PEOPLE MANY OF WHOM HELD SECURITY CLEARANCES. SUCH PEOPLE WOULD THINK ELLSBERG GUILTY AND COULD LOSE CLEARANCE IF THEY FOUND HIM INNOCENT. THE DEFENSE USED UP ALL THEIR PREEMPTORY CHALLENGES ON SUCH FOLKS AND WERE LEFT WITH A JURY THAT WAS TOO CONSERVATIVE.
THEN THE JUDGE INFORMED THE COURT THAT ONE OF THE DEFENSE LAWYERS HAD BEEN OVERHEARD IN AN F.B.I. WIRE-TAP OF AN EMBASSY PHONE LINE DISCUSSING THE CASE.
LEN ASKED THE JUDGE TO SUBPOENA TAPES OF THE WIRE-TAP FROM THE F.B.I., BUT THE JUDGE REFUSED.

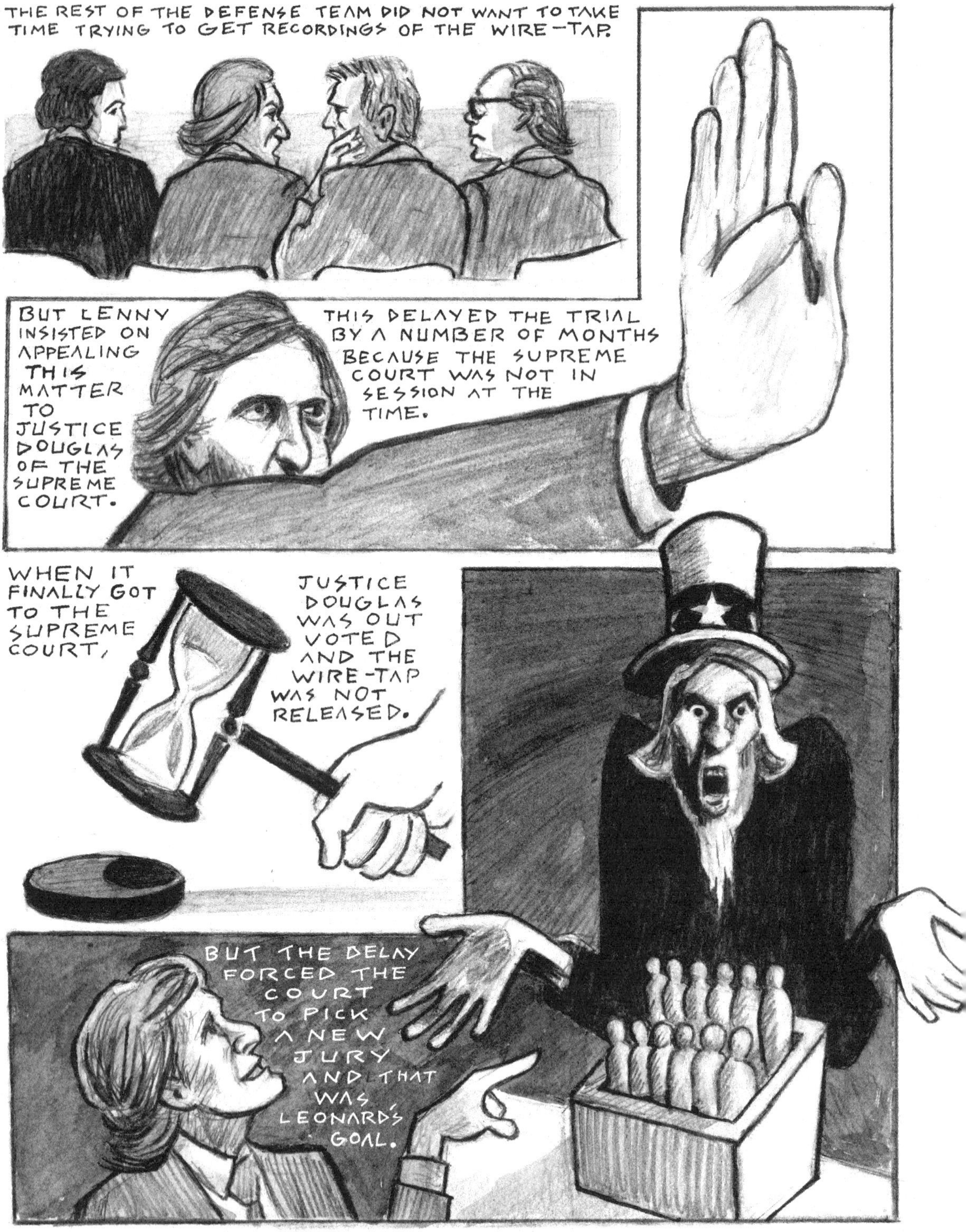
THE REST OF THE DEFENSE TEAM DID NOT WANT TO TAKE TIME TRYING TO GET RECORDINGS OF THE WIRE-TAP.
BUT LENNY INSISTED ON APPEALING THIS MATTER TO JUSTICE DOUGLAS OF THE SUPREME COURT.
THIS DELAYED THE TRIAL BY A NUMBER OF MONTHS BECAUSE THE SUPREME COURT WAS NOT IN SESSION AT THE TIME.
WHEN IT FINALLY GOT TO THE SUPREME COURT,
JUSTICE DOUGLAS WAS OUT VOTED AND THE WIRE-TAP WAS NOT RELEASED.
BUT THE DELAY FORCED THE COURT TO PICK A NEW JURY AND THAT WAS LEONARD'S GOAL.

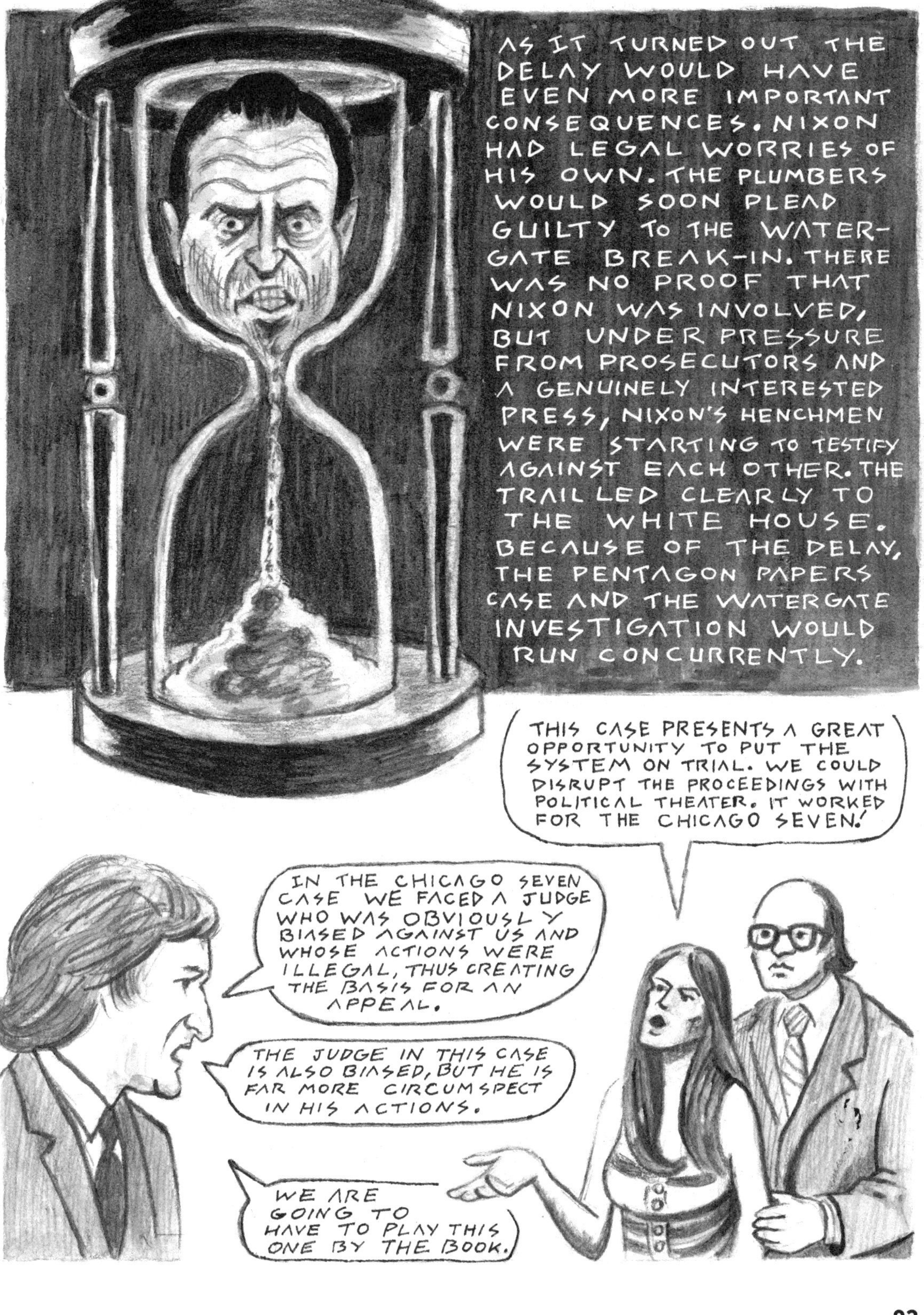
AS IT TURNED OUT THE DELAY WOULD HAVE EVEN MORE IMPORTANT CONSEQUENCES. NIXON HAD LEGAL WORRIES OF HIS OWN. THE PLUMBERS WOULD SOON PLEAD GUILTY TO THE WATER-GATE BREAK-IN. THERE WAS NO PROOF THAT NIXON WAS INVOLVED, BUT UNDER PRESSURE FROM PROSECUTORS AND A GENUINELY INTERESTED PRESS, NIXON'S HENCHMEN WERE STARTING TO TESTIFY AGAINST EACH OTHER. THE TRAIL LED CLEARLY TO THE WHITE HOUSE. BECAUSE OF THE DELAY, THE PENTAGON PAPERS CASE AND THE WATERGATE INVESTIGATION WOULD RUN CONCURRENTLY.
THIS CASE PRESENTS A GREAT OPPORTUNITY TO PUT THE SYSTEM ON TRIAL. WE COULD DISRUPT THE PROCEEDINGS WITH POLITICAL THEATER. IT WORKED FOR THE CHICAGO SEVEN!
IN THE CHICAGO SEVEN CASE WE FACED A JUDGE WHO WAS OBVIOUSLY BIASED AGAINST US AND WHOSE ACTIONS WERE ILLEGAL, THUS CREATING THE BASIS FOR AN APPEAL.
THE JUDGE IN THIS CASE IS ALSO BIASED, BUT HE IS FAR MORE CIRCUMSPECT IN HIS ACTIONS.
WE ARE GOING TO HAVE TO PLAY THIS ONE BY THE BOOK.

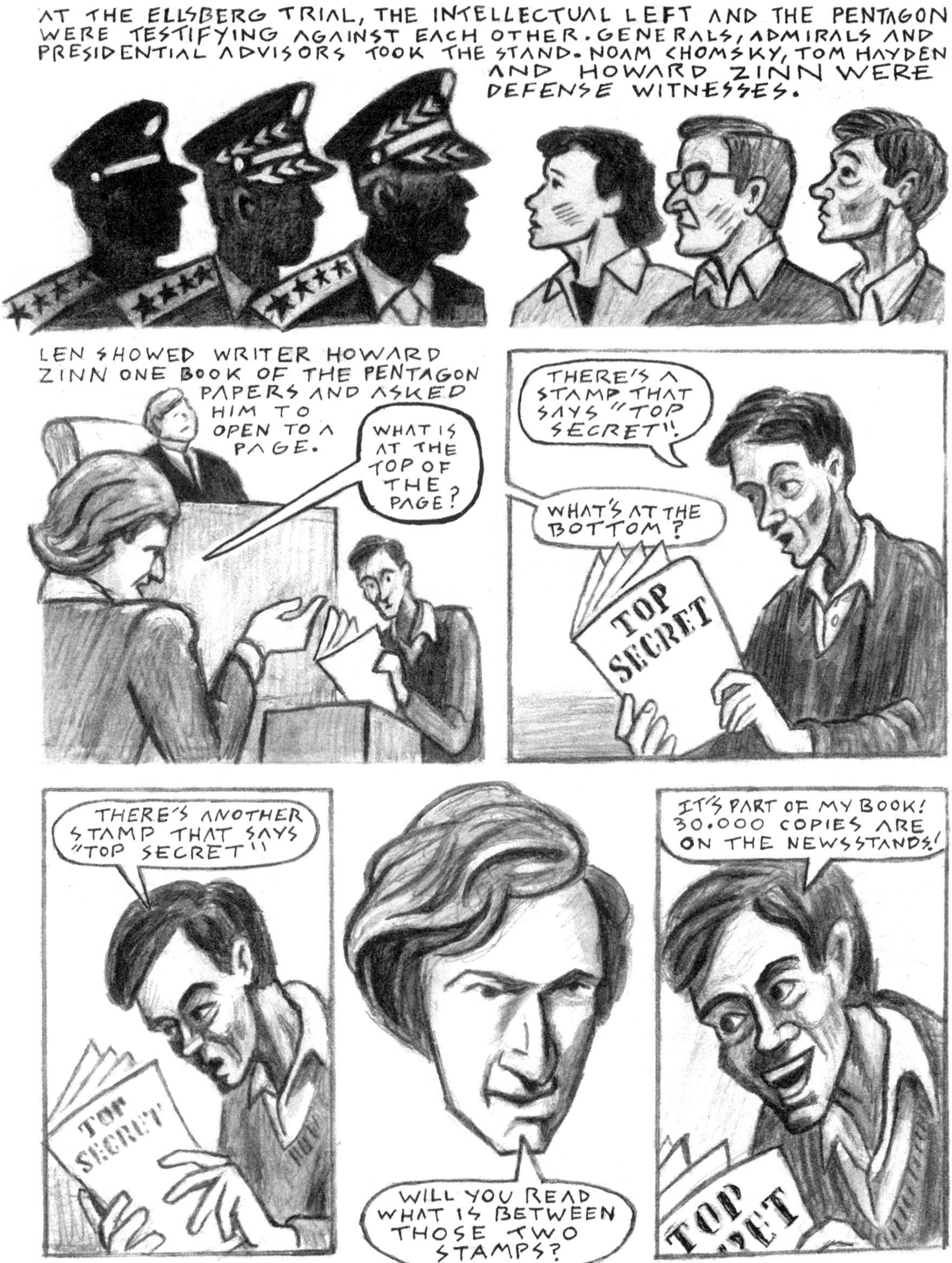
AT THE ELLSBERG TRIAL, THE INTELLECTUAL LEFT AND THE PENTAGON WERE TESTIFYING AGAINST EACH OTHER. GENERALS, ADMIRALS AND PRESIDENTIAL ADVISORS TOOK THE STAND. NOAM CHOMSKY, TOM HAYDEN AND HOWARD ZINN WERE DEFENSE WITNESSES.
LEN SHOWED WRITER HOWARD ZINN ONE BOOK OF THE PENTAGON PAPERS AND ASKED HIM TO OPEN TO A PAGE.
WHAT IS AT THE TOP OF THE PAGE?
THERE'S A STAMP THAT SAYS "TOP SECRET".
WHAT'S AT THE BOTTOM?
TOP SECRET
THERE'S ANOTHER STAMP THAT SAYS "TOP SECRET".
TOP SECRET
WILL YOU READ WHAT IS BETWEEN THOSE TWO STAMPS?
IT'S PART OF MY BOOK! 30.000 COPIES ARE ON THE NEWSSTANDS!

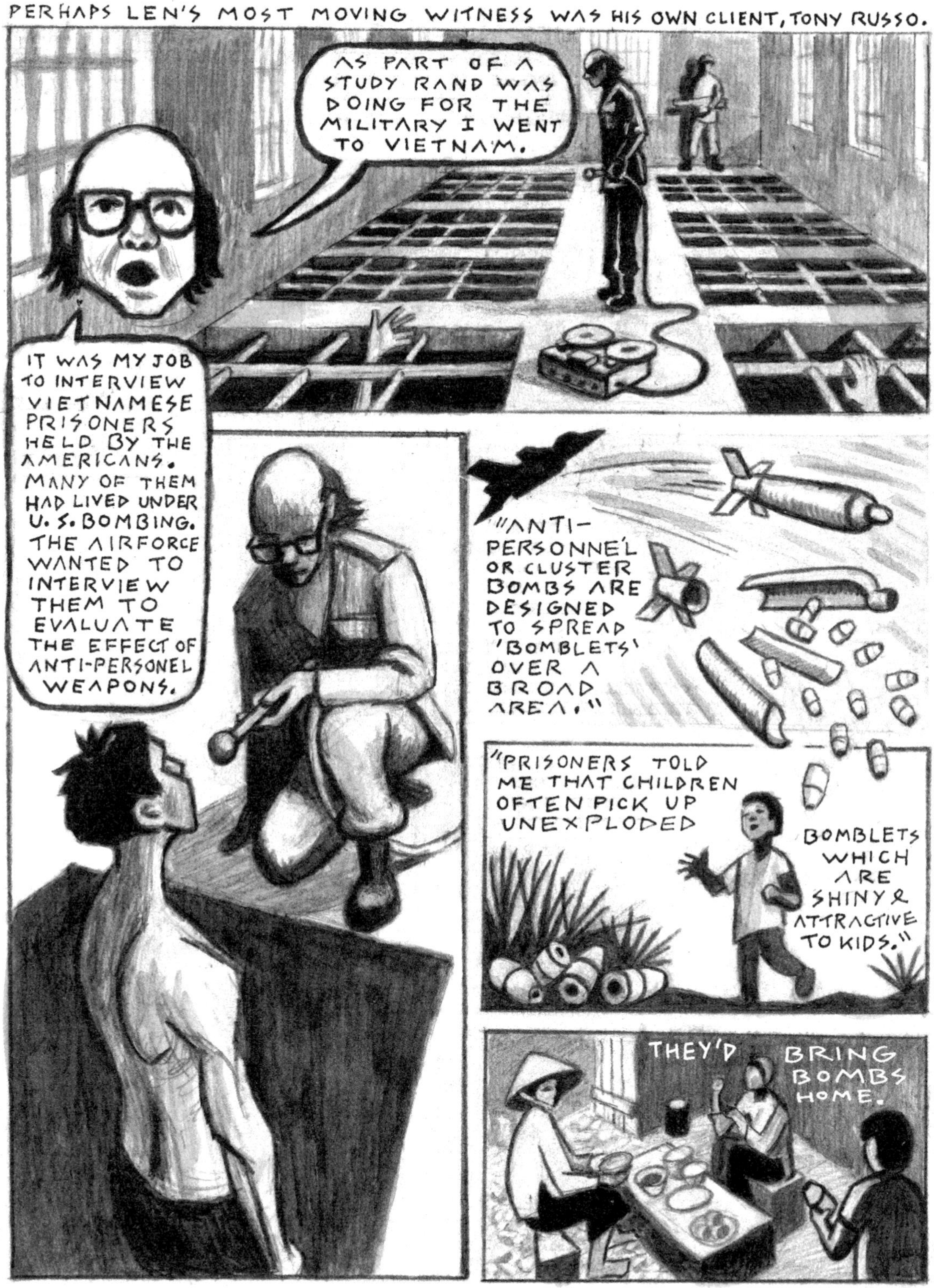
PERHAPS LEN'S MOST MOVING WITNESS WAS HIS OWN CLIENT, TONY RUSSO.
AS PART OF A STUDY RAND WAS DOING FOR THE MILITARY I WENT TO VIETNAM.
IT WAS MY JOB TO INTERVIEW VIETNAMESE PRISONERS HELD BY THE AMERICANS. MANY OF THEM HAD LIVED UNDER U.S. BOMBING. THE AIRFORCE WANTED TO INTERVIEW THEM TO EVALUATE THE EFFECT OF ANTI-PERSONEL WEAPONS.
"ANTI-PERSONNEL OR CLUSTER BOMBS ARE DESIGNED TO SPREAD 'BOMBLETS' OVER A BROAD AREA."
"PRISONERS TOLD ME THAT CHILDREN OFTEN PICK UP UNEXPLODED
BOMBLETS WHICH ARE SHINY & ATTRACTIVE TO KIDS."
THEY'D BRING BOMBS HOME.

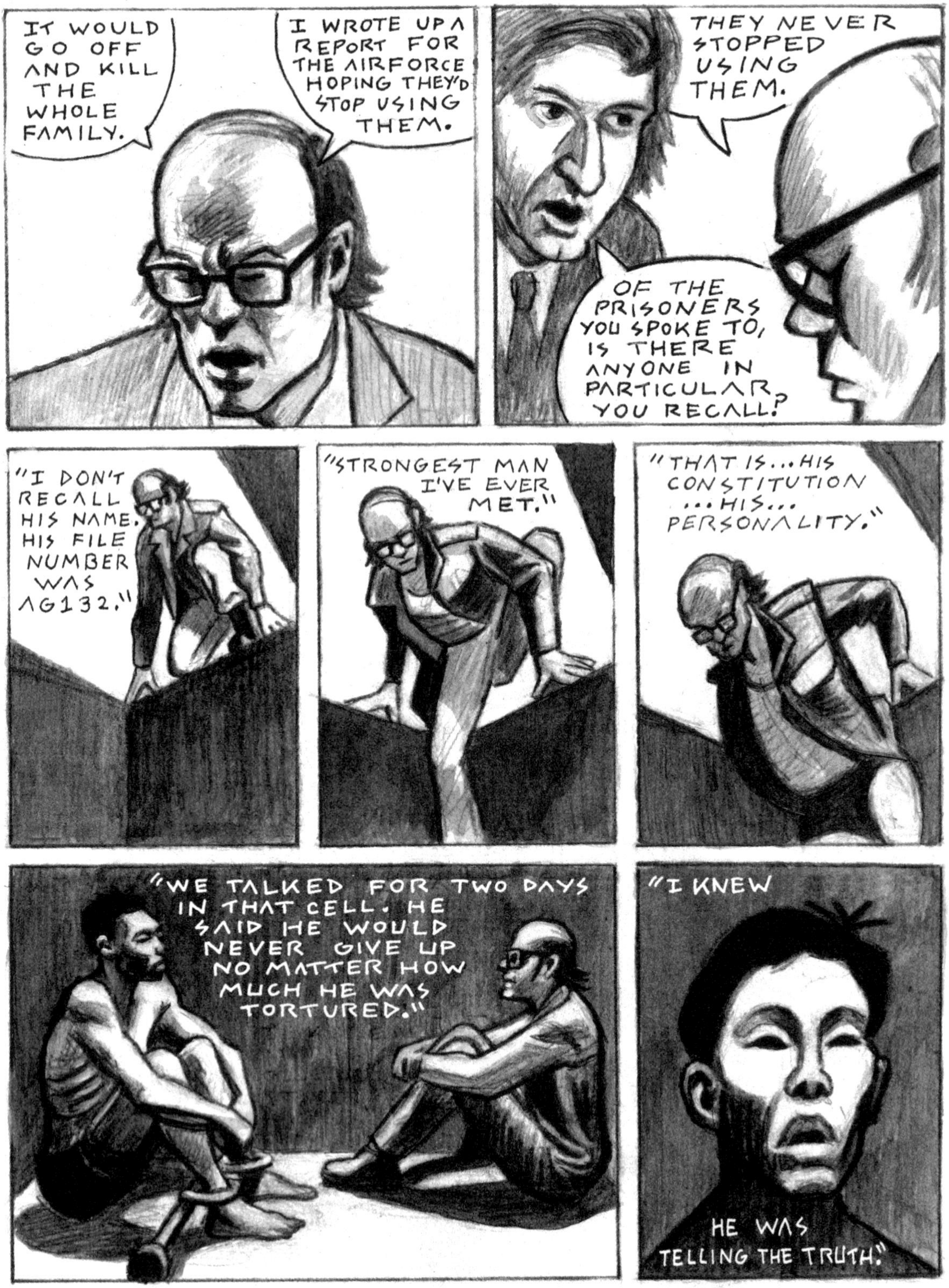

IT WOULD GO OFF AND KILL THE WHOLE FAMILY.
I WROTE UP A REPORT FOR THE AIRFORCE HOPING THEY'D STOP USING THEM.
THEY NEVER STOPPED USING THEM.
OF THE PRISONERS YOU SPOKE TO, IS THERE ANYONE IN PARTICULAR YOU RECALL?
"I DON'T RECALL HIS NAME. HIS FILE NUMBER WAS AG132."
"STRONGEST MAN I'VE EVER MET."
"THAT IS... HIS CONSTITUTION ...HIS... PERSONALITY."
"WE TALKED FOR TWO DAYS IN THAT CELL. HE SAID HE WOULD NEVER GIVE UP NO MATTER HOW MUCH HE WAS TORTURED."
"I KNEW
HE WAS TELLING THE TRUTH."

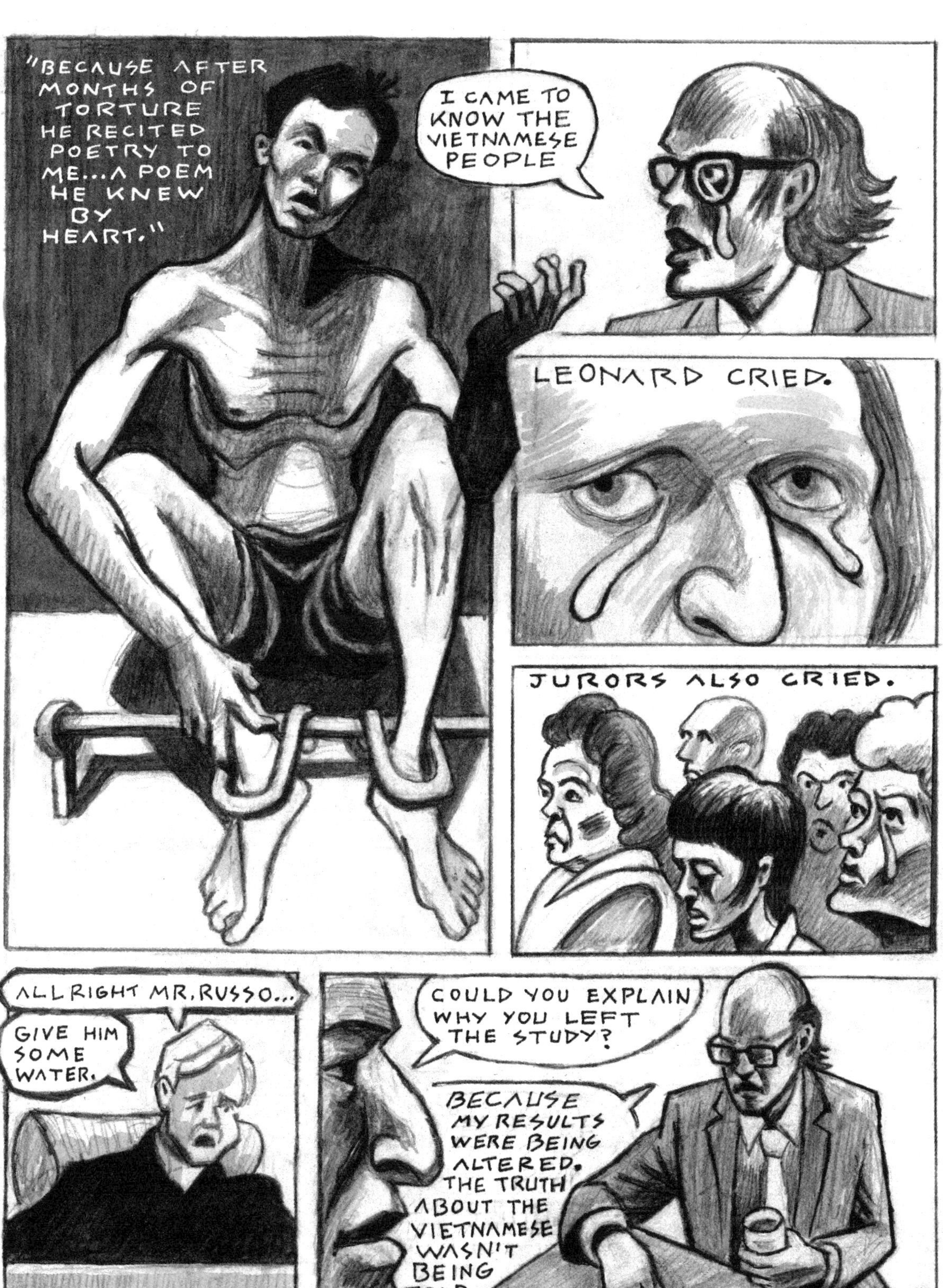
"BECAUSE AFTER MONTHS OF TORTURE HE RECITED POETRY TO ME...A POEM HE KNEW BY HEART."
I CAME TO KNOW THE VIETNAMESE PEOPLE
LEONARD CRIED.
JURORS ALSO CRIED.
ALLRIGHT MR. RUSSO...
GIVE HIM SOME WATER.
COULD YOU EXPLAIN WHY YOU LEFT THE STUDY?
BECAUSE MY RESULTS WERE BEING ALTERED. THE TRUTH ABOUT THE VIETNAMESE WASN'T BEING TOLD.

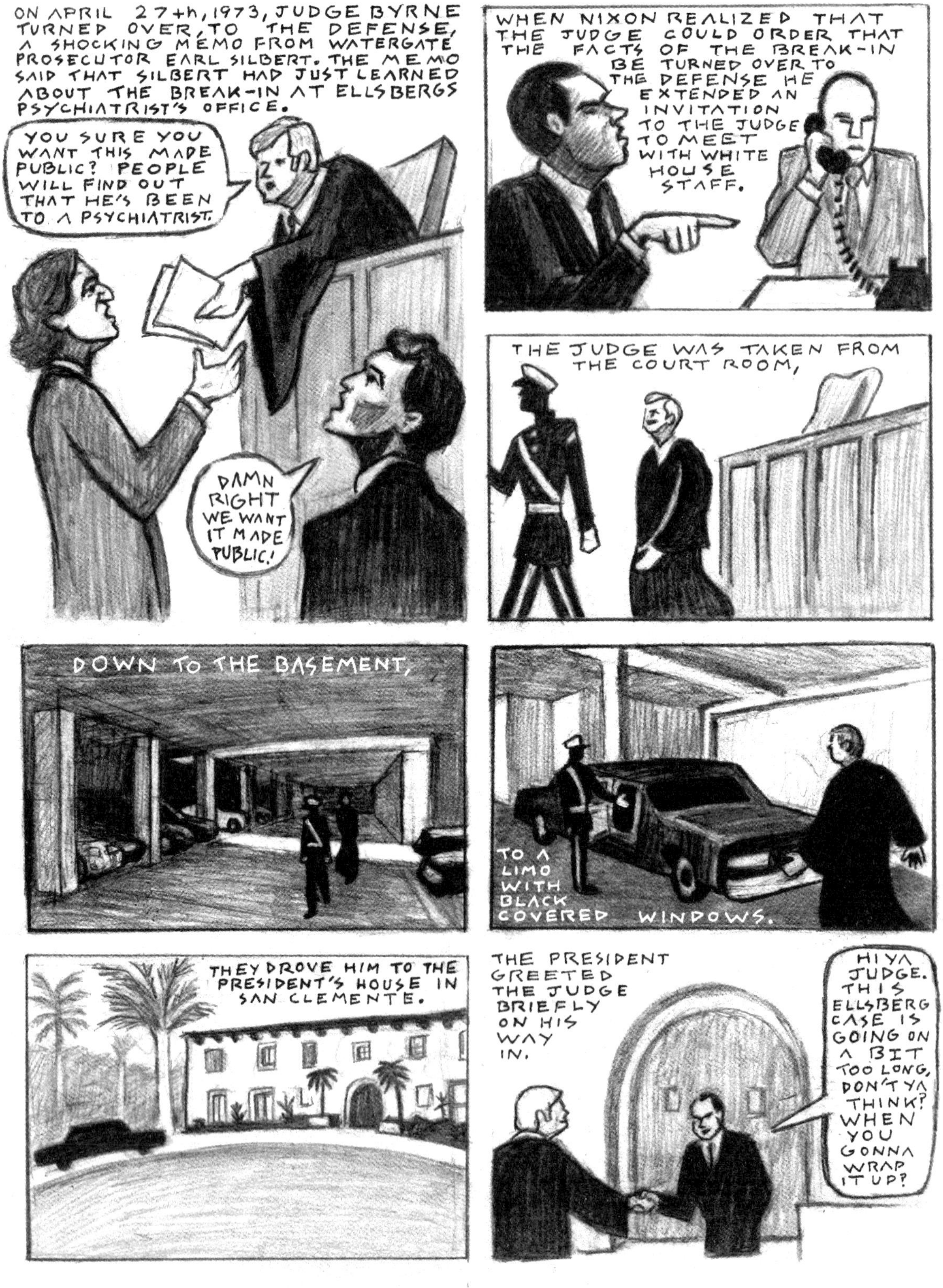

ON APRIL 27th, 1973, JUDGE BYRNE TURNED OVER, TO THE DEFENSE, A SHOCKING MEMO FROM WATERGATE PROSECUTOR EARL SILBERT. THE MEMO SAID THAT SILBERT HAD JUST LEARNED ABOUT THE BREAK-IN AT ELLSBERGS PSYCHIATRIST'S OFFICE.
YOU SURE YOU WANT THIS MADE PUBLIC? PEOPLE WILL FIND OUT THAT HE'S BEEN TO A PSYCHIATRIST.
DAMN RIGHT WE WANT IT MADE PUBLIC!
WHEN NIXON REALIZED THAT THE JUDGE COULD ORDER THAT THE FACTS OF THE BREAK-IN BE TURNED OVER TO THE DEFENSE HE EXTENDED AN INVITATION TO THE JUDGE TO MEET WITH WHITE HOUSE STAFF.
THE JUDGE WAS TAKEN FROM THE COURT ROOM,
DOWN TO THE BASEMENT,
TO A LIMO WITH BLACK COVERED WINDOWS.
THEY DROVE HIM TO THE PRESIDENT'S HOUSE IN SAN CLEMENTE.
THE PRESIDENT GREETED THE JUDGE BRIEFLY ON HIS WAY IN.
HIYA JUDGE. THIS ELLSBERG CASE IS GOING ON A BIT TOO LONG, DON'T YA THINK? WHEN YOU GONNA WRAP IT UP?

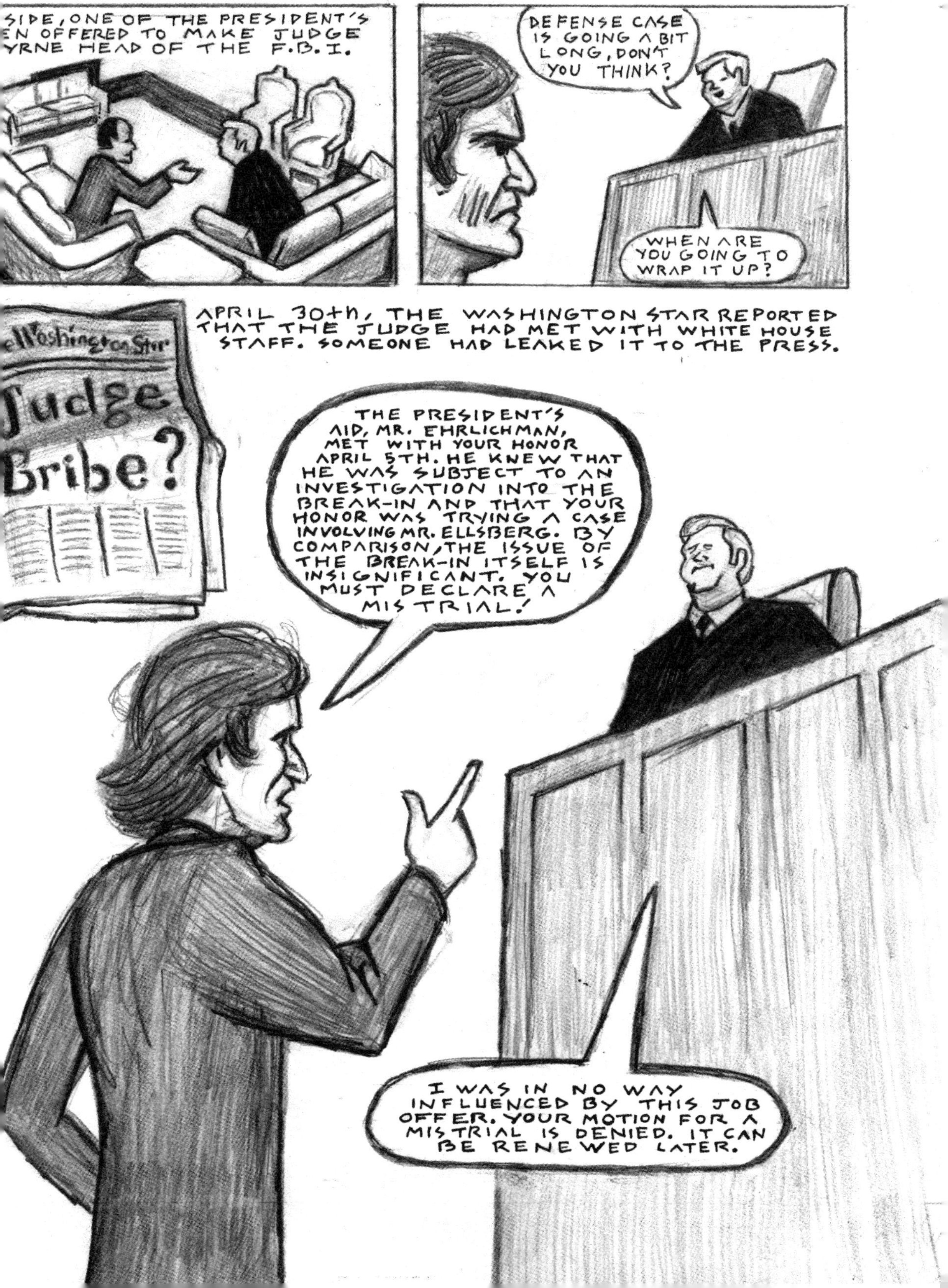
SIDE, ONE OF THE PRESIDENT'S
EN OFFERED TO MAKE JUDGE
YRNE HEAD OF THE F.B.I.
DEFENSE CASE IS GOING A BIT LONG, DON'T YOU THINK?
WHEN ARE YOU GOING TO WRAP IT UP?
APRIL 30th, THE WASHINGTON STAR REPORTED THAT THE JUDGE HAD MET WITH WHITE HOUSE STAFF. SOMEONE HAD LEAKED IT TO THE PRESS.
Washington Star
Judge Bribe?
THE PRESIDENT'S AID, MR. EHRLICHMAN, MET WITH YOUR HONOR APRIL 5TH. HE KNEW THAT HE WAS SUBJECT TO AN INVESTIGATION INTO THE BREAK-IN AND THAT YOUR HONOR WAS TRYING A CASE INVOLVING MR. ELLSBERG. BY COMPARISON, THE ISSUE OF THE BREAK-IN ITSELF IS INSIGNIFICANT. YOU MUST DECLARE A MISTRIAL!
I WAS IN NO WAY INFLUENCED BY THIS JOB OFFER. YOUR MOTION FOR A MISTRIAL IS DENIED. IT CAN BE RENEWED LATER.

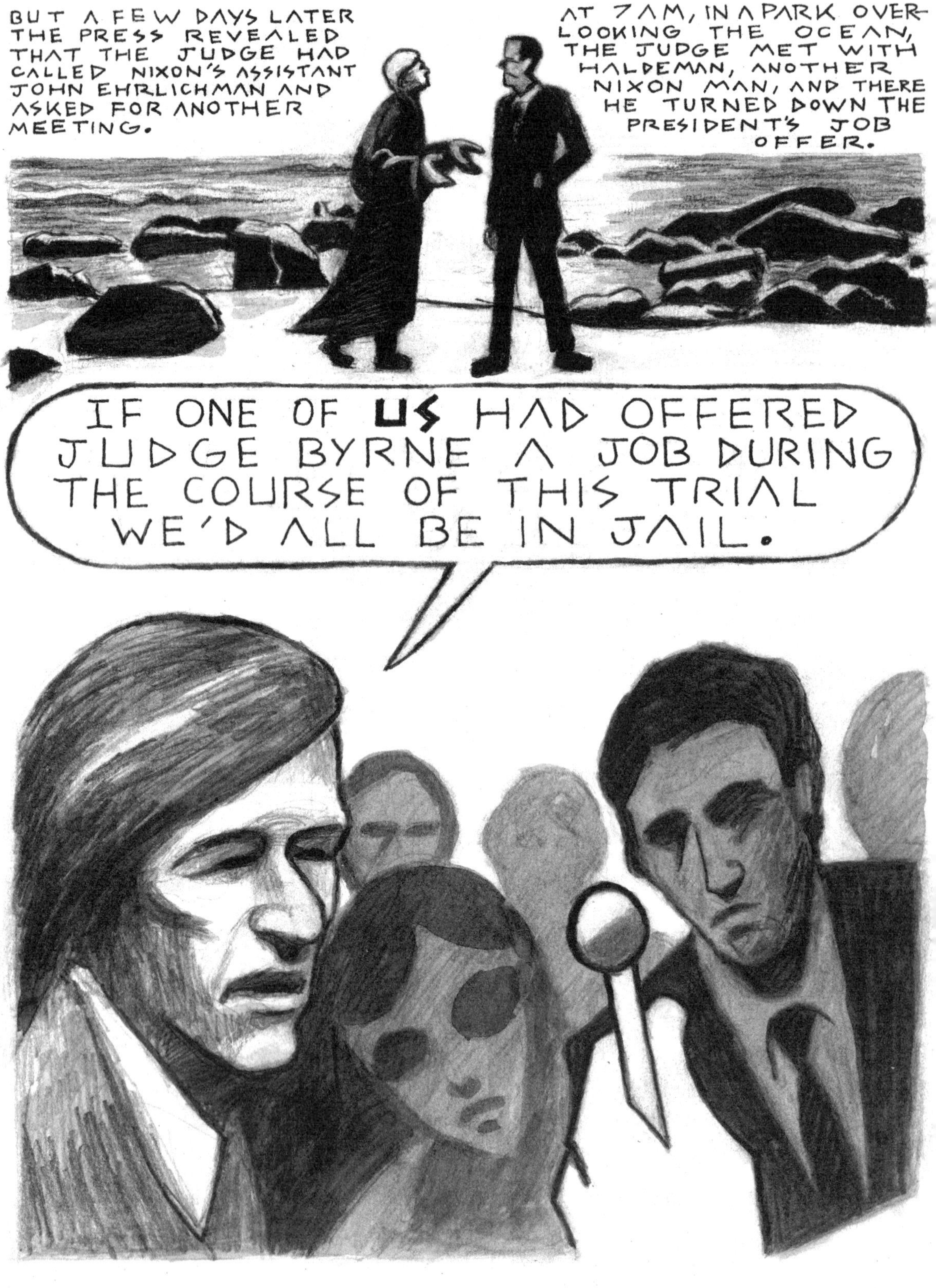
BUT A FEW DAYS LATER THE PRESS REVEALED THAT THE JUDGE HAD CALLED NIXON'S ASSISTANT JOHN EHRLICHMAN AND ASKED FOR ANOTHER MEETING.
AT 7AM, IN A PARK OVERLOOKING THE OCEAN, THE JUDGE MET WITH HALDEMAN, ANOTHER NIXON MAN, AND THERE HE TURNED DOWN THE PRESIDENT'S JOB OFFER.
IF ONE OF **US** HAD OFFERED JUDGE BYRNE A JOB DURING THE COURSE OF THIS TRIAL WE'D ALL BE IN JAIL.

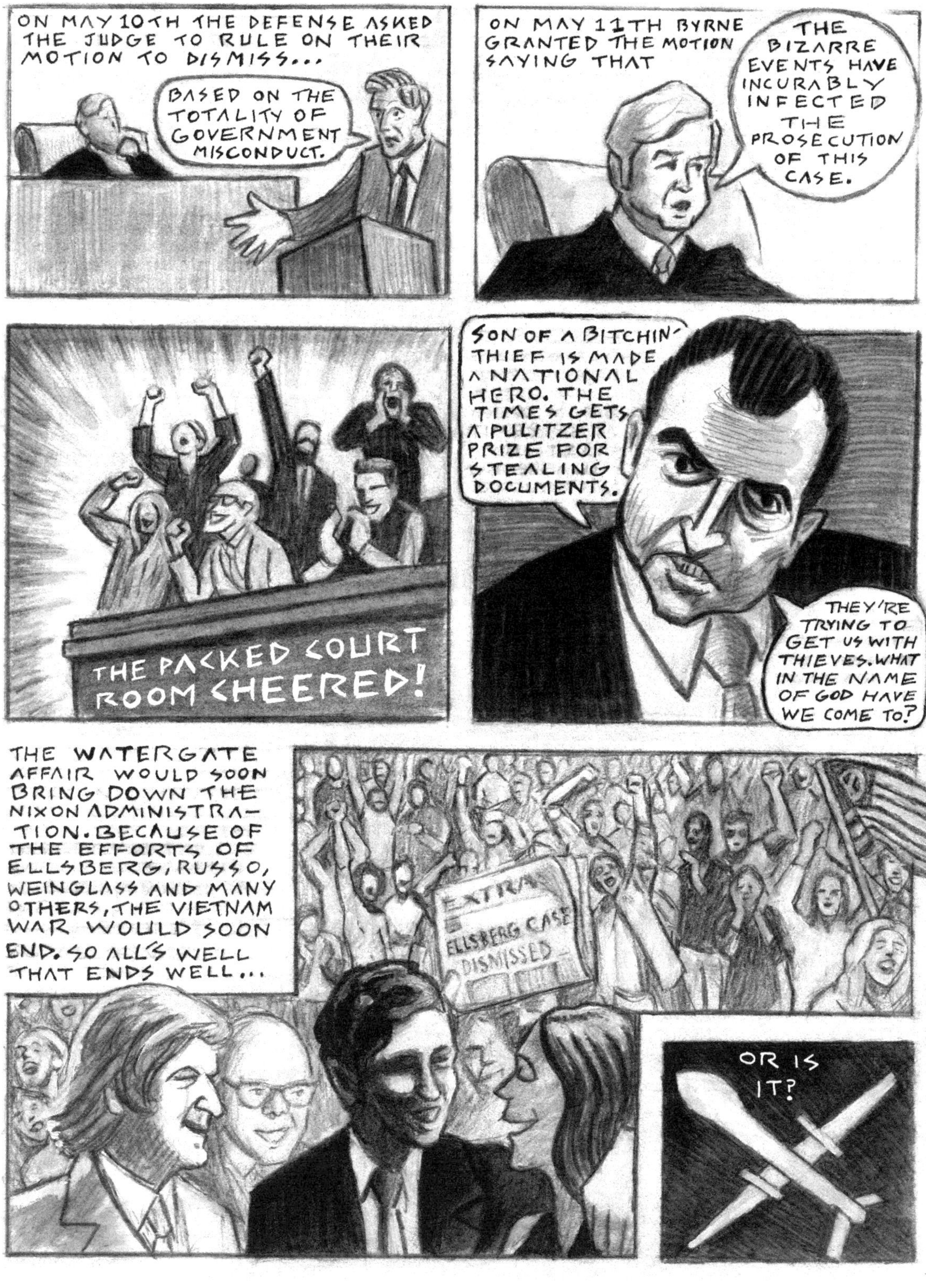
ON MAY 10TH THE DEFENSE ASKED THE JUDGE TO RULE ON THEIR MOTION TO DISMISS...
BASED ON THE TOTALITY OF GOVERNMENT MISCONDUCT.
ON MAY 11TH BYRNE GRANTED THE MOTION SAYING THAT
THE BIZARRE EVENTS HAVE INCURABLY INFECTED THE PROSECUTION OF THIS CASE.
THE PACKED COURT ROOM CHEERED!
SON OF A BITCHIN' THIEF IS MADE A NATIONAL HERO. THE TIMES GETS A PULITZER PRIZE FOR STEALING DOCUMENTS.
THEY'RE TRYING TO GET US WITH THIEVES. WHAT IN THE NAME OF GOD HAVE WE COME TO?
THE WATERGATE AFFAIR WOULD SOON BRING DOWN THE NIXON ADMINISTRA-TION. BECAUSE OF THE EFFORTS OF ELLSBERG, RUSSO, WEINGLASS AND MANY OTHERS, THE VIETNAM WAR WOULD SOON END. SO ALL'S WELL THAT ENDS WELL...
EXTRA
ELLSBERG CASE DISMISSED
OR IS IT?

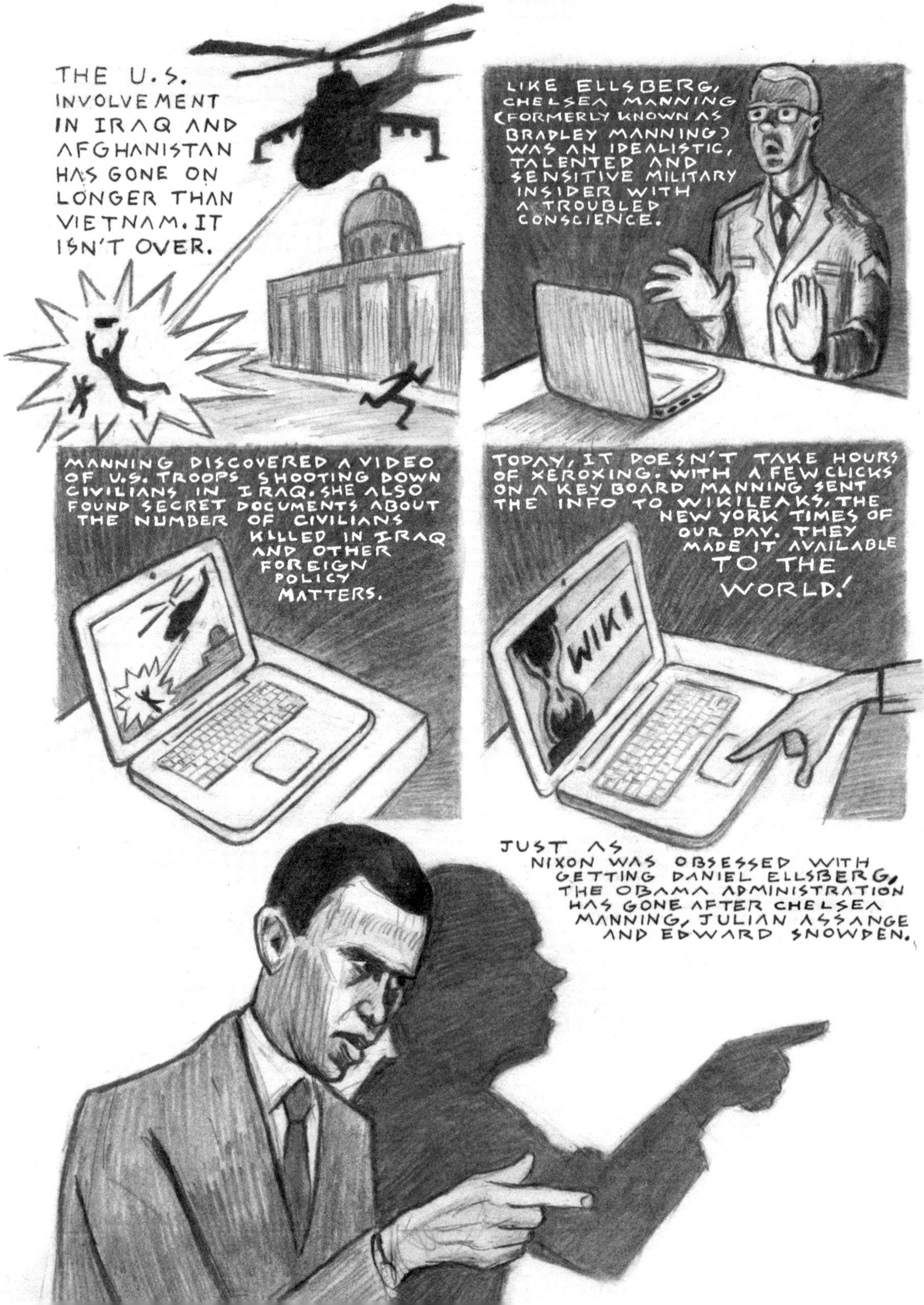
THE U.S. INVOLVEMENT IN IRAQ AND AFGHANISTAN HAS GONE ON LONGER THAN VIETNAM. IT ISN'T OVER.
LIKE ELLSBERG, CHELSEA MANNING (FORMERLY KNOWN AS BRADLEY MANNING) WAS AN IDEALISTIC, TALENTED AND SENSITIVE MILITARY INSIDER WITH A TROUBLED CONSCIENCE.
MANNING DISCOVERED A VIDEO OF U.S. TROOPS SHOOTING DOWN CIVILIANS IN IRAQ. SHE ALSO FOUND SECRET DOCUMENTS ABOUT THE NUMBER OF CIVILIANS KILLED IN IRAQ AND OTHER FOREIGN POLICY MATTERS.
TODAY, IT DOESN'T TAKE HOURS OF XEROXING. WITH A FEW CLICKS ON A KEYBOARD MANNING SENT THE INFO TO WIKILEAKS, THE NEW YORK TIMES OF OUR DAY. THEY MADE IT AVAILABLE TO THE WORLD!
WIKI
JUST AS NIXON WAS OBSESSED WITH GETTING DANIEL ELLSBERG, THE OBAMA ADMINISTRATION HAS GONE AFTER CHELSEA MANNING, JULIAN ASSANGE AND EDWARD SNOWDEN.

BECAUSE THERE WAS A CLEAR CUT VICTORY IN TIMES VS. U.S.

THE GOVERNMENT CANNOT LEGALLY SHUT DOWN WIKILEAKS. SO THEY HAVE HOUNDED WIKILEAKS' FOUNDER, JULIAN ASSANGE WITH SEXUAL CHARGES INSTEAD.

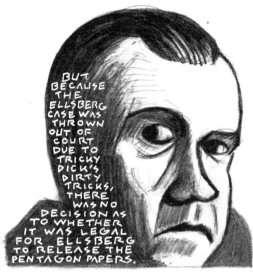

BUT BECAUSE THE ELLSBERG CASE WAS THROWN OUT OF COURT DUE TO TRICKY DICK'S DIRTY TRICKS, THERE WAS NO DECISION AS TO WHETHER IT WAS LEGAL FOR ELLSBERG TO RELEASE THE PENTAGON PAPERS.

SO MANNING WAS CONVICTED AND SENT TO PRISON. IS THIS NIXON'S REVENGE?

IN PRISON BRADLEY MANNING CHANGED GENDER DESIGNATION TO FEMALE.

SHE IS NOW CHELSEA MANNING.

DURING THE LAST YEARS OF HIS LIFE LEN WEINGLASS HAD A CONVERSATION WITH AN AGING DANIEL ELLSBERG, WHO ASKED HIM,...

WHAT CAN WE DO...

TO HELP MANNING & ASSANGE?

IN A DEMOCRACY DOES THE PUBLIC HAVE THE RIGHT TO

KNOW?

103

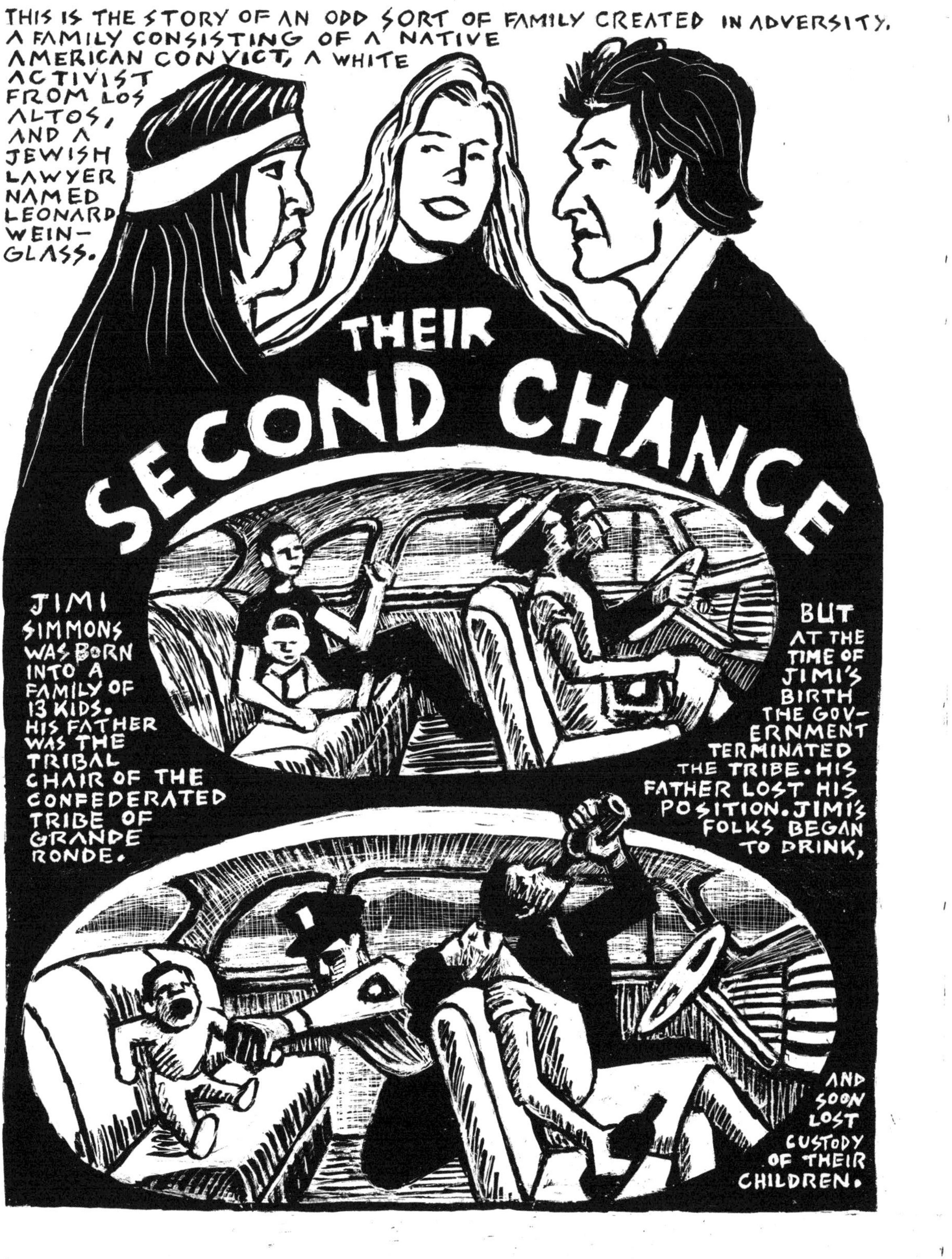
THIS IS THE STORY OF AN ODD SORT OF FAMILY CREATED IN ADVERSITY. A FAMILY CONSISTING OF A NATIVE AMERICAN CONVICT, A WHITE ACTIVIST FROM LOS ALTOS, AND A JEWISH LAWYER NAMED LEONARD WEIN-GLASS.
THEIR SECOND CHANCE
JIMI SIMMONS WAS BORN INTO A FAMILY OF 13 KIDS. HIS FATHER WAS THE TRIBAL CHAIR OF THE CONFEDERATED TRIBE OF GRANDE RONDE.
BUT AT THE TIME OF JIMI'S BIRTH THE GOV-ERNMENT TERMINATED THE TRIBE. HIS FATHER LOST HIS POSITION. JIMI'S FOLKS BEGAN TO DRINK,
AND SOON LOST CUSTODY OF THEIR CHILDREN.

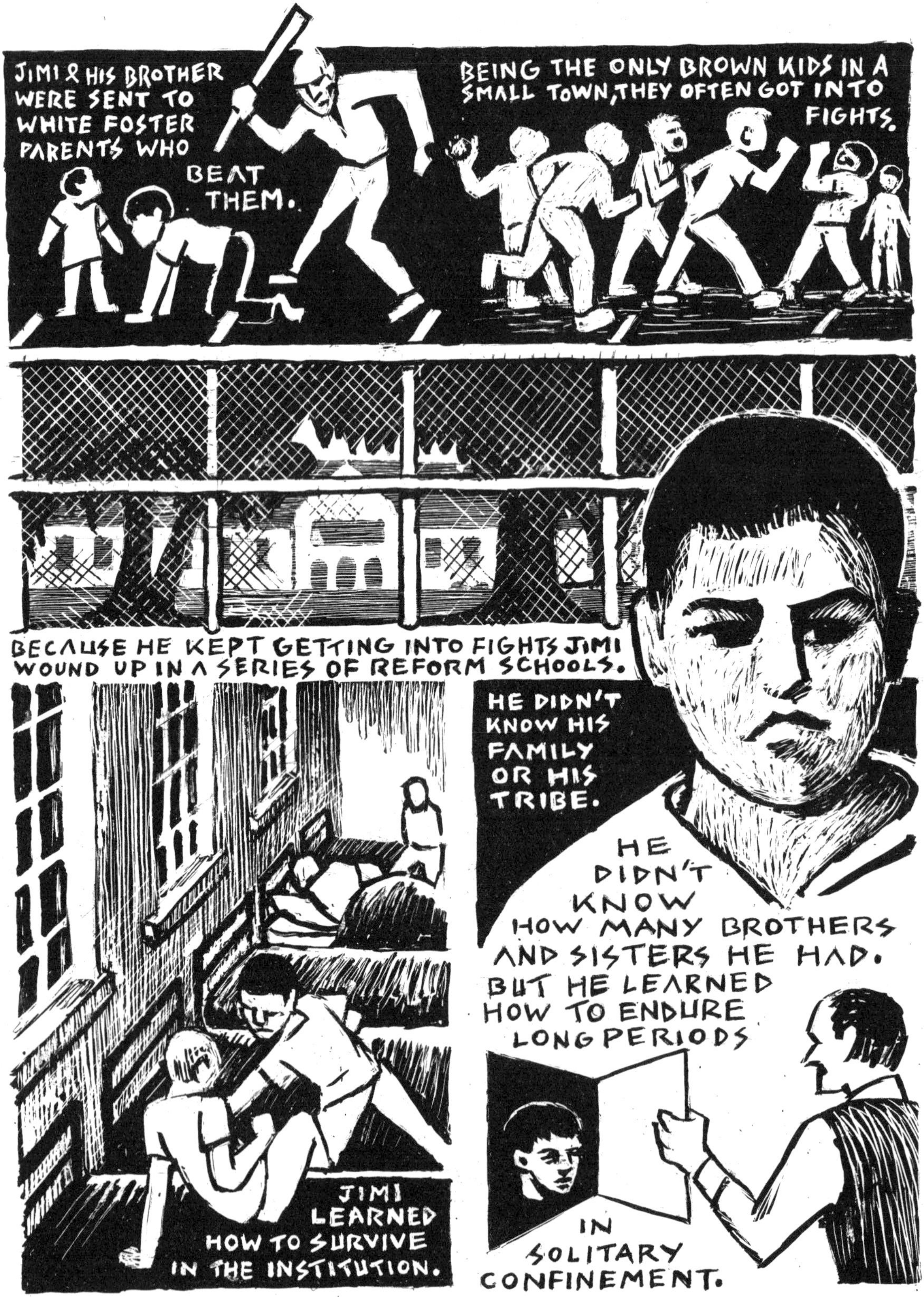
JIMI & HIS BROTHER WERE SENT TO WHITE FOSTER PARENTS WHO
BEAT THEM.
BEING THE ONLY BROWN KIDS IN A SMALL TOWN, THEY OFTEN GOT INTO FIGHTS.
BECAUSE HE KEPT GETTING INTO FIGHTS JIMI WOUND UP IN A SERIES OF REFORM SCHOOLS.
HE DIDN'T KNOW HIS FAMILY OR HIS TRIBE.
HE DIDN'T KNOW HOW MANY BROTHERS AND SISTERS HE HAD.
JIMI LEARNED HOW TO SURVIVE IN THE INSTITUTION.
BUT HE LEARNED HOW TO ENDURE LONG PERIODS
IN SOLITARY CONFINEMENT.

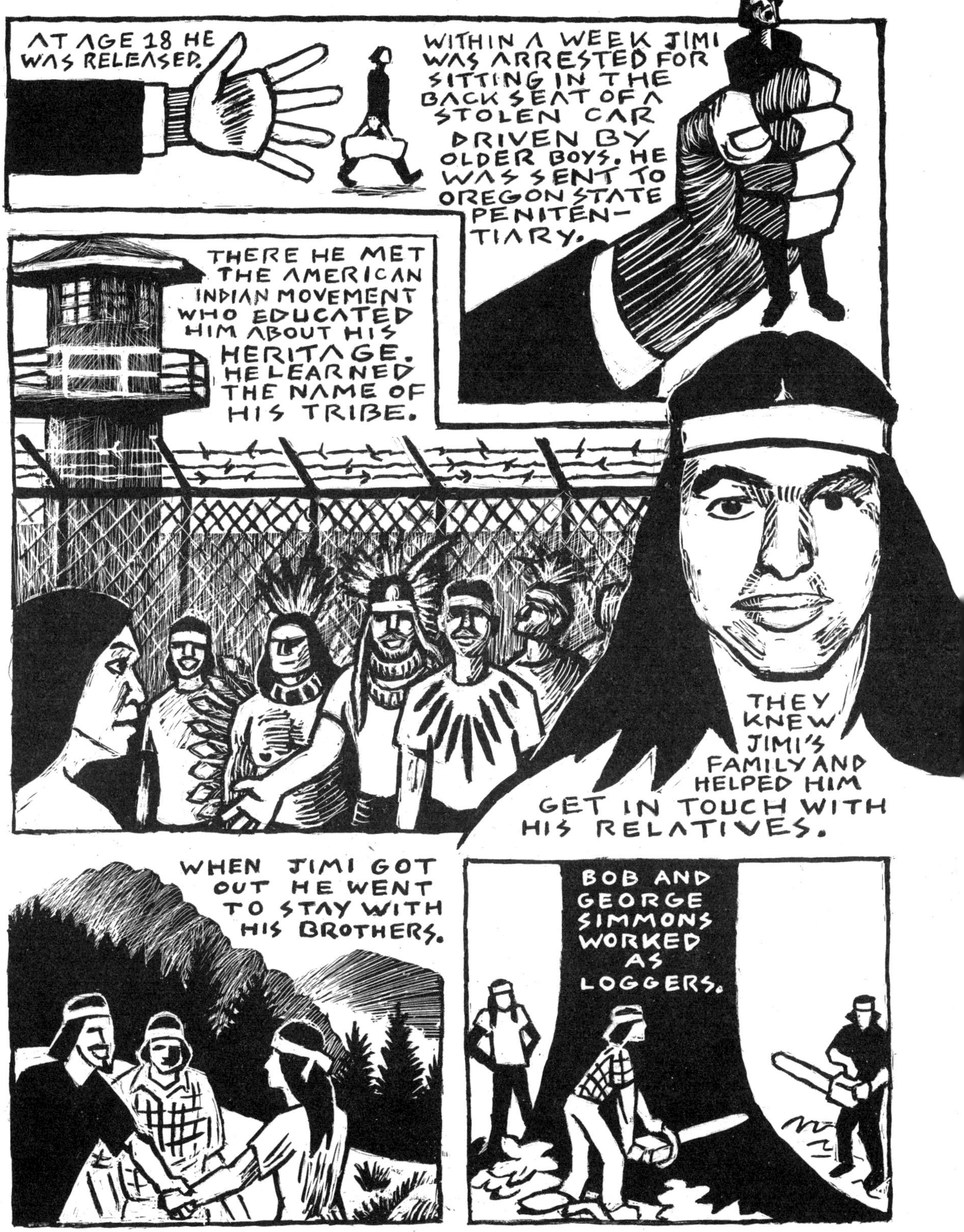
AT AGE 18 HE WAS RELEASED.
WITHIN A WEEK JIMI WAS ARRESTED FOR SITTING IN THE BACK SEAT OF A STOLEN CAR DRIVEN BY OLDER BOYS. HE WAS SENT TO OREGON STATE PENITENTIARY.
THERE HE MET THE AMERICAN INDIAN MOVEMENT WHO EDUCATED HIM ABOUT HIS HERITAGE. HE LEARNED THE NAME OF HIS TRIBE.
THEY KNEW JIMI'S FAMILY AND HELPED HIM GET IN TOUCH WITH HIS RELATIVES.
WHEN JIMI GOT OUT HE WENT TO STAY WITH HIS BROTHERS.
BOB AND GEORGE SIMMONS WORKED AS LOGGERS.

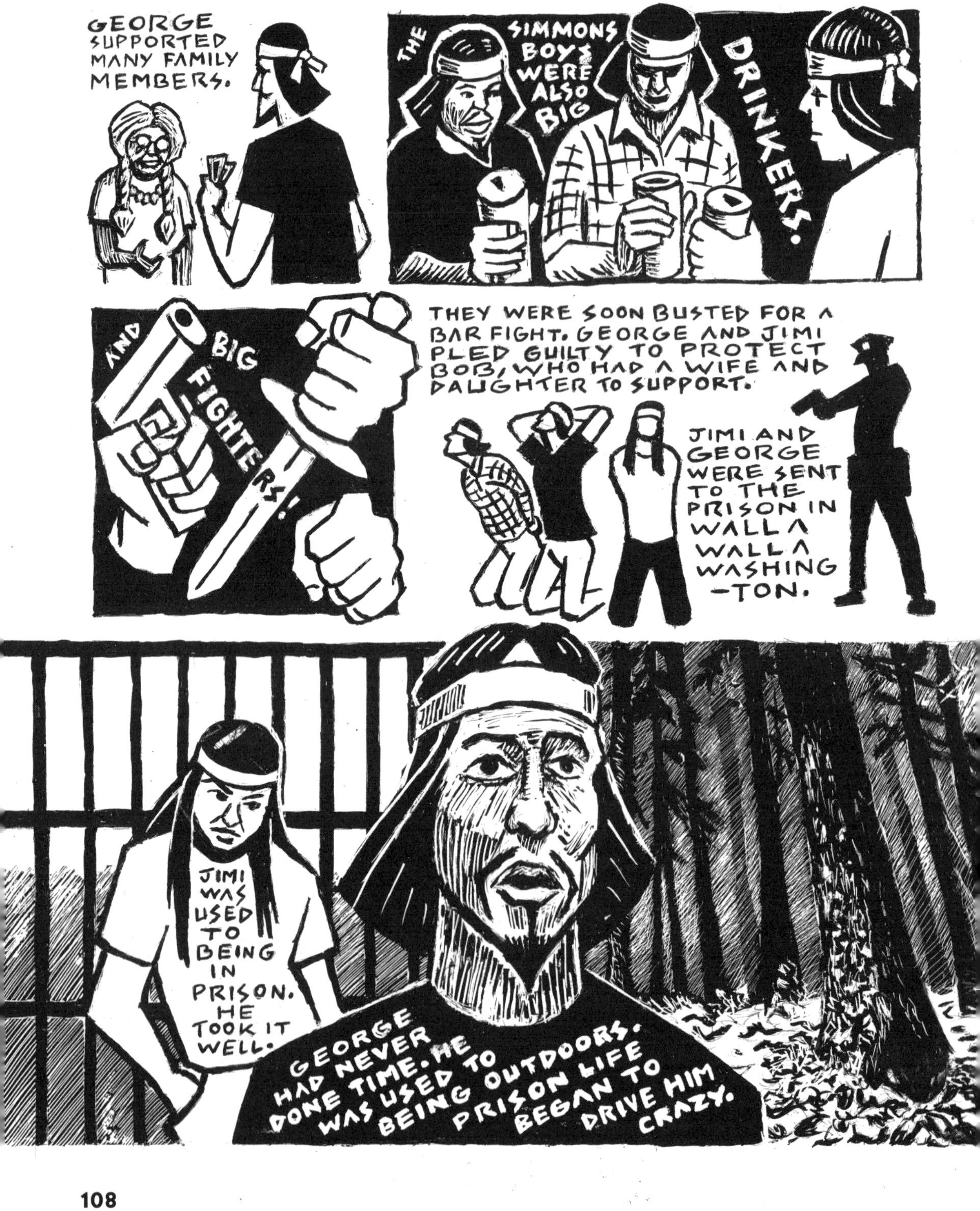
GEORGE SUPPORTED MANY FAMILY MEMBERS.
THE SIMMONS BOYS WERE ALSO BIG DRINKERS.
AND BIG FIGHTERS!
THEY WERE SOON BUSTED FOR A BAR FIGHT. GEORGE AND JIMI PLED GUILTY TO PROTECT BOB, WHO HAD A WIFE AND DAUGHTER TO SUPPORT.
JIMI AND GEORGE WERE SENT TO THE PRISON IN WALLA WALLA WASHING-TON.
JIMI WAS USED TO BEING IN PRISON. HE TOOK IT WELL.
GEORGE HAD NEVER DONE TIME. HE WAS USED TO BEING OUTDOORS. PRISON LIFE BEGAN TO DRIVE HIM CRAZY.

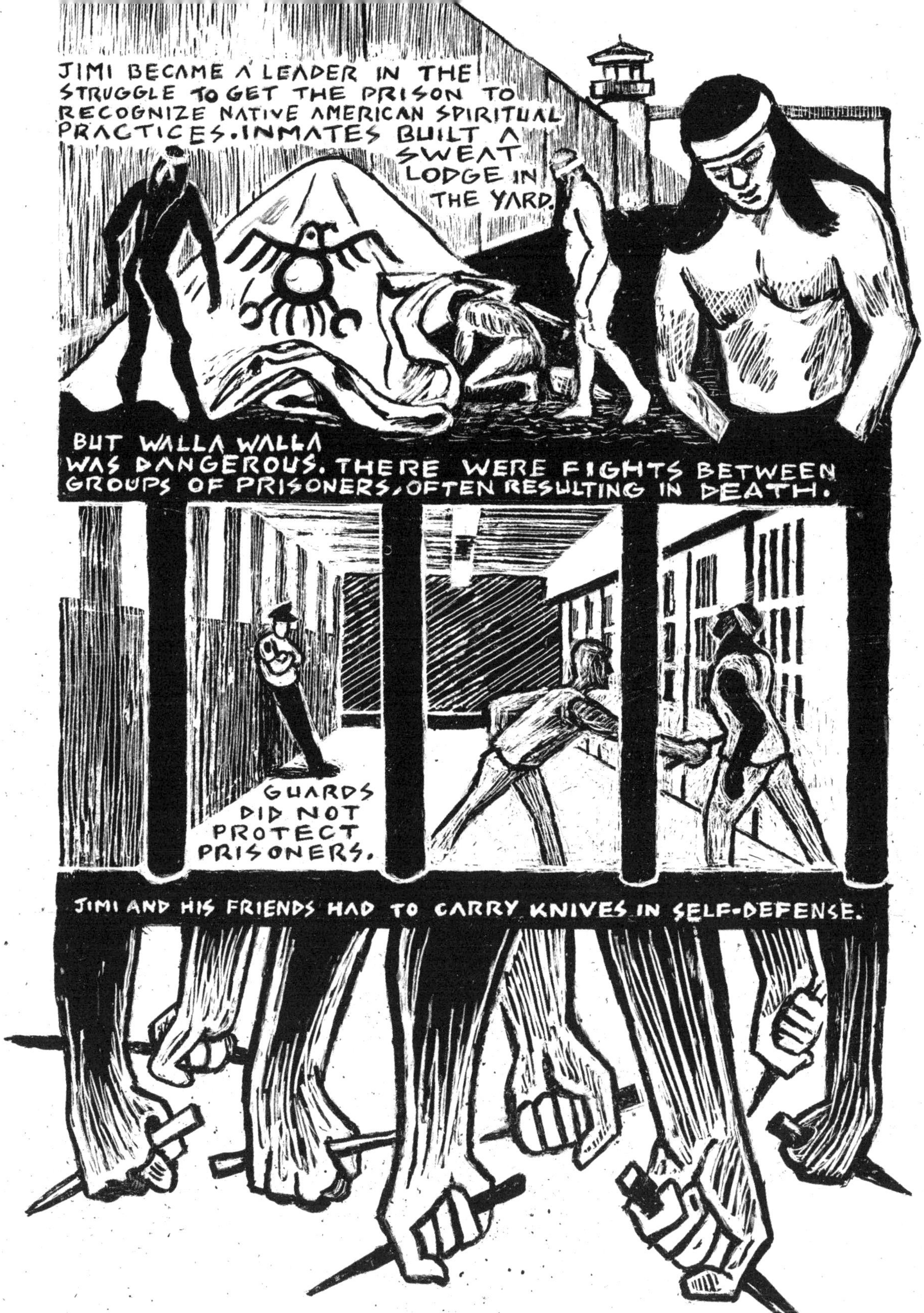
JIMI BECAME A LEADER IN THE STRUGGLE TO GET THE PRISON TO RECOGNIZE NATIVE AMERICAN SPIRITUAL PRACTICES. INMATES BUILT A SWEAT LODGE IN THE YARD.
BUT WALLA WALLA WAS DANGEROUS. THERE WERE FIGHTS BETWEEN GROUPS OF PRISONERS, OFTEN RESULTING IN DEATH.
GUARDS DID NOT PROTECT PRISONERS.
JIMI AND HIS FRIENDS HAD TO CARRY KNIVES IN SELF-DEFENSE.

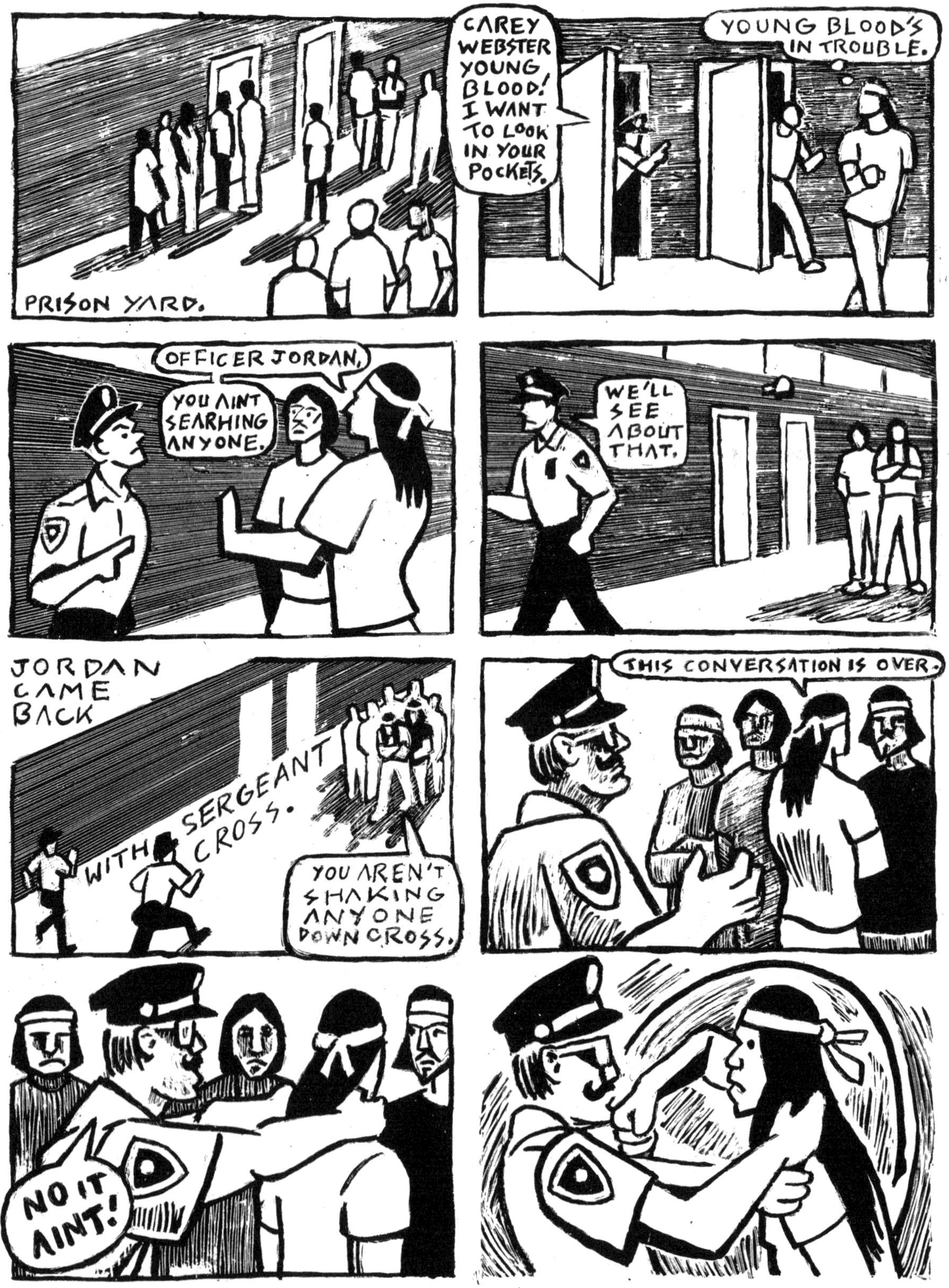
PRISON YARD.
CAREY WEBSTER YOUNG BLOOD! I WANT TO LOOK IN YOUR POCKETS.
YOUNG BLOOD'S IN TROUBLE.
OFFICER JORDAN,
YOU AINT SEARHING ANYONE.
WE'LL SEE ABOUT THAT.
JORDAN CAME BACK WITH SERGEANT CROSS.
YOU AREN'T SHAKING ANYONE DOWN CROSS.
THIS CONVERSATION IS OVER.
NO IT AINT!

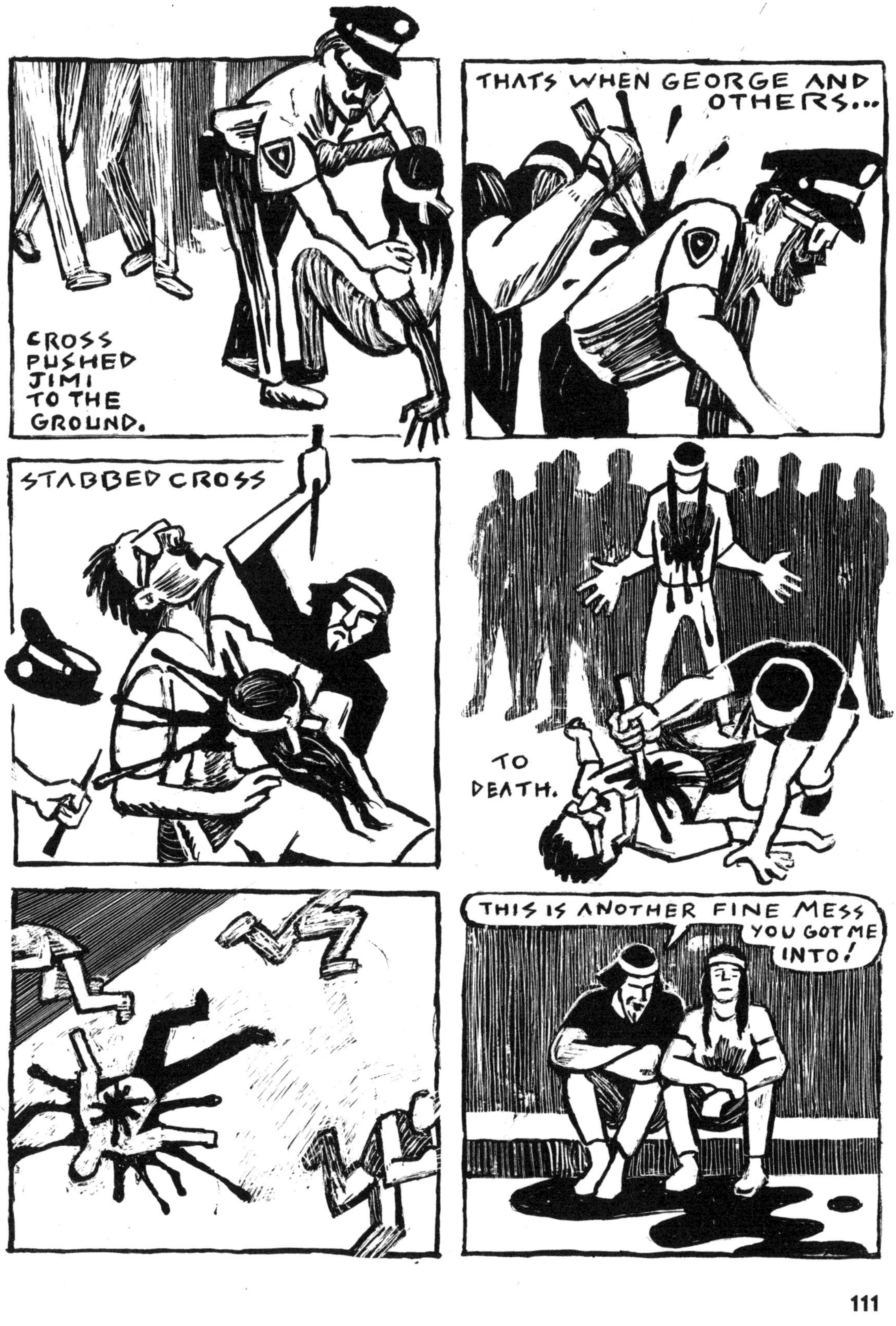
CROSS PUSHED JIMI TO THE GROUND.
THATS WHEN GEORGE AND OTHERS...
STABBED CROSS
TO DEATH.
THIS IS ANOTHER FINE MESS YOU GOT ME INTO!

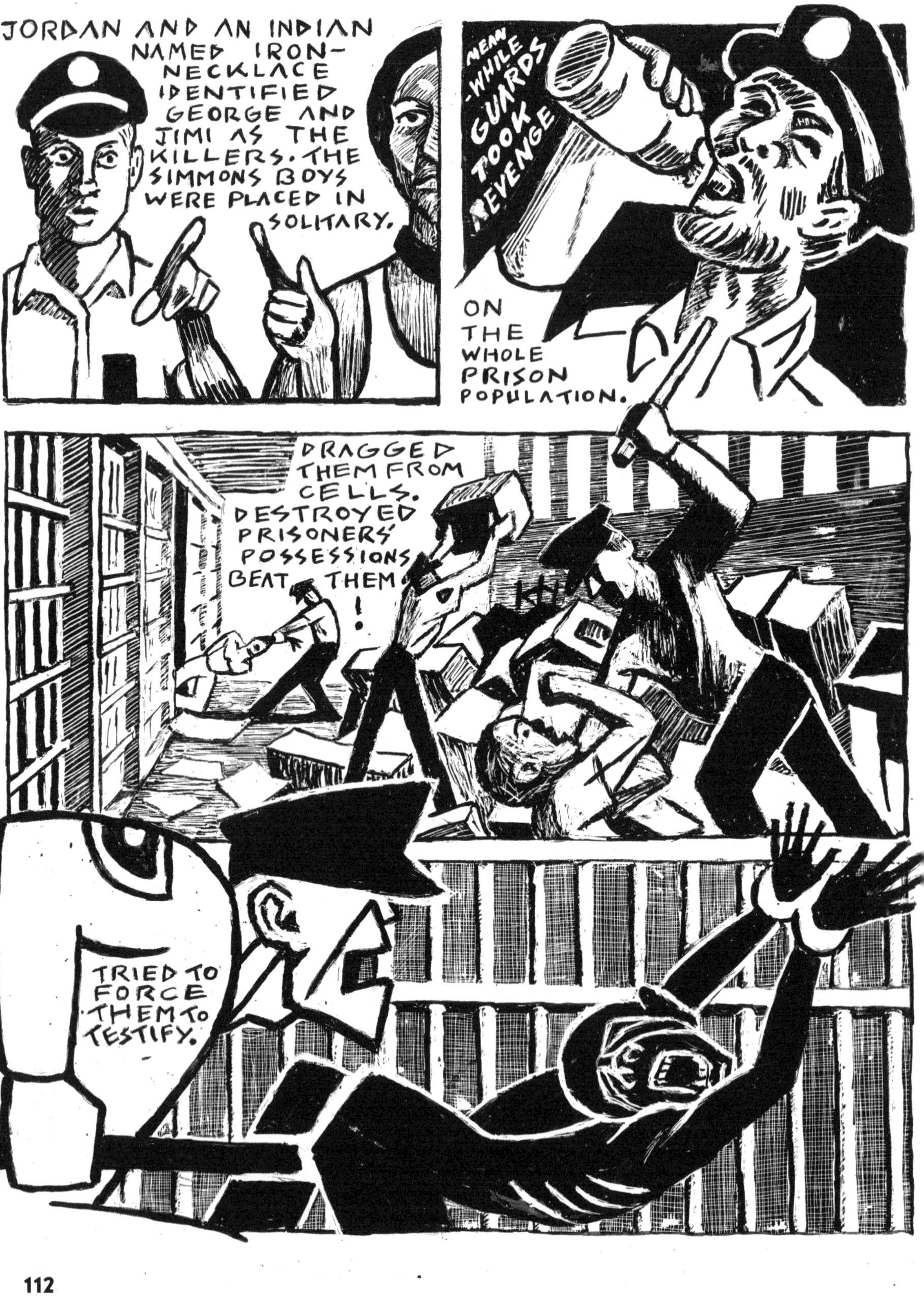
JORDAN AND AN INDIAN NAMED IRON-NECKLACE IDENTIFIED GEORGE AND JIMI AS THE KILLERS. THE SIMMONS BOYS WERE PLACED IN SOLITARY.
MEAN-WHILE GUARDS TOOK REVENGE
ON THE WHOLE PRISON POPULATION.
DRAGGED THEM FROM CELLS. DESTROYED PRISONERS' POSSESSIONS BEAT THEM!
TRIED TO FORCE THEM TO TESTIFY.

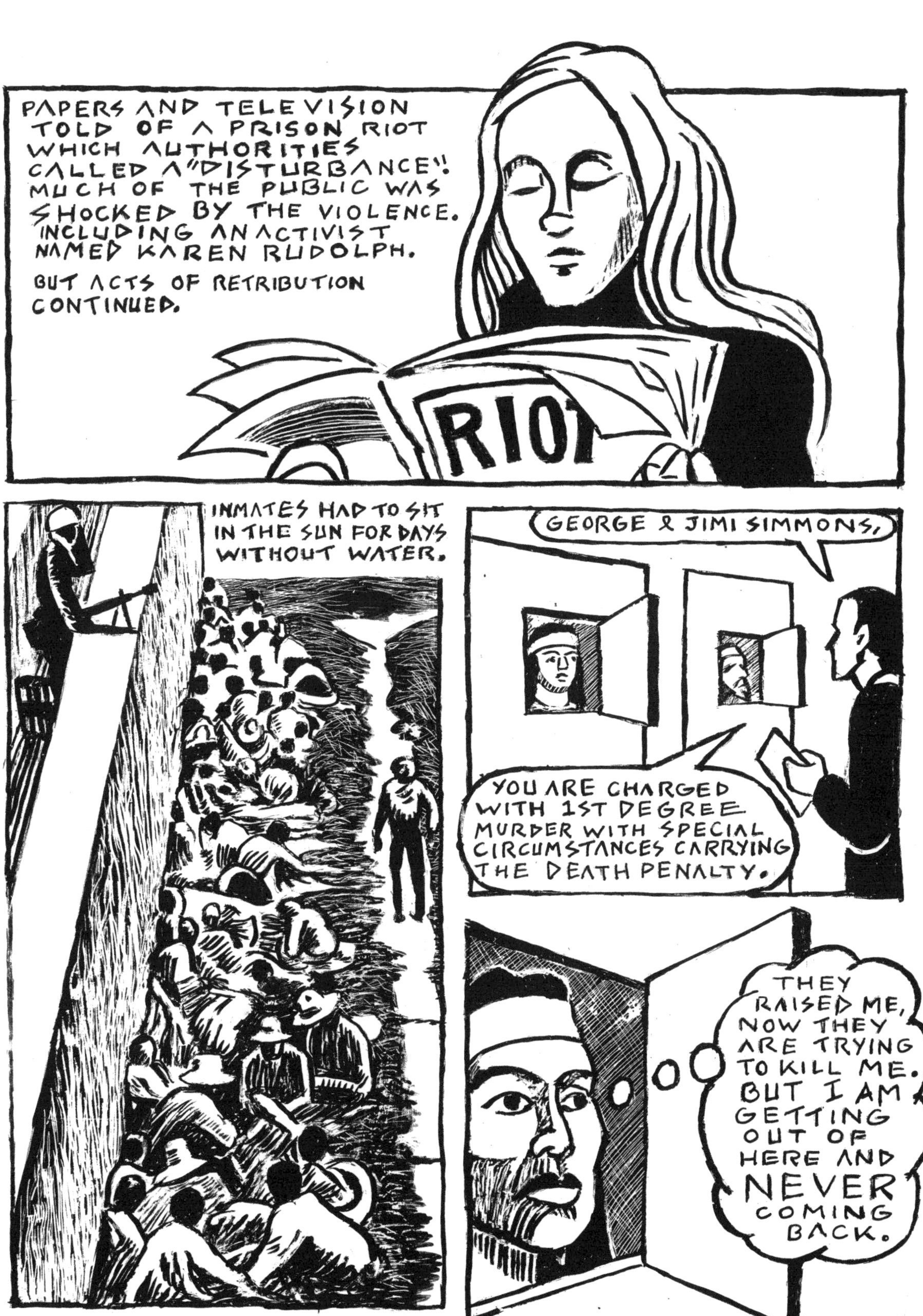
PAPERS AND TELEVISION TOLD OF A PRISON RIOT WHICH AUTHORITIES CALLED A "DISTURBANCE". MUCH OF THE PUBLIC WAS SHOCKED BY THE VIOLENCE. INCLUDING AN ACTIVIST NAMED KAREN RUDOLPH.
BUT ACTS OF RETRIBUTION CONTINUED.
RIOT
INMATES HAD TO SIT IN THE SUN FOR DAYS WITHOUT WATER.
GEORGE & JIMI SIMMONS,
YOU ARE CHARGED WITH 1ST DEGREE MURDER WITH SPECIAL CIRCUMSTANCES CARRYING THE DEATH PENALTY.
THEY RAISED ME, NOW THEY ARE TRYING TO KILL ME. BUT I AM GETTING OUT OF HERE AND NEVER COMING BACK.

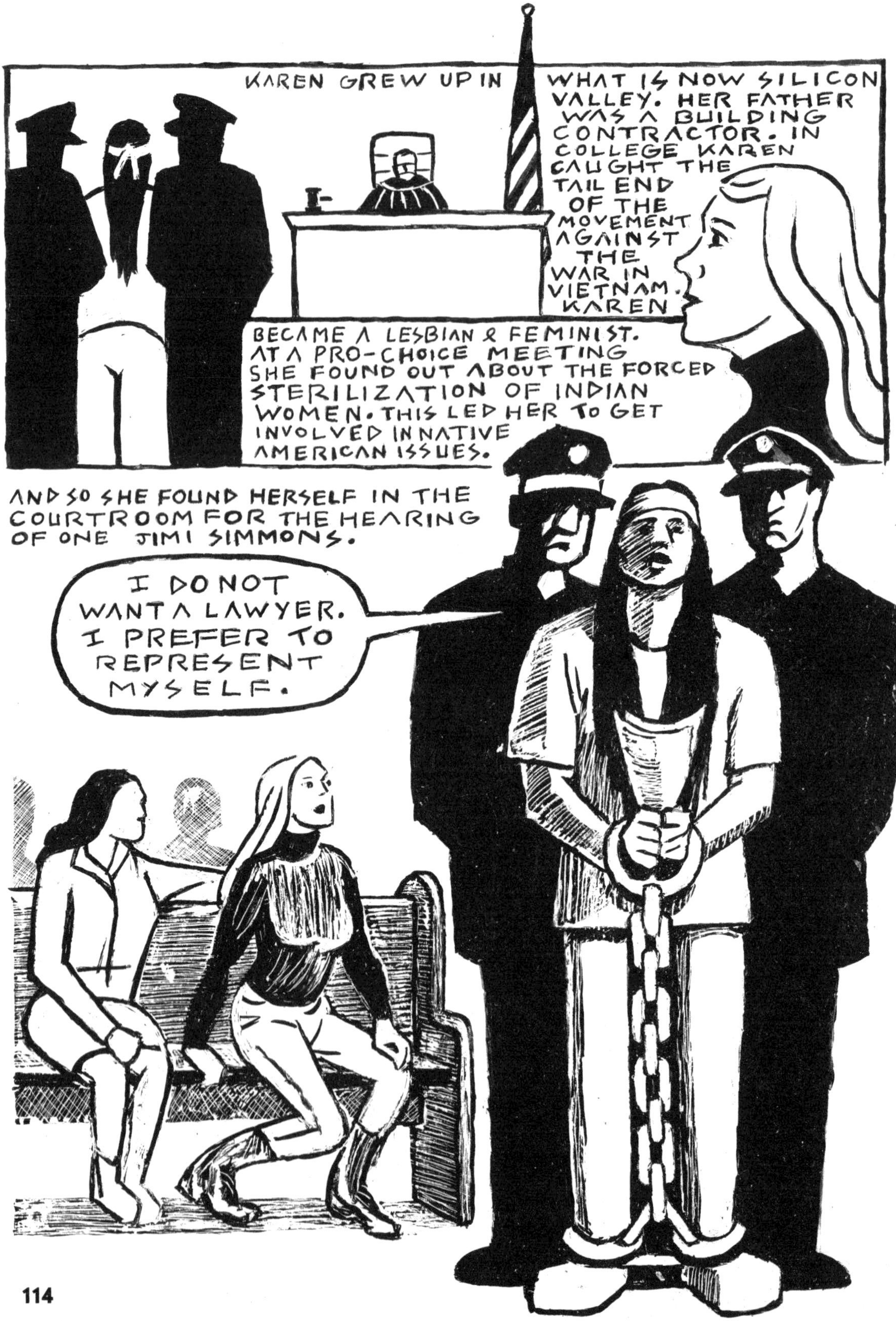
KAREN GREW UP IN
WHAT IS NOW SILICON VALLEY. HER FATHER WAS A BUILDING CONTRACTOR. IN COLLEGE KAREN CAUGHT THE TAIL END OF THE MOVEMENT AGAINST THE WAR IN VIETNAM. KAREN
BECAME A LESBIAN & FEMINIST. AT A PRO-CHOICE MEETING SHE FOUND OUT ABOUT THE FORCED STERILIZATION OF INDIAN WOMEN. THIS LED HER TO GET INVOLVED IN NATIVE AMERICAN ISSUES.
AND SO SHE FOUND HERSELF IN THE COURTROOM FOR THE HEARING OF ONE JIMI SIMMONS.
I DO NOT WANT A LAWYER. I PREFER TO REPRESENT MYSELF.

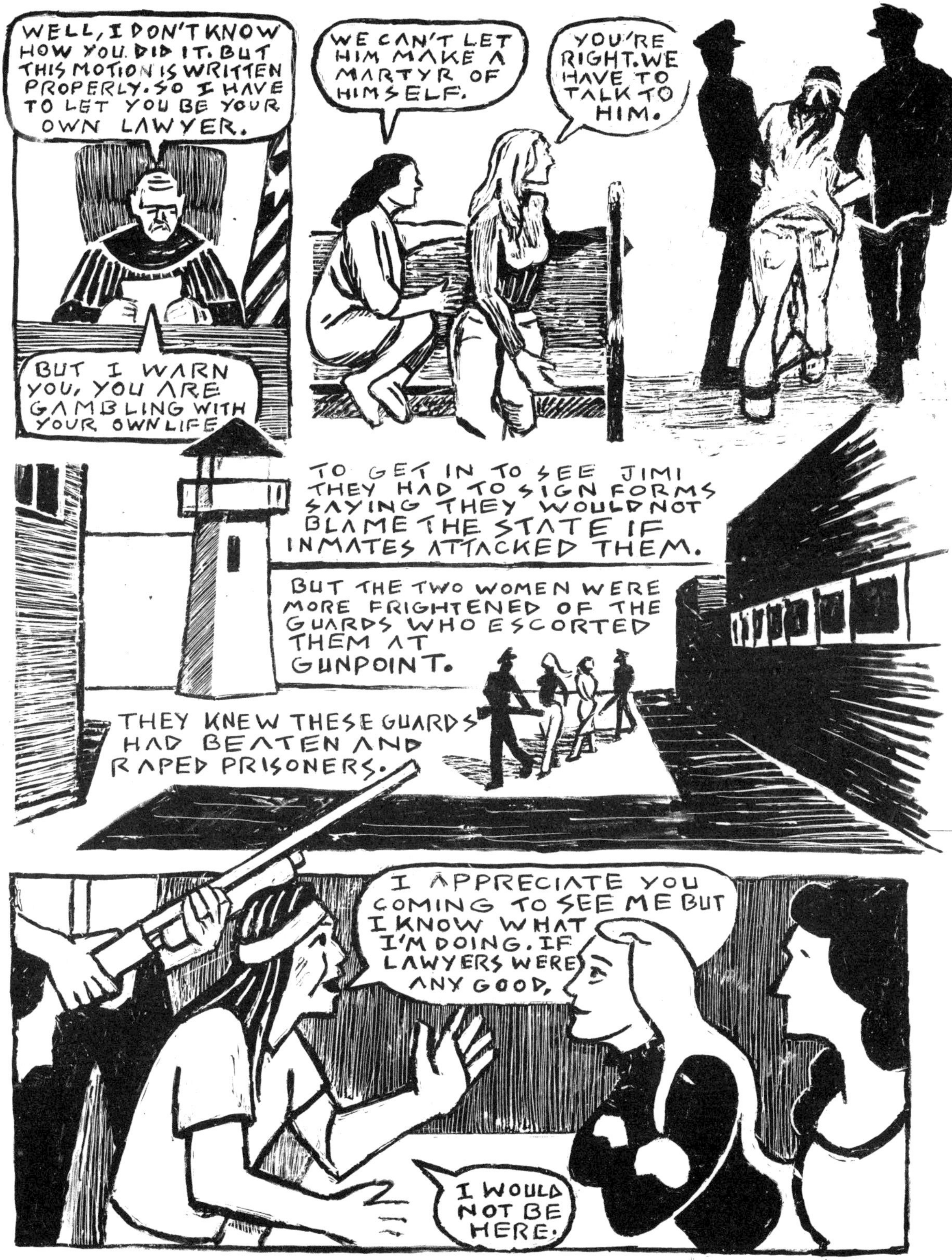
WELL, I DON'T KNOW HOW YOU DID IT. BUT THIS MOTION IS WRITTEN PROPERLY. SO I HAVE TO LET YOU BE YOUR OWN LAWYER.
BUT I WARN YOU, YOU ARE GAMBLING WITH YOUR OWN LIFE.
WE CAN'T LET HIM MAKE A MARTYR OF HIMSELF.
YOU'RE RIGHT. WE HAVE TO TALK TO HIM.
TO GET IN TO SEE JIMI THEY HAD TO SIGN FORMS SAYING THEY WOULD NOT BLAME THE STATE IF INMATES ATTACKED THEM.
BUT THE TWO WOMEN WERE MORE FRIGHTENED OF THE GUARDS WHO ESCORTED THEM AT GUNPOINT.
THEY KNEW THESE GUARDS HAD BEATEN AND RAPED PRISONERS.
I APPRECIATE YOU COMING TO SEE ME BUT I KNOW WHAT I'M DOING. IF LAWYERS WERE ANY GOOD,
I WOULD NOT BE HERE.

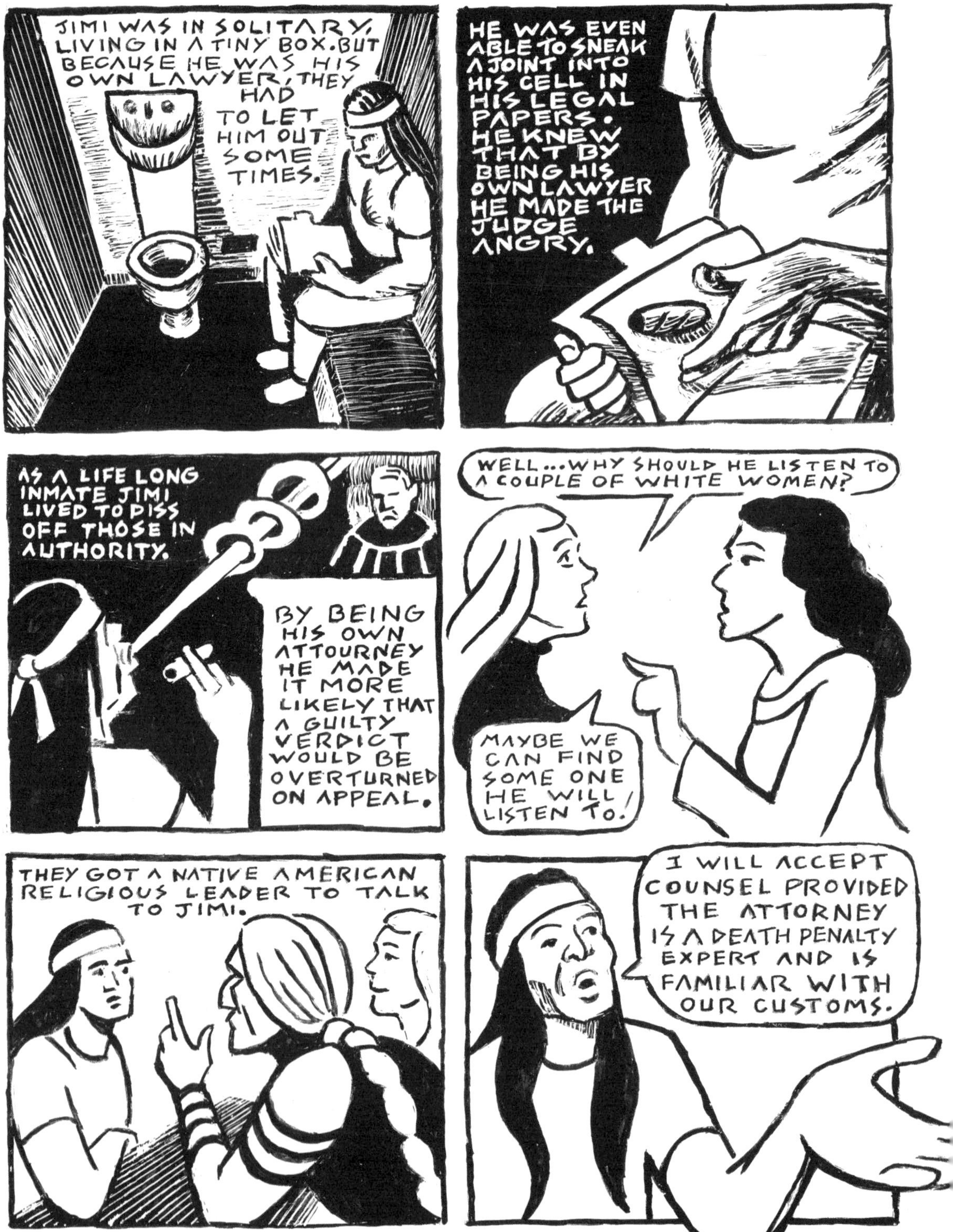
JIMI WAS IN SOLITARY, LIVING IN A TINY BOX. BUT BECAUSE HE WAS HIS OWN LAWYER, THEY HAD TO LET HIM OUT SOME TIMES.
HE WAS EVEN ABLE TO SNEAK A JOINT INTO HIS CELL IN HIS LEGAL PAPERS. HE KNEW THAT BY BEING HIS OWN LAWYER HE MADE THE JUDGE ANGRY.
AS A LIFE LONG INMATE JIMI LIVED TO DISS OFF THOSE IN AUTHORITY.
BY BEING HIS OWN ATTOURNEY HE MADE IT MORE LIKELY THAT A GUILTY VERDICT WOULD BE OVERTURNED ON APPEAL.
WELL...WHY SHOULD HE LISTEN TO A COUPLE OF WHITE WOMEN?
MAYBE WE CAN FIND SOME ONE HE WILL LISTEN TO.
THEY GOT A NATIVE AMERICAN RELIGIOUS LEADER TO TALK TO JIMI.
I WILL ACCEPT COUNSEL PROVIDED THE ATTORNEY IS A DEATH PENALTY EXPERT AND IS FAMILIAR WITH OUR CUSTOMS.

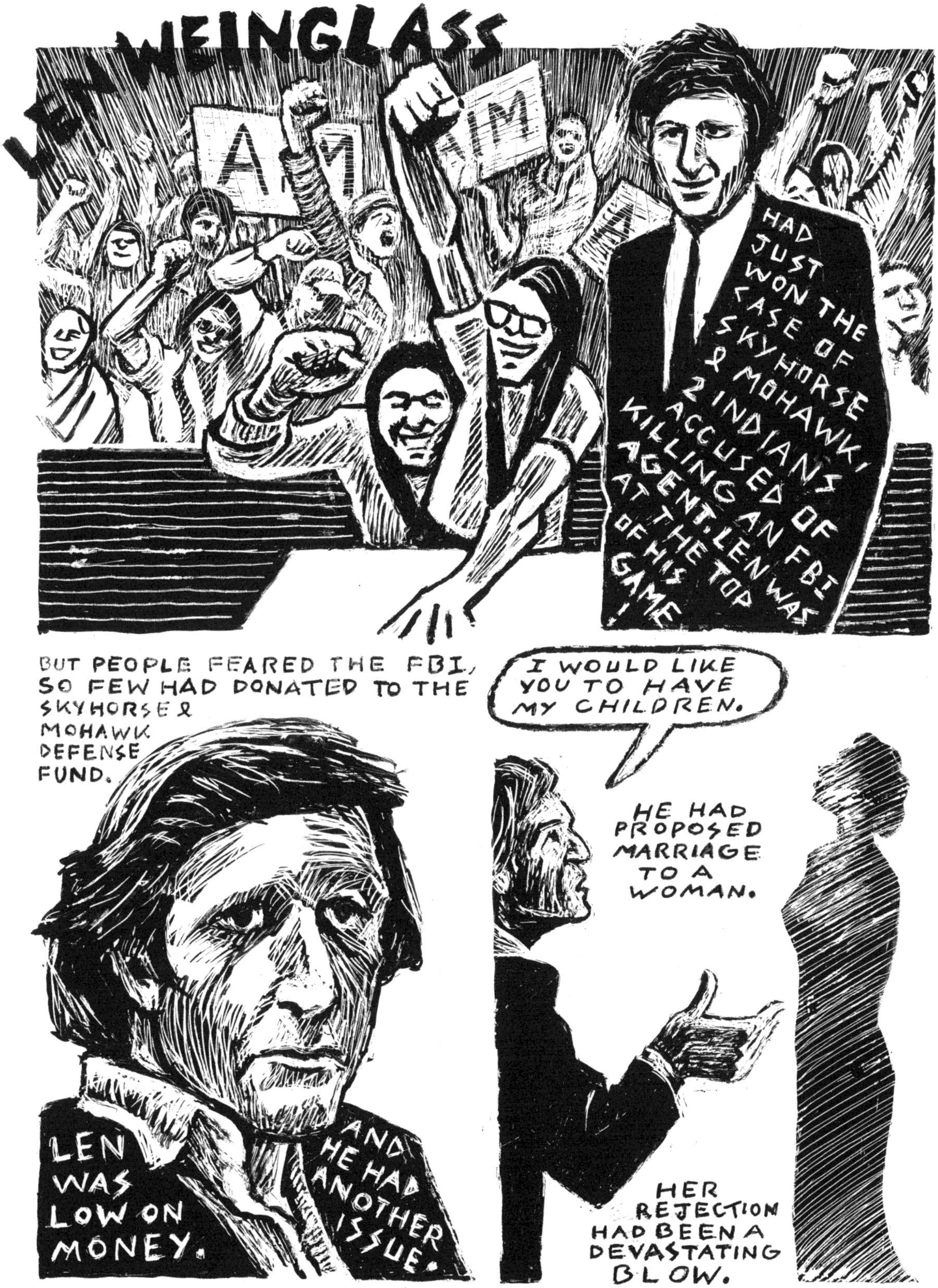
LEN WEINGLASS
AIM
AIM
HAD JUST WON THE CASE OF SKYHORSE & MOHAWK, 2 INDIANS ACCUSED OF KILLING AN FBI AGENT. LEN WAS AT THE TOP OF HIS GAME!
BUT PEOPLE FEARED THE FBI, SO FEW HAD DONATED TO THE SKYHORSE & MOHAWK DEFENSE FUND.
LEN WAS LOW ON MONEY.
AND HE HAD ANOTHER ISSUE.
I WOULD LIKE YOU TO HAVE MY CHILDREN.
HE HAD PROPOSED MARRIAGE TO A WOMAN.
HER REJECTION HAD BEEN A DEVASTATING BLOW.

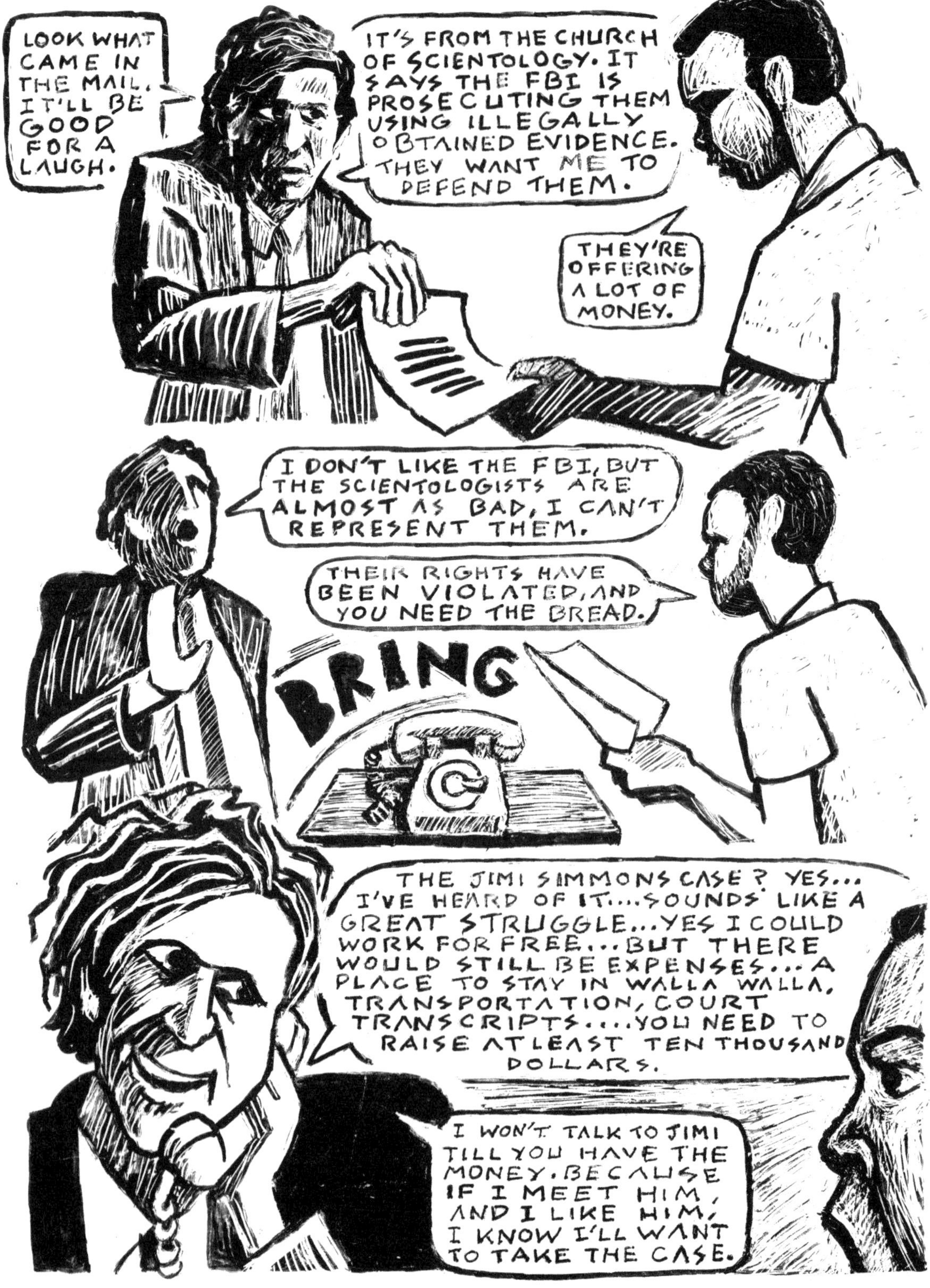
LOOK WHAT CAME IN THE MAIL. IT'LL BE GOOD FOR A LAUGH.
IT'S FROM THE CHURCH OF SCIENTOLOGY. IT SAYS THE FBI IS PROSECUTING THEM USING ILLEGALLY OBTAINED EVIDENCE. THEY WANT ME TO DEFEND THEM.
THEY'RE OFFERING A LOT OF MONEY.
I DON'T LIKE THE FBI, BUT THE SCIENTOLOGISTS ARE ALMOST AS BAD, I CAN'T REPRESENT THEM.
THEIR RIGHTS HAVE BEEN VIOLATED, AND YOU NEED THE BREAD.
BRING
THE JIMI SIMMONS CASE? YES... I'VE HEARD OF IT....SOUNDS LIKE A GREAT STRUGGLE...YES I COULD WORK FOR FREE...BUT THERE WOULD STILL BE EXPENSES...A PLACE TO STAY IN WALLA WALLA, TRANSPORTATION, COURT TRANSCRIPTS....YOU NEED TO RAISE AT LEAST TEN THOUSAND DOLLARS.
I WON'T TALK TO JIMI TILL YOU HAVE THE MONEY. BECAUSE IF I MEET HIM, AND I LIKE HIM, I KNOW I'LL WANT TO TAKE THE CASE.

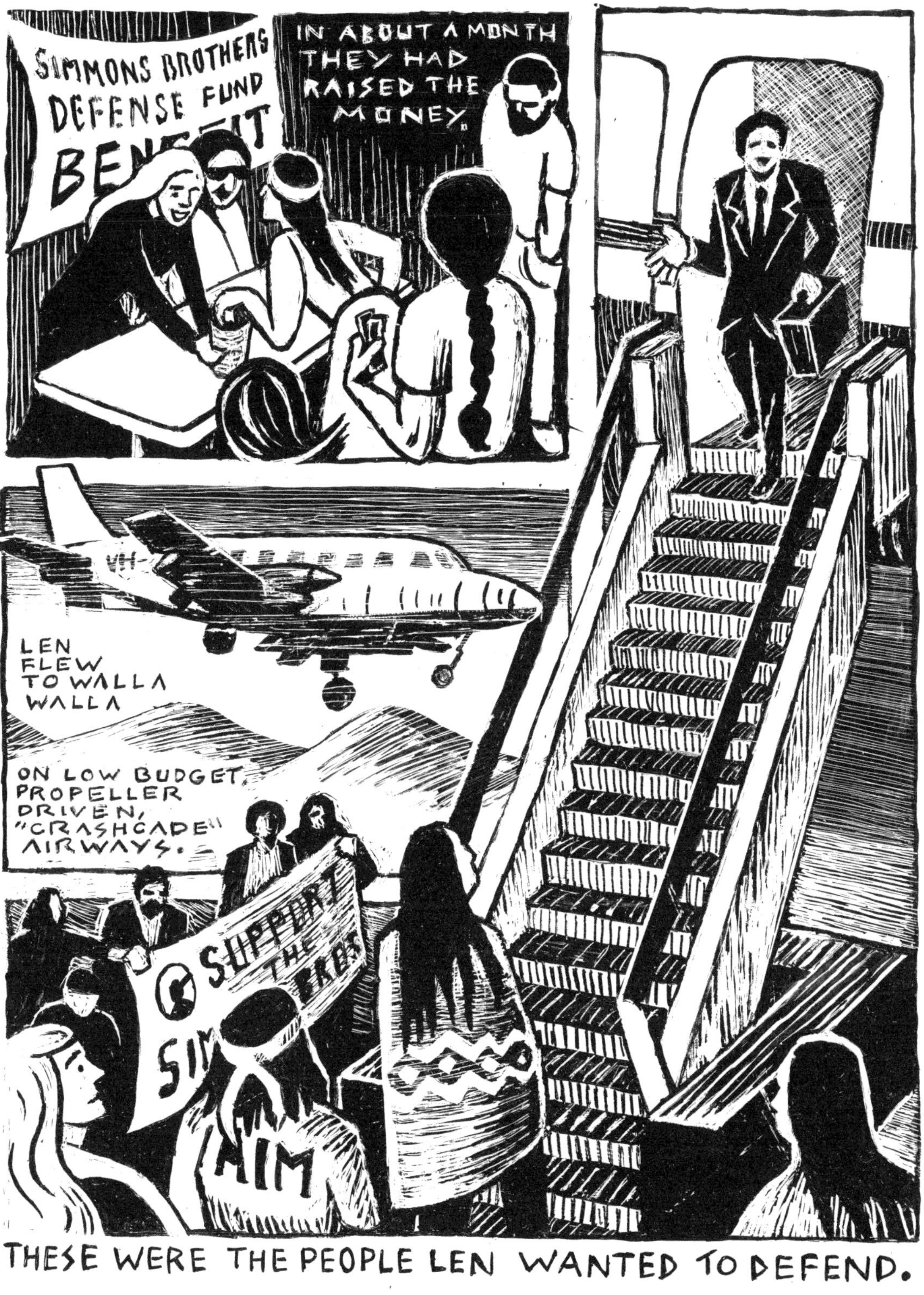
SIMMONS BROTHERS
DEFENSE FUND
IN ABOUT A MONTH THEY HAD RAISED THE MONEY.
LEN FLEW TO WALLA WALLA
ON LOW BUDGET, PROPELLER DRIVEN, "CRASHCADE" AIRWAYS.
SUPPORT THE BROS
AIM

THESE WERE THE PEOPLE LEN WANTED TO DEFEND.

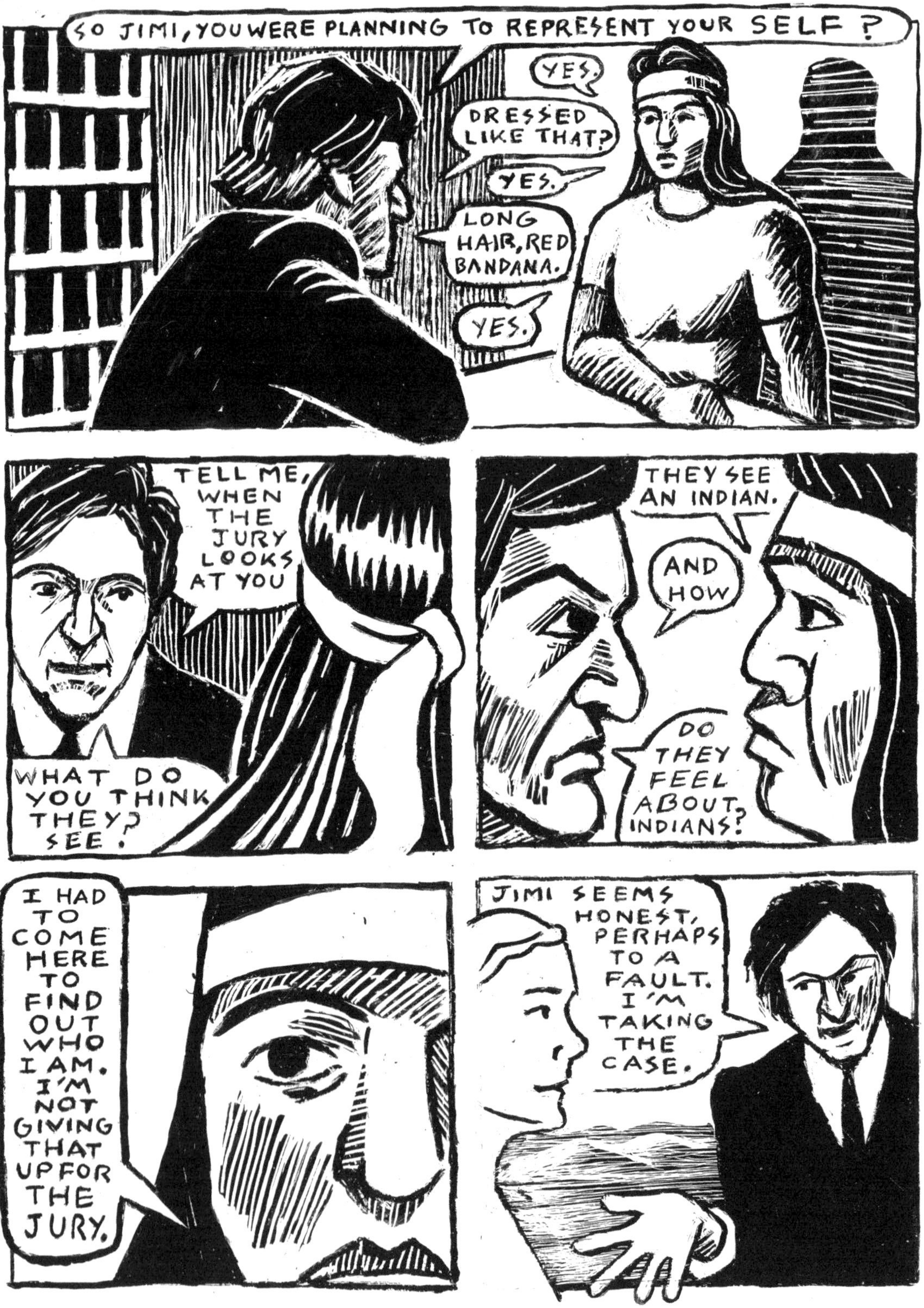
SO JIMI, YOU WERE PLANNING TO REPRESENT YOUR SELF?
YES.
DRESSED LIKE THAT?
YES.
LONG HAIR, RED BANDANA.
YES.
TELL ME, WHEN THE JURY LOOKS AT YOU
WHAT DO YOU THINK THEY SEE?
THEY SEE AN INDIAN.
AND HOW
DO THEY FEEL ABOUT INDIANS?
I HAD TO COME HERE TO FIND OUT WHO I AM. I'M NOT GIVING THAT UP FOR THE JURY.
JIMI SEEMS HONEST, PERHAPS TO A FAULT. I'M TAKING THE CASE.

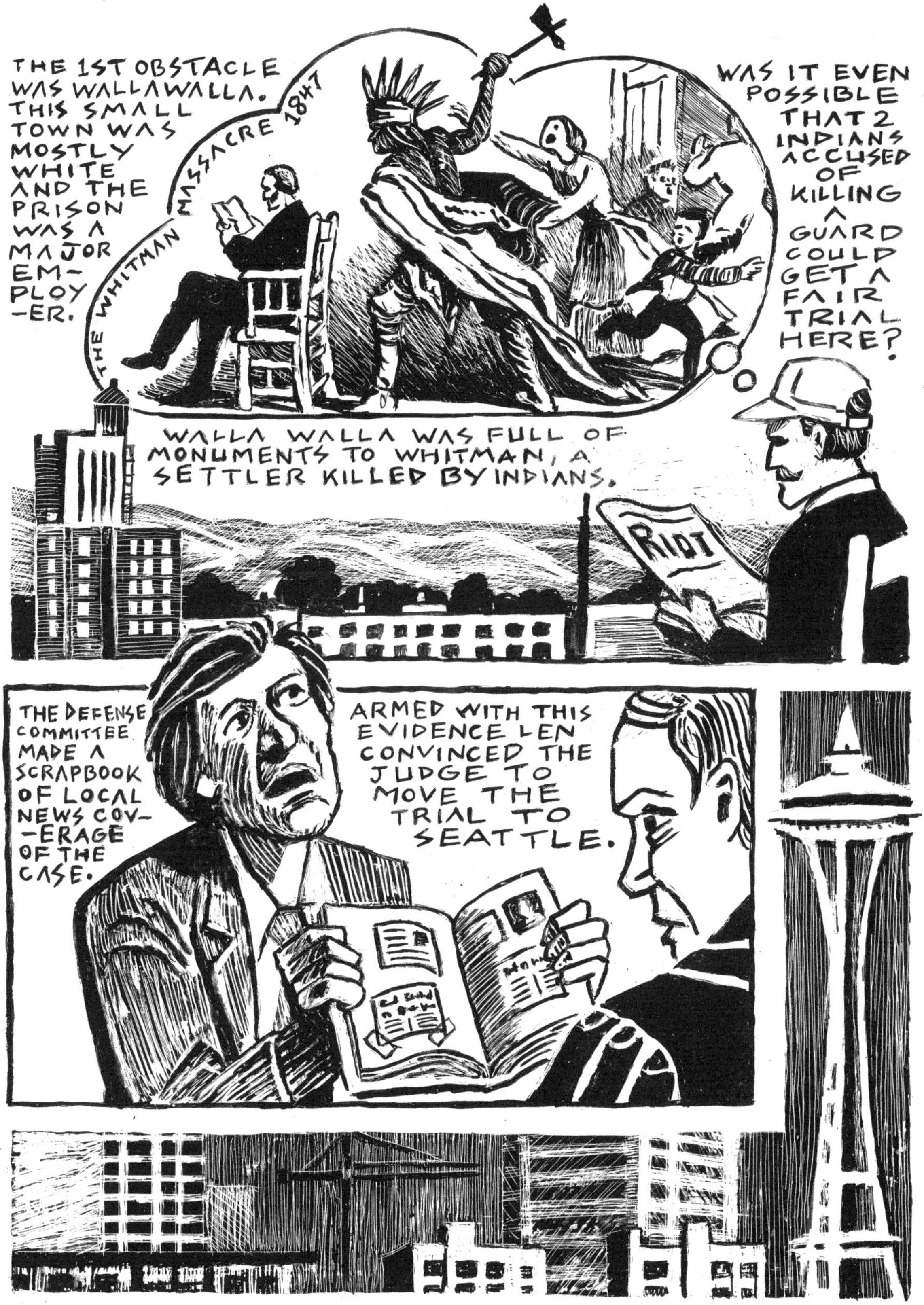
THE 1ST OBSTACLE WAS WALLAWALLA. THIS SMALL TOWN WAS MOSTLY WHITE AND THE PRISON WAS A MAJOR EM-PLOY-ER.
THE WHITMAN MASSACRE 1847
WAS IT EVEN POSSIBLE THAT 2 INDIANS ACCUSED OF KILLING A GUARD COULD GET A FAIR TRIAL HERE?
WALLA WALLA WAS FULL OF MONUMENTS TO WHITMAN, A SETTLER KILLED BY INDIANS.
RIOT
THE DEFENSE COMMITTEE MADE A SCRAPBOOK OF LOCAL NEWS COV--ERAGE OF THE CASE.
ARMED WITH THIS EVIDENCE LEN CONVINCED THE JUDGE TO MOVE THE TRIAL TO SEATTLE.

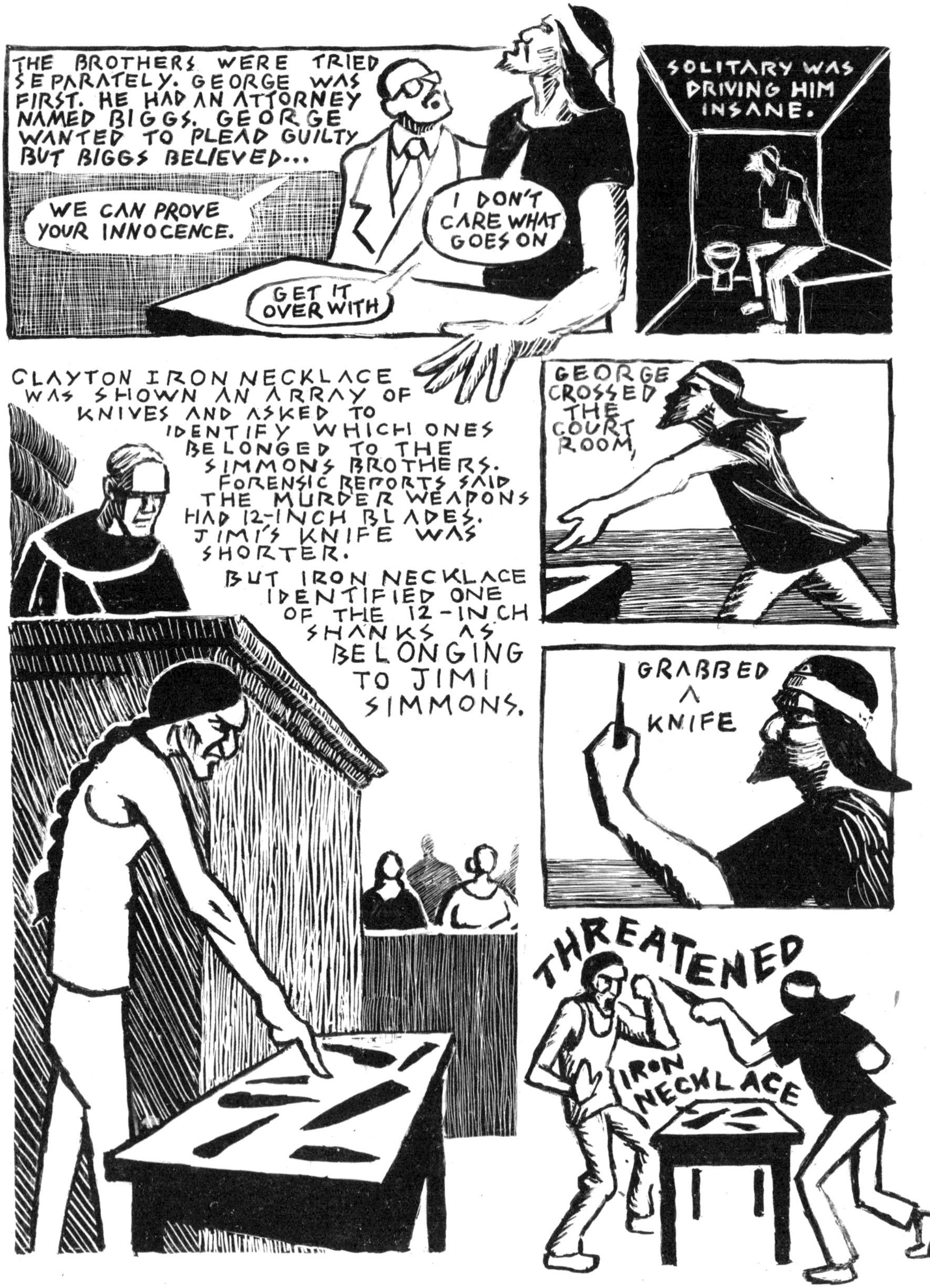
THE BROTHERS WERE TRIED SEPARATELY. GEORGE WAS FIRST. HE HAD AN ATTORNEY NAMED BIGGS. GEORGE WANTED TO PLEAD GUILTY BUT BIGGS BELIEVED...
WE CAN PROVE YOUR INNOCENCE.
I DON'T CARE WHAT GOES ON
GET IT OVER WITH
SOLITARY WAS DRIVING HIM INSANE.
CLAYTON IRON NECKLACE WAS SHOWN AN ARRAY OF KNIVES AND ASKED TO IDENTIFY WHICH ONES BELONGED TO THE SIMMONS BROTHERS.
FORENSIC REPORTS SAID THE MURDER WEAPONS HAD 12-INCH BLADES. JIMI'S KNIFE WAS SHORTER.
BUT IRON NECKLACE IDENTIFIED ONE OF THE 12-INCH SHANKS AS BELONGING TO JIMI SIMMONS.
GEORGE CROSSED THE COURT ROOM,
GRABBED A KNIFE
THREATENED
IRON NECKLACE

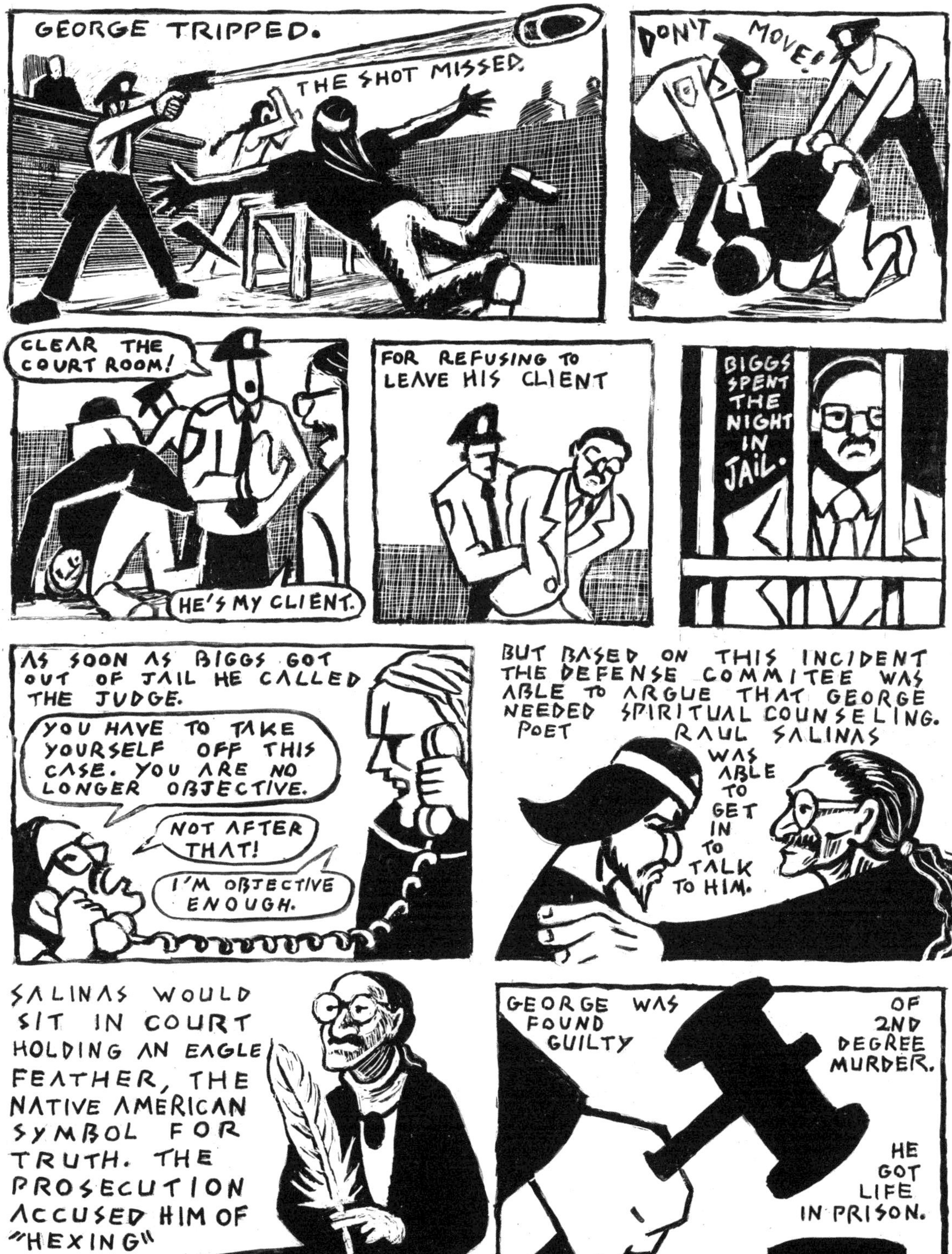
GEORGE TRIPPED.
THE SHOT MISSED.
DON'T MOVE!
CLEAR THE COURT ROOM!
HE'S MY CLIENT.
FOR REFUSING TO LEAVE HIS CLIENT
BIGGS SPENT THE NIGHT IN JAIL.
AS SOON AS BIGGS GOT OUT OF JAIL HE CALLED THE JUDGE.
YOU HAVE TO TAKE YOURSELF OFF THIS CASE. YOU ARE NO LONGER OBJECTIVE.
NOT AFTER THAT!
I'M OBJECTIVE ENOUGH.
BUT BASED ON THIS INCIDENT THE DEFENSE COMMITEE WAS ABLE TO ARGUE THAT GEORGE NEEDED SPIRITUAL COUNSELING.
POET RAUL SALINAS WAS ABLE TO GET IN TO TALK TO HIM.
SALINAS WOULD SIT IN COURT HOLDING AN EAGLE FEATHER, THE NATIVE AMERICAN SYMBOL FOR TRUTH. THE PROSECUTION ACCUSED HIM OF "HEXING" WITNESSES.
GEORGE WAS FOUND GUILTY OF 2ND DEGREE MURDER.
HE GOT LIFE IN PRISON.

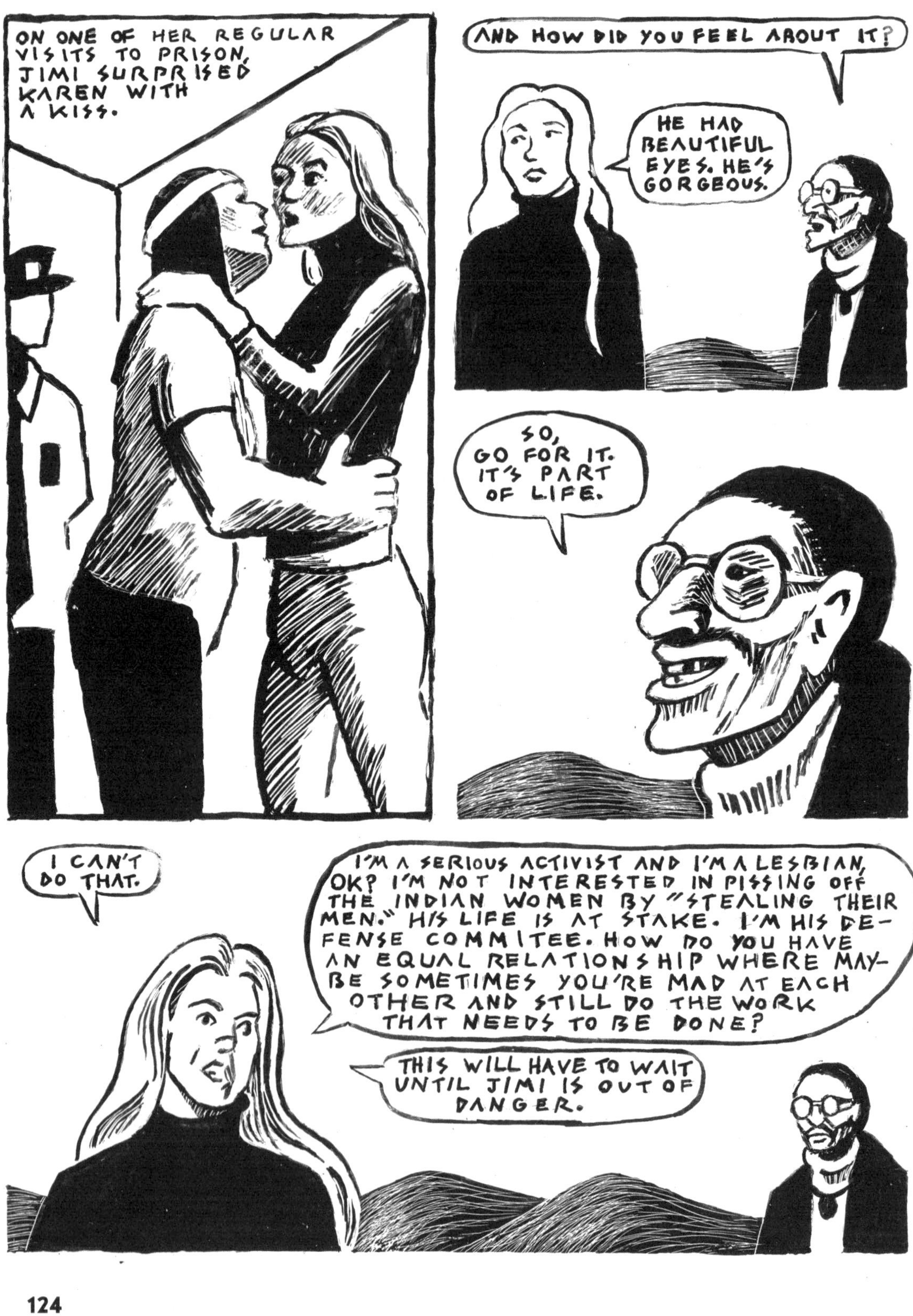
ON ONE OF HER REGULAR VISITS TO PRISON, JIMI SURPRISED KAREN WITH A KISS.
AND HOW DID YOU FEEL ABOUT IT?
HE HAD BEAUTIFUL EYES. HE'S GORGEOUS.
SO, GO FOR IT. IT'S PART OF LIFE.
I CAN'T DO THAT.
I'M A SERIOUS ACTIVIST AND I'M A LESBIAN, OK? I'M NOT INTERESTED IN PISSING OFF THE INDIAN WOMEN BY "STEALING THEIR MEN." HIS LIFE IS AT STAKE. I'M HIS DEFENSE COMMITEE. HOW DO YOU HAVE AN EQUAL RELATIONSHIP WHERE MAYBE SOMETIMES YOU'RE MAD AT EACH OTHER AND STILL DO THE WORK THAT NEEDS TO BE DONE?
THIS WILL HAVE TO WAIT UNTIL JIMI IS OUT OF DANGER.

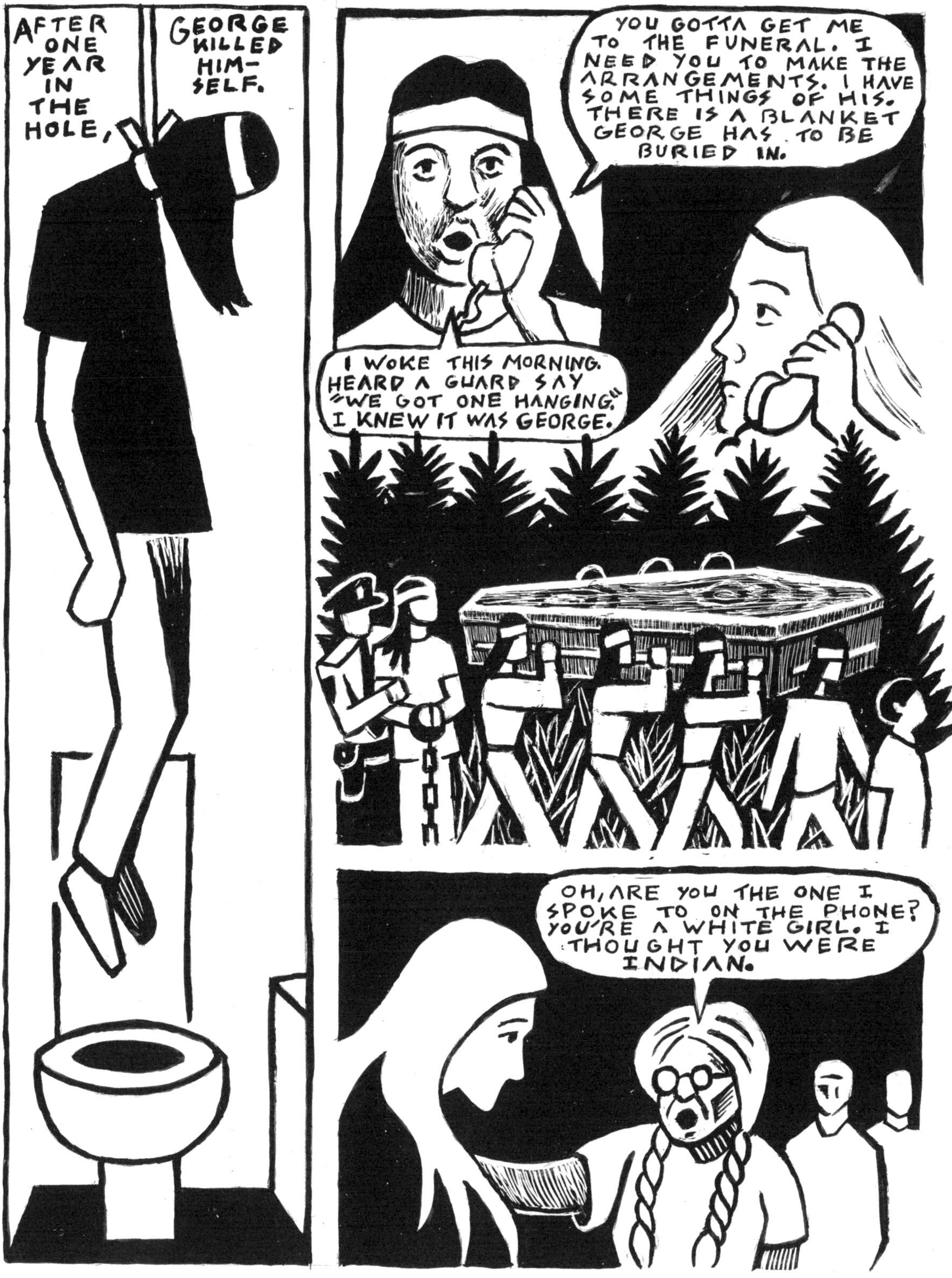
AFTER ONE YEAR IN THE HOLE,
GEORGE KILLED HIM-SELF.
YOU GOTTA GET ME TO THE FUNERAL. I NEED YOU TO MAKE THE ARRANGEMENTS. I HAVE SOME THINGS OF HIS. THERE IS A BLANKET GEORGE HAS TO BE BURIED IN.
I WOKE THIS MORNING. HEARD A GUARD SAY "WE GOT ONE HANGING." I KNEW IT WAS GEORGE.
OH, ARE YOU THE ONE I SPOKE TO ON THE PHONE? YOU'RE A WHITE GIRL. I THOUGHT YOU WERE INDIAN.

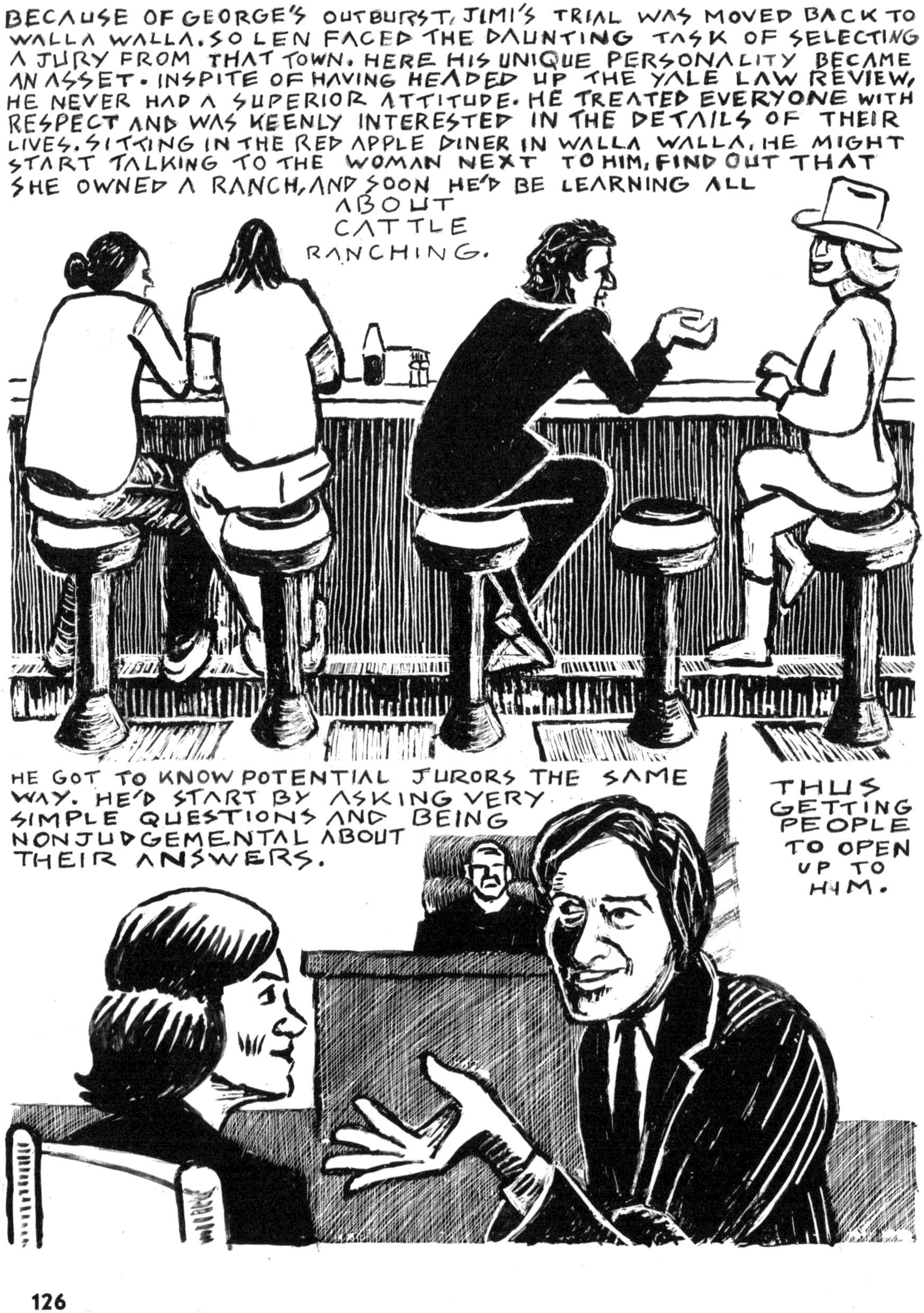
BECAUSE OF GEORGE'S OUTBURST, JIMI'S TRIAL WAS MOVED BACK TO WALLA WALLA. SO LEN FACED THE DAUNTING TASK OF SELECTING A JURY FROM THAT TOWN. HERE HIS UNIQUE PERSONALITY BECAME AN ASSET. INSPITE OF HAVING HEADED UP THE YALE LAW REVIEW, HE NEVER HAD A SUPERIOR ATTITUDE. HE TREATED EVERYONE WITH RESPECT AND WAS KEENLY INTERESTED IN THE DETAILS OF THEIR LIVES. SITTING IN THE RED APPLE DINER IN WALLA WALLA, HE MIGHT START TALKING TO THE WOMAN NEXT TO HIM, FIND OUT THAT SHE OWNED A RANCH, AND SOON HE'D BE LEARNING ALL ABOUT CATTLE RANCHING.
HE GOT TO KNOW POTENTIAL JURORS THE SAME WAY. HE'D START BY ASKING VERY SIMPLE QUESTIONS AND BEING NONJUDGEMENTAL ABOUT THEIR ANSWERS.
THUS GETTING PEOPLE TO OPEN UP TO HIM.

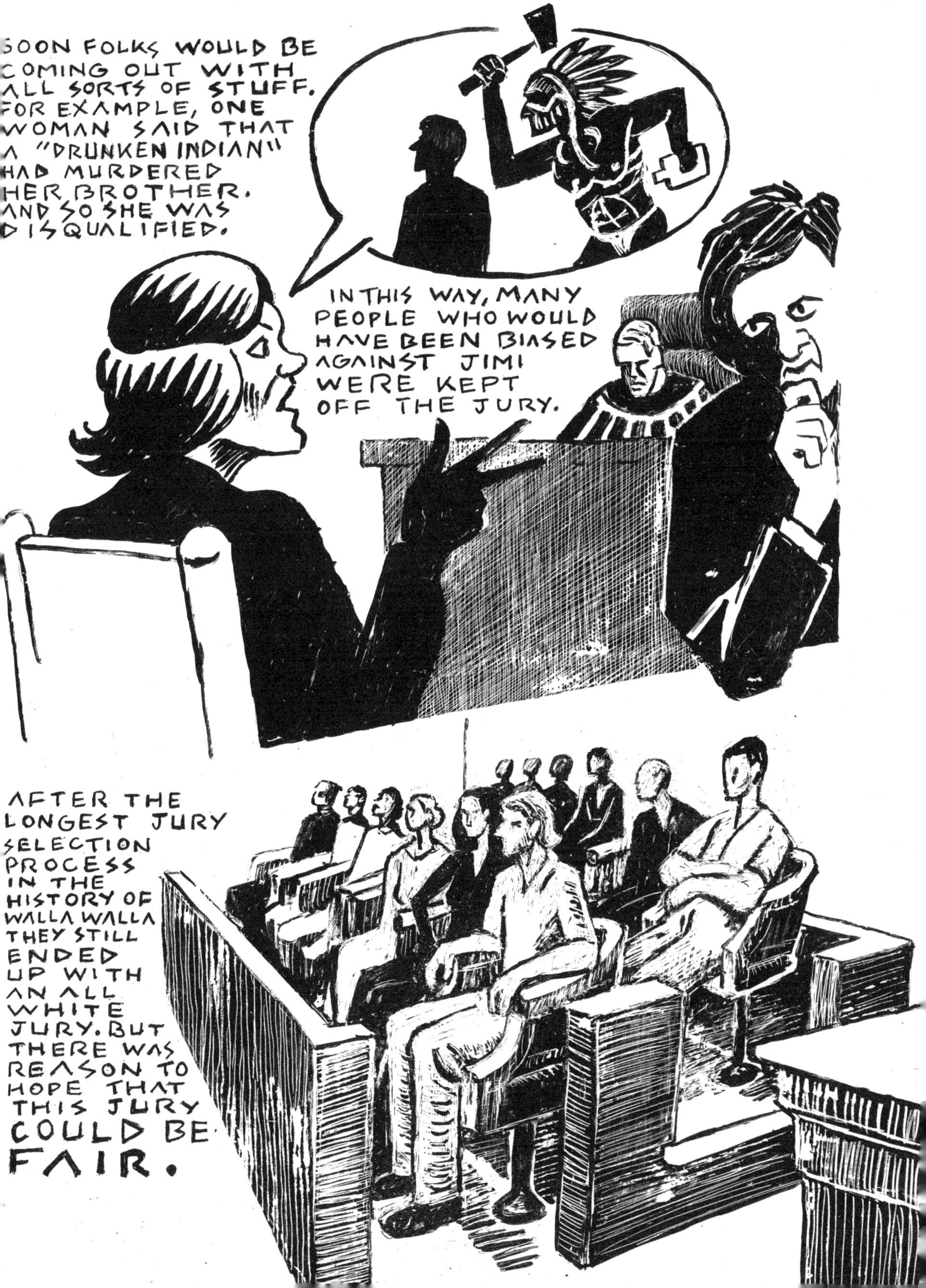
SOON FOLKS WOULD BE COMING OUT WITH ALL SORTS OF STUFF. FOR EXAMPLE, ONE WOMAN SAID THAT A "DRUNKEN INDIAN" HAD MURDERED HER BROTHER. AND SO SHE WAS DISQUALIFIED.
IN THIS WAY, MANY PEOPLE WHO WOULD HAVE BEEN BIASED AGAINST JIMI WERE KEPT OFF THE JURY.
AFTER THE LONGEST JURY SELECTION PROCESS IN THE HISTORY OF WALLA WALLA THEY STILL ENDED UP WITH AN ALL WHITE JURY. BUT THERE WAS REASON TO HOPE THAT THIS JURY COULD BE FAIR.

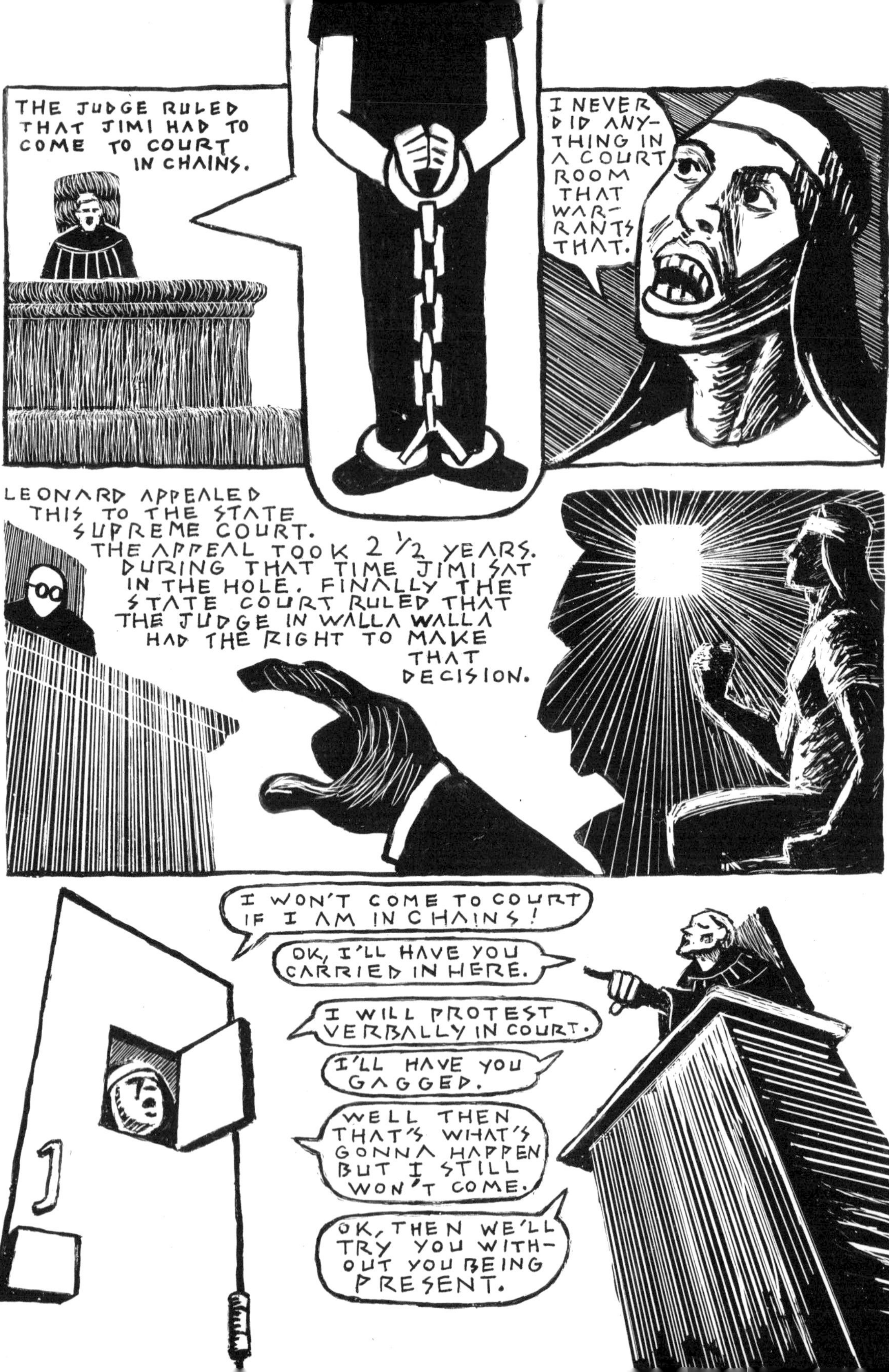
THE JUDGE RULED THAT JIMI HAD TO COME TO COURT IN CHAINS.
I NEVER DID ANYTHING IN A COURT ROOM THAT WARRANTS THAT.
LEONARD APPEALED THIS TO THE STATE SUPREME COURT. THE APPEAL TOOK 2 1/2 YEARS. DURING THAT TIME JIMI SAT IN THE HOLE. FINALLY THE STATE COURT RULED THAT THE JUDGE IN WALLA WALLA HAD THE RIGHT TO MAKE THAT DECISION.
I WON'T COME TO COURT IF I AM IN CHAINS!
OK, I'LL HAVE YOU CARRIED IN HERE.
I WILL PROTEST VERBALLY IN COURT.
I'LL HAVE YOU GAGGED.
WELL THEN THAT'S WHAT'S GONNA HAPPEN BUT I STILL WON'T COME.
OK, THEN WE'LL TRY YOU WITHOUT YOU BEING PRESENT.

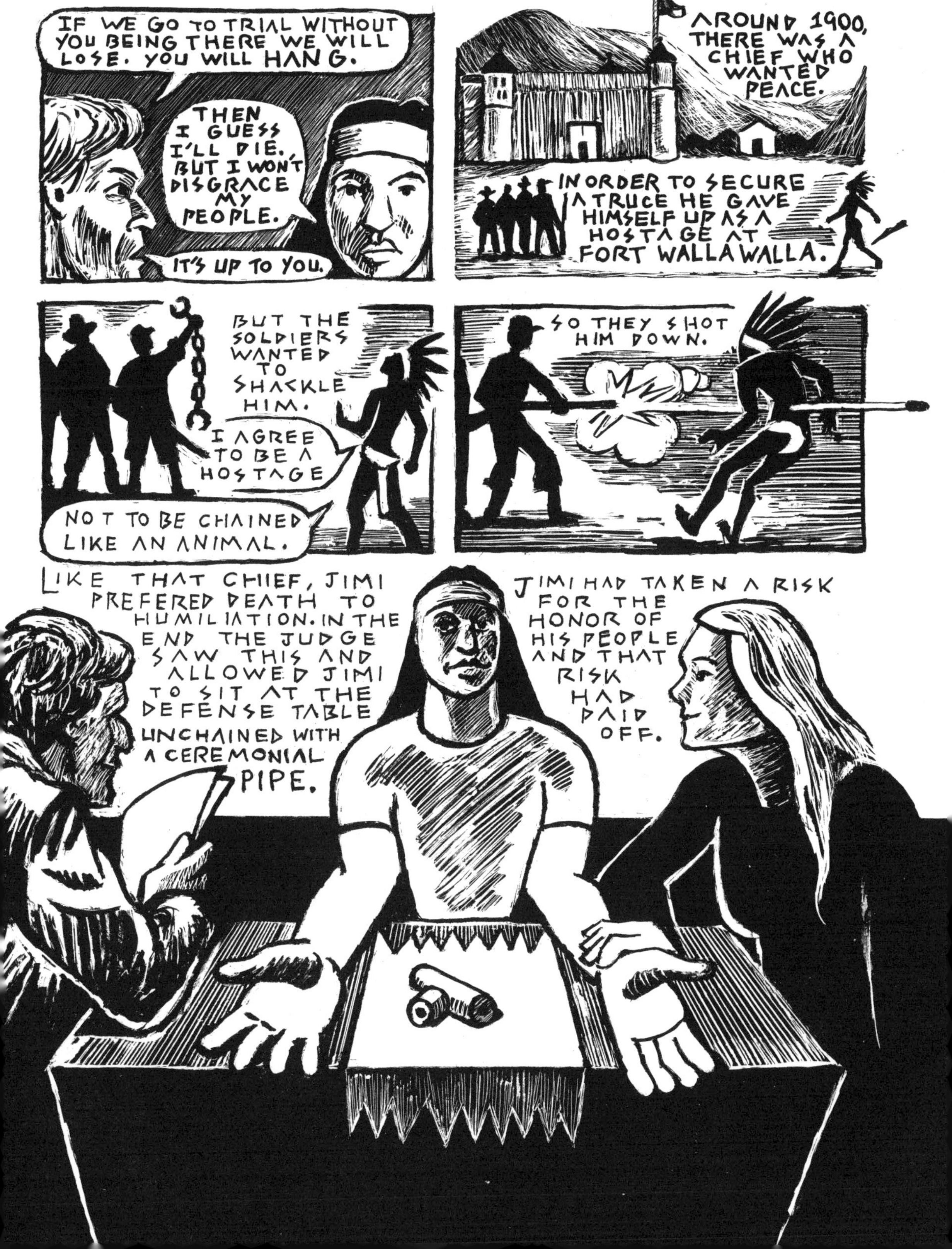
IF WE GO TO TRIAL WITHOUT YOU BEING THERE WE WILL LOSE. YOU WILL HANG.
THEN I GUESS I'LL DIE... BUT I WON'T DISGRACE MY PEOPLE.
IT'S UP TO YOU.
AROUND 1900, THERE WAS A CHIEF WHO WANTED PEACE.
IN ORDER TO SECURE A TRUCE HE GAVE HIMSELF UP AS A HOSTAGE AT FORT WALLA WALLA.
BUT THE SOLDIERS WANTED TO SHACKLE HIM.
I AGREE TO BE A HOSTAGE
NOT TO BE CHAINED LIKE AN ANIMAL.
SO THEY SHOT HIM DOWN.
LIKE THAT CHIEF, JIMI PREFERED DEATH TO HUMILIATION. IN THE END THE JUDGE SAW THIS AND ALLOWED JIMI TO SIT AT THE DEFENSE TABLE UNCHAINED WITH A CEREMONIAL PIPE.
JIMI HAD TAKEN A RISK FOR THE HONOR OF HIS PEOPLE AND THAT RISK HAD PAID OFF.

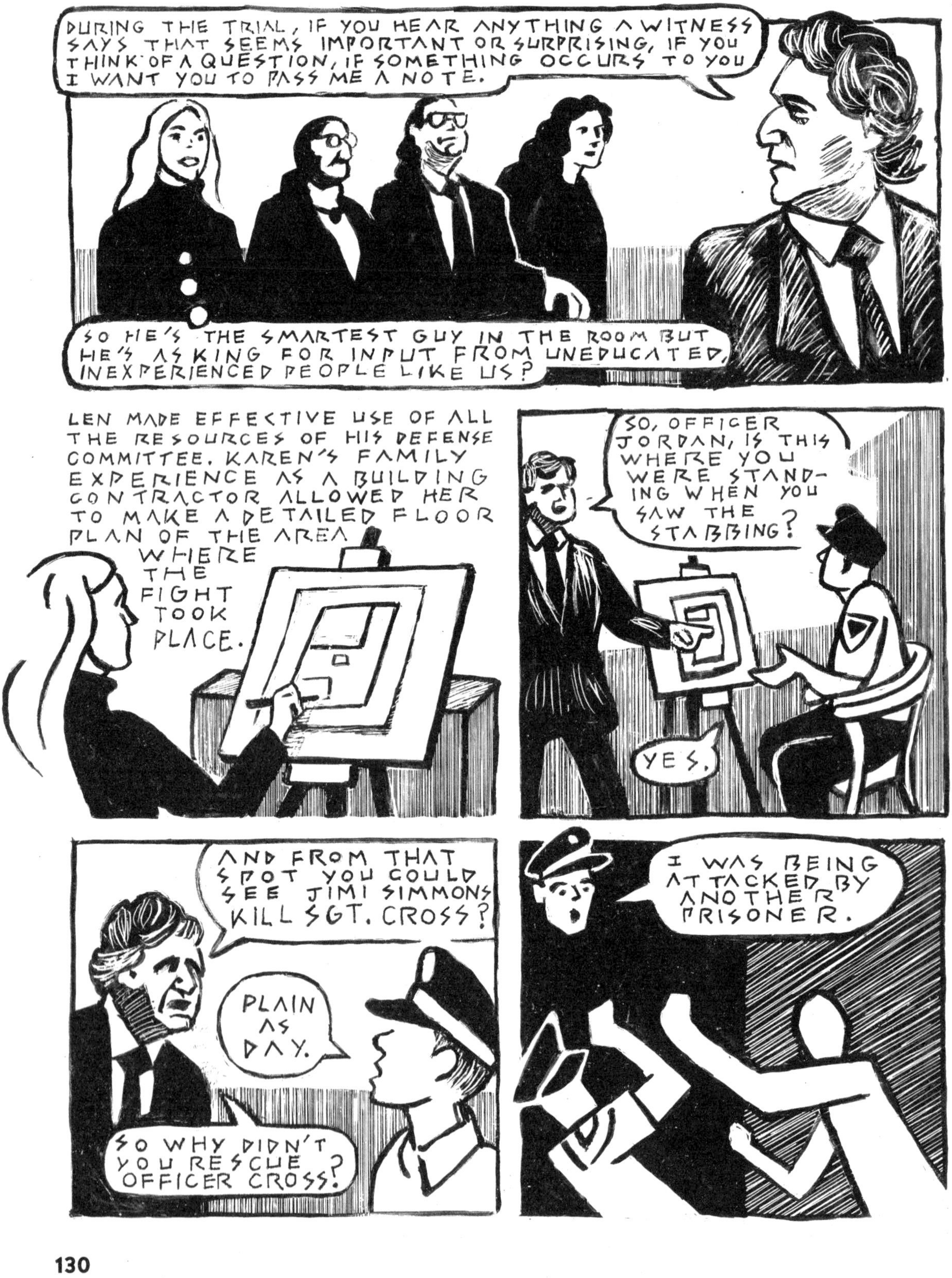
DURING THE TRIAL, IF YOU HEAR ANYTHING A WITNESS SAYS THAT SEEMS IMPORTANT OR SURPRISING, IF YOU THINK OF A QUESTION, IF SOMETHING OCCURS TO YOU I WANT YOU TO PASS ME A NOTE.
SO HE'S THE SMARTEST GUY IN THE ROOM BUT HE'S ASKING FOR INPUT FROM UNEDUCATED, INEXPERIENCED PEOPLE LIKE US?
LEN MADE EFFECTIVE USE OF ALL THE RESOURCES OF HIS DEFENSE COMMITTEE. KAREN'S FAMILY EXPERIENCE AS A BUILDING CONTRACTOR ALLOWED HER TO MAKE A DETAILED FLOOR PLAN OF THE AREA WHERE THE FIGHT TOOK PLACE.
SO, OFFICER JORDAN, IS THIS WHERE YOU WERE STANDING WHEN YOU SAW THE STABBING?
YES.
AND FROM THAT SPOT YOU COULD SEE JIMI SIMMONS KILL SGT. CROSS?
PLAIN AS DAY.
SO WHY DIDN'T YOU RESCUE OFFICER CROSS?
I WAS BEING ATTACKED BY ANOTHER PRISONER.

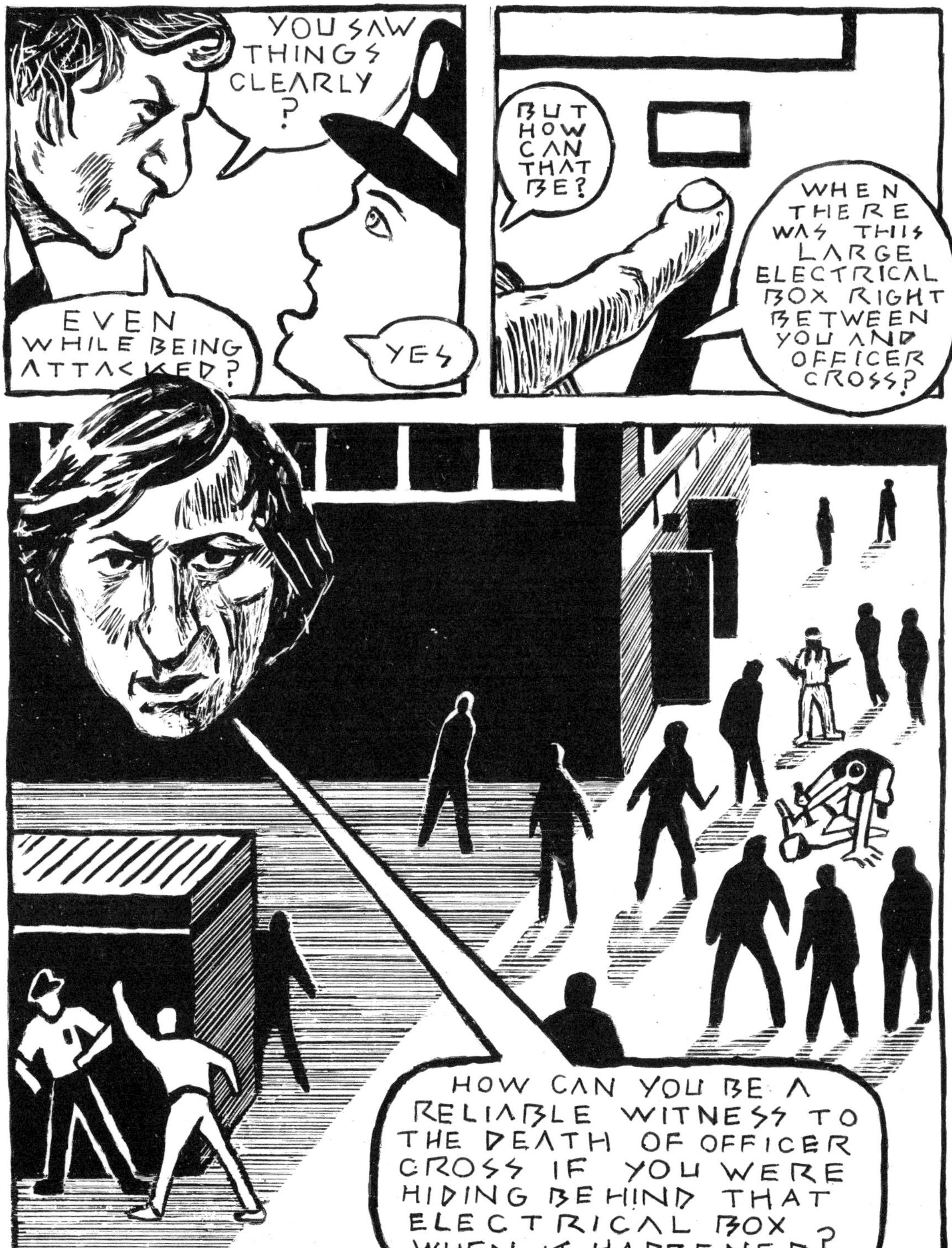
YOU SAW THINGS CLEARLY ?
EVEN WHILE BEING ATTACKED?
YES
BUT HOW CAN THAT BE?
WHEN THERE WAS THIS LARGE ELECTRICAL BOX RIGHT BETWEEN YOU AND OFFICER CROSS?
HOW CAN YOU BE A RELIABLE WITNESS TO THE DEATH OF OFFICER CROSS IF YOU WERE HIDING BEHIND THAT ELECTRICAL BOX WHEN IT HAPPENED?

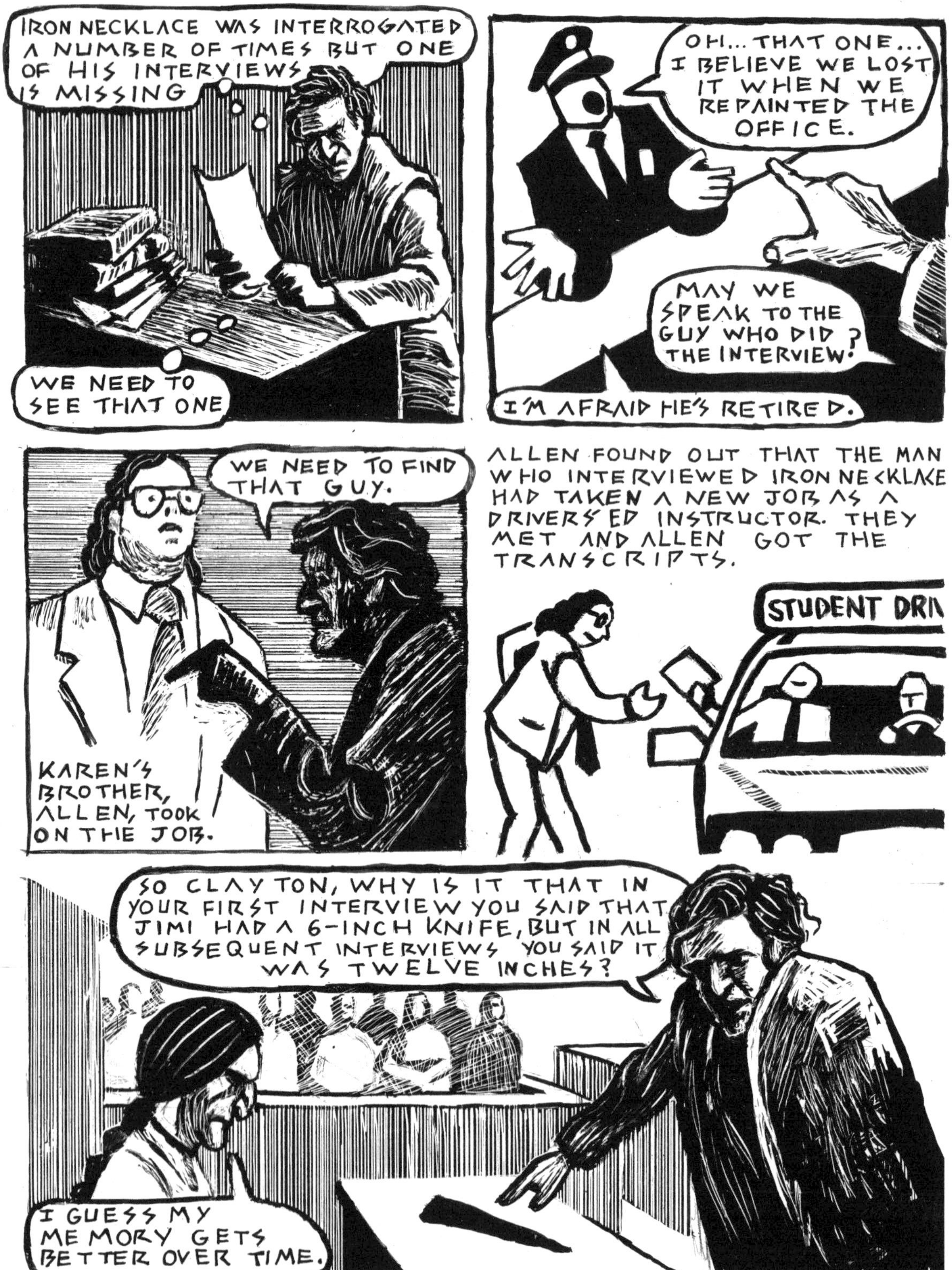
IRON NECKLACE WAS INTERROGATED A NUMBER OF TIMES BUT ONE OF HIS INTERVIEWS IS MISSING
WE NEED TO SEE THAT ONE
OH... THAT ONE... I BELIEVE WE LOST IT WHEN WE REPAINTED THE OFFICE.
MAY WE SPEAK TO THE GUY WHO DID THE INTERVIEW?
I'M AFRAID HE'S RETIRED.
WE NEED TO FIND THAT GUY.
KAREN'S BROTHER, ALLEN, TOOK ON THE JOB.
ALLEN FOUND OUT THAT THE MAN WHO INTERVIEWED IRON NECKLACE HAD TAKEN A NEW JOB AS A DRIVERS ED INSTRUCTOR. THEY MET AND ALLEN GOT THE TRANSCRIPTS.
STUDENT DRI
SO CLAYTON, WHY IS IT THAT IN YOUR FIRST INTERVIEW YOU SAID THAT JIMI HAD A 6-INCH KNIFE, BUT IN ALL SUBSEQUENT INTERVIEWS YOU SAID IT WAS TWELVE INCHES?
I GUESS MY MEMORY GETS BETTER OVER TIME.

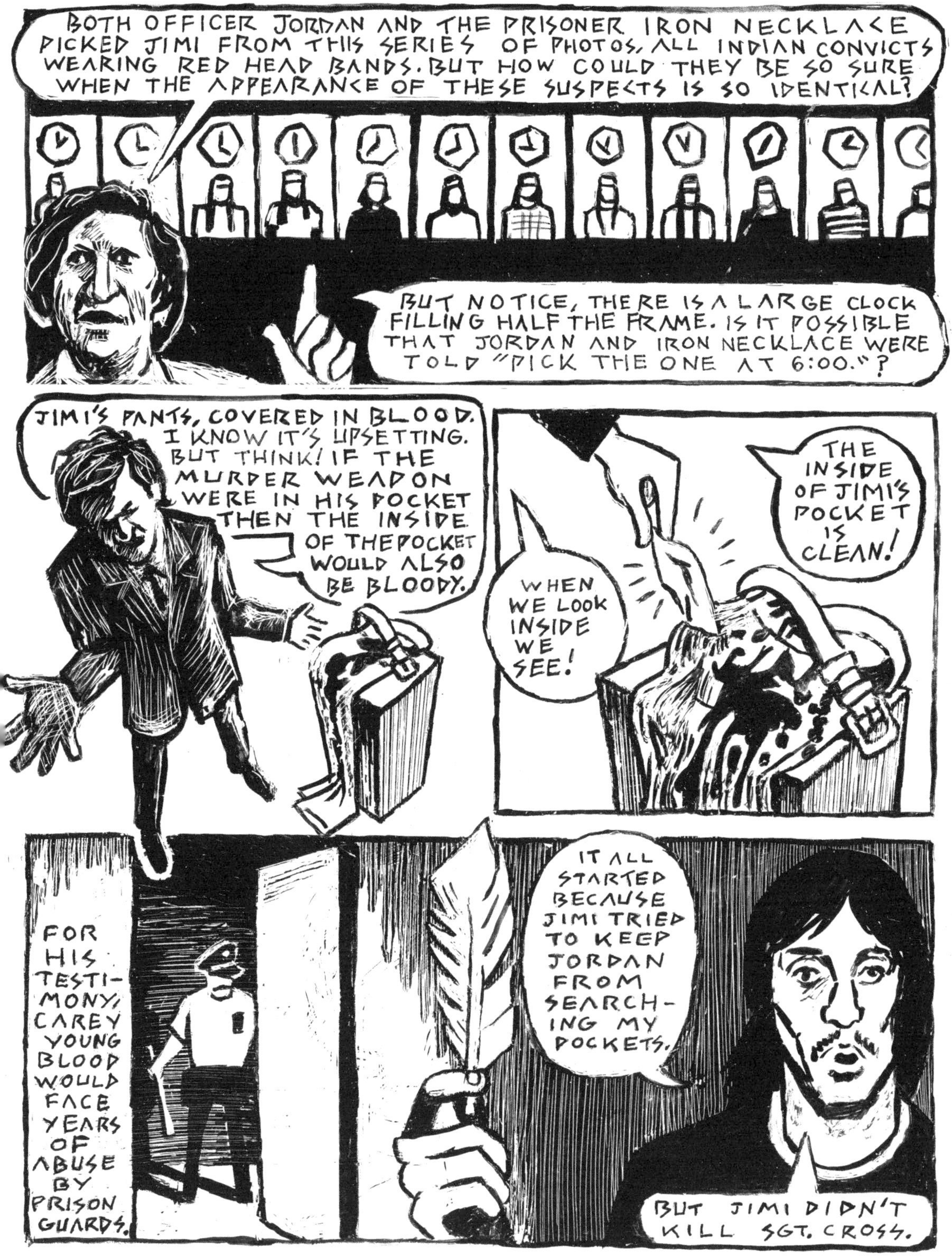
BOTH OFFICER JORDAN AND THE PRISONER IRON NECKLACE PICKED JIMI FROM THIS SERIES OF PHOTOS, ALL INDIAN CONVICTS WEARING RED HEAD BANDS. BUT HOW COULD THEY BE SO SURE WHEN THE APPEARANCE OF THESE SUSPECTS IS SO IDENTICAL?
BUT NOTICE, THERE IS A LARGE CLOCK FILLING HALF THE FRAME. IS IT POSSIBLE THAT JORDAN AND IRON NECKLACE WERE TOLD "PICK THE ONE AT 6:00."?
JIMI'S PANTS, COVERED IN BLOOD. I KNOW IT'S UPSETTING. BUT THINK! IF THE MURDER WEAPON WERE IN HIS POCKET THEN THE INSIDE OF THE POCKET WOULD ALSO BE BLOODY.
WHEN WE LOOK INSIDE WE SEE!
THE INSIDE OF JIMI'S POCKET IS CLEAN!
FOR HIS TESTIMONY, CAREY YOUNG BLOOD WOULD FACE YEARS OF ABUSE BY PRISON GUARDS.
IT ALL STARTED BECAUSE JIMI TRIED TO KEEP JORDAN FROM SEARCHING MY POCKETS.
BUT JIMI DIDN'T KILL SGT. CROSS.

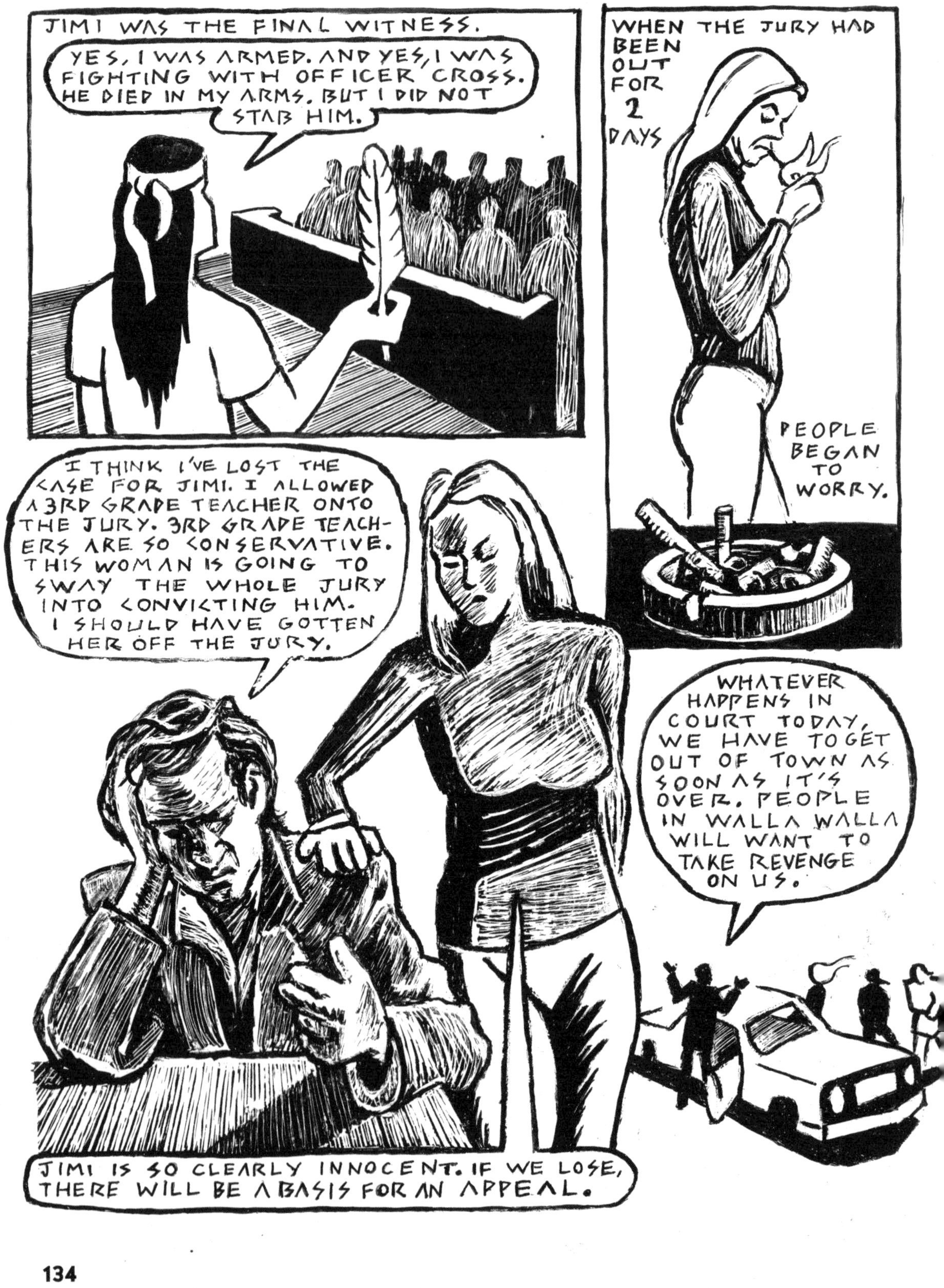
JIMI WAS THE FINAL WITNESS.
YES, I WAS ARMED. AND YES, I WAS FIGHTING WITH OFFICER CROSS. HE DIED IN MY ARMS, BUT I DID NOT STAB HIM.
WHEN THE JURY HAD BEEN OUT FOR 2 DAYS
PEOPLE BEGAN TO WORRY.
I THINK I'VE LOST THE CASE FOR JIMI. I ALLOWED A 3RD GRADE TEACHER ONTO THE JURY. 3RD GRADE TEACHERS ARE SO CONSERVATIVE. THIS WOMAN IS GOING TO SWAY THE WHOLE JURY INTO CONVICTING HIM. I SHOULD HAVE GOTTEN HER OFF THE JURY.
WHATEVER HAPPENS IN COURT TODAY, WE HAVE TO GET OUT OF TOWN AS SOON AS IT'S OVER. PEOPLE IN WALLA WALLA WILL WANT TO TAKE REVENGE ON US.
JIMI IS SO CLEARLY INNOCENT. IF WE LOSE, THERE WILL BE A BASIS FOR AN APPEAL.

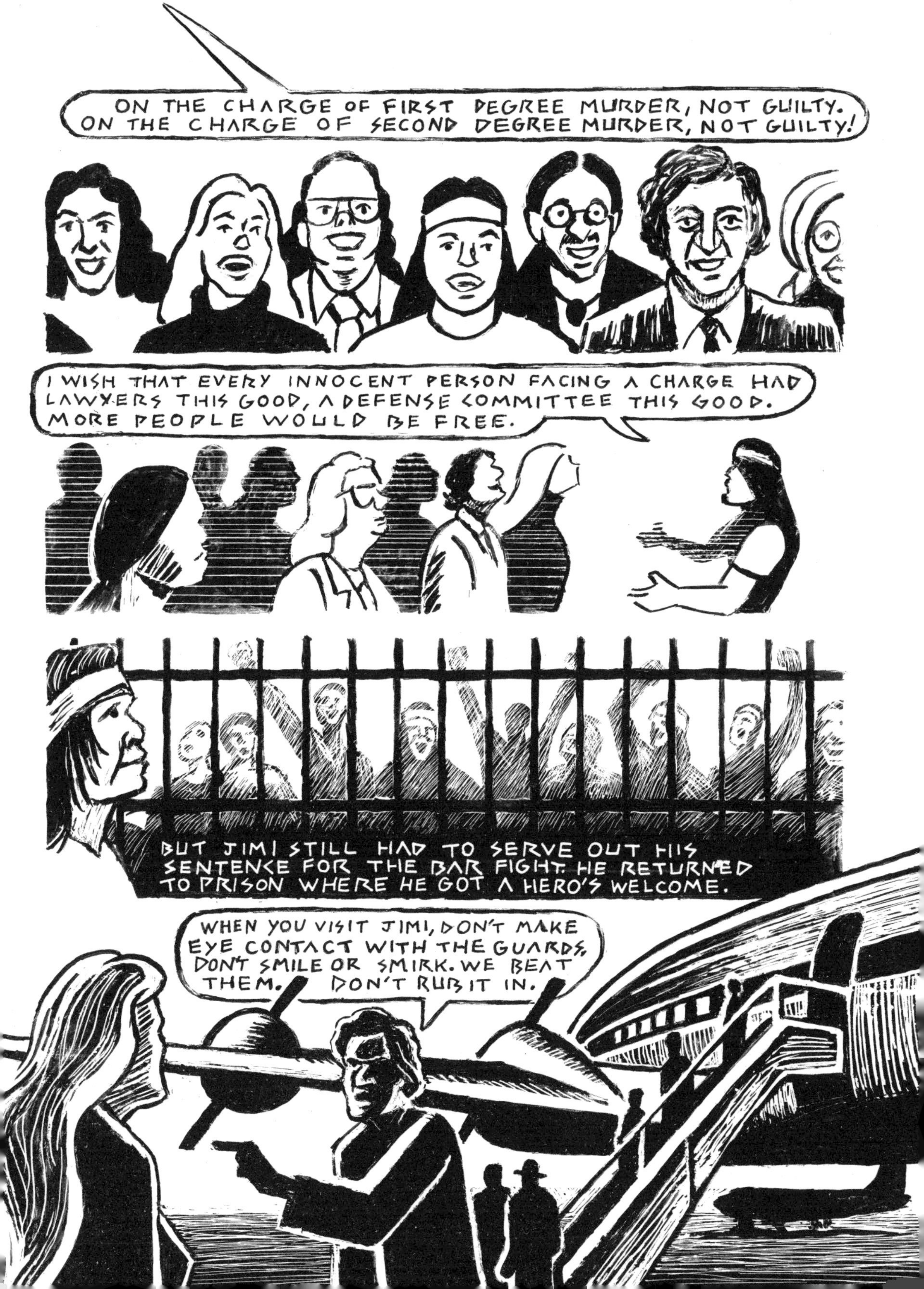
ON THE CHARGE OF FIRST DEGREE MURDER, NOT GUILTY. ON THE CHARGE OF SECOND DEGREE MURDER, NOT GUILTY!
I WISH THAT EVERY INNOCENT PERSON FACING A CHARGE HAD LAWYERS THIS GOOD, A DEFENSE COMMITTEE THIS GOOD. MORE PEOPLE WOULD BE FREE.
BUT JIMI STILL HAD TO SERVE OUT HIS SENTENCE FOR THE BAR FIGHT. HE RETURNED TO PRISON WHERE HE GOT A HERO'S WELCOME.
WHEN YOU VISIT JIMI, DON'T MAKE EYE CONTACT WITH THE GUARDS, DON'T SMILE OR SMIRK. WE BEAT THEM. DON'T RUB IT IN.

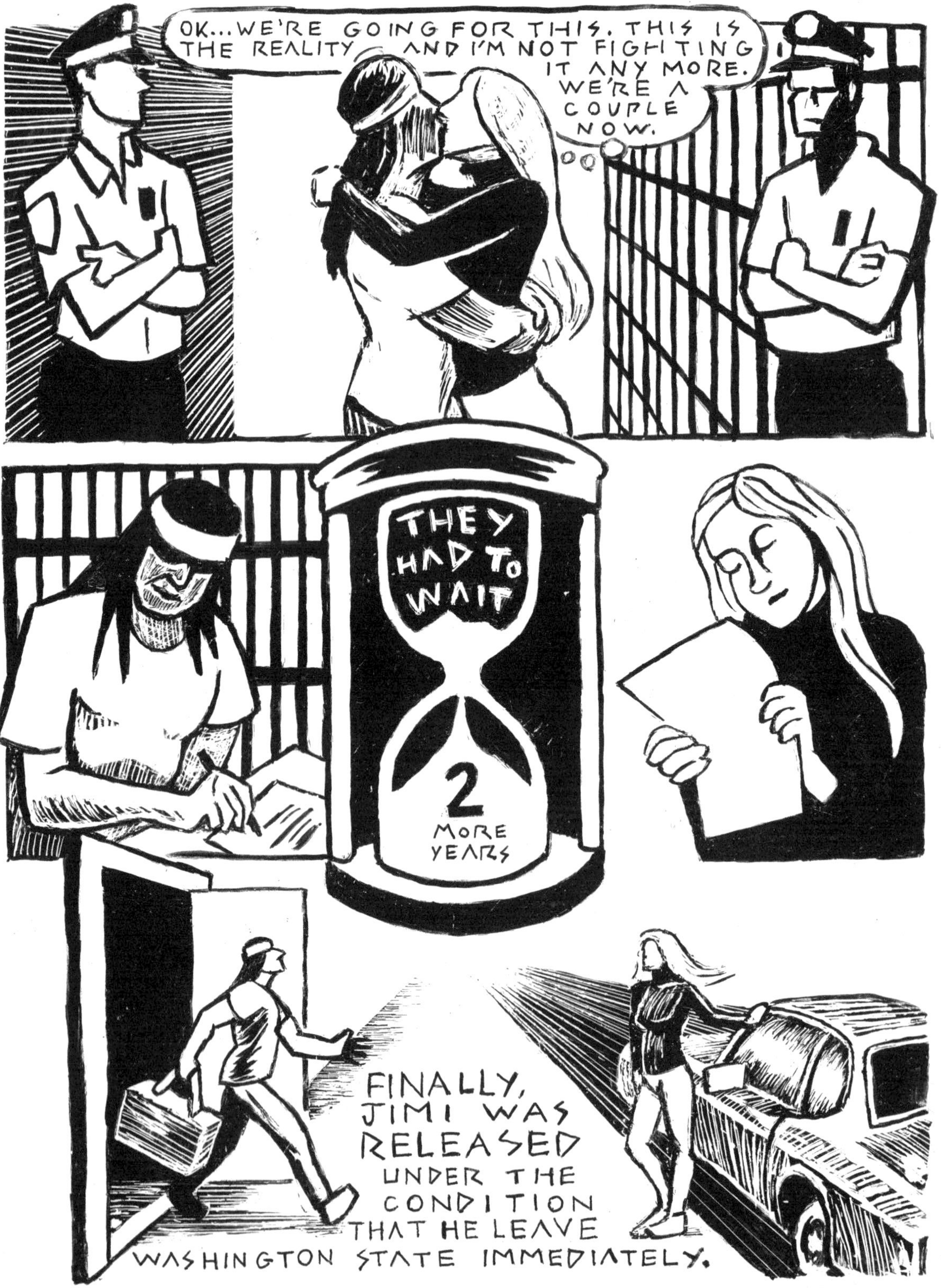
OK... WE'RE GOING FOR THIS. THIS IS THE REALITY AND I'M NOT FIGHTING IT ANY MORE. WE'RE A COUPLE NOW.
THEY HAD TO WAIT
2 MORE YEARS
FINALLY, JIMI WAS RELEASED UNDER THE CONDITION THAT HE LEAVE WASHINGTON STATE IMMEDIATELY.

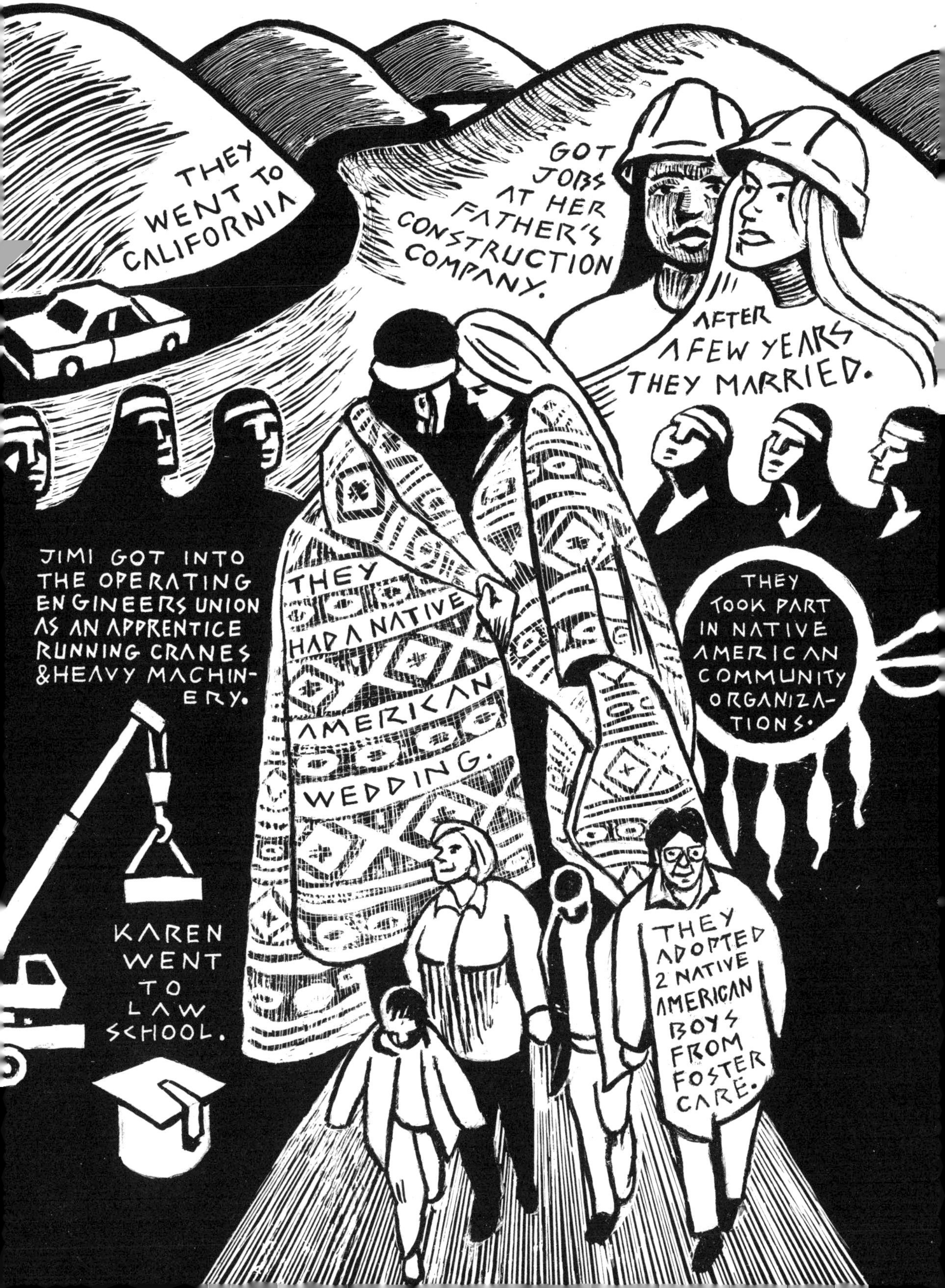
THEY WENT TO CALIFORNIA
GOT JOBS AT HER FATHER'S CONSTRUCTION COMPANY.
AFTER A FEW YEARS THEY MARRIED.
JIMI GOT INTO THE OPERATING ENGINEERS UNION AS AN APPRENTICE RUNNING CRANES &HEAVY MACHIN-ERY.
THEY HAD A NATIVE AMERICAN WEDDING.
THEY TOOK PART IN NATIVE AMERICAN COMMUNITY ORGANIZA-TIONS.
KAREN WENT TO LAW SCHOOL.
THEY ADOPTED 2 NATIVE AMERICAN BOYS FROM FOSTER CARE.

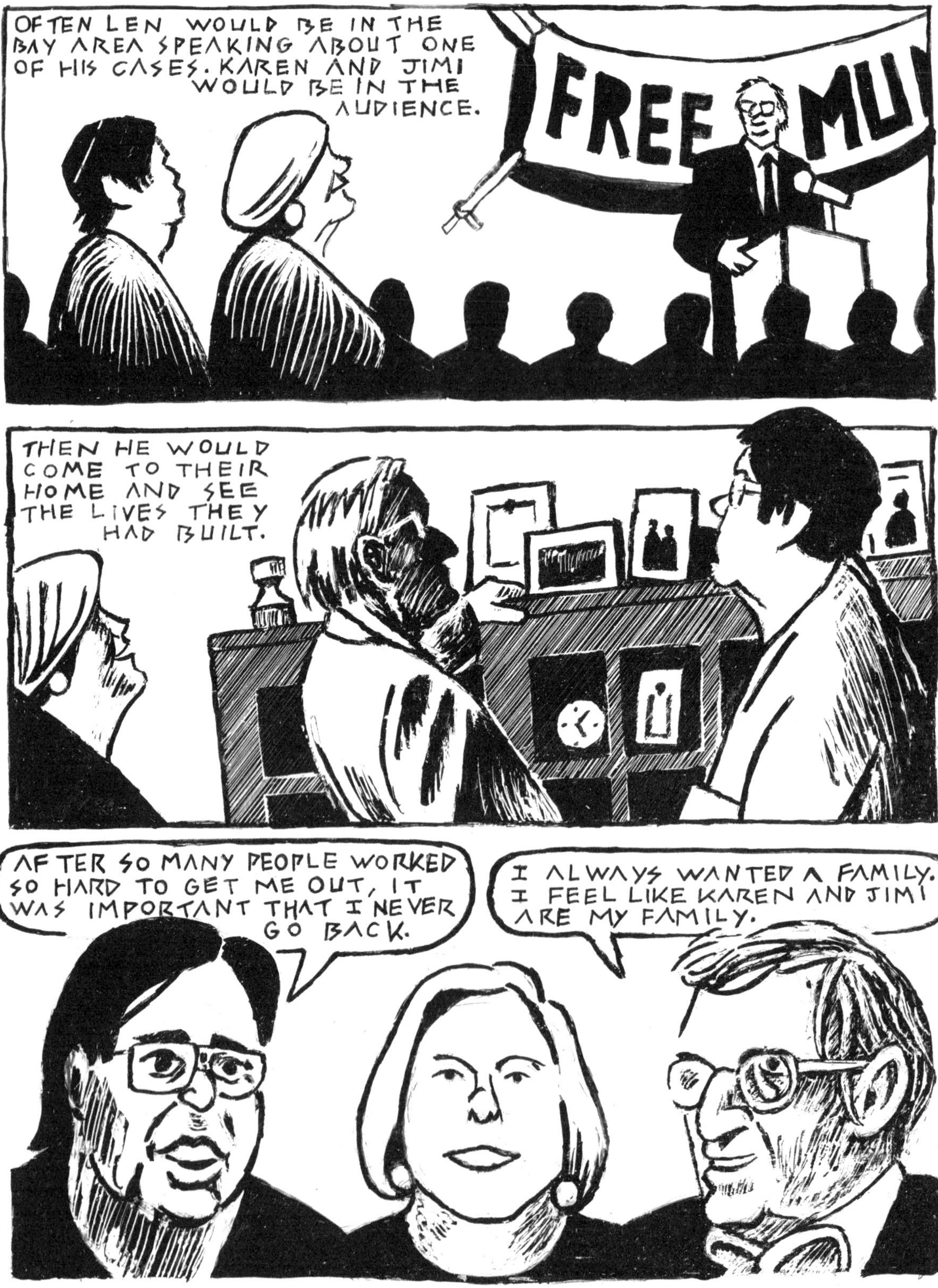

OFTEN LEN WOULD BE IN THE BAY AREA SPEAKING ABOUT ONE OF HIS CASES. KAREN AND JIMI WOULD BE IN THE AUDIENCE.
FREE MU
THEN HE WOULD COME TO THEIR HOME AND SEE THE LIVES THEY HAD BUILT.
AFTER SO MANY PEOPLE WORKED SO HARD TO GET ME OUT, IT WAS IMPORTANT THAT I NEVER GO BACK.
I ALWAYS WANTED A FAMILY. I FEEL LIKE KAREN AND JIMI ARE MY FAMILY.

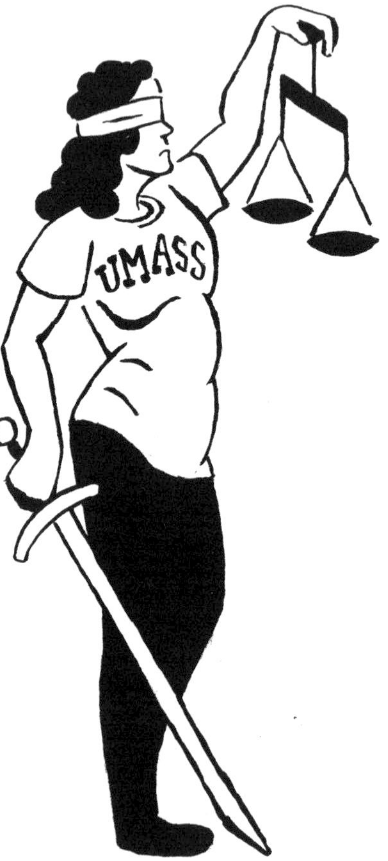
UMASS

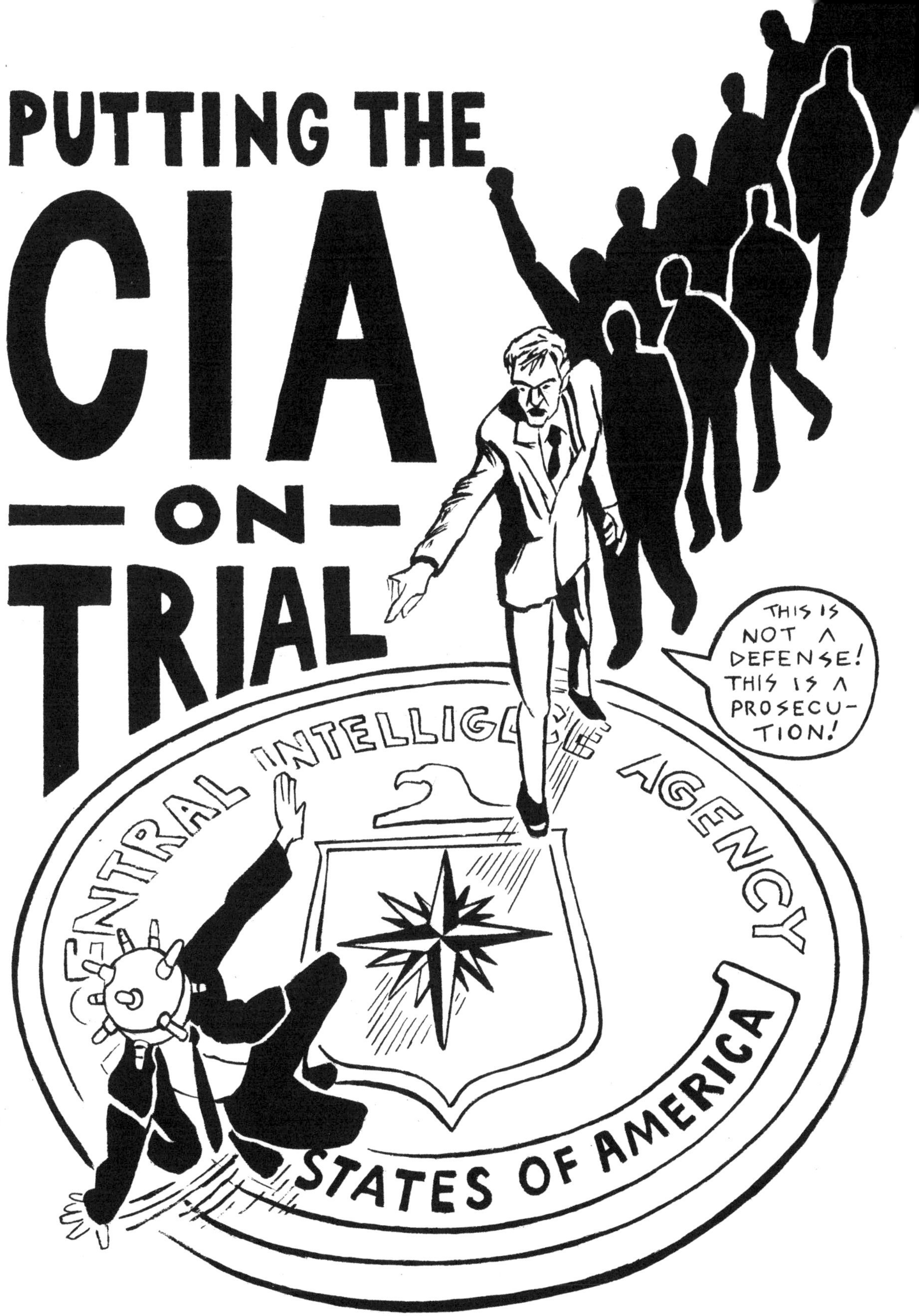
PUTTING THE
CIA
— ON —
TRIAL
CENTRAL INTELLIGENCE AGENCY
STATES OF AMERICA
THIS IS NOT A DEFENSE! THIS IS A PROSECUTION!

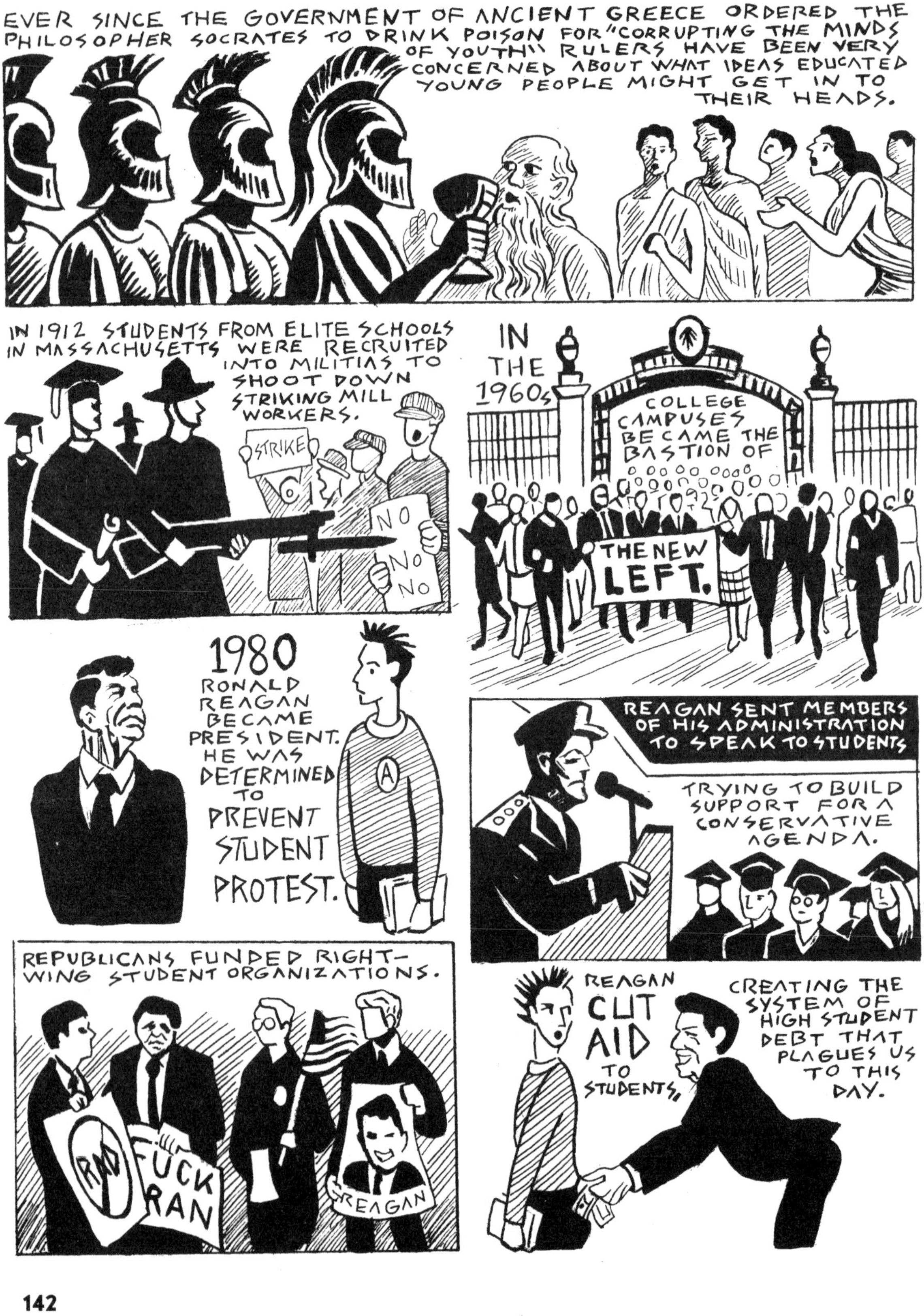
EVER SINCE THE GOVERNMENT OF ANCIENT GREECE ORDERED THE PHILOSOPHER SOCRATES TO DRINK POISON FOR "CORRUPTING THE MINDS OF YOUTH" RULERS HAVE BEEN VERY CONCERNED ABOUT WHAT IDEAS EDUCATED YOUNG PEOPLE MIGHT GET IN TO THEIR HEADS.
IN 1912 STUDENTS FROM ELITE SCHOOLS IN MASSACHUSETTS WERE RECRUITED INTO MILITIAS TO SHOOT DOWN STRIKING MILL WORKERS.
STRIKE
NO NO NO
IN THE 1960s COLLEGE CAMPUSES BECAME THE BASTION OF
THE NEW LEFT.
1980 RONALD REAGAN BECAME PRESIDENT. HE WAS DETERMINED TO PREVENT STUDENT PROTEST.
A
REAGAN SENT MEMBERS OF HIS ADMINISTRATION TO SPEAK TO STUDENTS
TRYING TO BUILD SUPPORT FOR A CONSERVATIVE AGENDA.
REPUBLICANS FUNDED RIGHT-WING STUDENT ORGANIZATIONS.
FUCK RAN
REAGAN
REAGAN CUT AID TO STUDENTS,
CREATING THE SYSTEM OF HIGH STUDENT DEBT THAT PLAGUES US TO THIS DAY.

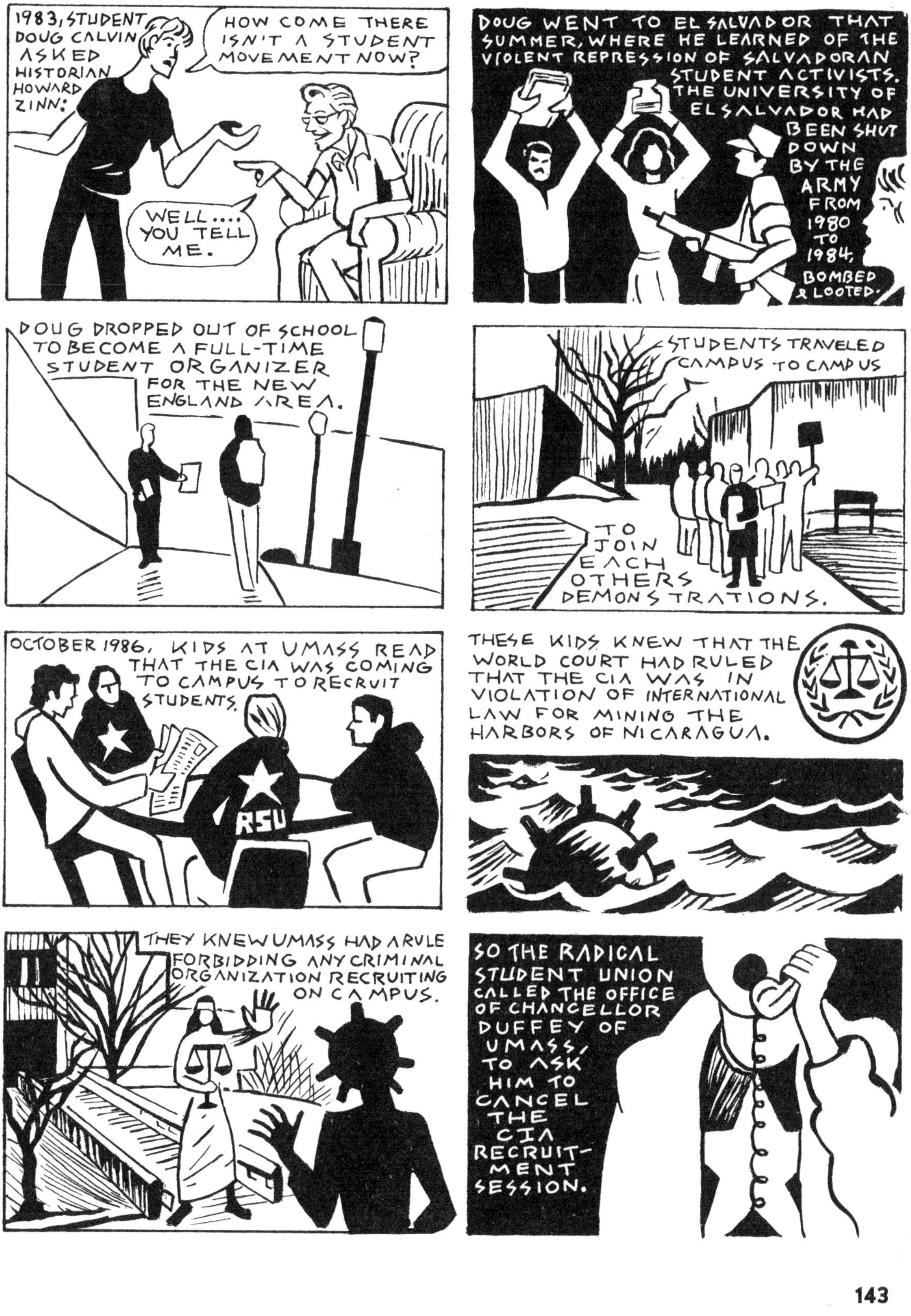
1983, STUDENT DOUG CALVIN ASKED HISTORIAN HOWARD ZINN:
HOW COME THERE ISN'T A STUDENT MOVEMENT NOW?
WELL.... YOU TELL ME.
DOUG WENT TO EL SALVADOR THAT SUMMER, WHERE HE LEARNED OF THE VIOLENT REPRESSION OF SALVADORAN STUDENT ACTIVISTS. THE UNIVERSITY OF EL SALVADOR HAD BEEN SHUT DOWN BY THE ARMY FROM 1980 TO 1984, BOMBED & LOOTED.
DOUG DROPPED OUT OF SCHOOL TO BECOME A FULL-TIME STUDENT ORGANIZER FOR THE NEW ENGLAND AREA.
STUDENTS TRAVELED CAMPUS TO CAMPUS
TO JOIN EACH OTHERS DEMONSTRATIONS.
OCTOBER 1986, KIDS AT UMASS READ THAT THE CIA WAS COMING TO CAMPUS TO RECRUIT STUDENTS.
RSU
THESE KIDS KNEW THAT THE WORLD COURT HAD RULED THAT THE CIA WAS IN VIOLATION OF INTERNATIONAL LAW FOR MINING THE HARBORS OF NICARAGUA.
THEY KNEW UMASS HAD A RULE FORBIDDING ANY CRIMINAL ORGANIZATION RECRUITING ON CAMPUS.
SO THE RADICAL STUDENT UNION CALLED THE OFFICE OF CHANCELLOR DUFFEY OF UMASS, TO ASK HIM TO CANCEL THE CIA RECRUITMENT SESSION.

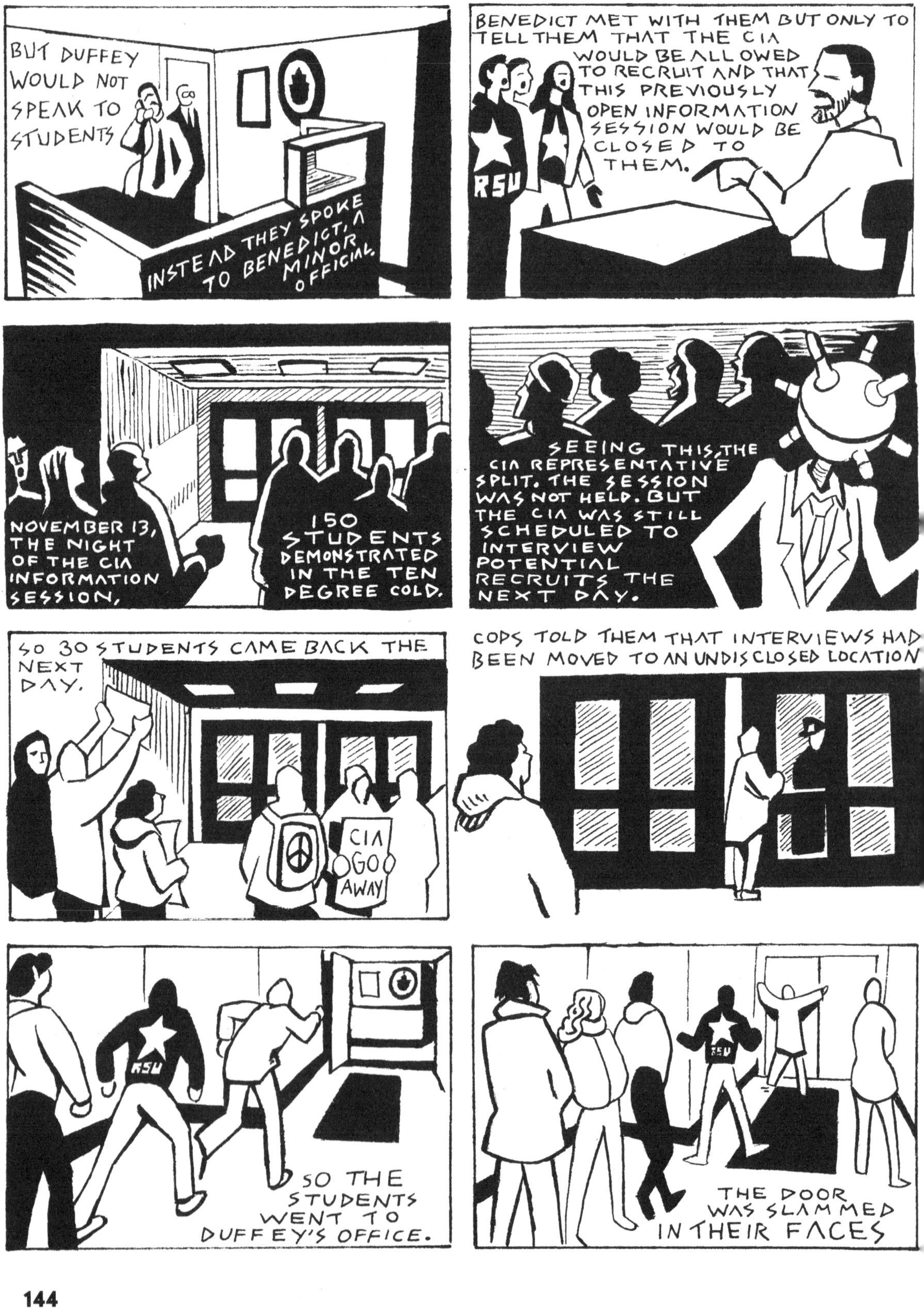
BUT DUFFEY WOULD NOT SPEAK TO STUDENTS
INSTEAD THEY SPOKE TO BENEDICT, A MINOR OFFICIAL.
BENEDICT MET WITH THEM BUT ONLY TO TELL THEM THAT THE CIA WOULD BE ALLOWED TO RECRUIT AND THAT THIS PREVIOUSLY OPEN INFORMATION SESSION WOULD BE CLOSED TO THEM.
RSU
NOVEMBER 13, THE NIGHT OF THE CIA INFORMATION SESSION,
150 STUDENTS DEMONSTRATED IN THE TEN DEGREE COLD.
SEEING THIS, THE CIA REPRESENTATIVE SPLIT. THE SESSION WAS NOT HELD. BUT THE CIA WAS STILL SCHEDULED TO INTERVIEW POTENTIAL RECRUITS THE NEXT DAY.
SO 30 STUDENTS CAME BACK THE NEXT DAY.
CIA GO AWAY
COPS TOLD THEM THAT INTERVIEWS HAD BEEN MOVED TO AN UNDISCLOSED LOCATION
RSU
SO THE STUDENTS WENT TO DUFFEY'S OFFICE.
RSU
THE DOOR WAS SLAMMED IN THEIR FACES

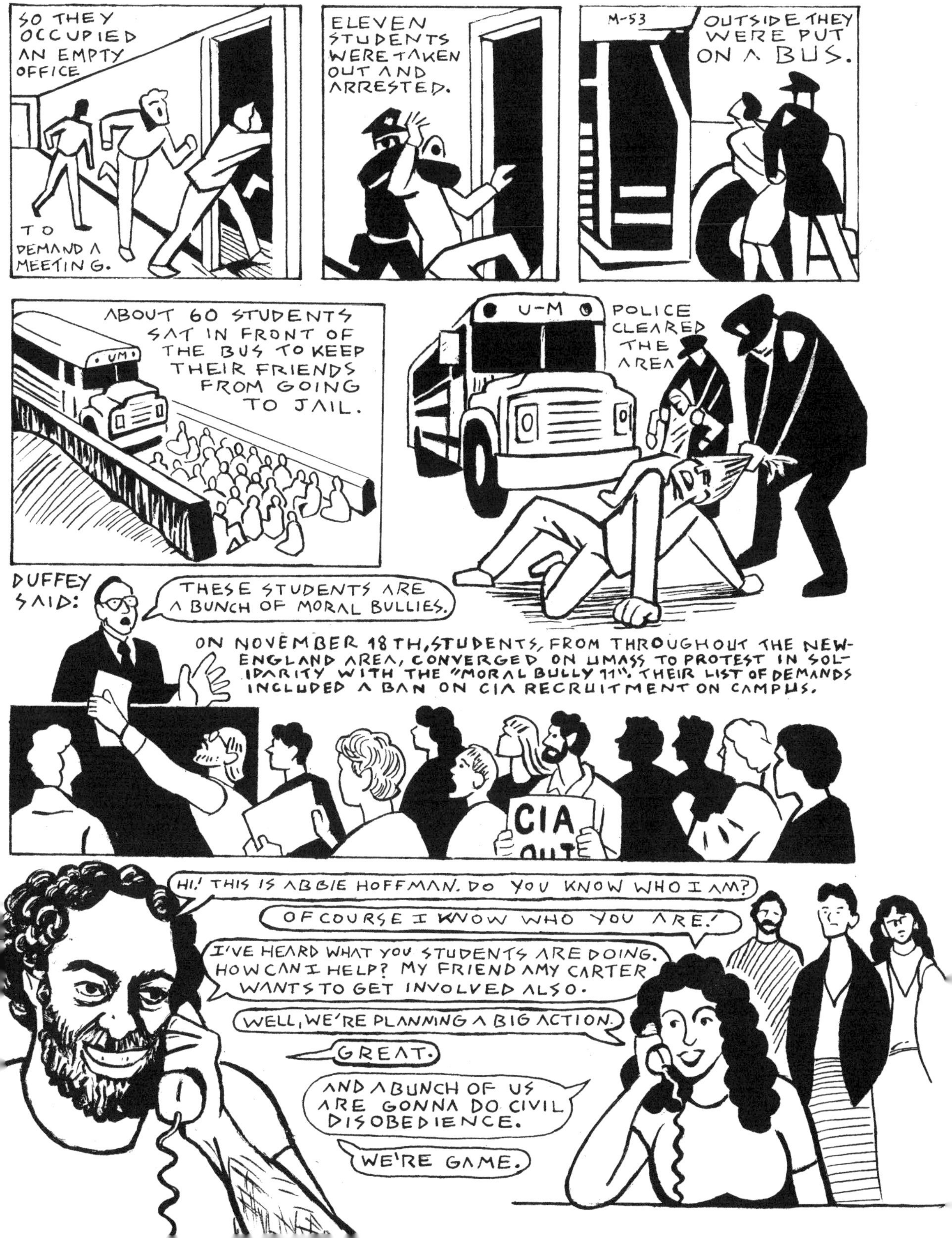
SO THEY OCCUPIED AN EMPTY OFFICE
TO DEMAND A MEETING.
ELEVEN STUDENTS WERE TAKEN OUT AND ARRESTED.
M-53
OUTSIDE THEY WERE PUT ON A BUS.
ABOUT 60 STUDENTS SAT IN FRONT OF THE BUS TO KEEP THEIR FRIENDS FROM GOING TO JAIL.
UM
U-M
POLICE CLEARED THE AREA
DUFFEY SAID:
THESE STUDENTS ARE A BUNCH OF MORAL BULLIES.
ON NOVEMBER 18TH, STUDENTS, FROM THROUGHOUT THE NEW-ENGLAND AREA, CONVERGED ON UMASS TO PROTEST IN SOLIDARITY WITH THE "MORAL BULLY 11". THEIR LIST OF DEMANDS INCLUDED A BAN ON CIA RECRUITMENT ON CAMPUS.
CIA OUT
HI! THIS IS ABBIE HOFFMAN. DO YOU KNOW WHO I AM?
OF COURSE I KNOW WHO YOU ARE!
I'VE HEARD WHAT YOU STUDENTS ARE DOING. HOW CAN I HELP? MY FRIEND AMY CARTER WANTS TO GET INVOLVED ALSO.
WELL, WE'RE PLANNING A BIG ACTION.
GREAT.
AND A BUNCH OF US ARE GONNA DO CIVIL DISOBEDIENCE.
WE'RE GAME.

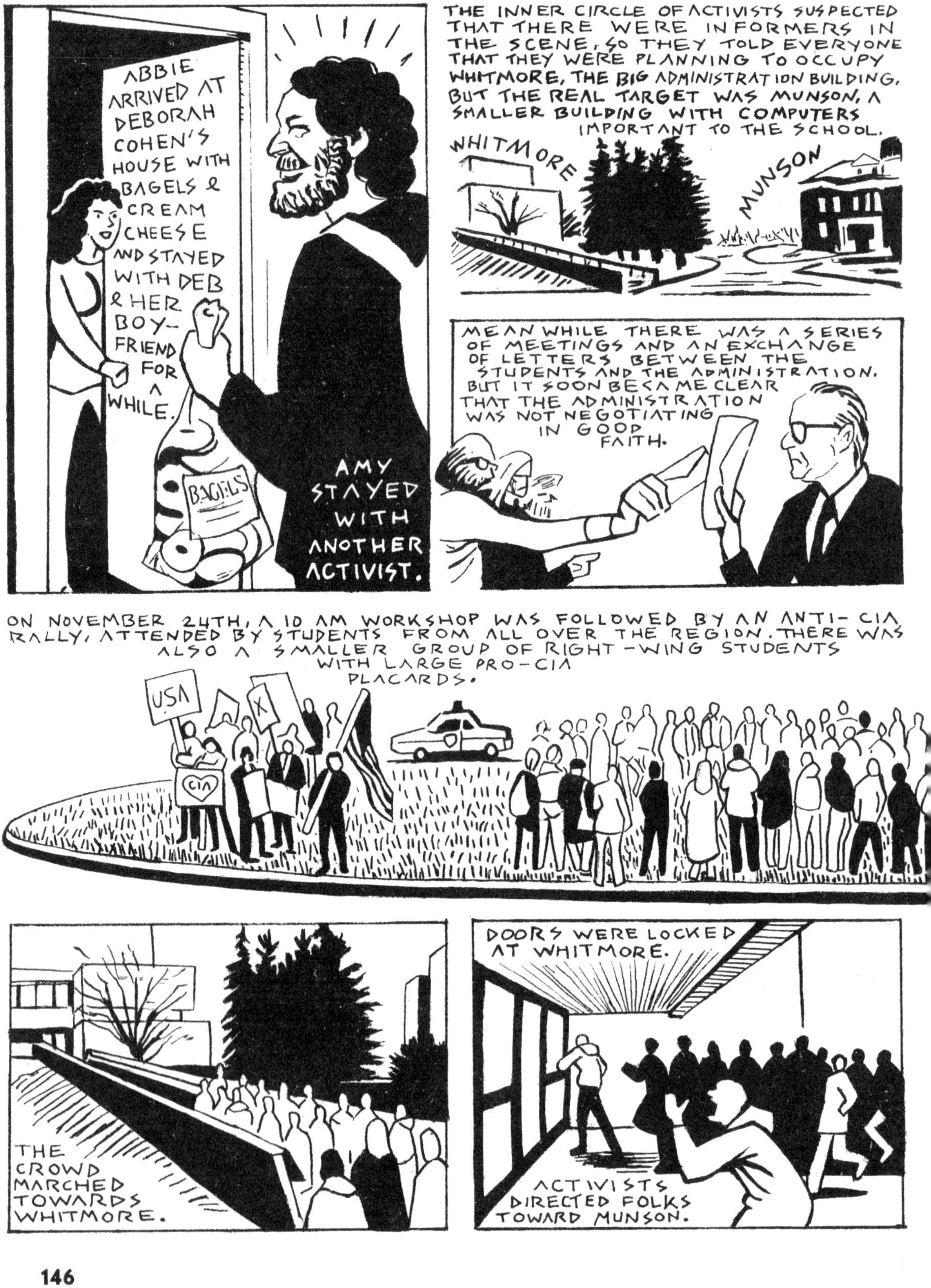
ABBIE ARRIVED AT DEBORAH COHEN'S HOUSE WITH BAGELS & CREAM CHEESE AND STAYED WITH DEB & HER BOY-FRIEND FOR A WHILE.
BAGELS
AMY STAYED WITH ANOTHER ACTIVIST.
THE INNER CIRCLE OF ACTIVISTS SUSPECTED THAT THERE WERE INFORMERS IN THE SCENE, SO THEY TOLD EVERYONE THAT THEY WERE PLANNING TO OCCUPY WHITMORE, THE BIG ADMINISTRATION BUILDING. BUT THE REAL TARGET WAS MUNSON, A SMALLER BUILDING WITH COMPUTERS IMPORTANT TO THE SCHOOL.
WHITMORE
MUNSON
MEANWHILE THERE WAS A SERIES OF MEETINGS AND AN EXCHANGE OF LETTERS BETWEEN THE STUDENTS AND THE ADMINISTRATION. BUT IT SOON BECAME CLEAR THAT THE ADMINISTRATION WAS NOT NEGOTIATING IN GOOD FAITH.
ON NOVEMBER 24TH, A 10 AM WORKSHOP WAS FOLLOWED BY AN ANTI-CIA RALLY, ATTENDED BY STUDENTS FROM ALL OVER THE REGION. THERE WAS ALSO A SMALLER GROUP OF RIGHT-WING STUDENTS WITH LARGE PRO-CIA PLACARDS.
USA
X
CIA
THE CROWD MARCHED TOWARDS WHITMORE.
DOORS WERE LOCKED AT WHITMORE.
ACTIVISTS DIRECTED FOLKS TOWARD MUNSON.

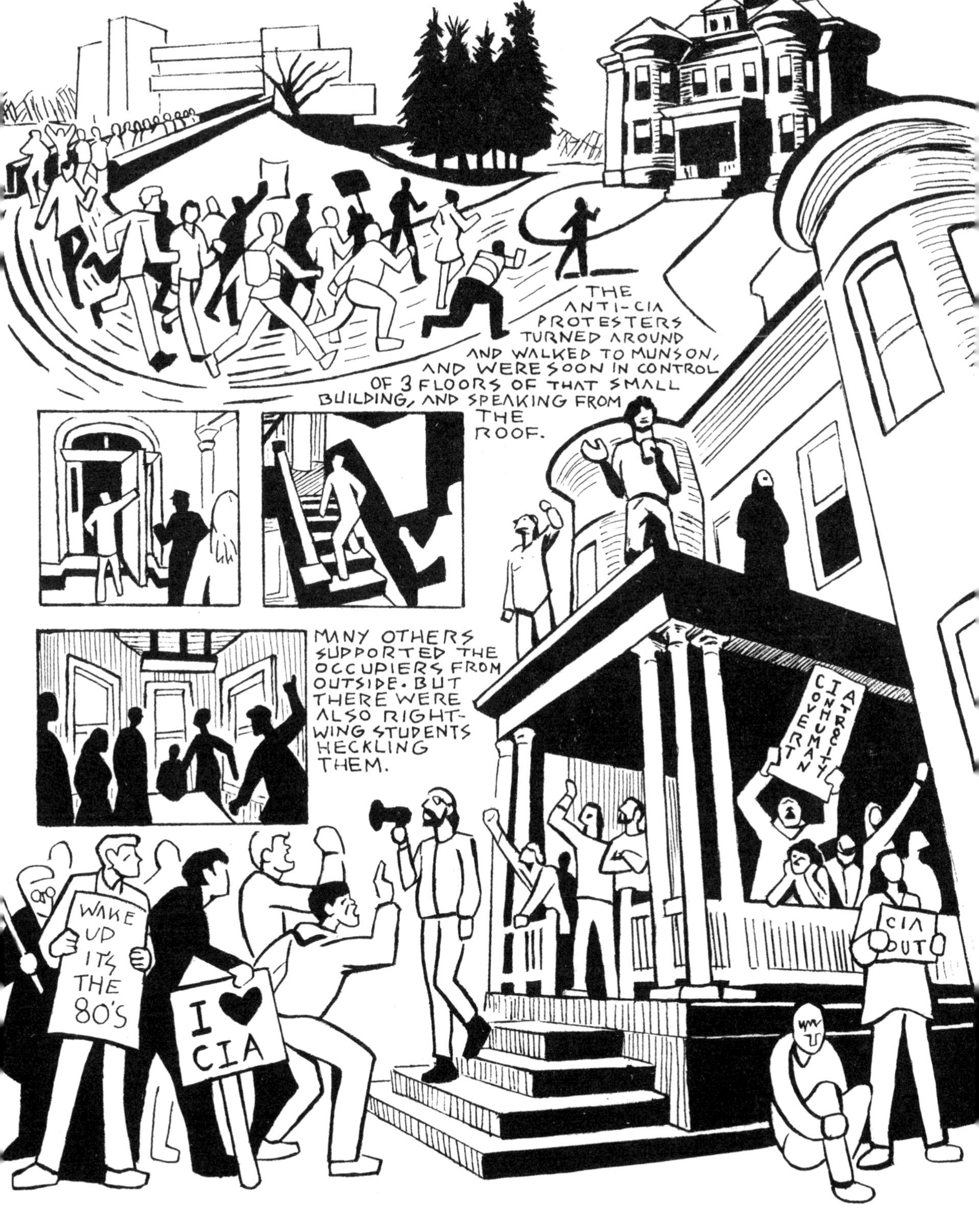
THE ANTI-CIA PROTESTERS TURNED AROUND AND WALKED TO MUNSON, AND WERE SOON IN CONTROL OF 3 FLOORS OF THAT SMALL BUILDING, AND SPEAKING FROM THE ROOF.
MANY OTHERS SUPPORTED THE OCCUPIERS FROM OUTSIDE. BUT THERE WERE ALSO RIGHT-WING STUDENTS HECKLING THEM.
COVERT INHUMAN ATROCITY
WAKE UP IT'S THE 80'S
I ♥ CIA
CIA OUT

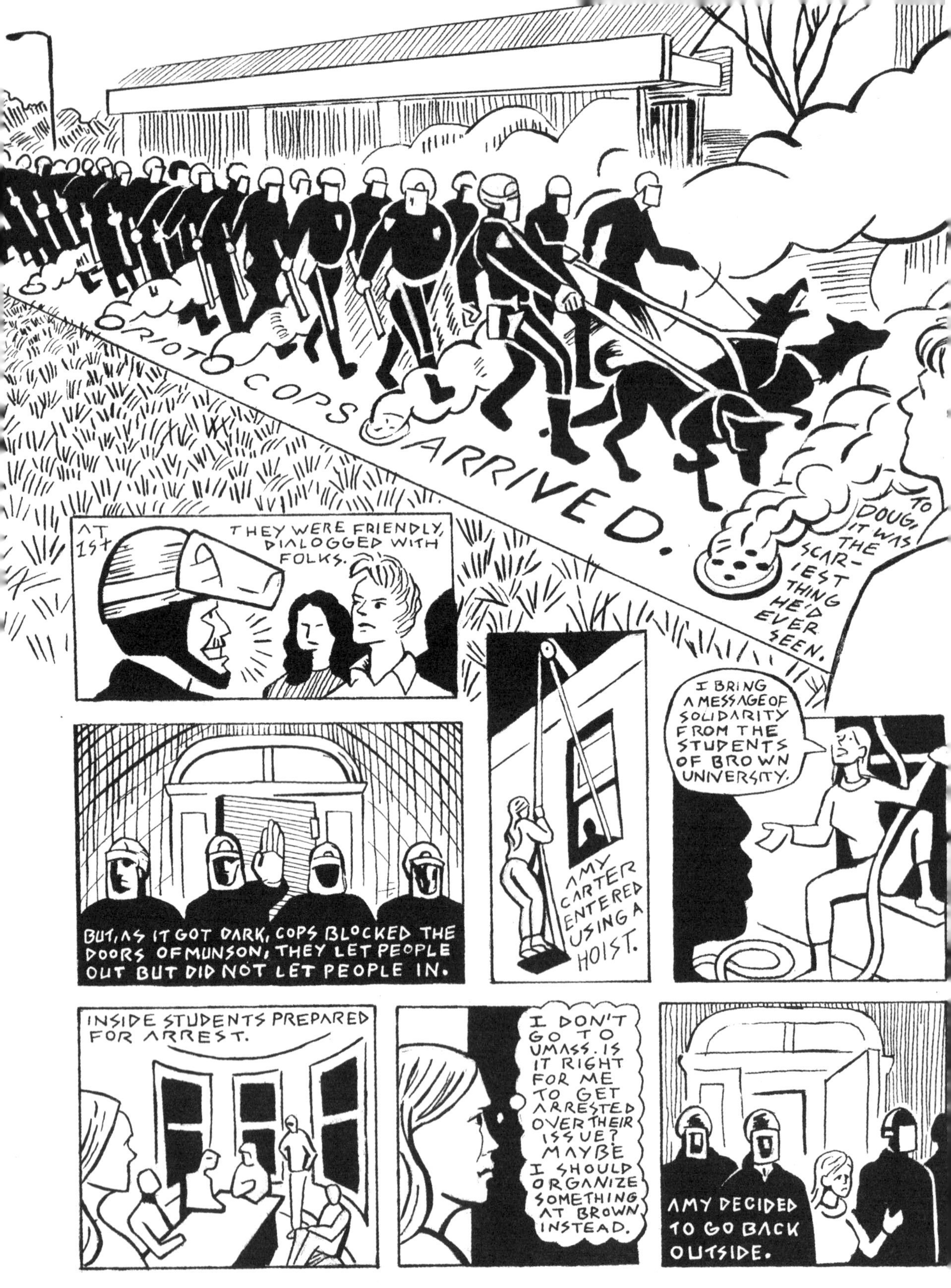
RIOT COPS ARRIVED.
TO DOUG, IT WAS THE SCARIEST THING HE'D EVER SEEN.
AT 1st
THEY WERE FRIENDLY, DIALOGGED WITH FOLKS.
BUT, AS IT GOT DARK, COPS BLOCKED THE DOORS OF MUNSON, THEY LET PEOPLE OUT BUT DID NOT LET PEOPLE IN.
AMY CARTER ENTERED USING A HOIST.
I BRING A MESSAGE OF SOLIDARITY FROM THE STUDENTS OF BROWN UNIVERSITY.
INSIDE STUDENTS PREPARED FOR ARREST.
I DON'T GO TO UMASS. IS IT RIGHT FOR ME TO GET ARRESTED OVER THEIR ISSUE? MAYBE I SHOULD ORGANIZE SOMETHING AT BROWN INSTEAD.
AMY DECIDED TO GO BACK OUTSIDE.

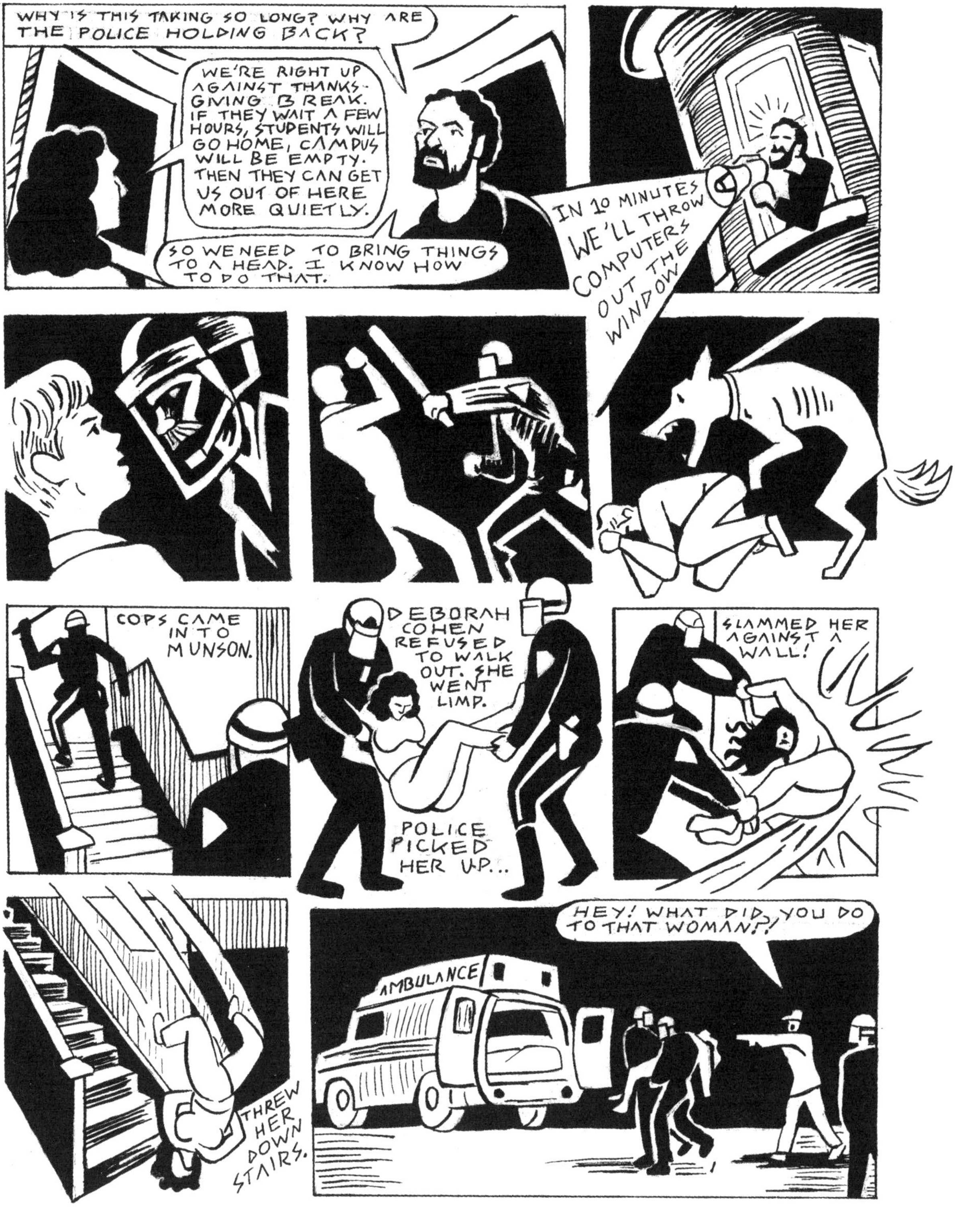
WHY IS THIS TAKING SO LONG? WHY ARE THE POLICE HOLDING BACK?
WE'RE RIGHT UP AGAINST THANKSGIVING BREAK. IF THEY WAIT A FEW HOURS, STUDENTS WILL GO HOME, CAMPUS WILL BE EMPTY. THEN THEY CAN GET US OUT OF HERE MORE QUIETLY.
SO WE NEED TO BRING THINGS TO A HEAD. I KNOW HOW TO DO THAT.
IN 10 MINUTES WE'LL THROW COMPUTERS OUT THE WINDOW
COPS CAME IN TO MUNSON.
DEBORAH COHEN REFUSED TO WALK OUT. SHE WENT LIMP.
POLICE PICKED HER UP...
SLAMMED HER AGAINST A WALL!
THREW HER DOWN STAIRS.
AMBULANCE
HEY! WHAT DID YOU DO TO THAT WOMAN?!

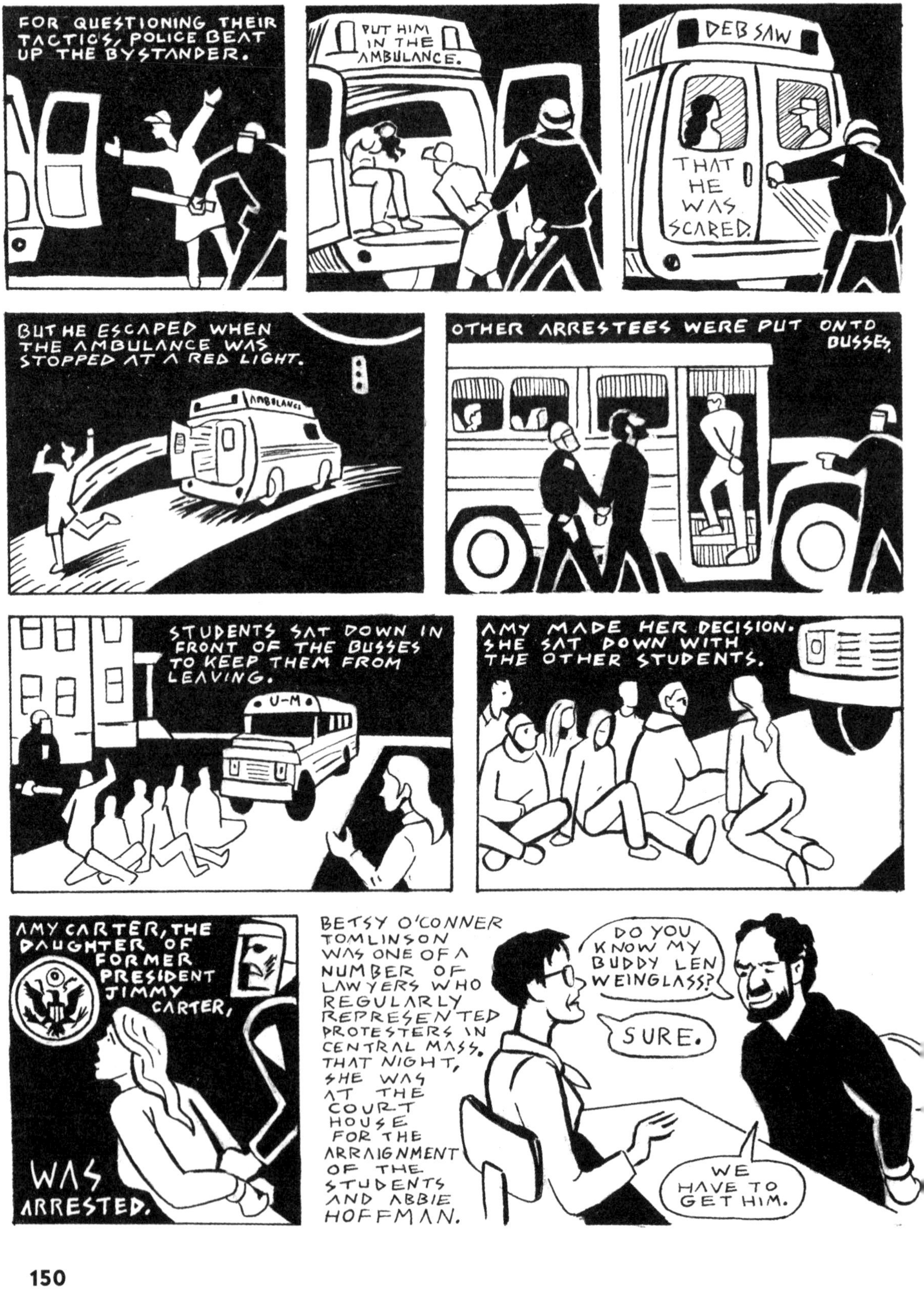

FOR QUESTIONING THEIR TACTICS, POLICE BEAT UP THE BYSTANDER.
PUT HIM IN THE AMBULANCE.
DEB SAW
THAT HE WAS SCARED.
BUT HE ESCAPED WHEN THE AMBULANCE WAS STOPPED AT A RED LIGHT.
AMBULANCE
OTHER ARRESTEES WERE PUT ONTO BUSSES.
STUDENTS SAT DOWN IN FRONT OF THE BUSSES TO KEEP THEM FROM LEAVING.
U-M
AMY MADE HER DECISION. SHE SAT DOWN WITH THE OTHER STUDENTS.
AMY CARTER, THE DAUGHTER OF FORMER PRESIDENT JIMMY CARTER,
WAS ARRESTED.
BETSY O'CONNER TOMLINSON WAS ONE OF A NUMBER OF LAWYERS WHO REGULARLY REPRESENTED PROTESTERS IN CENTRAL MASS. THAT NIGHT, SHE WAS AT THE COURT HOUSE FOR THE ARRAIGNMENT OF THE STUDENTS AND ABBIE HOFFMAN.
DO YOU KNOW MY BUDDY LEN WEINGLASS?
SURE.
WE HAVE TO GET HIM.

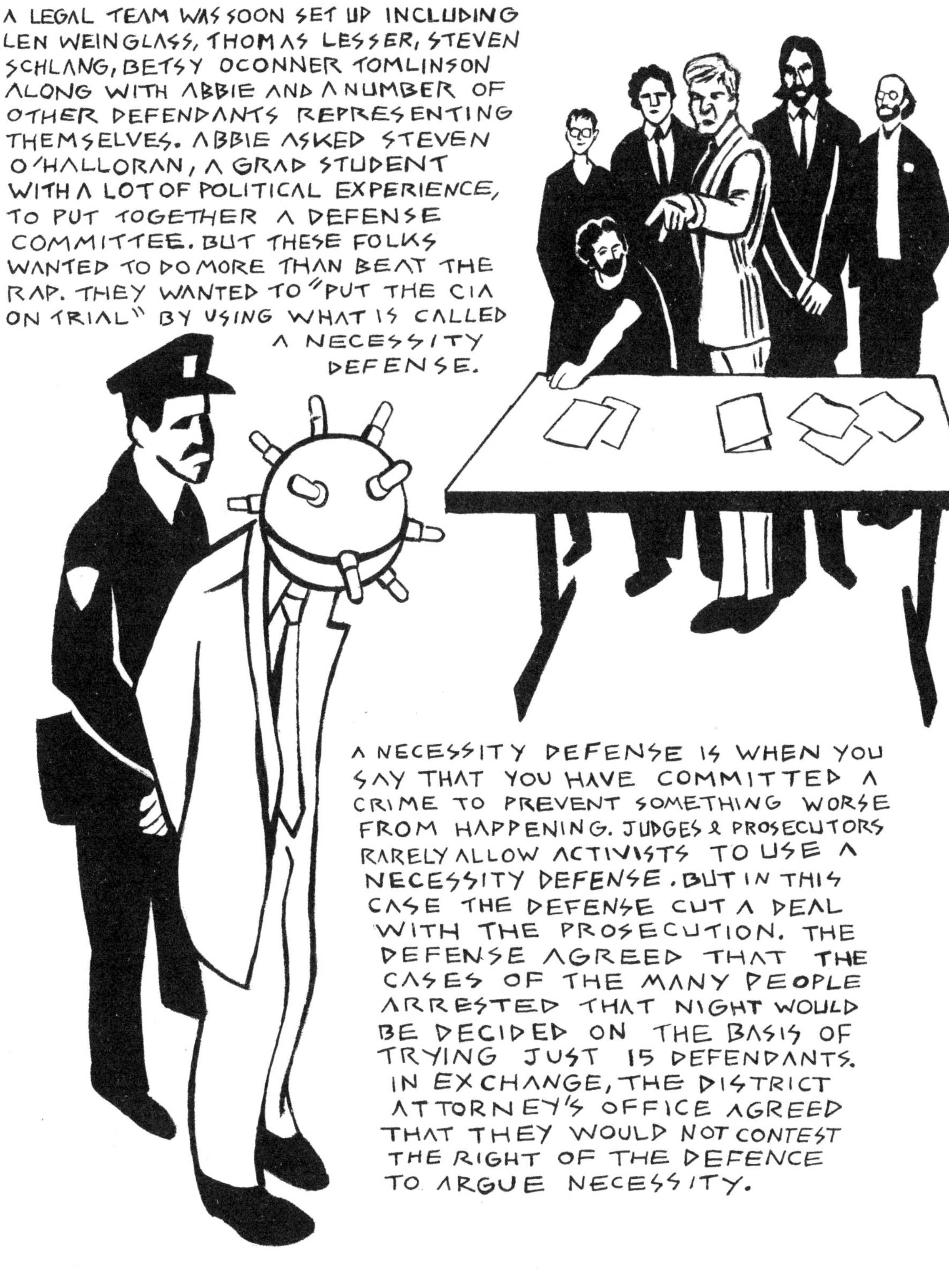
A LEGAL TEAM WAS SOON SET UP INCLUDING LEN WEINGLASS, THOMAS LESSER, STEVEN SCHLANG, BETSY OCONNER TOMLINSON ALONG WITH ABBIE AND A NUMBER OF OTHER DEFENDANTS REPRESENTING THEMSELVES. ABBIE ASKED STEVEN O'HALLORAN, A GRAD STUDENT WITH A LOT OF POLITICAL EXPERIENCE, TO PUT TOGETHER A DEFENSE COMMITTEE. BUT THESE FOLKS WANTED TO DO MORE THAN BEAT THE RAP. THEY WANTED TO "PUT THE CIA ON TRIAL" BY USING WHAT IS CALLED A NECESSITY DEFENSE.
A NECESSITY DEFENSE IS WHEN YOU SAY THAT YOU HAVE COMMITTED A CRIME TO PREVENT SOMETHING WORSE FROM HAPPENING. JUDGES & PROSECUTORS RARELY ALLOW ACTIVISTS TO USE A NECESSITY DEFENSE. BUT IN THIS CASE THE DEFENSE CUT A DEAL WITH THE PROSECUTION. THE DEFENSE AGREED THAT THE CASES OF THE MANY PEOPLE ARRESTED THAT NIGHT WOULD BE DECIDED ON THE BASIS OF TRYING JUST 15 DEFENDANTS. IN EXCHANGE, THE DISTRICT ATTORNEY'S OFFICE AGREED THAT THEY WOULD NOT CONTEST THE RIGHT OF THE DEFENCE TO ARGUE NECESSITY.

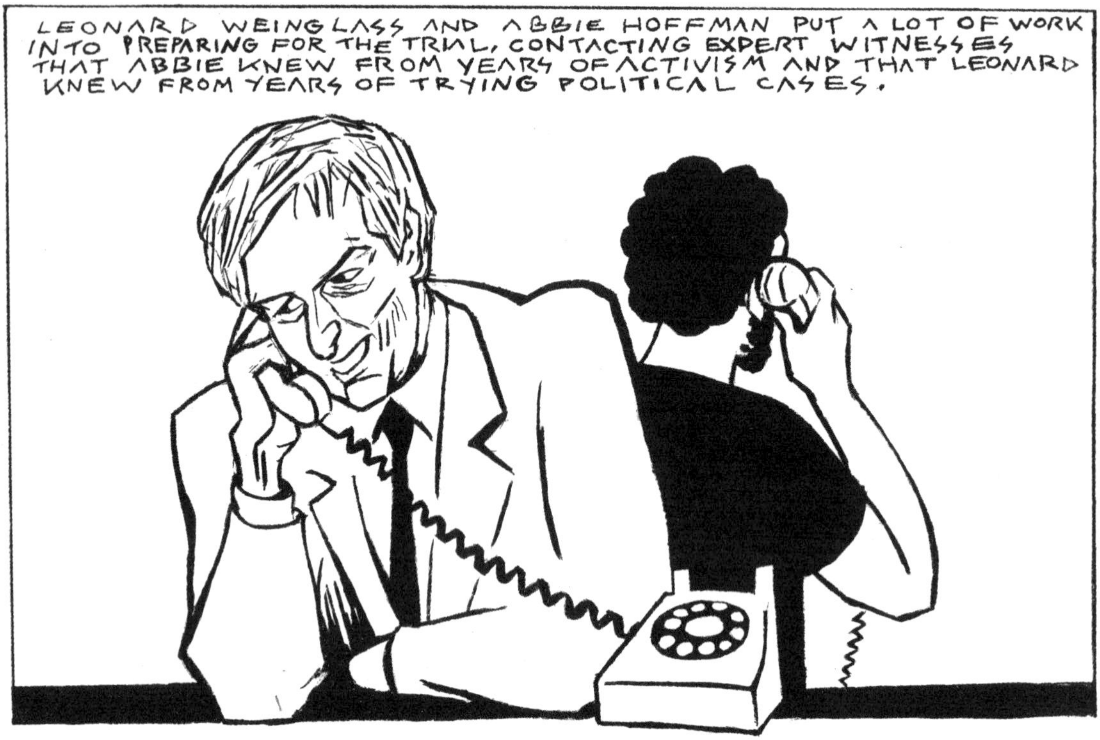
LEONARD WEINGLASS AND ABBIE HOFFMAN PUT A LOT OF WORK INTO PREPARING FOR THE TRIAL, CONTACTING EXPERT WITNESSES THAT ABBIE KNEW FROM YEARS OF ACTIVISM AND THAT LEONARD KNEW FROM YEARS OF TRYING POLITICAL CASES.

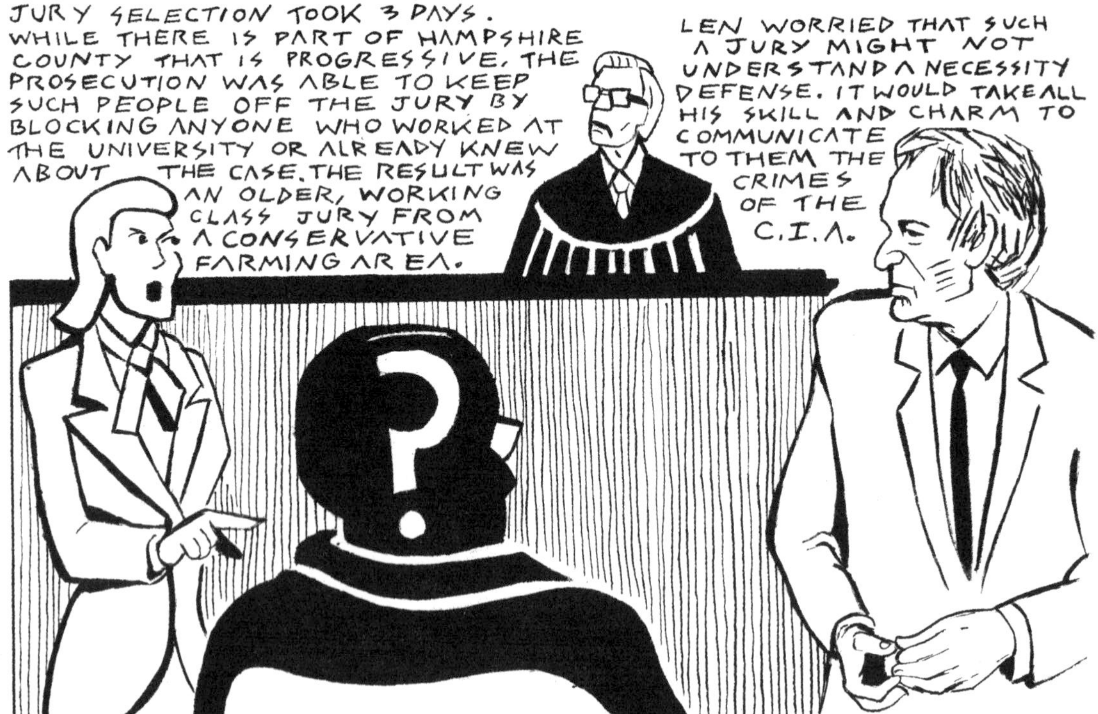
JURY SELECTION TOOK 3 DAYS. WHILE THERE IS PART OF HAMPSHIRE COUNTY THAT IS PROGRESSIVE, THE PROSECUTION WAS ABLE TO KEEP SUCH PEOPLE OFF THE JURY BY BLOCKING ANYONE WHO WORKED AT THE UNIVERSITY OR ALREADY KNEW ABOUT THE CASE. THE RESULT WAS AN OLDER, WORKING CLASS JURY FROM A CONSERVATIVE FARMING AREA.
LEN WORRIED THAT SUCH A JURY MIGHT NOT UNDERSTAND A NECESSITY DEFENSE. IT WOULD TAKE ALL HIS SKILL AND CHARM TO COMMUNICATE TO THEM THE CRIMES OF THE C.I.A.

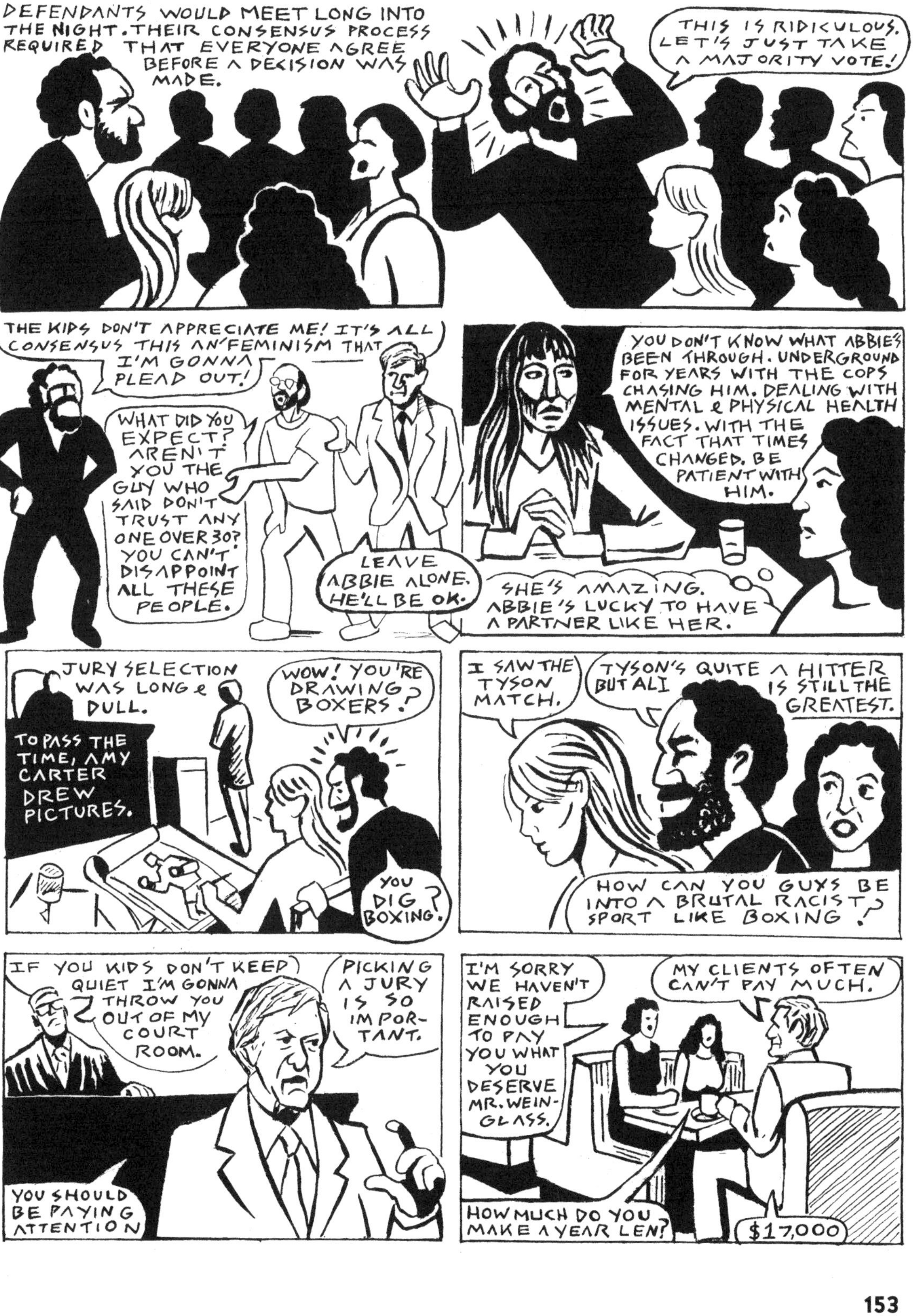
DEFENDANTS WOULD MEET LONG INTO THE NIGHT. THEIR CONSENSUS PROCESS REQUIRED THAT EVERYONE AGREE BEFORE A DECISION WAS MADE.
THIS IS RIDICULOUS. LET'S JUST TAKE A MAJORITY VOTE!
THE KIDS DON'T APPRECIATE ME! IT'S ALL CONSENSUS THIS AN' FEMINISM THAT — I'M GONNA PLEAD OUT!
WHAT DID YOU EXPECT? AREN'T YOU THE GUY WHO SAID DON'T TRUST ANY ONE OVER 30? YOU CAN'T DISAPPOINT ALL THESE PEOPLE.
LEAVE ABBIE ALONE. HE'LL BE OK.
YOU DON'T KNOW WHAT ABBIE'S BEEN THROUGH. UNDERGROUND FOR YEARS WITH THE COPS CHASING HIM. DEALING WITH MENTAL & PHYSICAL HEALTH ISSUES. WITH THE FACT THAT TIMES CHANGED. BE PATIENT WITH HIM.
SHE'S AMAZING. ABBIE'S LUCKY TO HAVE A PARTNER LIKE HER.
JURY SELECTION WAS LONG & DULL.
TO PASS THE TIME, AMY CARTER DREW PICTURES.
WOW! YOU'RE DRAWING BOXERS?
YOU DIG BOXING?
I SAW THE TYSON MATCH.
TYSON'S QUITE A HITTER BUT ALI IS STILL THE GREATEST.
HOW CAN YOU GUYS BE INTO A BRUTAL RACIST SPORT LIKE BOXING?
IF YOU KIDS DON'T KEEP QUIET I'M GONNA THROW YOU OUT OF MY COURT ROOM.
PICKING A JURY IS SO IMPORTANT.
YOU SHOULD BE PAYING ATTENTION
I'M SORRY WE HAVEN'T RAISED ENOUGH TO PAY YOU WHAT YOU DESERVE MR. WEINGLASS.
MY CLIENTS OFTEN CAN'T PAY MUCH.
HOW MUCH DO YOU MAKE A YEAR LEN?
$17,000

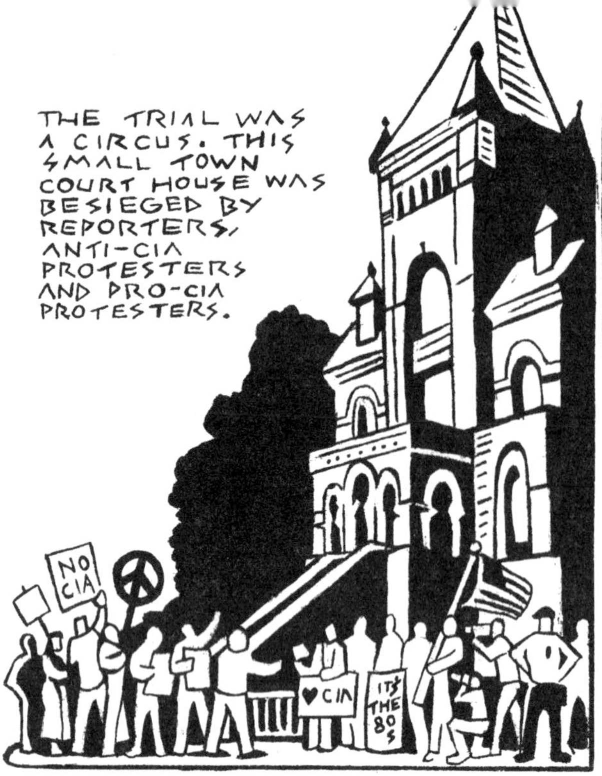
THE TRIAL WAS A CIRCUS. THIS SMALL TOWN COURT HOUSE WAS BESIEGED BY REPORTERS, ANTI-CIA PROTESTERS AND PRO-CIA PROTESTERS.
NO CIA
♥ CIA
IT'S THE 80'S

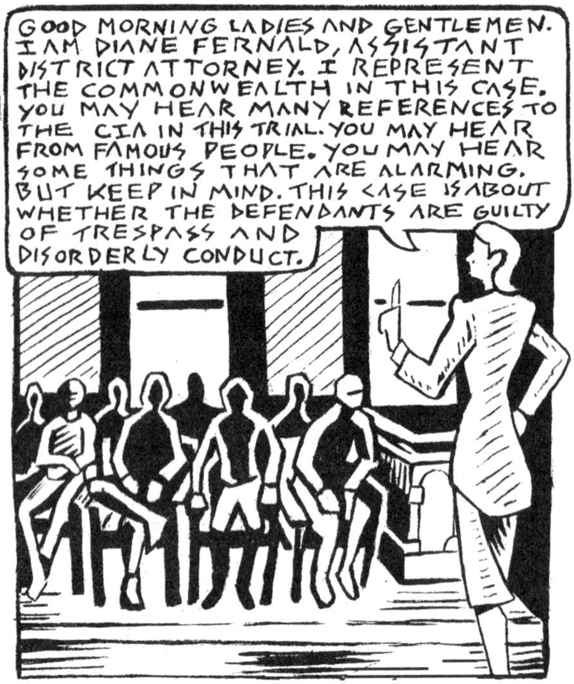
GOOD MORNING LADIES AND GENTLEMEN. I AM DIANE FERNALD, ASSISTANT DISTRICT ATTORNEY. I REPRESENT THE COMMONWEALTH IN THIS CASE. YOU MAY HEAR MANY REFERENCES TO THE CIA IN THIS TRIAL. YOU MAY HEAR FROM FAMOUS PEOPLE. YOU MAY HEAR SOME THINGS THAT ARE ALARMING. BUT KEEP IN MIND. THIS CASE IS ABOUT WHETHER THE DEFENDANTS ARE GUILTY OF TRESPASS AND DISORDERLY CONDUCT.

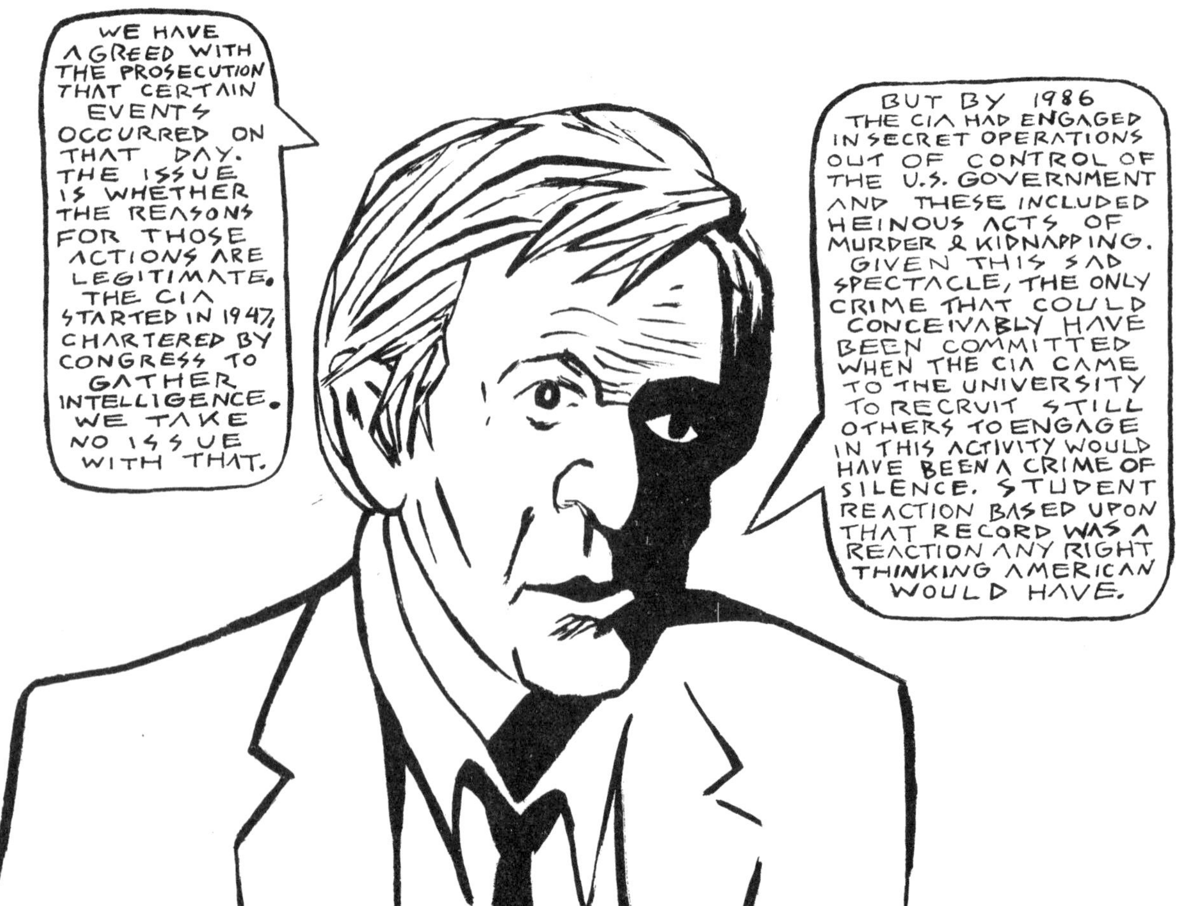
WE HAVE AGREED WITH THE PROSECUTION THAT CERTAIN EVENTS OCCURRED ON THAT DAY. THE ISSUE IS WHETHER THE REASONS FOR THOSE ACTIONS ARE LEGITIMATE. THE CIA STARTED IN 1947, CHARTERED BY CONGRESS TO GATHER INTELLIGENCE. WE TAKE NO ISSUE WITH THAT.
BUT BY 1986 THE CIA HAD ENGAGED IN SECRET OPERATIONS OUT OF CONTROL OF THE U.S. GOVERNMENT AND THESE INCLUDED HEINOUS ACTS OF MURDER & KIDNAPPING. GIVEN THIS SAD SPECTACLE, THE ONLY CRIME THAT COULD CONCEIVABLY HAVE BEEN COMMITTED WHEN THE CIA CAME TO THE UNIVERSITY TO RECRUIT STILL OTHERS TO ENGAGE IN THIS ACTIVITY WOULD HAVE BEEN A CRIME OF SILENCE. STUDENT REACTION BASED UPON THAT RECORD WAS A REACTION ANY RIGHT THINKING AMERICAN WOULD HAVE.

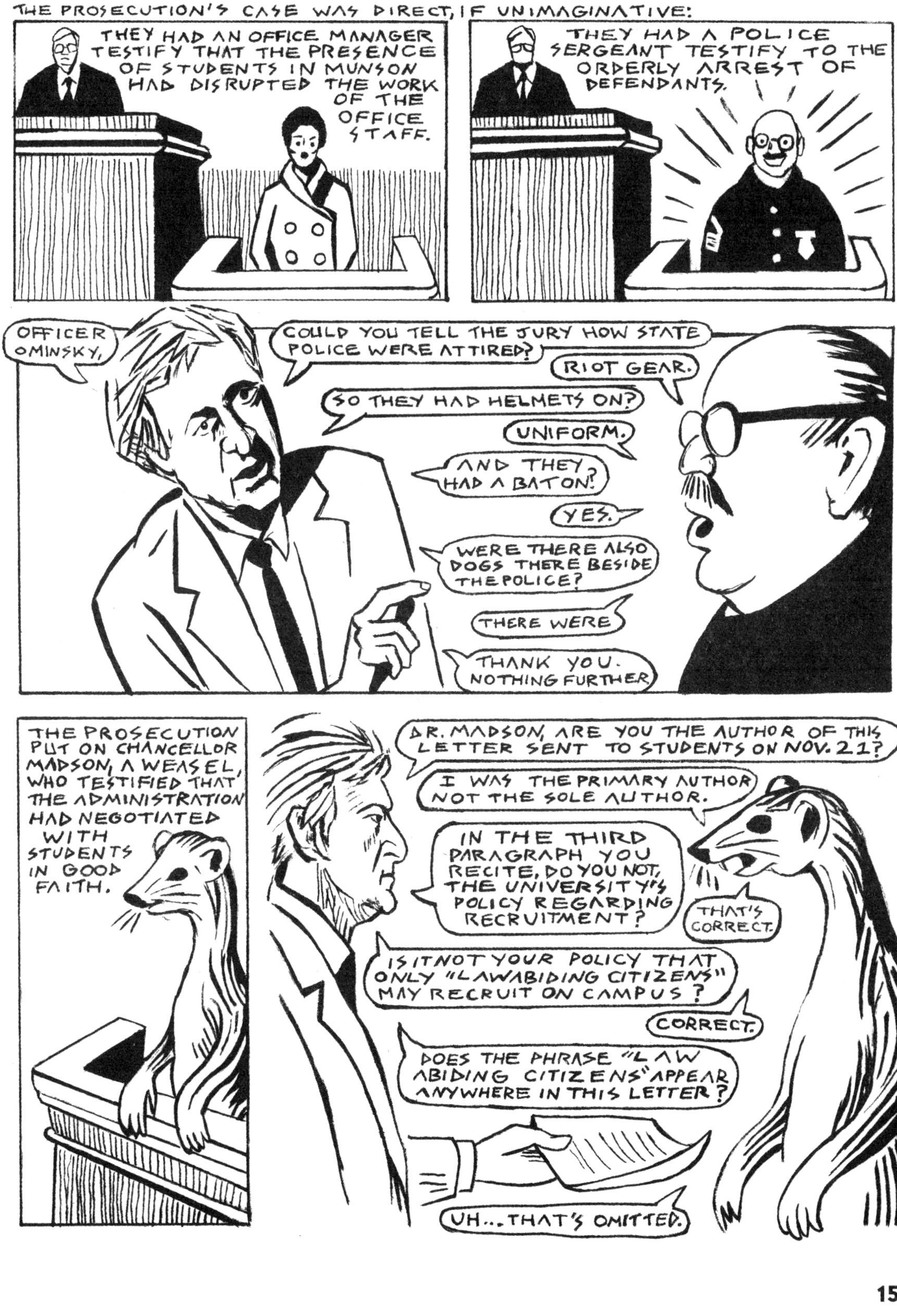
THE PROSECUTION'S CASE WAS DIRECT, IF UNIMAGINATIVE:
THEY HAD AN OFFICE MANAGER TESTIFY THAT THE PRESENCE OF STUDENTS IN MUNSON HAD DISRUPTED THE WORK OF THE OFFICE STAFF.
THEY HAD A POLICE SERGEANT TESTIFY TO THE ORDERLY ARREST OF DEFENDANTS.
OFFICER OMINSKY,
COULD YOU TELL THE JURY HOW STATE POLICE WERE ATTIRED?
RIOT GEAR.
SO THEY HAD HELMETS ON?
UNIFORM.
AND THEY HAD A BATON?
YES.
WERE THERE ALSO DOGS THERE BESIDE THE POLICE?
THERE WERE
THANK YOU. NOTHING FURTHER
THE PROSECUTION PUT ON CHANCELLOR MADSON, A WEASEL, WHO TESTIFIED THAT THE ADMINISTRATION HAD NEGOTIATED WITH STUDENTS IN GOOD FAITH.
DR. MADSON, ARE YOU THE AUTHOR OF THIS LETTER SENT TO STUDENTS ON NOV. 21?
I WAS THE PRIMARY AUTHOR NOT THE SOLE AUTHOR.
IN THE THIRD PARAGRAPH YOU RECITE, DO YOU NOT, THE UNIVERSITY'S POLICY REGARDING RECRUITMENT?
THAT'S CORRECT.
IS IT NOT YOUR POLICY THAT ONLY "LAWABIDING CITIZENS" MAY RECRUIT ON CAMPUS?
CORRECT.
DOES THE PHRASE "LAW ABIDING CITIZENS" APPEAR ANYWHERE IN THIS LETTER?
UH...THAT'S OMITTED.

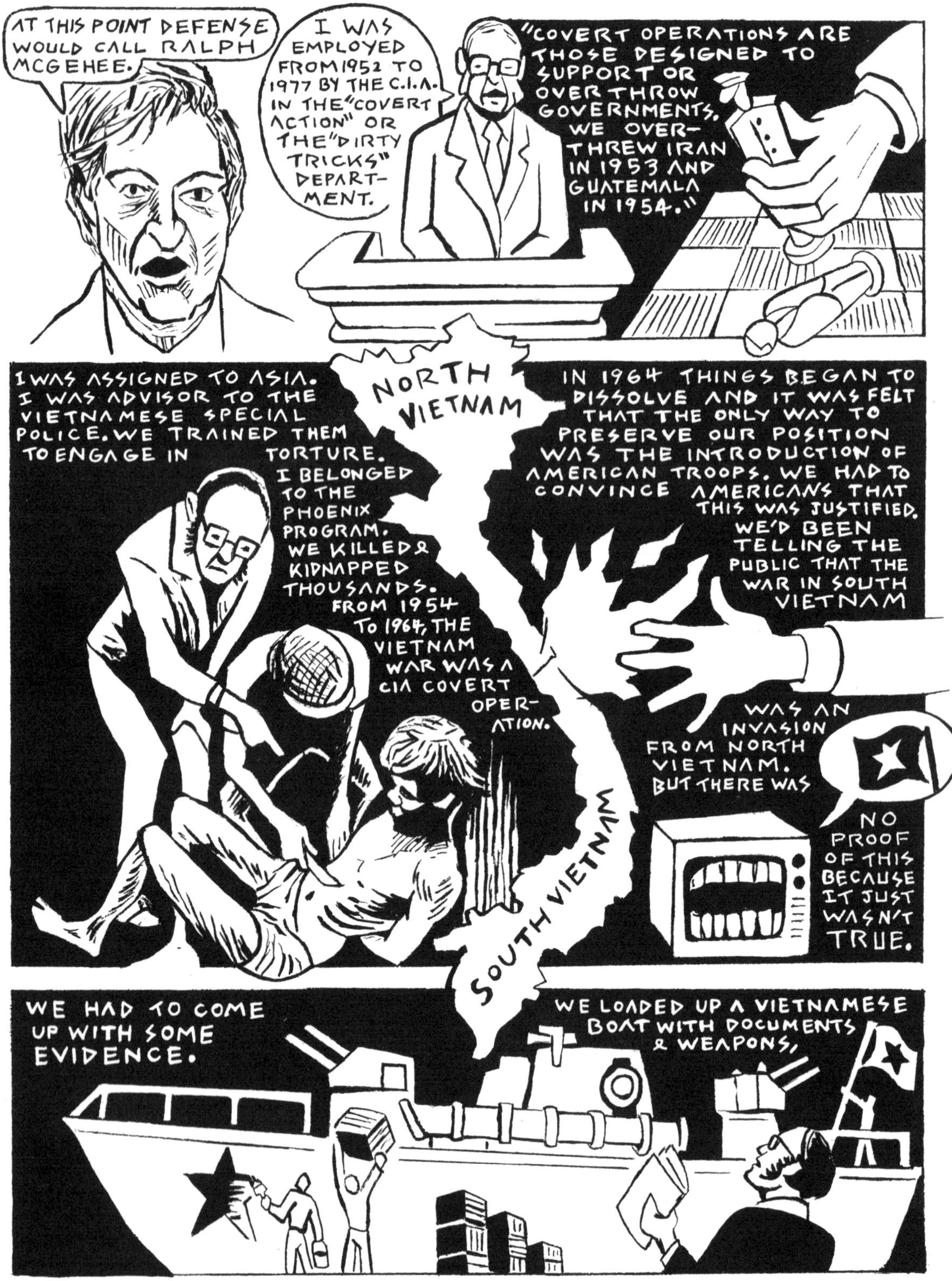
AT THIS POINT DEFENSE WOULD CALL RALPH MCGEHEE.
I WAS EMPLOYED FROM 1952 TO 1977 BY THE C.I.A. IN THE "COVERT ACTION" OR THE "DIRTY TRICKS" DEPARTMENT.
"COVERT OPERATIONS ARE THOSE DESIGNED TO SUPPORT OR OVERTHROW GOVERNMENTS. WE OVERTHREW IRAN IN 1953 AND GUATEMALA IN 1954."
I WAS ASSIGNED TO ASIA. I WAS ADVISOR TO THE VIETNAMESE SPECIAL POLICE. WE TRAINED THEM TO ENGAGE IN TORTURE. I BELONGED TO THE PHOENIX PROGRAM. WE KILLED & KIDNAPPED THOUSANDS. FROM 1954 TO 1964, THE VIETNAM WAR WAS A CIA COVERT OPERATION.
NORTH VIETNAM
SOUTH VIETNAM
IN 1964 THINGS BEGAN TO DISSOLVE AND IT WAS FELT THAT THE ONLY WAY TO PRESERVE OUR POSITION WAS THE INTRODUCTION OF AMERICAN TROOPS. WE HAD TO CONVINCE AMERICANS THAT THIS WAS JUSTIFIED.
WE'D BEEN TELLING THE PUBLIC THAT THE WAR IN SOUTH VIETNAM
WAS AN INVASION FROM NORTH VIETNAM. BUT THERE WAS
NO PROOF OF THIS BECAUSE IT JUST WASN'T TRUE.
WE HAD TO COME UP WITH SOME EVIDENCE.
WE LOADED UP A VIETNAMESE BOAT WITH DOCUMENTS & WEAPONS,

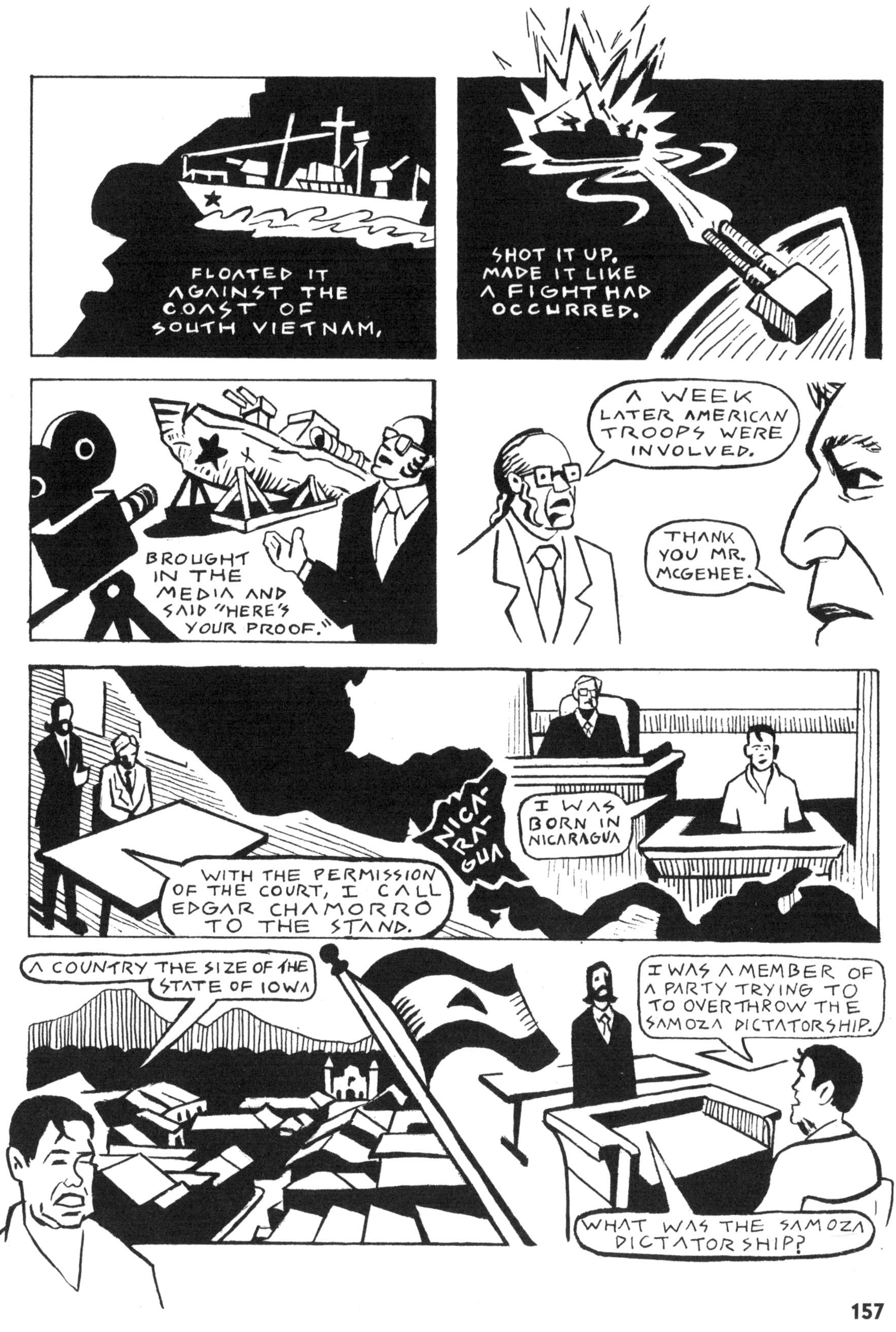
FLOATED IT AGAINST THE COAST OF SOUTH VIETNAM,
SHOT IT UP. MADE IT LIKE A FIGHT HAD OCCURRED.
BROUGHT IN THE MEDIA AND SAID "HERE'S YOUR PROOF."
A WEEK LATER AMERICAN TROOPS WERE INVOLVED.
THANK YOU MR. MCGEHEE.
WITH THE PERMISSION OF THE COURT, I CALL EDGAR CHAMORRO TO THE STAND.
NICA-RA-GUA
I WAS BORN IN NICARAGUA
A COUNTRY THE SIZE OF THE STATE OF IOWA
I WAS A MEMBER OF A PARTY TRYING TO TO OVERTHROW THE SAMOZA DICTATORSHIP.
WHAT WAS THE SAMOZA DICTATORSHIP?

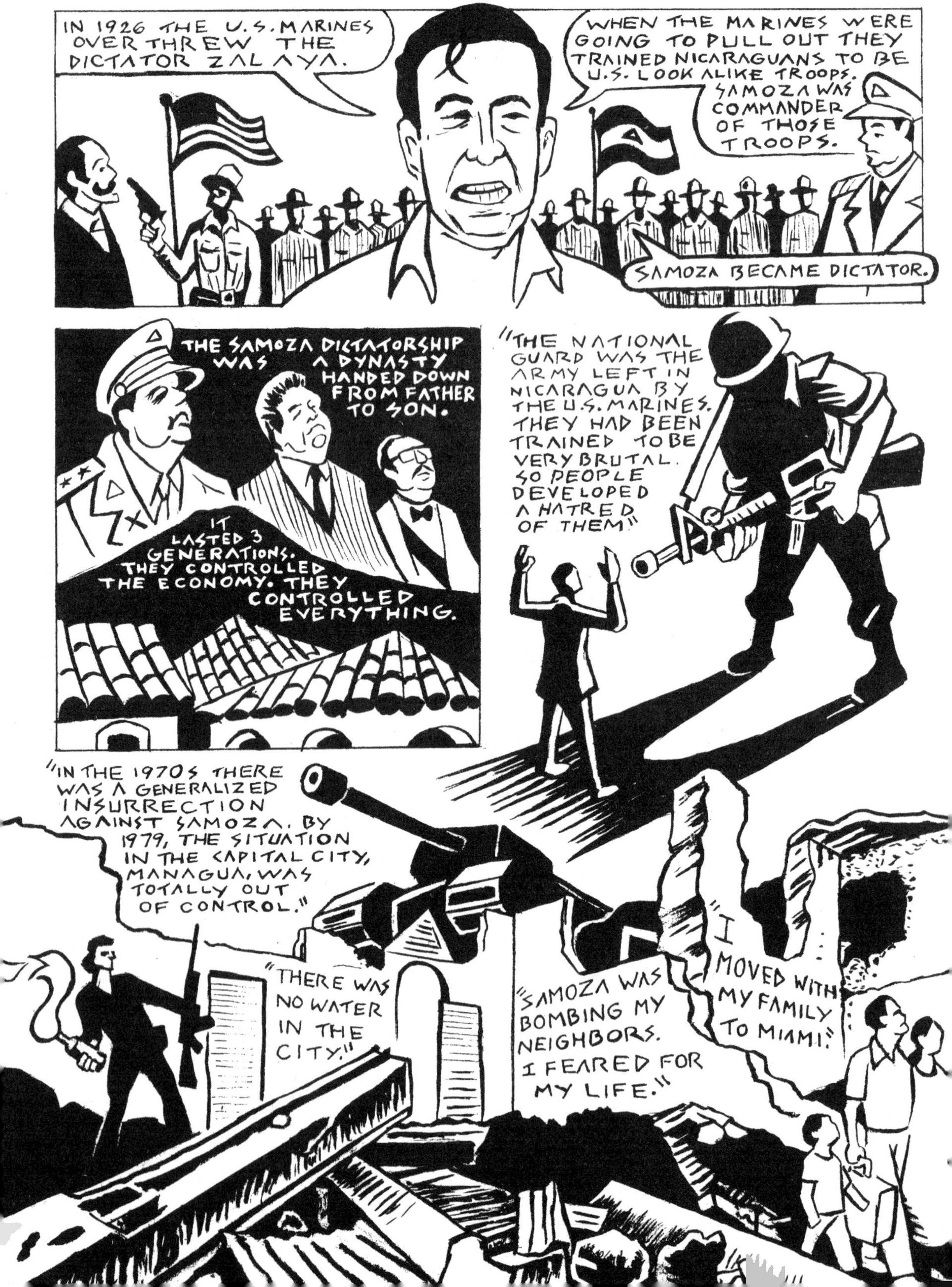

IN 1926 THE U.S. MARINES OVERTHREW THE DICTATOR ZALAYA.
WHEN THE MARINES WERE GOING TO PULL OUT THEY TRAINED NICARAGUANS TO BE U.S. LOOK ALIKE TROOPS.
SAMOZA WAS COMMANDER OF THOSE TROOPS.
SAMOZA BECAME DICTATOR.
THE SAMOZA DICTATORSHIP WAS A DYNASTY HANDED DOWN FROM FATHER TO SON.
IT LASTED 3 GENERATIONS. THEY CONTROLLED THE ECONOMY. THEY CONTROLLED EVERYTHING.
"THE NATIONAL GUARD WAS THE ARMY LEFT IN NICARAGUA BY THE U.S. MARINES. THEY HAD BEEN TRAINED TO BE VERY BRUTAL. SO PEOPLE DEVELOPED A HATRED OF THEM"
"IN THE 1970S THERE WAS A GENERALIZED INSURRECTION AGAINST SAMOZA. BY 1979, THE SITUATION IN THE CAPITAL CITY, MANAGUA, WAS TOTALLY OUT OF CONTROL."
"THERE WAS NO WATER IN THE CITY."
"SAMOZA WAS BOMBING MY NEIGHBORS. I FEARED FOR MY LIFE."
"I MOVED WITH MY FAMILY TO MIAMI."

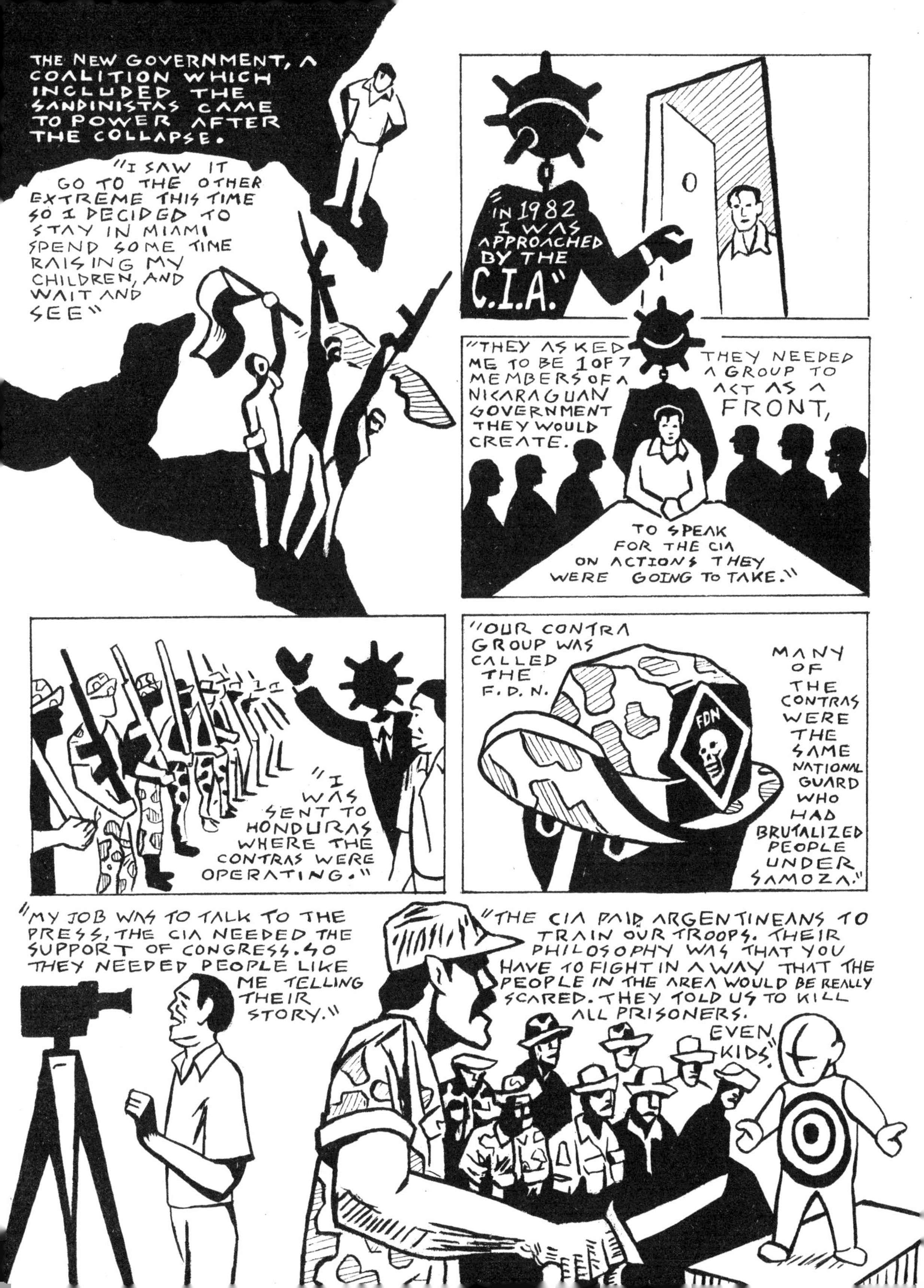
THE NEW GOVERNMENT, A COALITION WHICH INCLUDED THE SANDINISTAS CAME TO POWER AFTER THE COLLAPSE.
"I SAW IT GO TO THE OTHER EXTREME THIS TIME SO I DECIDED TO STAY IN MIAMI SPEND SOME TIME RAISING MY CHILDREN, AND WAIT AND SEE"
"IN 1982 I WAS APPROACHED BY THE C.I.A."
"THEY ASKED ME TO BE 1 OF 7 MEMBERS OF A NICARAGUAN GOVERNMENT THEY WOULD CREATE.
THEY NEEDED A GROUP TO ACT AS A FRONT,
TO SPEAK FOR THE CIA ON ACTIONS THEY WERE GOING TO TAKE."
"I WAS SENT TO HONDURAS WHERE THE CONTRAS WERE OPERATING."
"OUR CONTRA GROUP WAS CALLED THE F.D.N.
FDN
MANY OF THE CONTRAS WERE THE SAME NATIONAL GUARD WHO HAD BRUTALIZED PEOPLE UNDER SAMOZA."
"MY JOB WAS TO TALK TO THE PRESS. THE CIA NEEDED THE SUPPORT OF CONGRESS. SO THEY NEEDED PEOPLE LIKE ME TELLING THEIR STORY."
"THE CIA PAID ARGENTINEANS TO TRAIN OUR TROOPS. THEIR PHILOSOPHY WAS THAT YOU HAVE TO FIGHT IN A WAY THAT THE PEOPLE IN THE AREA WOULD BE REALLY SCARED. THEY TOLD US TO KILL ALL PRISONERS.
EVEN KIDS."

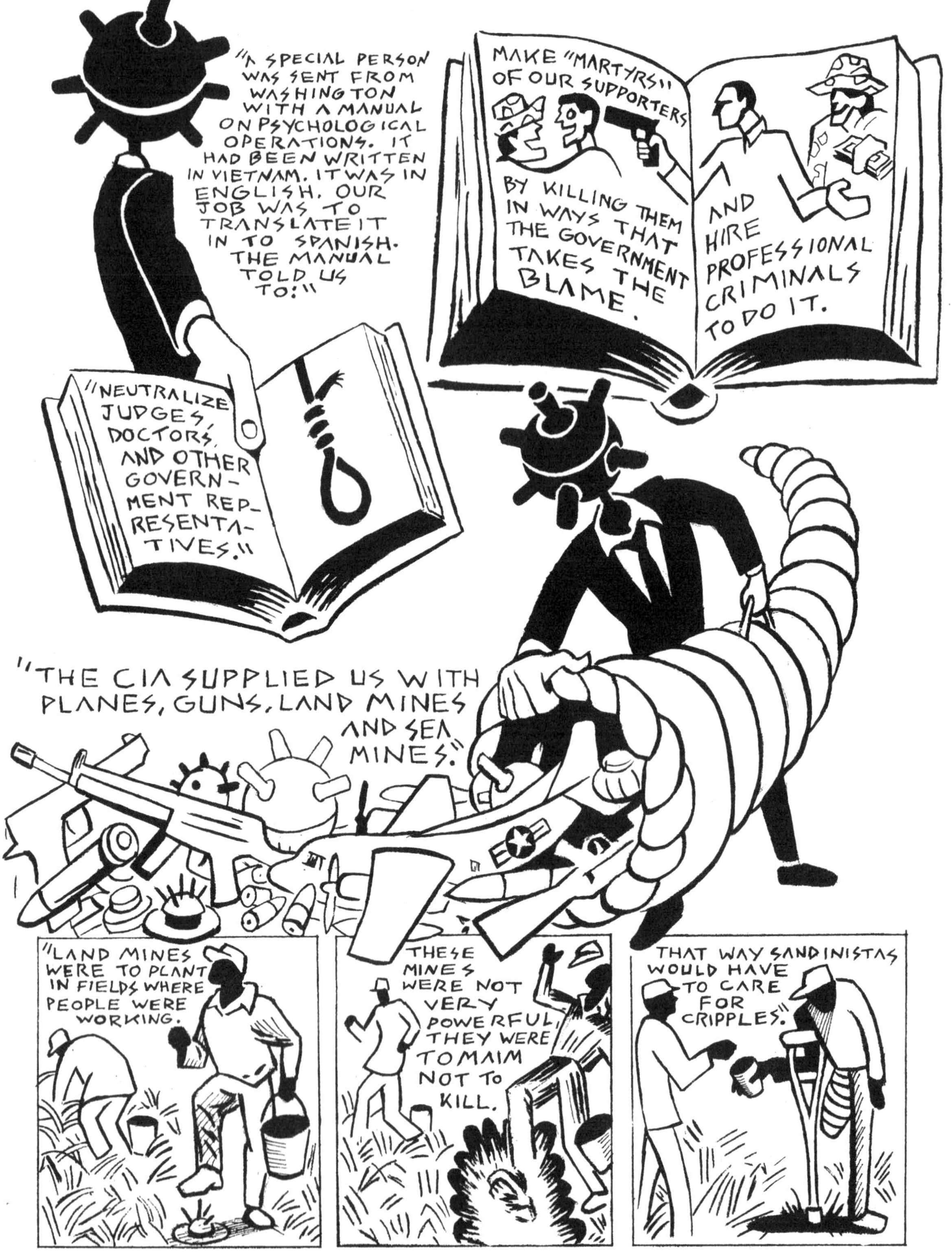
"A SPECIAL PERSON WAS SENT FROM WASHINGTON WITH A MANUAL ON PSYCHOLOGICAL OPERATIONS. IT HAD BEEN WRITTEN IN VIETNAM. IT WAS IN ENGLISH. OUR JOB WAS TO TRANSLATE IT IN TO SPANISH. THE MANUAL TOLD US TO:"
MAKE "MARTYRS" OF OUR SUPPORTERS
BY KILLING THEM IN WAYS THAT THE GOVERNMENT TAKES THE BLAME.
AND HIRE PROFESSIONAL CRIMINALS TO DO IT.
"NEUTRALIZE JUDGES, DOCTORS, AND OTHER GOVERNMENT REPRESENTATIVES."
"THE CIA SUPPLIED US WITH PLANES, GUNS, LAND MINES AND SEA MINES."
"LAND MINES WERE TO PLANT IN FIELDS WHERE PEOPLE WERE WORKING.
THESE MINES WERE NOT VERY POWERFUL, THEY WERE TO MAIM NOT TO KILL.
THAT WAY SANDINISTAS WOULD HAVE TO CARE FOR CRIPPLES."

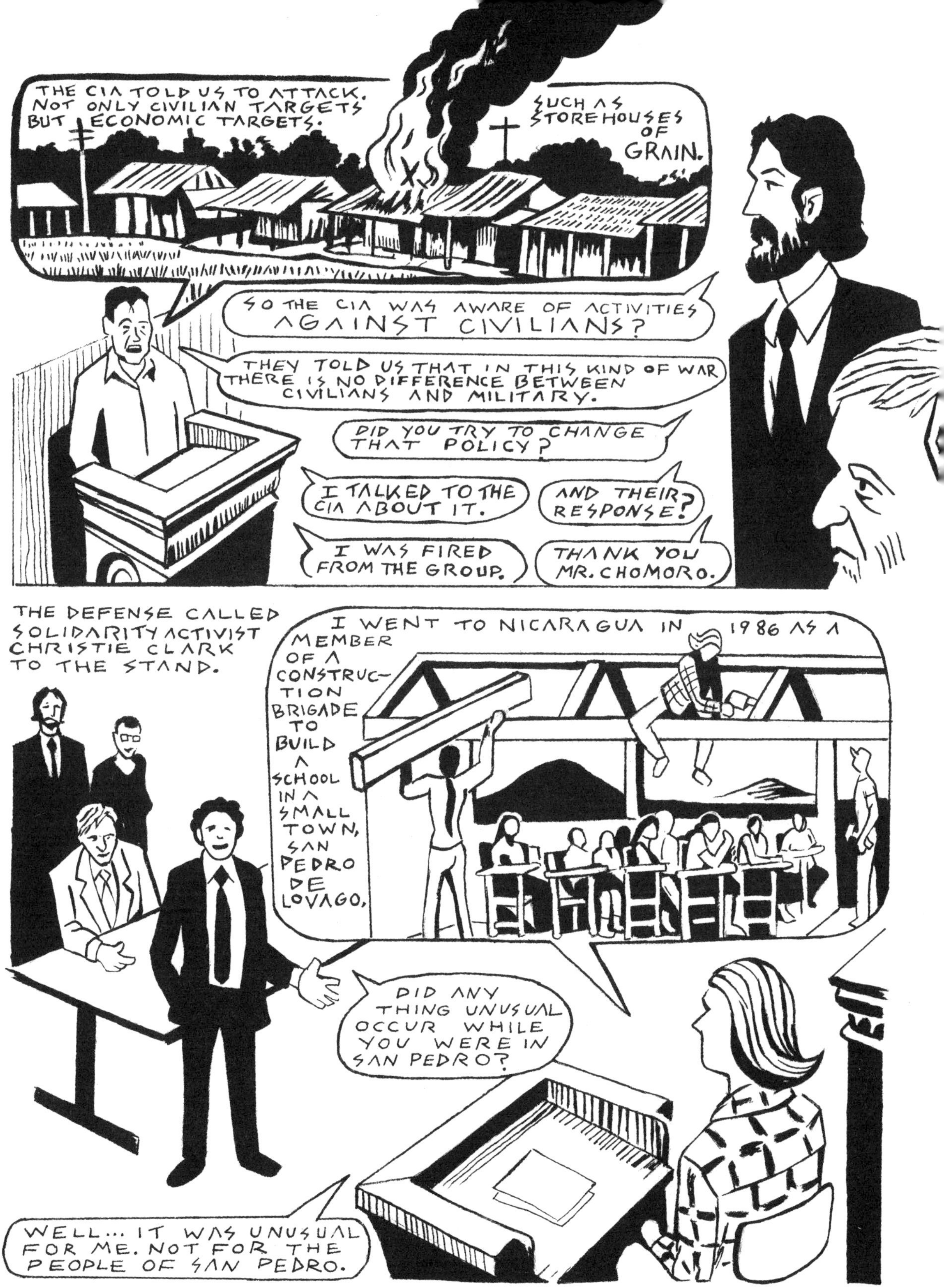

THE CIA TOLD US TO ATTACK. NOT ONLY CIVILIAN TARGETS BUT ECONOMIC TARGETS.
SUCH AS STOREHOUSES OF GRAIN.
SO THE CIA WAS AWARE OF ACTIVITIES AGAINST CIVILIANS?
THEY TOLD US THAT IN THIS KIND OF WAR THERE IS NO DIFFERENCE BETWEEN CIVILIANS AND MILITARY.
DID YOU TRY TO CHANGE THAT POLICY?
I TALKED TO THE CIA ABOUT IT.
AND THEIR RESPONSE?
I WAS FIRED FROM THE GROUP.
THANK YOU MR. CHOMORO.
THE DEFENSE CALLED SOLIDARITY ACTIVIST CHRISTIE CLARK TO THE STAND.
I WENT TO NICARAGUA IN 1986 AS A MEMBER OF A CONSTRUCTION BRIGADE TO BUILD A SCHOOL IN A SMALL TOWN, SAN PEDRO DE LOVAGO,
DID ANY THING UNUSUAL OCCUR WHILE YOU WERE IN SAN PEDRO?
WELL... IT WAS UNUSUAL FOR ME. NOT FOR THE PEOPLE OF SAN PEDRO.

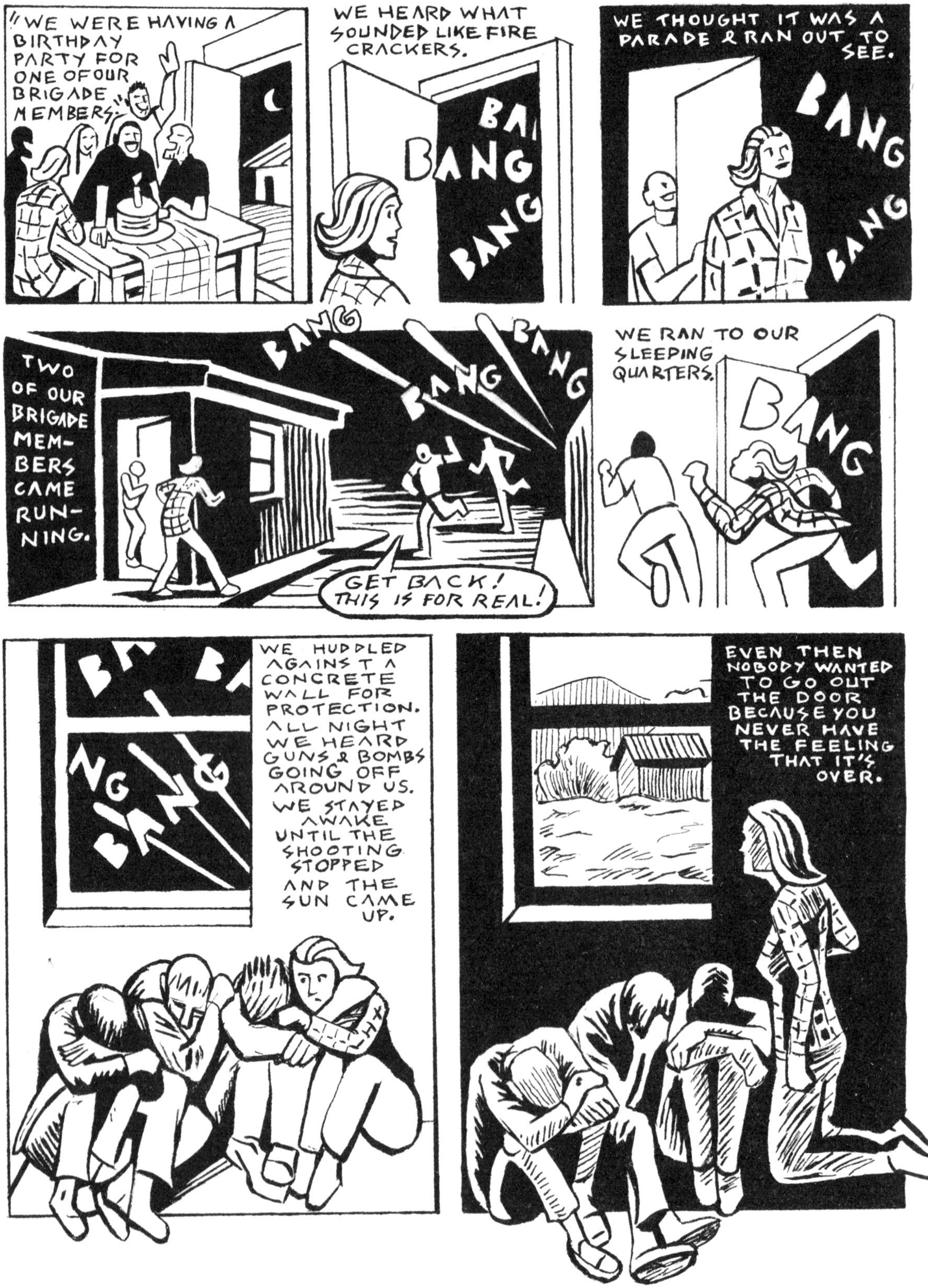
"WE WERE HAVING A BIRTHDAY PARTY FOR ONE OF OUR BRIGADE MEMBERS.
WE HEARD WHAT SOUNDED LIKE FIRE CRACKERS.
BANG
BANG
WE THOUGHT IT WAS A PARADE & RAN OUT TO SEE.
BANG
BANG
TWO OF OUR BRIGADE MEM-BERS CAME RUN-NING.
BANG
BANG
BANG
GET BACK! THIS IS FOR REAL!
WE RAN TO OUR SLEEPING QUARTERS.
BANG
WE HUDDLED AGAINST A CONCRETE WALL FOR PROTECTION. ALL NIGHT WE HEARD GUNS & BOMBS GOING OFF AROUND US. WE STAYED AWAKE UNTIL THE SHOOTING STOPPED AND THE SUN CAME UP.
EVEN THEN NOBODY WANTED TO GO OUT THE DOOR BECAUSE YOU NEVER HAVE THE FEELING THAT IT'S OVER.

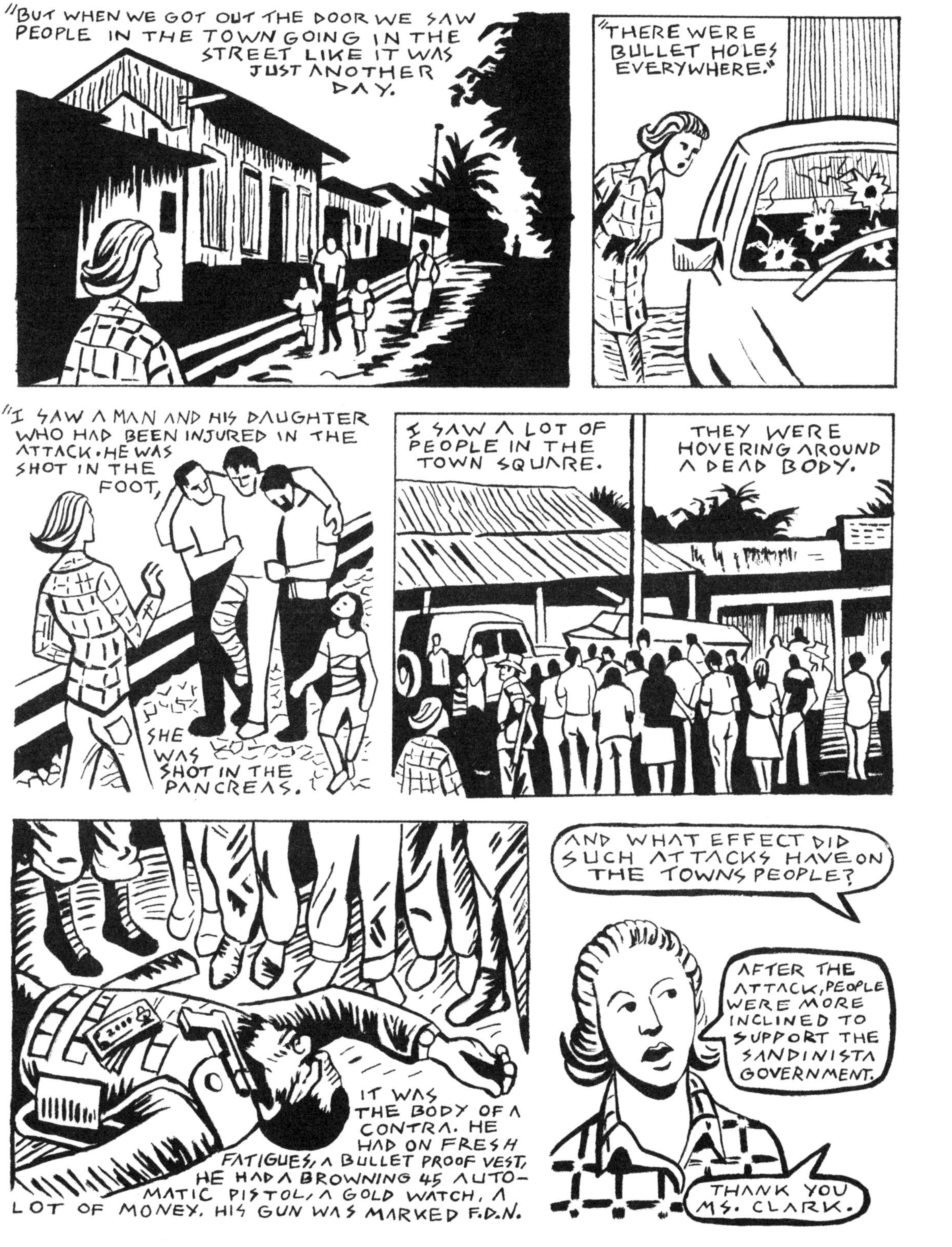
"BUT WHEN WE GOT OUT THE DOOR WE SAW PEOPLE IN THE TOWN GOING IN THE STREET LIKE IT WAS JUST ANOTHER DAY.
"THERE WERE BULLET HOLES EVERYWHERE."
"I SAW A MAN AND HIS DAUGHTER WHO HAD BEEN INJURED IN THE ATTACK. HE WAS SHOT IN THE FOOT,
SHE WAS SHOT IN THE PANCREAS.
I SAW A LOT OF PEOPLE IN THE TOWN SQUARE.
THEY WERE HOVERING AROUND A DEAD BODY.
IT WAS THE BODY OF A CONTRA. HE HAD ON FRESH FATIGUES, A BULLET PROOF VEST, HE HAD A BROWNING 45 AUTO-MATIC PISTOL, A GOLD WATCH, A LOT OF MONEY. HIS GUN WAS MARKED F.D.N.
AND WHAT EFFECT DID SUCH ATTACKS HAVE ON THE TOWNSPEOPLE?
AFTER THE ATTACK, PEOPLE WERE MORE INCLINED TO SUPPORT THE SANDINISTA GOVERNMENT.
THANK YOU MS. CLARK.

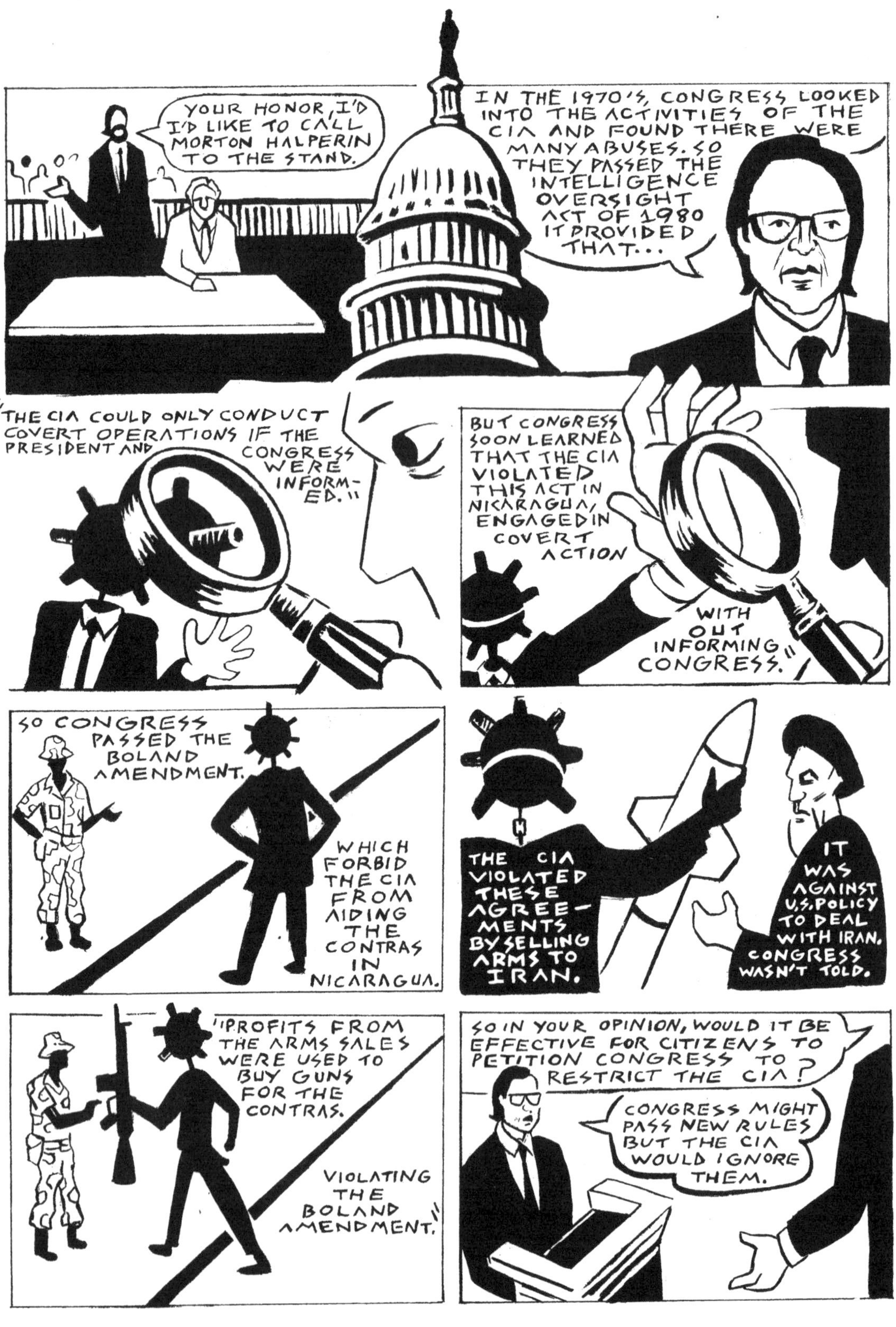
YOUR HONOR, I'D I'D LIKE TO CALL MORTON HALPERIN TO THE STAND.
IN THE 1970'S, CONGRESS LOOKED INTO THE ACTIVITIES OF THE CIA AND FOUND THERE WERE MANY ABUSES. SO THEY PASSED THE INTELLIGENCE OVERSIGHT ACT OF 1980 IT PROVIDED THAT...
"THE CIA COULD ONLY CONDUCT COVERT OPERATIONS IF THE PRESIDENT AND CONGRESS WERE INFORM-ED."
BUT CONGRESS SOON LEARNED THAT THE CIA VIOLATED THIS ACT IN NICARAGUA, ENGAGED IN COVERT ACTION
WITH OUT INFORMING CONGRESS."
SO CONGRESS PASSED THE BOLAND AMENDMENT.
WHICH FORBID THE CIA FROM AIDING THE CONTRAS IN NICARAGUA.
THE CIA VIOLATED THESE AGREE-MENTS BY SELLING ARMS TO IRAN.
IT WAS AGAINST U.S. POLICY TO DEAL WITH IRAN. CONGRESS WASN'T TOLD.
"PROFITS FROM THE ARMS SALES WERE USED TO BUY GUNS FOR THE CONTRAS.
VIOLATING THE BOLAND AMENDMENT."
SO IN YOUR OPINION, WOULD IT BE EFFECTIVE FOR CITIZENS TO PETITION CONGRESS TO RESTRICT THE CIA?
CONGRESS MIGHT PASS NEW RULES BUT THE CIA WOULD IGNORE THEM.

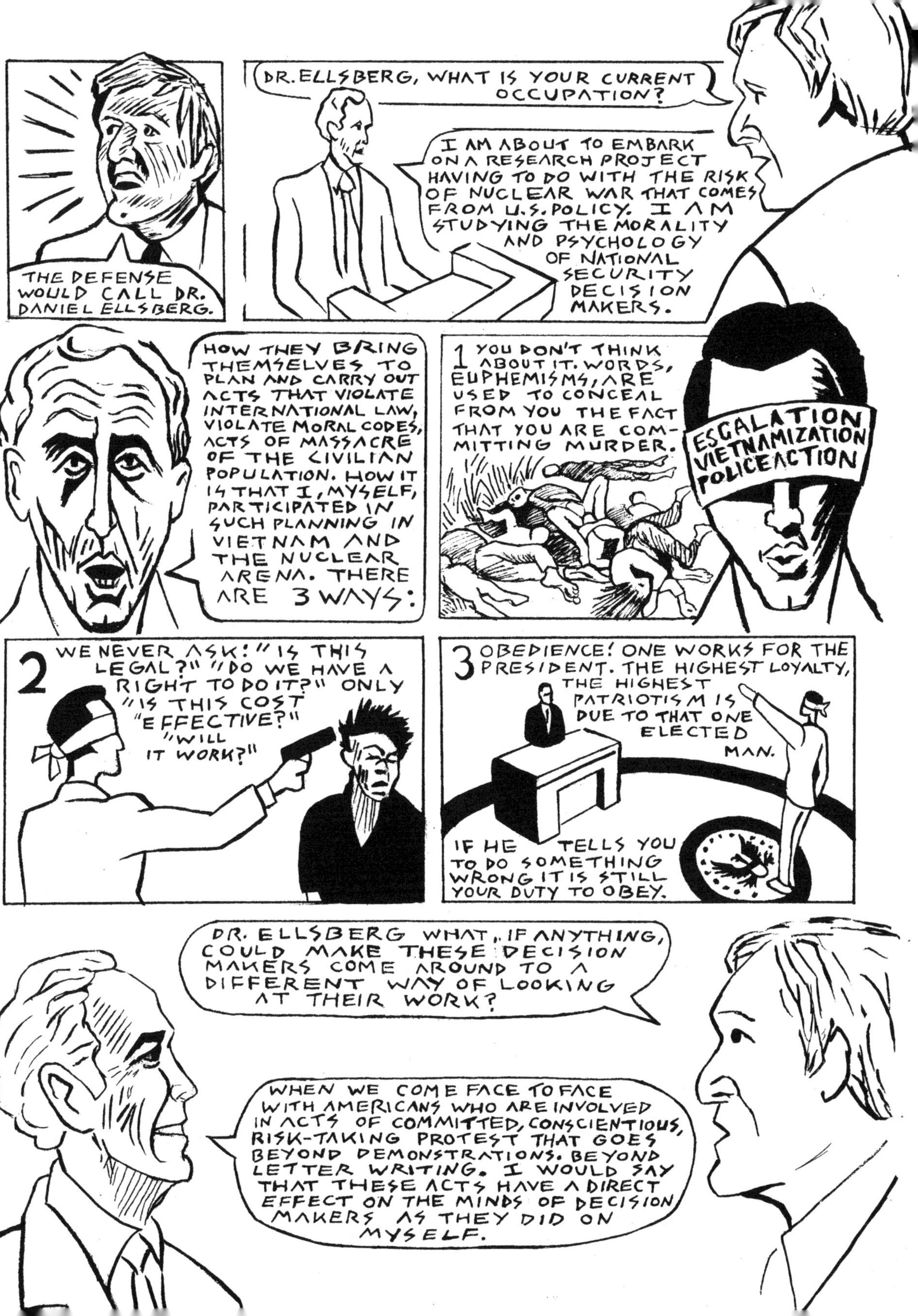
THE DEFENSE WOULD CALL DR. DANIEL ELLSBERG.
DR. ELLSBERG, WHAT IS YOUR CURRENT OCCUPATION?
I AM ABOUT TO EMBARK ON A RESEARCH PROJECT HAVING TO DO WITH THE RISK OF NUCLEAR WAR THAT COMES FROM U.S. POLICY. I AM STUDYING THE MORALITY AND PSYCHOLOGY OF NATIONAL SECURITY DECISION MAKERS.
HOW THEY BRING THEMSELVES TO PLAN AND CARRY OUT ACTS THAT VIOLATE INTERNATIONAL LAW, VIOLATE MORAL CODES, ACTS OF MASSACRE OF THE CIVILIAN POPULATION. HOW IT IS THAT I, MYSELF, PARTICIPATED IN SUCH PLANNING IN VIETNAM AND THE NUCLEAR ARENA. THERE ARE 3 WAYS:
1 YOU DON'T THINK ABOUT IT. WORDS, EUPHEMISMS, ARE USED TO CONCEAL FROM YOU THE FACT THAT YOU ARE COMMITTING MURDER.
ESCALATION VIETNAMIZATION POLICE ACTION
2 WE NEVER ASK: "IS THIS LEGAL?" "DO WE HAVE A RIGHT TO DO IT?" ONLY "IS THIS COST EFFECTIVE?" "WILL IT WORK?"
3 OBEDIENCE! ONE WORKS FOR THE PRESIDENT. THE HIGHEST LOYALTY, THE HIGHEST PATRIOTISM IS DUE TO THAT ONE ELECTED MAN.
IF HE TELLS YOU TO DO SOMETHING WRONG IT IS STILL YOUR DUTY TO OBEY.
DR. ELLSBERG WHAT, IF ANYTHING, COULD MAKE THESE DECISION MAKERS COME AROUND TO A DIFFERENT WAY OF LOOKING AT THEIR WORK?
WHEN WE COME FACE TO FACE WITH AMERICANS WHO ARE INVOLVED IN ACTS OF COMMITTED, CONSCIENTIOUS, RISK-TAKING PROTEST THAT GOES BEYOND DEMONSTRATIONS. BEYOND LETTER WRITING. I WOULD SAY THAT THESE ACTS HAVE A DIRECT EFFECT ON THE MINDS OF DECISION MAKERS AS THEY DID ON MYSELF.

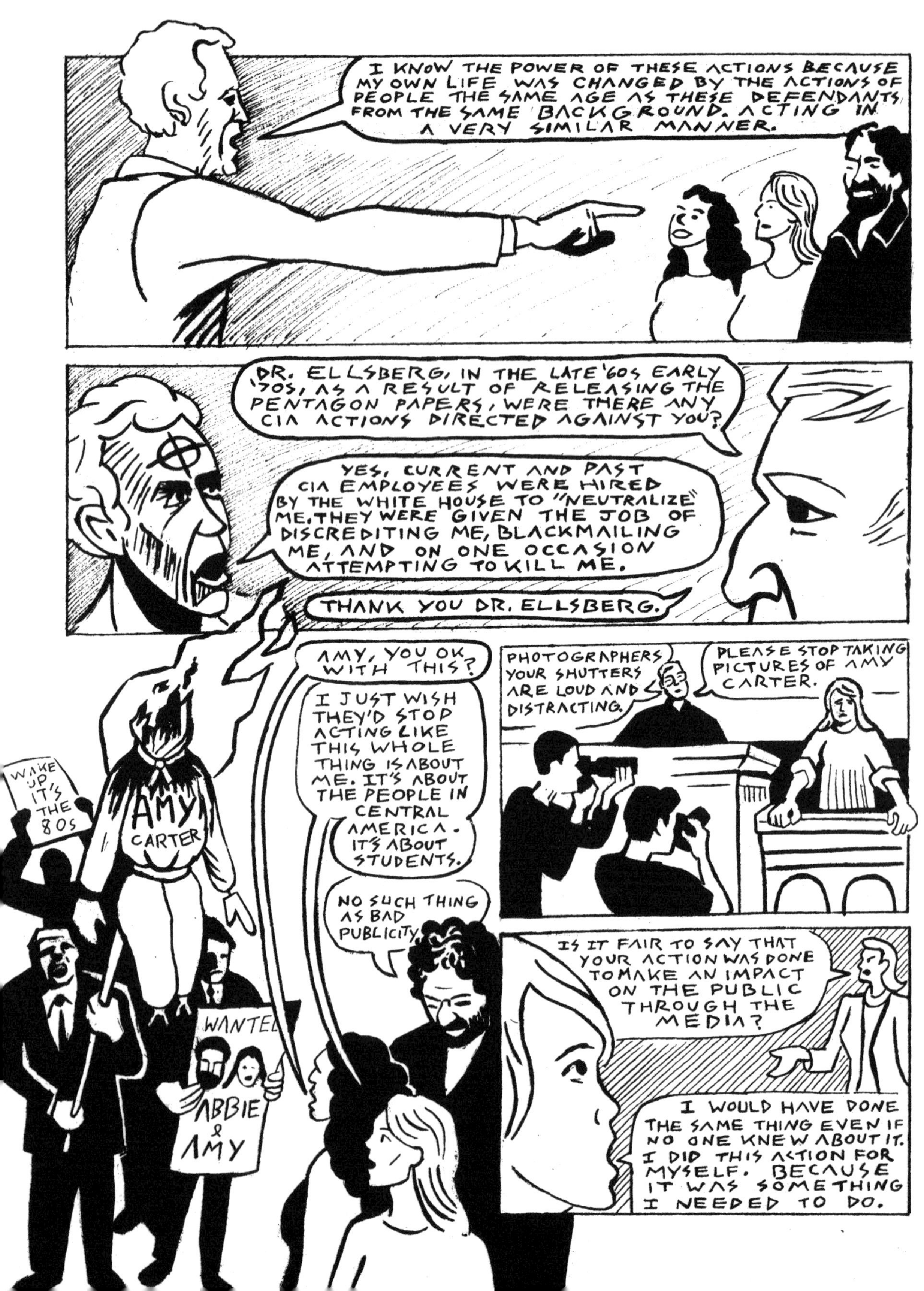

I KNOW THE POWER OF THESE ACTIONS BECAUSE MY OWN LIFE WAS CHANGED BY THE ACTIONS OF PEOPLE THE SAME AGE AS THESE DEFENDANTS FROM THE SAME BACKGROUND. ACTING IN A VERY SIMILAR MANNER.
DR. ELLSBERG, IN THE LATE '60s EARLY '70s, AS A RESULT OF RELEASING THE PENTAGON PAPERS, WERE THERE ANY CIA ACTIONS DIRECTED AGAINST YOU?
YES. CURRENT AND PAST CIA EMPLOYEES WERE HIRED BY THE WHITE HOUSE TO "NEUTRALIZE" ME. THEY WERE GIVEN THE JOB OF DISCREDITING ME, BLACKMAILING ME, AND ON ONE OCCASION ATTEMPTING TO KILL ME.
THANK YOU DR. ELLSBERG.
WAKE UP IT'S THE 80s
AMY CARTER
AMY, YOU OK WITH THIS?
I JUST WISH THEY'D STOP ACTING LIKE THIS WHOLE THING IS ABOUT ME. IT'S ABOUT THE PEOPLE IN CENTRAL AMERICA. IT'S ABOUT STUDENTS.
NO SUCH THING AS BAD PUBLICITY
WANTED
ABBIE & AMY
PHOTOGRAPHERS YOUR SHUTTERS ARE LOUD AND DISTRACTING.
PLEASE STOP TAKING PICTURES OF AMY CARTER.
IS IT FAIR TO SAY THAT YOUR ACTION WAS DONE TO MAKE AN IMPACT ON THE PUBLIC THROUGH THE MEDIA?
I WOULD HAVE DONE THE SAME THING EVEN IF NO ONE KNEW ABOUT IT. I DID THIS ACTION FOR MYSELF. BECAUSE IT WAS SOMETHING I NEEDED TO DO.

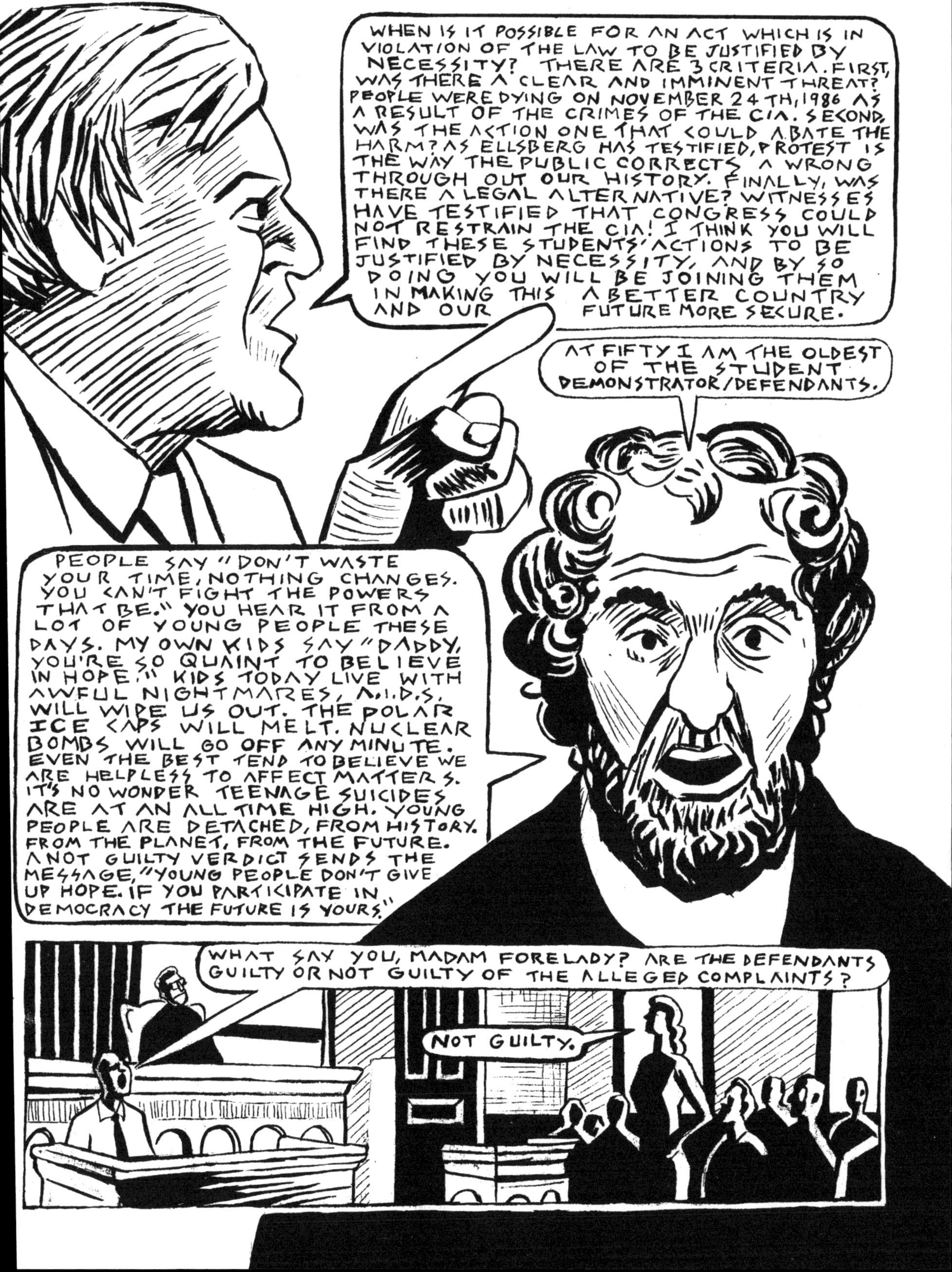
WHEN IS IT POSSIBLE FOR AN ACT WHICH IS IN VIOLATION OF THE LAW TO BE JUSTIFIED BY NECESSITY? THERE ARE 3 CRITERIA. FIRST, WAS THERE A CLEAR AND IMMINENT THREAT? PEOPLE WERE DYING ON NOVEMBER 24TH, 1986 AS A RESULT OF THE CRIMES OF THE CIA. SECOND, WAS THE ACTION ONE THAT COULD ABATE THE HARM? AS ELLSBERG HAS TESTIFIED, PROTEST IS THE WAY THE PUBLIC CORRECTS A WRONG THROUGH OUT OUR HISTORY. FINALLY, WAS THERE A LEGAL ALTERNATIVE? WITNESSES HAVE TESTIFIED THAT CONGRESS COULD NOT RESTRAIN THE CIA! I THINK YOU WILL FIND THESE STUDENTS' ACTIONS TO BE JUSTIFIED BY NECESSITY, AND BY SO DOING YOU WILL BE JOINING THEM IN MAKING THIS A BETTER COUNTRY AND OUR FUTURE MORE SECURE.
AT FIFTY I AM THE OLDEST OF THE STUDENT DEMONSTRATOR/DEFENDANTS.
PEOPLE SAY "DON'T WASTE YOUR TIME, NOTHING CHANGES. YOU CAN'T FIGHT THE POWERS THAT BE." YOU HEAR IT FROM A LOT OF YOUNG PEOPLE THESE DAYS. MY OWN KIDS SAY "DADDY, YOU'RE SO QUAINT TO BELIEVE IN HOPE." KIDS TODAY LIVE WITH AWFUL NIGHTMARES, A.I.D.S. WILL WIPE US OUT. THE POLAR ICE CAPS WILL MELT. NUCLEAR BOMBS WILL GO OFF ANY MINUTE. EVEN THE BEST TEND TO BELIEVE WE ARE HELPLESS TO AFFECT MATTERS. IT'S NO WONDER TEENAGE SUICIDES ARE AT AN ALL TIME HIGH. YOUNG PEOPLE ARE DETACHED, FROM HISTORY. FROM THE PLANET, FROM THE FUTURE. A NOT GUILTY VERDICT SENDS THE MESSAGE, "YOUNG PEOPLE DON'T GIVE UP HOPE. IF YOU PARTICIPATE IN DEMOCRACY THE FUTURE IS YOURS."
WHAT SAY YOU, MADAM FORELADY? ARE THE DEFENDANTS GUILTY OR NOT GUILTY OF THE ALLEGED COMPLAINTS?
NOT GUILTY.

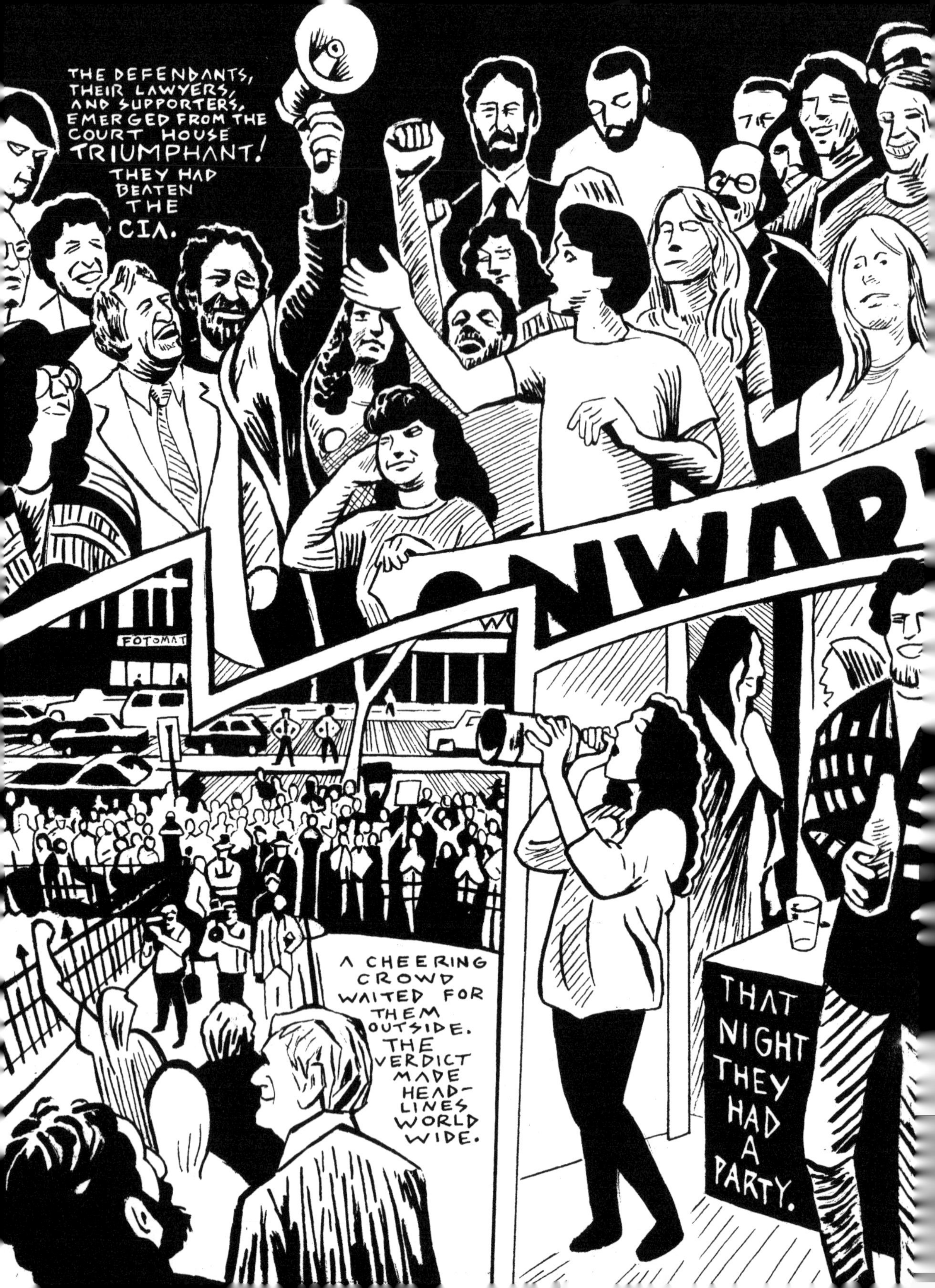
THE DEFENDANTS, THEIR LAWYERS, AND SUPPORTERS, EMERGED FROM THE COURT HOUSE TRIUMPHANT! THEY HAD BEATEN THE CIA.
ONWAR
FOTOMAT
A CHEERING CROWD WAITED FOR THEM OUTSIDE. THE VERDICT MADE HEAD-LINES WORLD WIDE.
THAT NIGHT THEY HAD A PARTY.

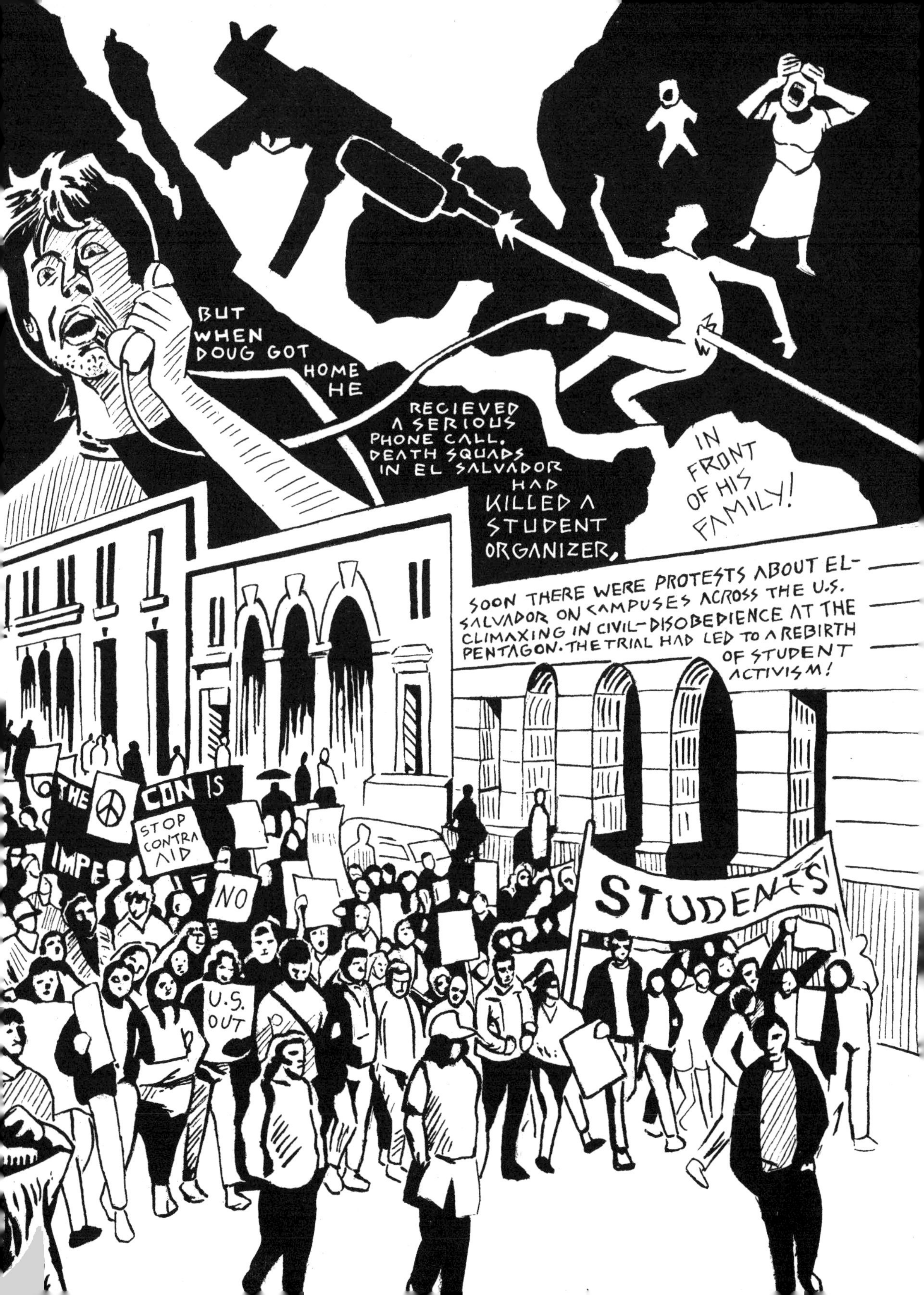

BUT WHEN DOUG GOT HOME HE RECIEVED A SERIOUS PHONE CALL. DEATH SQUADS IN EL SALVADOR HAD KILLED A STUDENT ORGANIZER,
IN FRONT OF HIS FAMILY!
SOON THERE WERE PROTESTS ABOUT EL-SALVADOR ON CAMPUSES ACROSS THE U.S. CLIMAXING IN CIVIL-DISOBEDIENCE AT THE PENTAGON. THE TRIAL HAD LED TO A REBIRTH OF STUDENT ACTIVISM!
THE CON IS IMPE
STOP CONTRA AID
NO
U.S. OUT
STUDENTS

IN 2002 LEONARD WEINGLASS EXPLAINED

THE PATRIOT ACT

THE BEGINNING OF THE END...

OF CIVIL LIBERTIES AS WE KNOW THEM

DID NOT HAPPEN OVERNIGHT ON 9-11

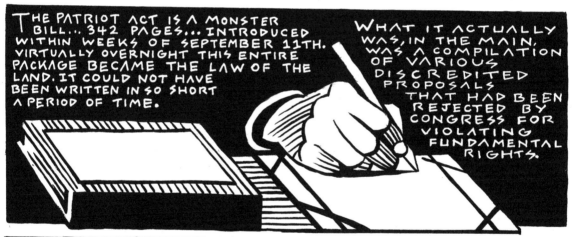

THE PATRIOT ACT IS A MONSTER BILL... 342 PAGES... INTRODUCED WITHIN WEEKS OF SEPTEMBER 11TH. VIRTUALLY OVERNIGHT THIS ENTIRE PACKAGE BECAME THE LAW OF THE LAND. IT COULD NOT HAVE BEEN WRITTEN IN SO SHORT A PERIOD OF TIME.

WHAT IT ACTUALLY WAS, IN THE MAIN, WAS A COMPILATION OF VARIOUS DISCREDITED PROPOSALS THAT HAD BEEN REJECTED BY CONGRESS FOR VIOLATING FUNDAMENTAL RIGHTS.

TO FULLY UNDERSTAND WHAT'S HAPPENING WE HAVE TO GO BACK TO 1972. AT THAT TIME NIXON SOUGHT PERMISSION FROM THE SUPREME COURT TO WIRE-TAP AMERICANS WITHOUT A WARRANT ON THE GROUNDS OF NATIONAL SECURITY.

THE COURT DIDN'T BUY IT.

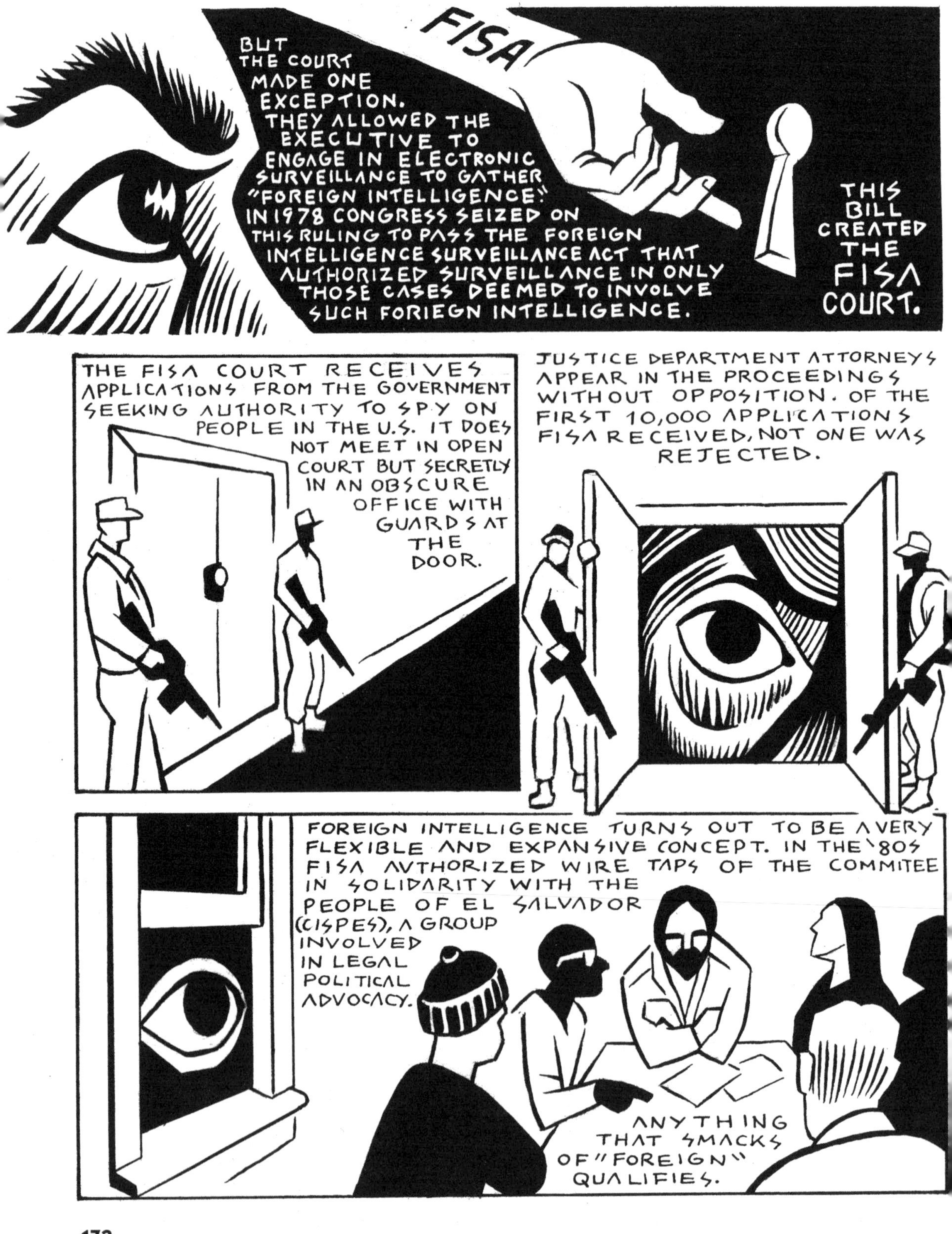
FISA
BUT THE COURT MADE ONE EXCEPTION. THEY ALLOWED THE EXECUTIVE TO ENGAGE IN ELECTRONIC SURVEILLANCE TO GATHER "FOREIGN INTELLIGENCE." IN 1978 CONGRESS SEIZED ON THIS RULING TO PASS THE FOREIGN INTELLIGENCE SURVEILLANCE ACT THAT AUTHORIZED SURVEILLANCE IN ONLY THOSE CASES DEEMED TO INVOLVE SUCH FORIEGN INTELLIGENCE.
THIS BILL CREATED THE FISA COURT.
THE FISA COURT RECEIVES APPLICATIONS FROM THE GOVERNMENT SEEKING AUTHORITY TO SPY ON PEOPLE IN THE U.S. IT DOES NOT MEET IN OPEN COURT BUT SECRETLY IN AN OBSCURE OFFICE WITH GUARDS AT THE DOOR.
JUSTICE DEPARTMENT ATTORNEYS APPEAR IN THE PROCEEDINGS WITHOUT OPPOSITION. OF THE FIRST 10,000 APPLICATIONS FISA RECEIVED, NOT ONE WAS REJECTED.
FOREIGN INTELLIGENCE TURNS OUT TO BE A VERY FLEXIBLE AND EXPANSIVE CONCEPT. IN THE '80s FISA AUTHORIZED WIRE TAPS OF THE COMMITEE IN SOLIDARITY WITH THE PEOPLE OF EL SALVADOR (CISPES), A GROUP INVOLVED IN LEGAL POLITICAL ADVOCACY.
ANYTHING THAT SMACKS OF "FOREIGN" QUALIFIES.

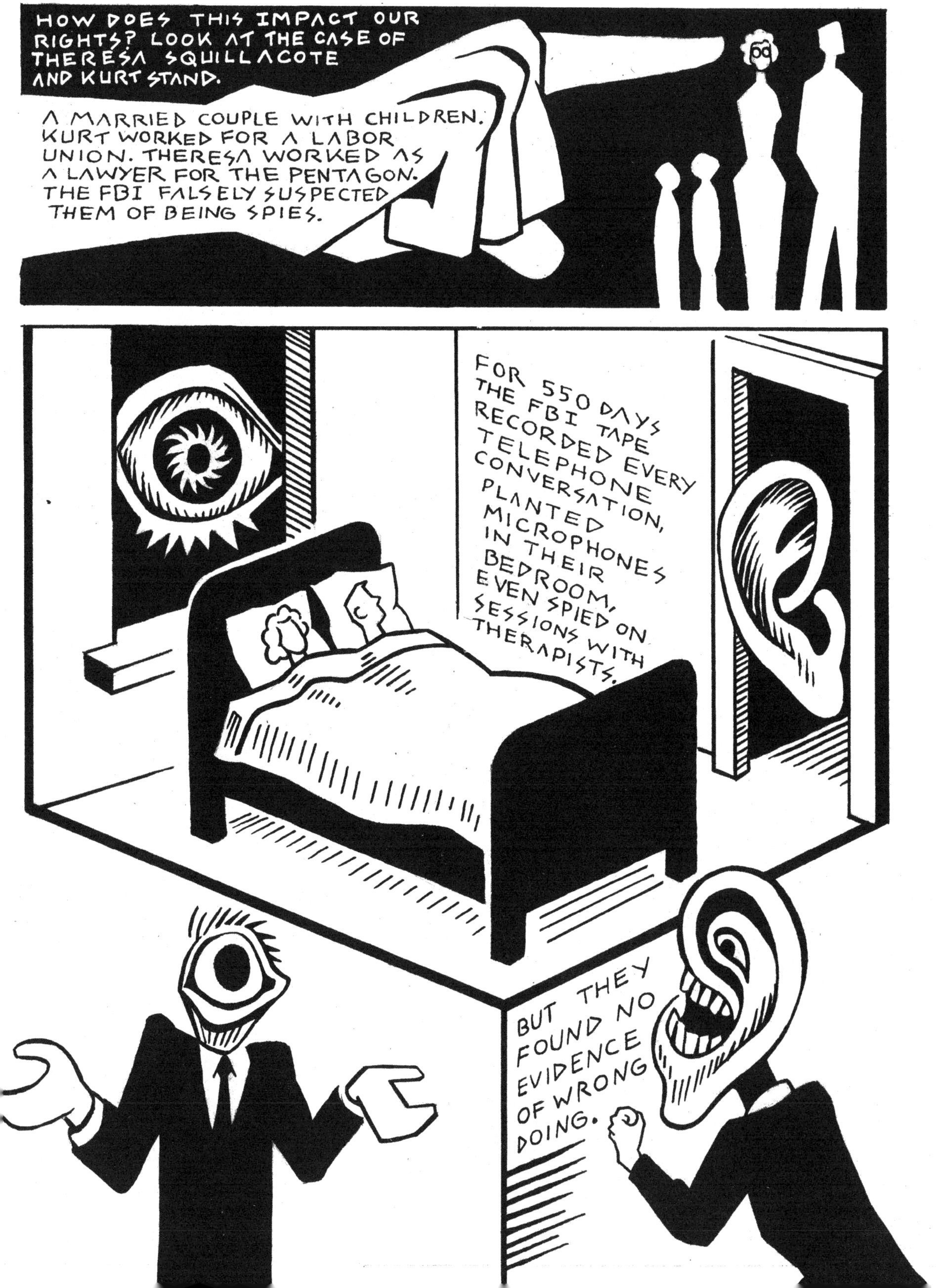
HOW DOES THIS IMPACT OUR RIGHTS? LOOK AT THE CASE OF THERESA SQUILLACOTE AND KURT STAND.
A MARRIED COUPLE WITH CHILDREN. KURT WORKED FOR A LABOR UNION. THERESA WORKED AS A LAWYER FOR THE PENTAGON. THE FBI FALSELY SUSPECTED THEM OF BEING SPIES.
FOR 550 DAYS THE FBI TAPE RECORDED EVERY TELEPHONE CONVERSATION, PLANTED MICROPHONES IN THEIR BEDROOM, EVEN SPIED ON SESSIONS WITH THERAPISTS.
BUT THEY FOUND NO EVIDENCE OF WRONG DOING.

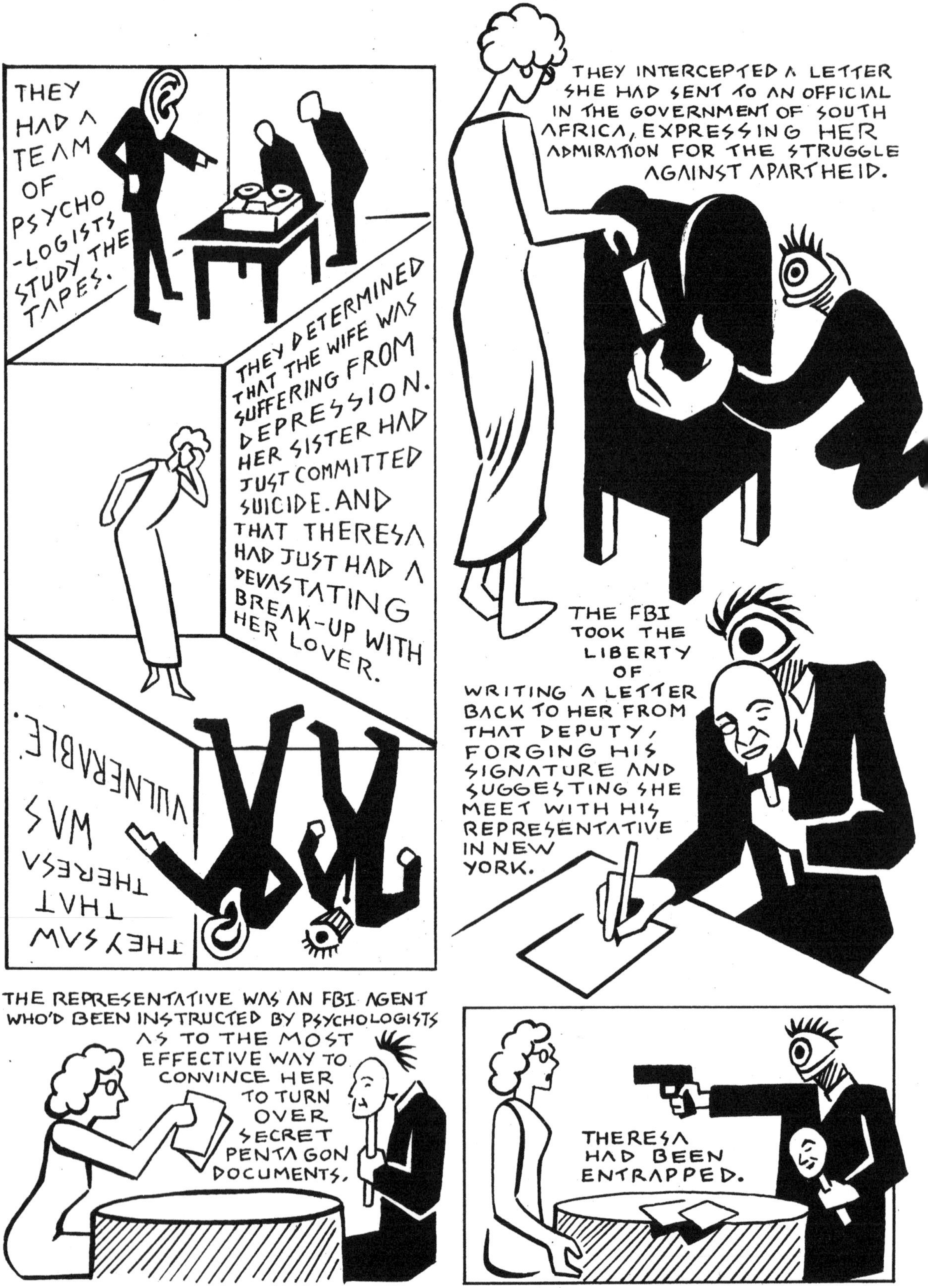
THEY HAD A TEAM OF PSYCHO PSYCHO-LOGISTS STUDY THE TAPES.
THEY DETERMINED THAT THE WIFE WAS SUFFERING FROM DEPRESSION. HER SISTER HAD JUST COMMITTED SUICIDE. AND THAT THERESA HAD JUST HAD A DEVASTATING BREAK-UP WITH HER LOVER.
THEY SAW THAT THERESA WAS VULNERABLE.
THEY INTERCEPTED A LETTER SHE HAD SENT TO AN OFFICIAL IN THE GOVERNMENT OF SOUTH AFRICA, EXPRESSING HER ADMIRATION FOR THE STRUGGLE AGAINST APARTHEID.
THE FBI TOOK THE LIBERTY OF WRITING A LETTER BACK TO HER FROM THAT DEPUTY, FORGING HIS SIGNATURE AND SUGGESTING SHE MEET WITH HIS REPRESENTATIVE IN NEW YORK.
THE REPRESENTATIVE WAS AN FBI AGENT WHO'D BEEN INSTRUCTED BY PSYCHOLOGISTS AS TO THE MOST EFFECTIVE WAY TO CONVINCE HER TO TURN OVER SECRET PENTAGON DOCUMENTS.
THERESA HAD BEEN ENTRAPPED.

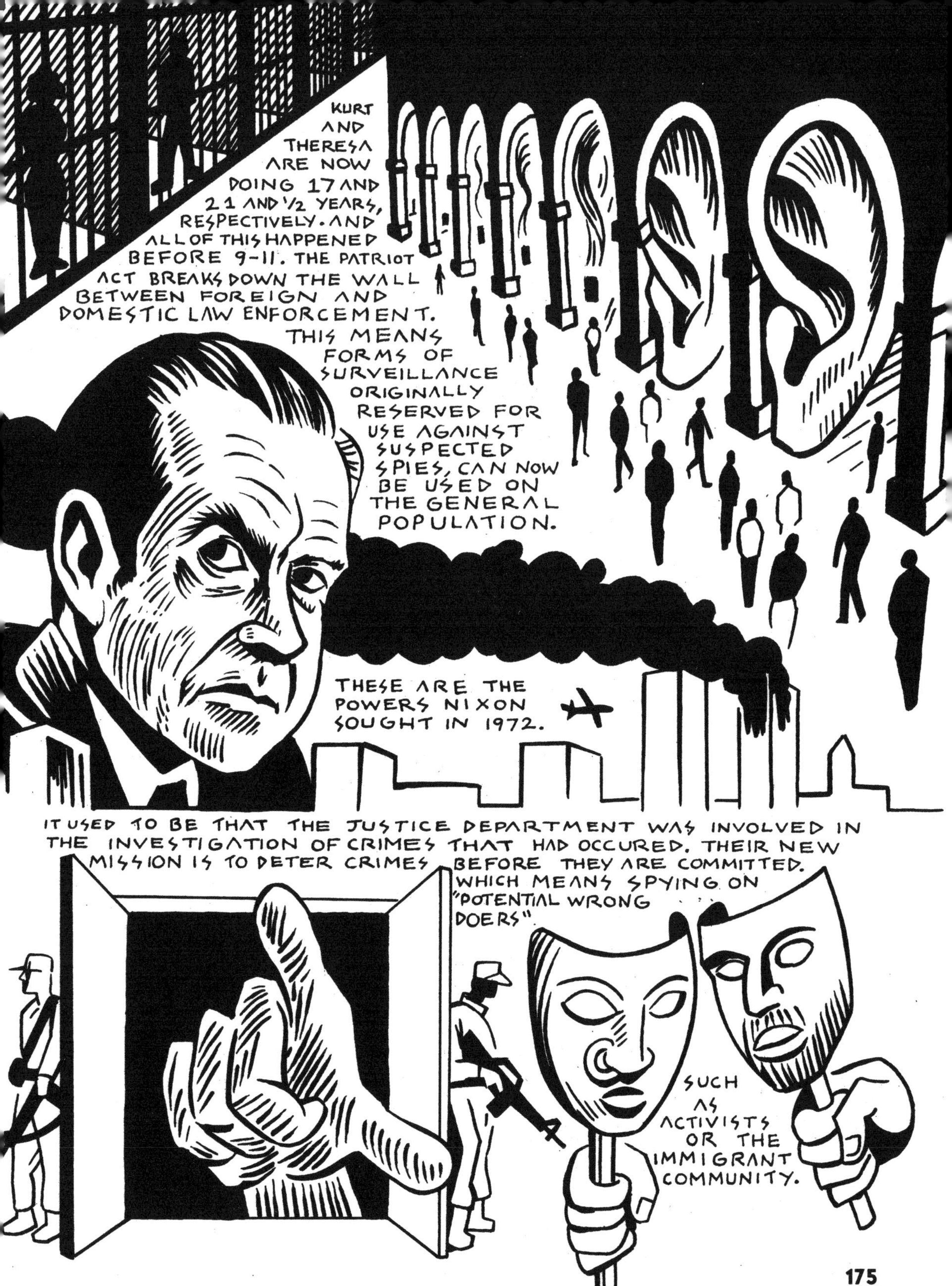
KURT AND THERESA ARE NOW DOING 17 AND 21 AND 1/2 YEARS, RESPECTIVELY. AND ALL OF THIS HAPPENED BEFORE 9-11. THE PATRIOT ACT BREAKS DOWN THE WALL BETWEEN FOREIGN AND DOMESTIC LAW ENFORCEMENT.
THIS MEANS FORMS OF SURVEILLANCE ORIGINALLY RESERVED FOR USE AGAINST SUSPECTED SPIES, CAN NOW BE USED ON THE GENERAL POPULATION.
THESE ARE THE POWERS NIXON SOUGHT IN 1972.
IT USED TO BE THAT THE JUSTICE DEPARTMENT WAS INVOLVED IN THE INVESTIGATION OF CRIMES THAT HAD OCCURED. THEIR NEW MISSION IS TO DETER CRIMES BEFORE THEY ARE COMMITTED.
WHICH MEANS SPYING ON "POTENTIAL WRONG DOERS"
SUCH AS ACTIVISTS OR THE IMMIGRANT COMMUNITY.

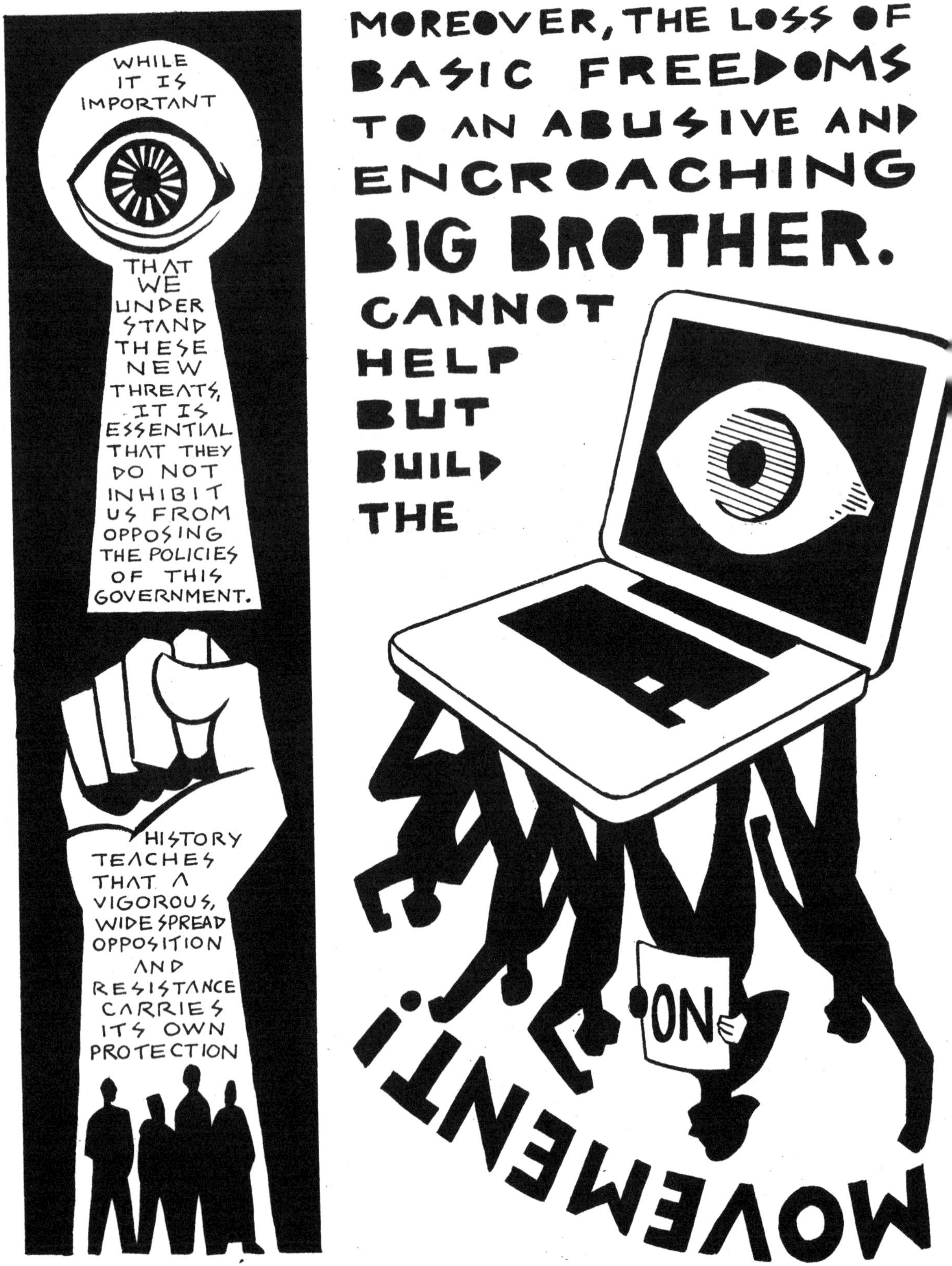

WHILE IT IS IMPORTANT THAT WE UNDERSTAND THESE NEW THREATS, IT IS ESSENTIAL THAT THEY DO NOT INHIBIT US FROM OPPOSING THE POLICIES OF THIS GOVERNMENT.
HISTORY TEACHES THAT A VIGOROUS, WIDESPREAD OPPOSITION AND RESISTANCE CARRIES ITS OWN PROTECTION
MOREOVER, THE LOSS OF BASIC FREEDOMS TO AN ABUSIVE AND ENCROACHING BIG BROTHER.
CANNOT HELP BUT BUILD THE
MOVEMENT!
ON

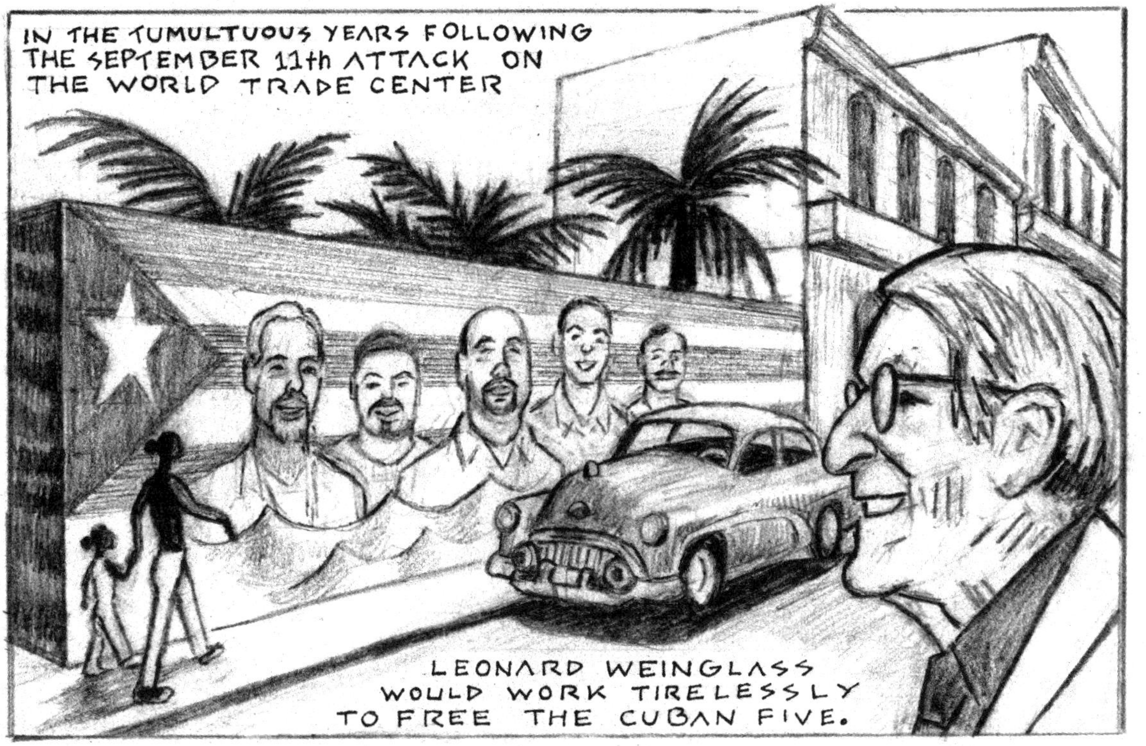
IN THE TUMULTUOUS YEARS FOLLOWING THE SEPTEMBER 11th ATTACK ON THE WORLD TRADE CENTER
LEONARD WEINGLASS WOULD WORK TIRELESSLY TO FREE THE CUBAN FIVE.

A MAN OF GREAT HOPES

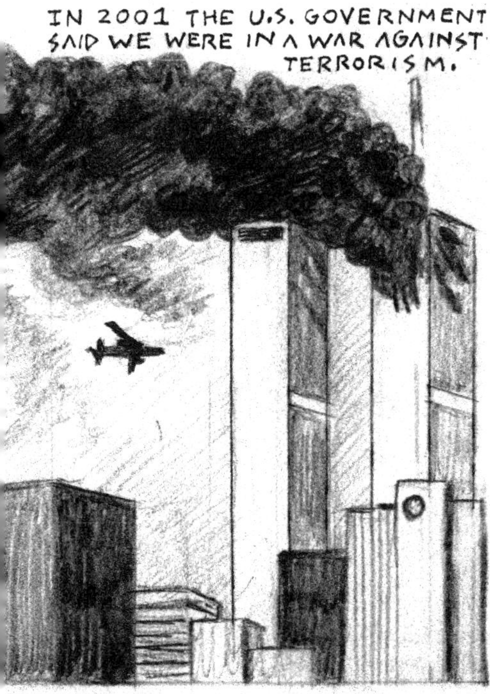
IN 2001 THE U.S. GOVERNMENT SAID WE WERE IN A WAR AGAINST TERRORISM.

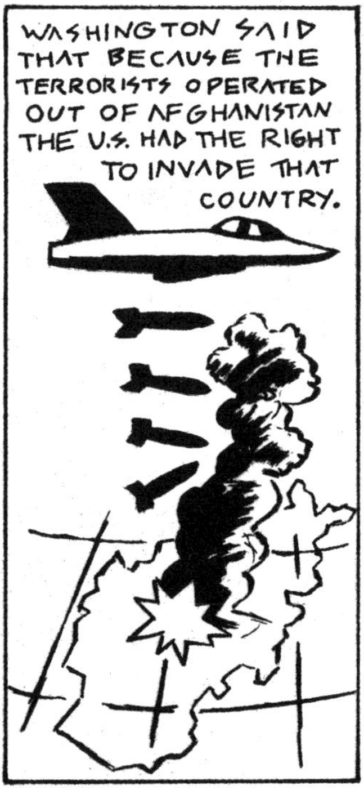
WASHINGTON SAID THAT BECAUSE THE TERRORISTS OPERATED OUT OF AFGHANISTAN THE U.S. HAD THE RIGHT TO INVADE THAT COUNTRY.

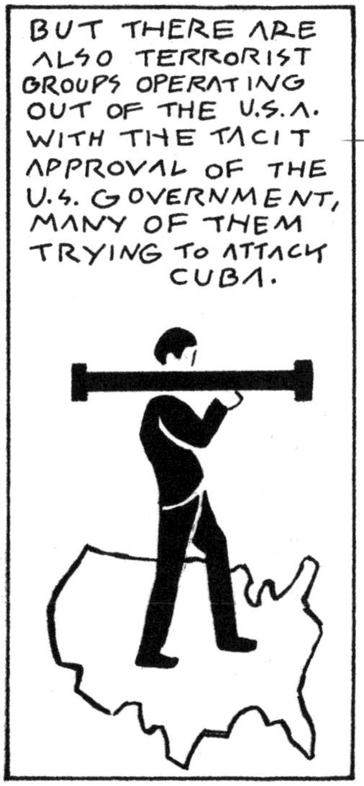
BUT THERE ARE ALSO TERRORIST GROUPS OPERATING OUT OF THE U.S.A. WITH THE TACIT APPROVAL OF THE U.S. GOVERNMENT, MANY OF THEM TRYING TO ATTACK CUBA.

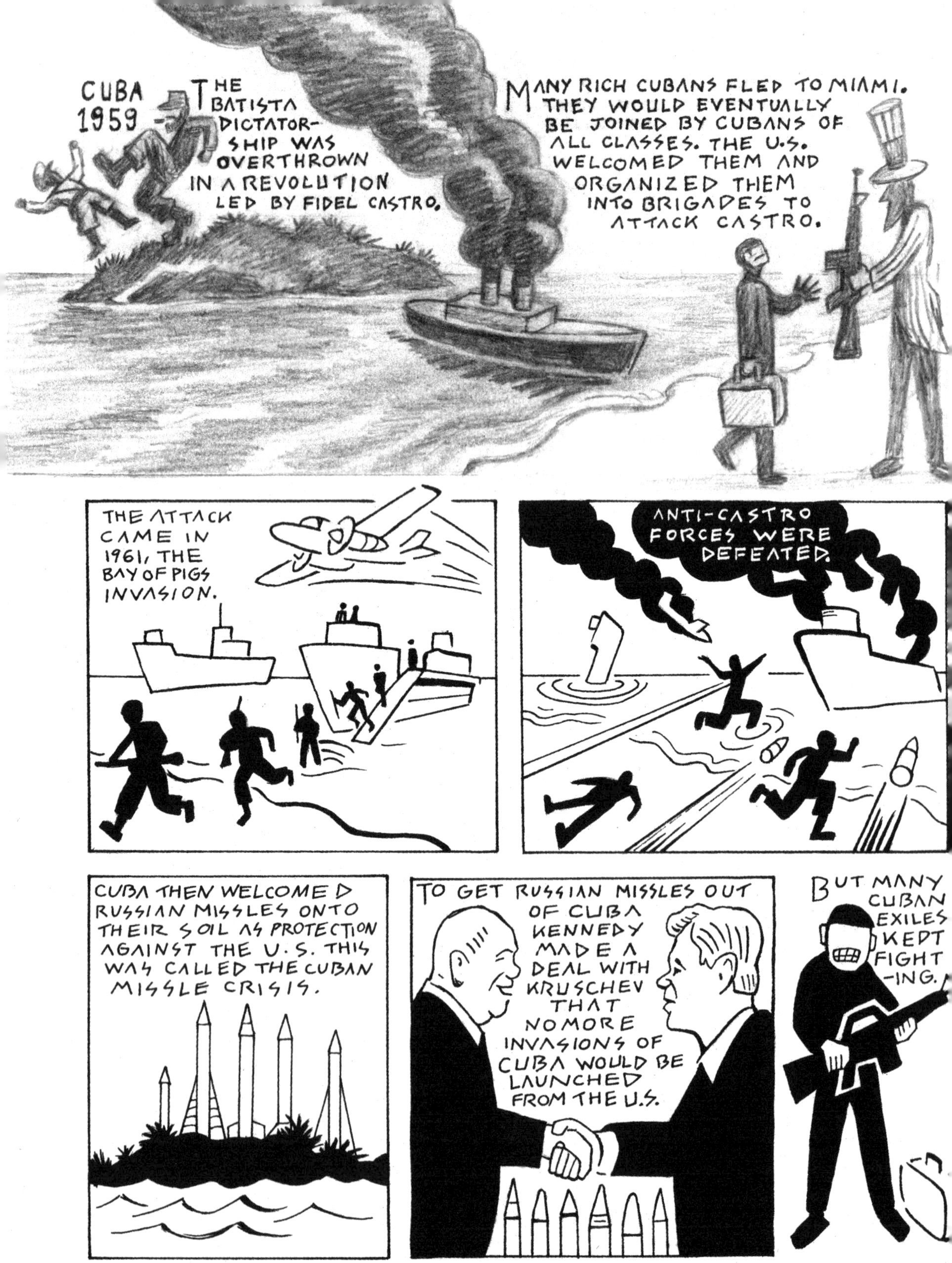
CUBA 1959 - THE BATISTA DICTATORSHIP WAS OVERTHROWN IN A REVOLUTION LED BY FIDEL CASTRO.
MANY RICH CUBANS FLED TO MIAMI. THEY WOULD EVENTUALLY BE JOINED BY CUBANS OF ALL CLASSES. THE U.S. WELCOMED THEM AND ORGANIZED THEM INTO BRIGADES TO ATTACK CASTRO.
THE ATTACK CAME IN 1961, THE BAY OF PIGS INVASION.
ANTI-CASTRO FORCES WERE DEFEATED.
CUBA THEN WELCOMED RUSSIAN MISSLES ONTO THEIR SOIL AS PROTECTION AGAINST THE U.S. THIS WAS CALLED THE CUBAN MISSLE CRISIS.
TO GET RUSSIAN MISSLES OUT OF CUBA KENNEDY MADE A DEAL WITH KRUSCHEV THAT NOMORE INVASIONS OF CUBA WOULD BE LAUNCHED FROM THE U.S.
BUT MANY CUBAN EXILES KEPT FIGHT-ING.

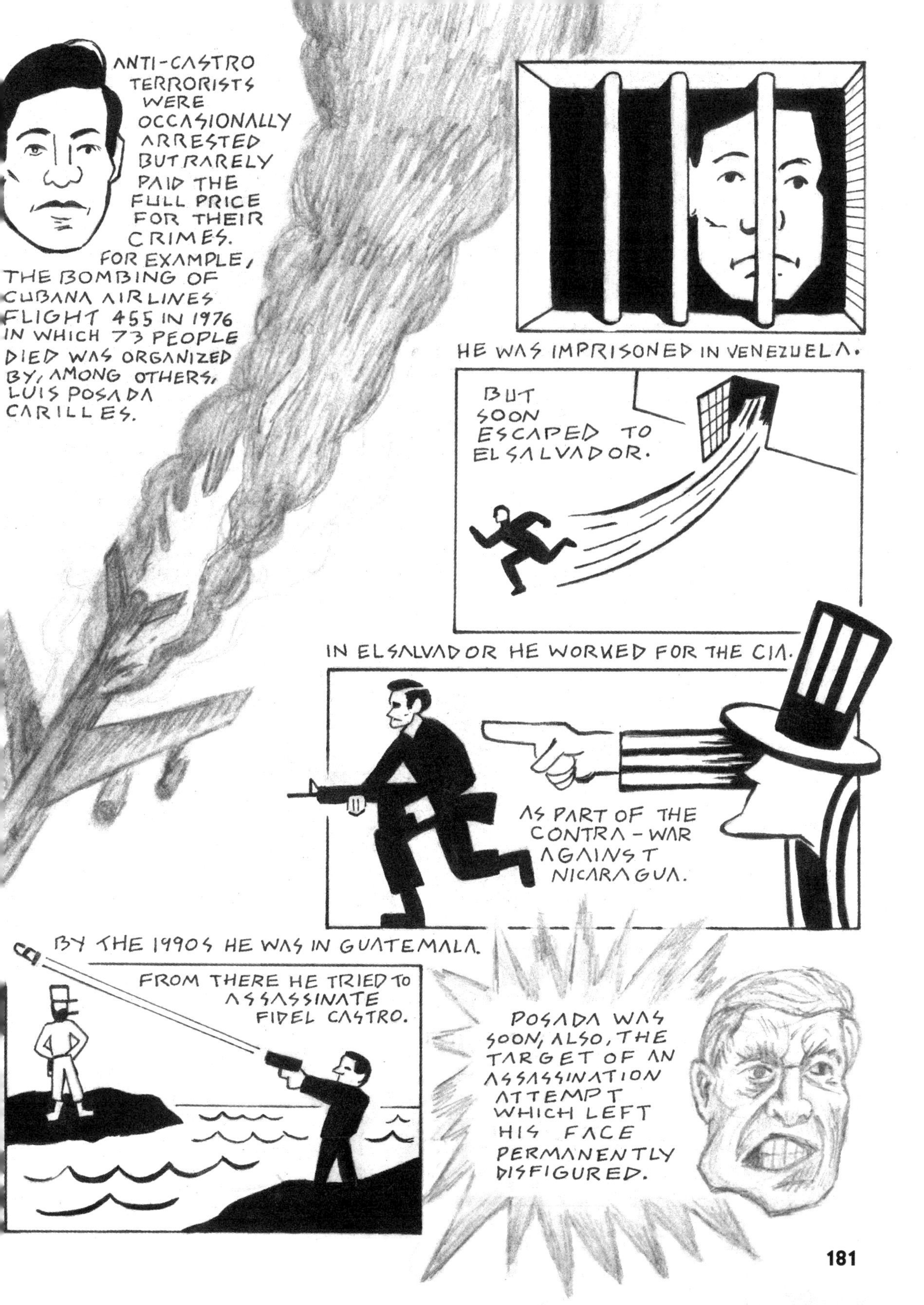
ANTI-CASTRO TERRORISTS WERE OCCASIONALLY ARRESTED BUT RARELY PAID THE FULL PRICE FOR THEIR CRIMES.
FOR EXAMPLE, THE BOMBING OF CUBANA AIRLINES FLIGHT 455 IN 1976 IN WHICH 73 PEOPLE DIED WAS ORGANIZED BY, AMONG OTHERS, LUIS POSADA CARILLES.
HE WAS IMPRISONED IN VENEZUELA.
BUT SOON ESCAPED TO EL SALVADOR.
IN EL SALVADOR HE WORKED FOR THE CIA.
AS PART OF THE CONTRA-WAR AGAINST NICARAGUA.
BY THE 1990S HE WAS IN GUATEMALA.
FROM THERE HE TRIED TO ASSASSINATE FIDEL CASTRO.
POSADA WAS SOON, ALSO, THE TARGET OF AN ASSASSINATION ATTEMPT WHICH LEFT HIS FACE PERMANENTLY DISFIGURED.

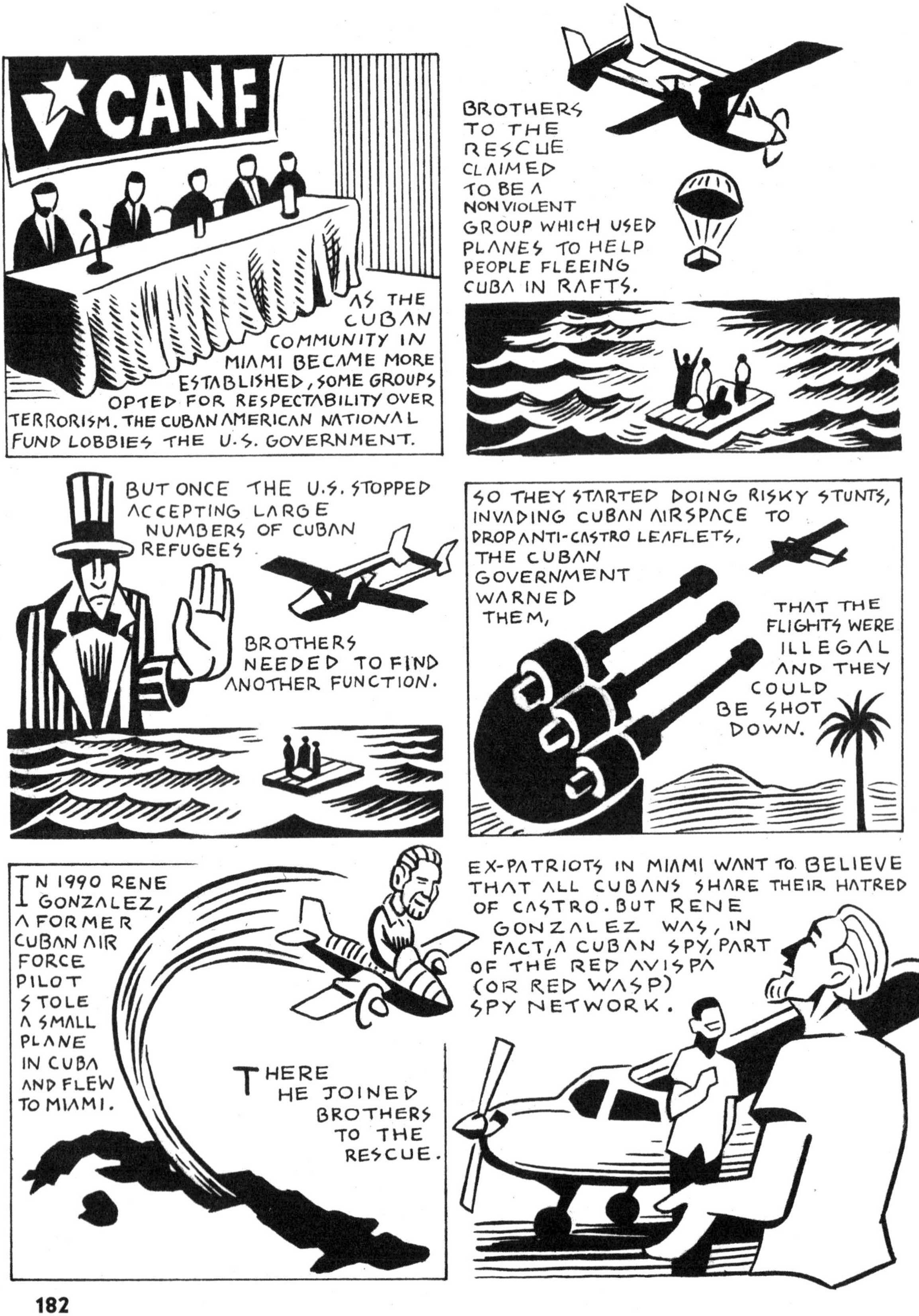
CANF
AS THE CUBAN COMMUNITY IN MIAMI BECAME MORE ESTABLISHED, SOME GROUPS OPTED FOR RESPECTABILITY OVER TERRORISM. THE CUBAN AMERICAN NATIONAL FUND LOBBIES THE U.S. GOVERNMENT.
BROTHERS TO THE RESCUE CLAIMED TO BE A NONVIOLENT GROUP WHICH USED PLANES TO HELP PEOPLE FLEEING CUBA IN RAFTS.
BUT ONCE THE U.S. STOPPED ACCEPTING LARGE NUMBERS OF CUBAN REFUGEES
BROTHERS NEEDED TO FIND ANOTHER FUNCTION.
SO THEY STARTED DOING RISKY STUNTS, INVADING CUBAN AIRSPACE TO DROP ANTI-CASTRO LEAFLETS.
THE CUBAN GOVERNMENT WARNED THEM,
THAT THE FLIGHTS WERE ILLEGAL AND THEY COULD BE SHOT DOWN.
IN 1990 RENE GONZALEZ, A FORMER CUBAN AIR FORCE PILOT STOLE A SMALL PLANE IN CUBA AND FLEW TO MIAMI.
THERE HE JOINED BROTHERS TO THE RESCUE.
EX-PATRIOTS IN MIAMI WANT TO BELIEVE THAT ALL CUBANS SHARE THEIR HATRED OF CASTRO. BUT RENE GONZALEZ WAS, IN FACT, A CUBAN SPY, PART OF THE RED AVISPA (OR RED WASP) SPY NETWORK.

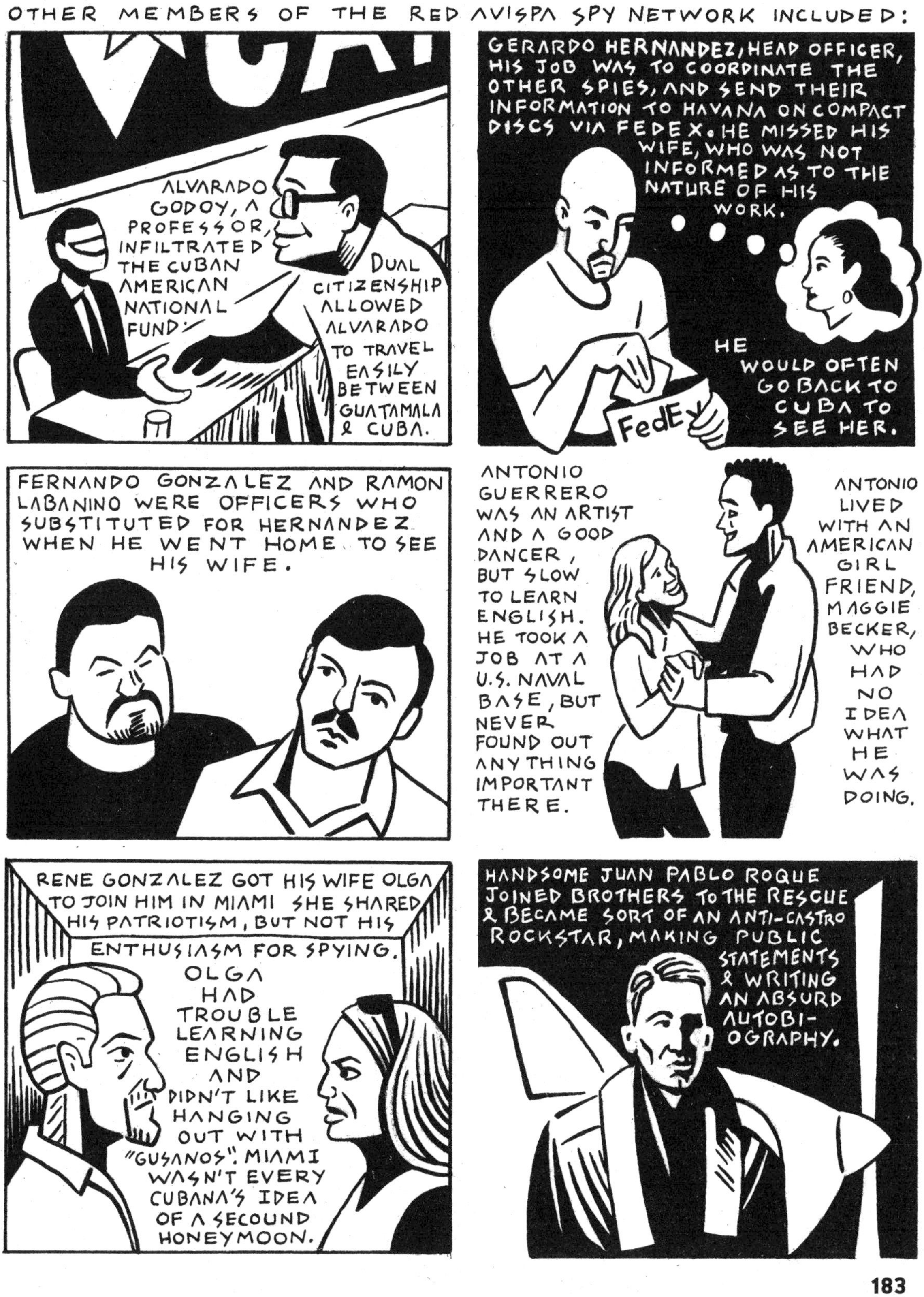
OTHER MEMBERS OF THE RED AVISPA SPY NETWORK INCLUDED:
ALVARADO GODOY, A PROFESSOR, INFILTRATED THE CUBAN AMERICAN NATIONAL FUND.
DUAL CITIZENSHIP ALLOWED ALVARADO TO TRAVEL EASILY BETWEEN GUATAMALA & CUBA.
GERARDO HERNANDEZ, HEAD OFFICER, HIS JOB WAS TO COORDINATE THE OTHER SPIES, AND SEND THEIR INFORMATION TO HAVANA ON COMPACT DISCS VIA FEDEX. HE MISSED HIS WIFE, WHO WAS NOT INFORMED AS TO THE NATURE OF HIS WORK.
FedE
HE WOULD OFTEN GO BACK TO CUBA TO SEE HER.
FERNANDO GONZALEZ AND RAMON LABANINO WERE OFFICERS WHO SUBSTITUTED FOR HERNANDEZ WHEN HE WENT HOME TO SEE HIS WIFE.
ANTONIO GUERRERO WAS AN ARTIST AND A GOOD DANCER, BUT SLOW TO LEARN ENGLISH. HE TOOK A JOB AT A U.S. NAVAL BASE, BUT NEVER FOUND OUT ANYTHING IMPORTANT THERE.
ANTONIO LIVED WITH AN AMERICAN GIRL FRIEND, MAGGIE BECKER, WHO HAD NO IDEA WHAT HE WAS DOING.
RENE GONZALEZ GOT HIS WIFE OLGA TO JOIN HIM IN MIAMI SHE SHARED HIS PATRIOTISM, BUT NOT HIS ENTHUSIASM FOR SPYING.
OLGA HAD TROUBLE LEARNING ENGLISH AND DIDN'T LIKE HANGING OUT WITH "GUSANOS". MIAMI WASN'T EVERY CUBANA'S IDEA OF A SECOUND HONEYMOON.
HANDSOME JUAN PABLO ROQUE JOINED BROTHERS TO THE RESCUE & BECAME SORT OF AN ANTI-CASTRO ROCKSTAR, MAKING PUBLIC STATEMENTS & WRITING AN ABSURD AUTOBIOGRAPHY.

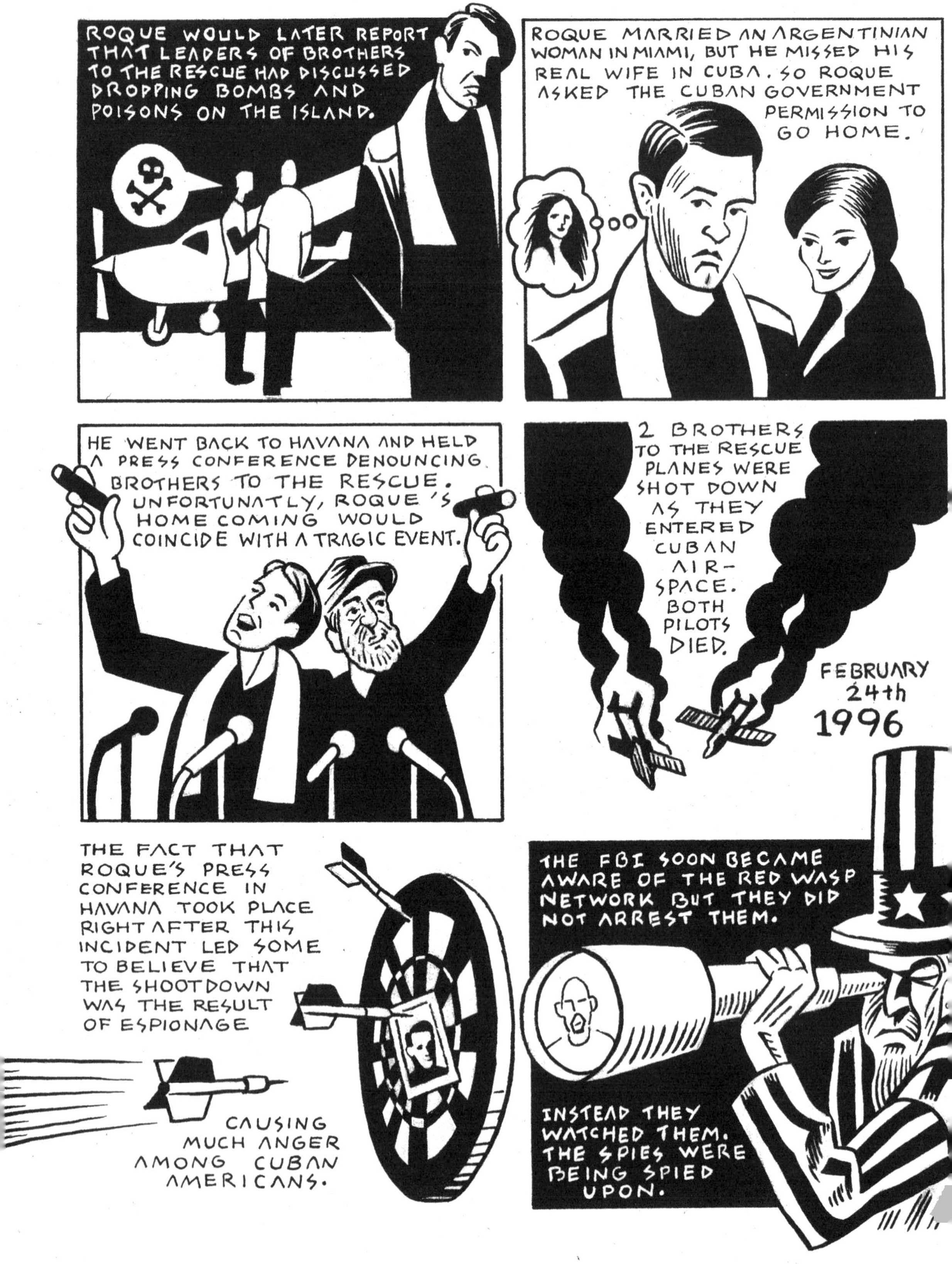
ROQUE WOULD LATER REPORT THAT LEADERS OF BROTHERS TO THE RESCUE HAD DISCUSSED DROPPING BOMBS AND POISONS ON THE ISLAND.
ROQUE MARRIED AN ARGENTINIAN WOMAN IN MIAMI, BUT HE MISSED HIS REAL WIFE IN CUBA. SO ROQUE ASKED THE CUBAN GOVERNMENT PERMISSION TO GO HOME.
HE WENT BACK TO HAVANA AND HELD A PRESS CONFERENCE DENOUNCING BROTHERS TO THE RESCUE. UNFORTUNATLY, ROQUE'S HOME COMING WOULD COINCIDE WITH A TRAGIC EVENT.
2 BROTHERS TO THE RESCUE PLANES WERE SHOT DOWN AS THEY ENTERED CUBAN AIR-SPACE. BOTH PILOTS DIED.
FEBRUARY 24th 1996
THE FACT THAT ROQUE'S PRESS CONFERENCE IN HAVANA TOOK PLACE RIGHT AFTER THIS INCIDENT LED SOME TO BELIEVE THAT THE SHOOTDOWN WAS THE RESULT OF ESPIONAGE
CAUSING MUCH ANGER AMONG CUBAN AMERICANS.
THE FBI SOON BECAME AWARE OF THE RED WASP NETWORK BUT THEY DID NOT ARREST THEM.
INSTEAD THEY WATCHED THEM. THE SPIES WERE BEING SPIED UPON.

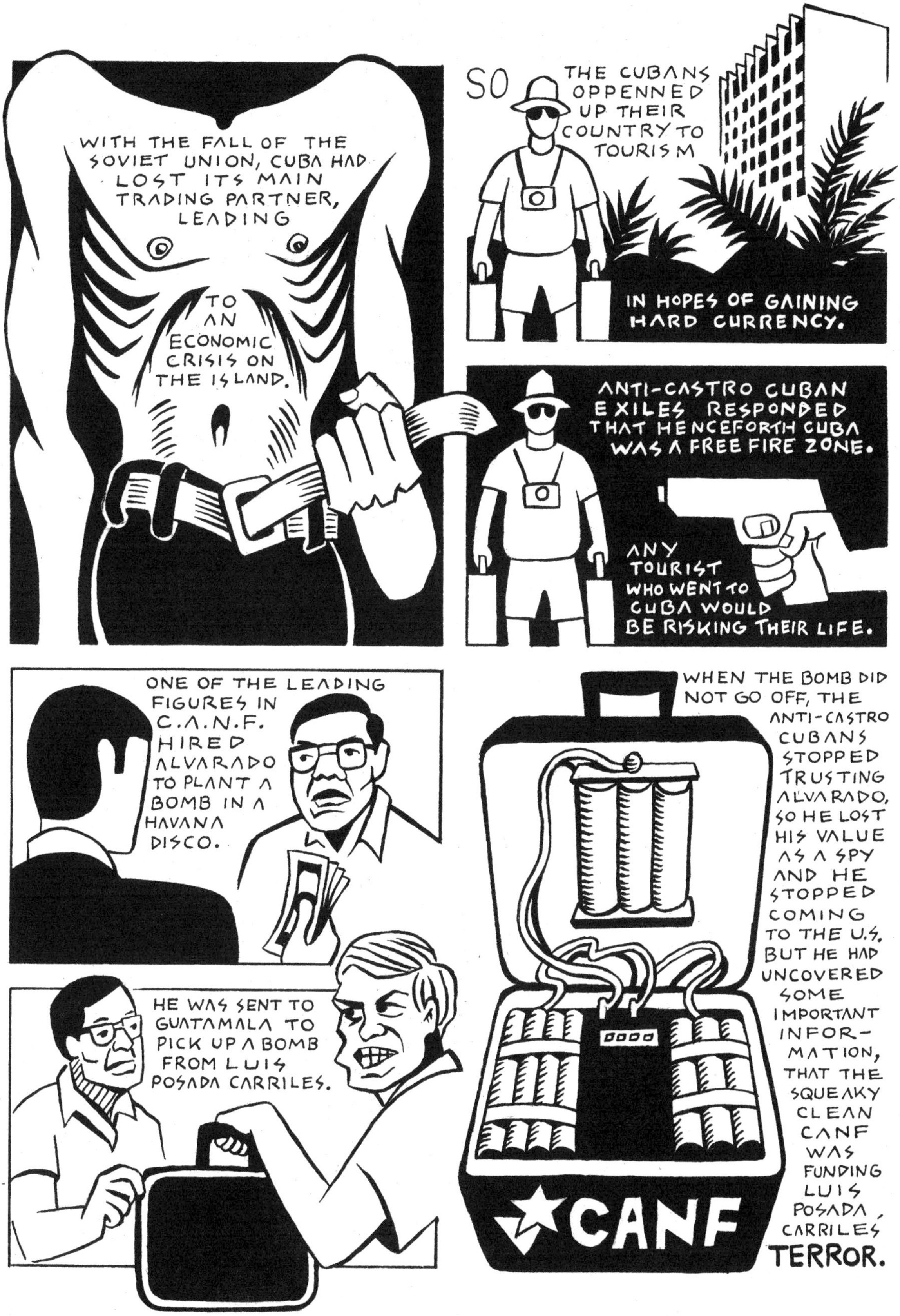
WITH THE FALL OF THE SOVIET UNION, CUBA HAD LOST ITS MAIN TRADING PARTNER, LEADING
TO AN ECONOMIC CRISIS ON THE ISLAND.
SO THE CUBANS OPPENNED UP THEIR COUNTRY TO TOURISM
IN HOPES OF GAINING HARD CURRENCY.
ANTI-CASTRO CUBAN EXILES RESPONDED THAT HENCEFORTH CUBA WAS A FREE FIRE ZONE.
ANY TOURIST WHO WENT TO CUBA WOULD BE RISKING THEIR LIFE.
ONE OF THE LEADING FIGURES IN C.A.N.F. HIRED ALVARADO TO PLANT A BOMB IN A HAVANA DISCO.
HE WAS SENT TO GUATAMALA TO PICK UP A BOMB FROM LUIS POSADA CARRILES.
WHEN THE BOMB DID NOT GO OFF, THE ANTI-CASTRO CUBANS STOPPED TRUSTING ALVARADO, SO HE LOST HIS VALUE AS A SPY AND HE STOPPED COMING TO THE U.S. BUT HE HAD UNCOVERED SOME IMPORTANT INFOR-MATION, THAT THE SQUEAKY CLEAN CANF WAS FUNDING LUIS POSADA CARRILES' TERROR.
CANF

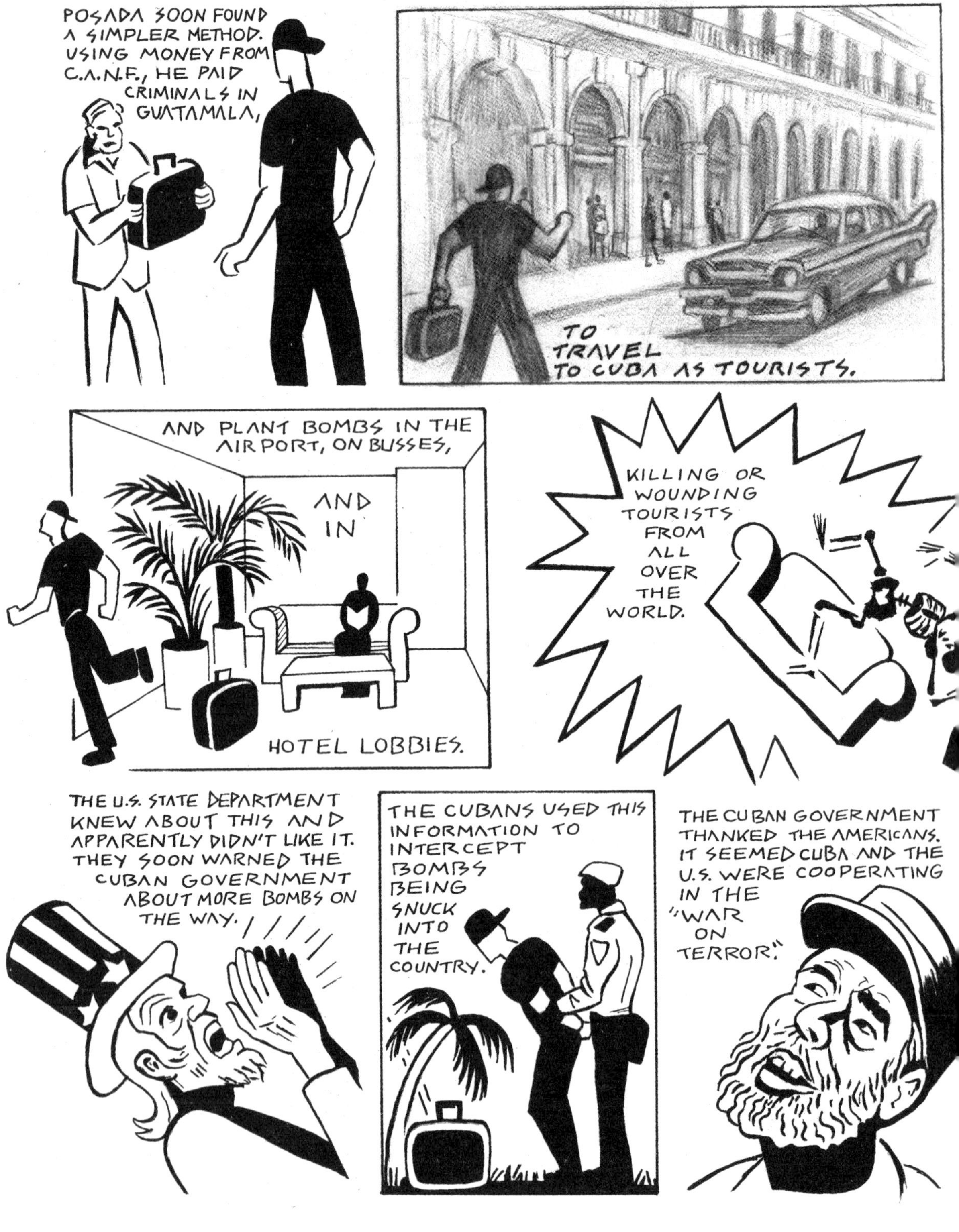
POSADA SOON FOUND A SIMPLER METHOD. USING MONEY FROM C.A.N.F., HE PAID CRIMINALS IN GUATAMALA,
TO TRAVEL TO CUBA AS TOURISTS.
AND PLANT BOMBS IN THE AIRPORT, ON BUSSES,
AND IN
HOTEL LOBBIES.
KILLING OR WOUNDING TOURISTS FROM ALL OVER THE WORLD.
THE U.S. STATE DEPARTMENT KNEW ABOUT THIS AND APPARENTLY DIDN'T LIKE IT. THEY SOON WARNED THE CUBAN GOVERNMENT ABOUT MORE BOMBS ON THE WAY.
THE CUBANS USED THIS INFORMATION TO INTERCEPT BOMBS BEING SNUCK INTO THE COUNTRY.
THE CUBAN GOVERNMENT THANKED THE AMERICANS. IT SEEMED CUBA AND THE U.S. WERE COOPERATING IN THE "WAR ON TERROR."

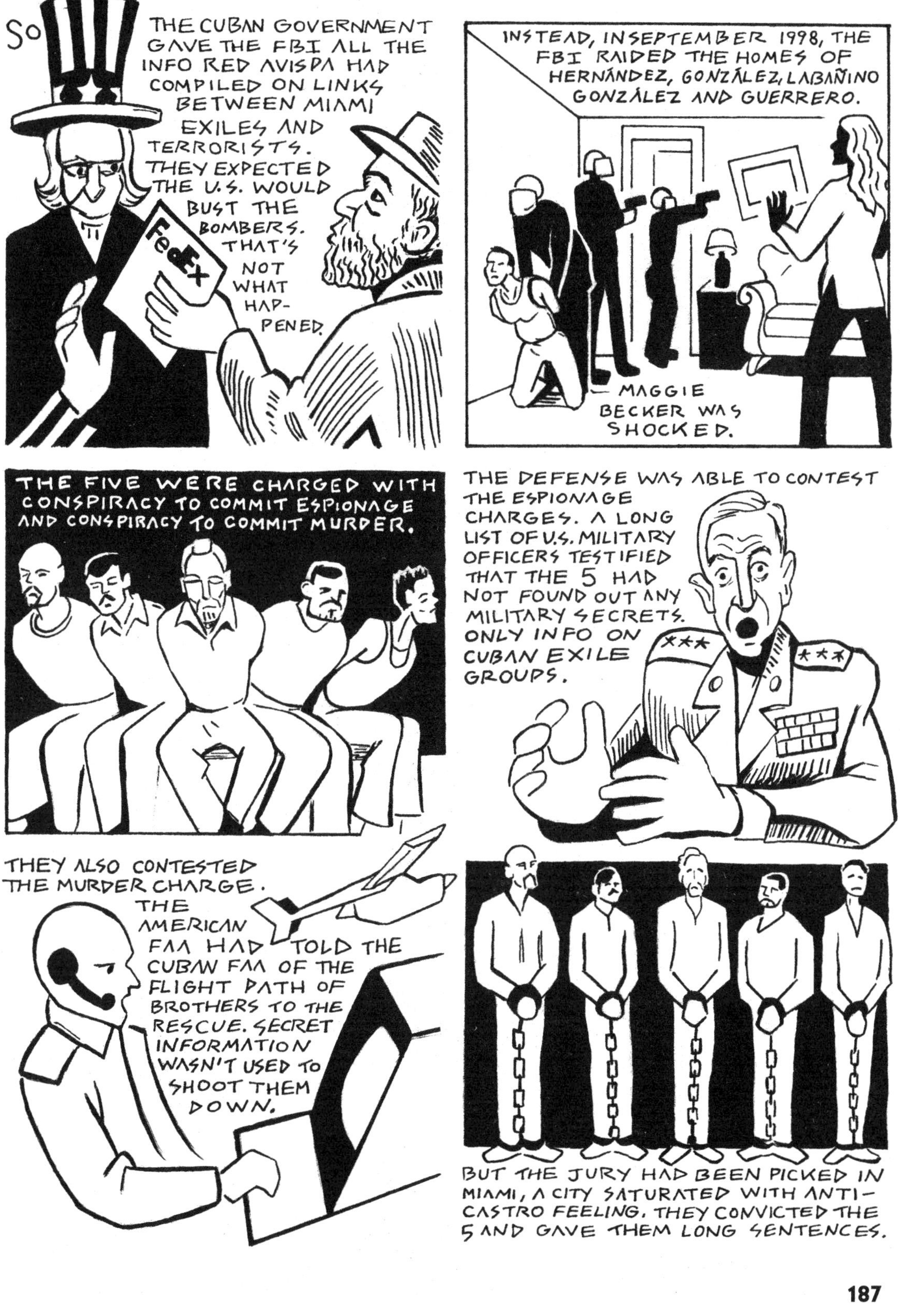
SO THE CUBAN GOVERNMENT GAVE THE FBI ALL THE INFO RED AVISPA HAD COMPILED ON LINKS BETWEEN MIAMI EXILES AND TERRORISTS. THEY EXPECTED THE U.S. WOULD BUST THE BOMBERS. THAT'S NOT WHAT HAPPENED.
FedEx
INSTEAD, IN SEPTEMBER 1998, THE FBI RAIDED THE HOMES OF HERNÁNDEZ, GONZÁLEZ, LABAÑINO GONZÁLEZ AND GUERRERO.
MAGGIE BECKER WAS SHOCKED.
THE FIVE WERE CHARGED WITH CONSPIRACY TO COMMIT ESPIONAGE AND CONSPIRACY TO COMMIT MURDER.
THE DEFENSE WAS ABLE TO CONTEST THE ESPIONAGE CHARGES. A LONG LIST OF U.S. MILITARY OFFICERS TESTIFIED THAT THE 5 HAD NOT FOUND OUT ANY MILITARY SECRETS. ONLY INFO ON CUBAN EXILE GROUPS.
THEY ALSO CONTESTED THE MURDER CHARGE. THE AMERICAN FAA HAD TOLD THE CUBAN FAA OF THE FLIGHT PATH OF BROTHERS TO THE RESCUE. SECRET INFORMATION WASN'T USED TO SHOOT THEM DOWN.
BUT THE JURY HAD BEEN PICKED IN MIAMI, A CITY SATURATED WITH ANTI-CASTRO FEELING. THEY CONVICTED THE 5 AND GAVE THEM LONG SENTENCES.

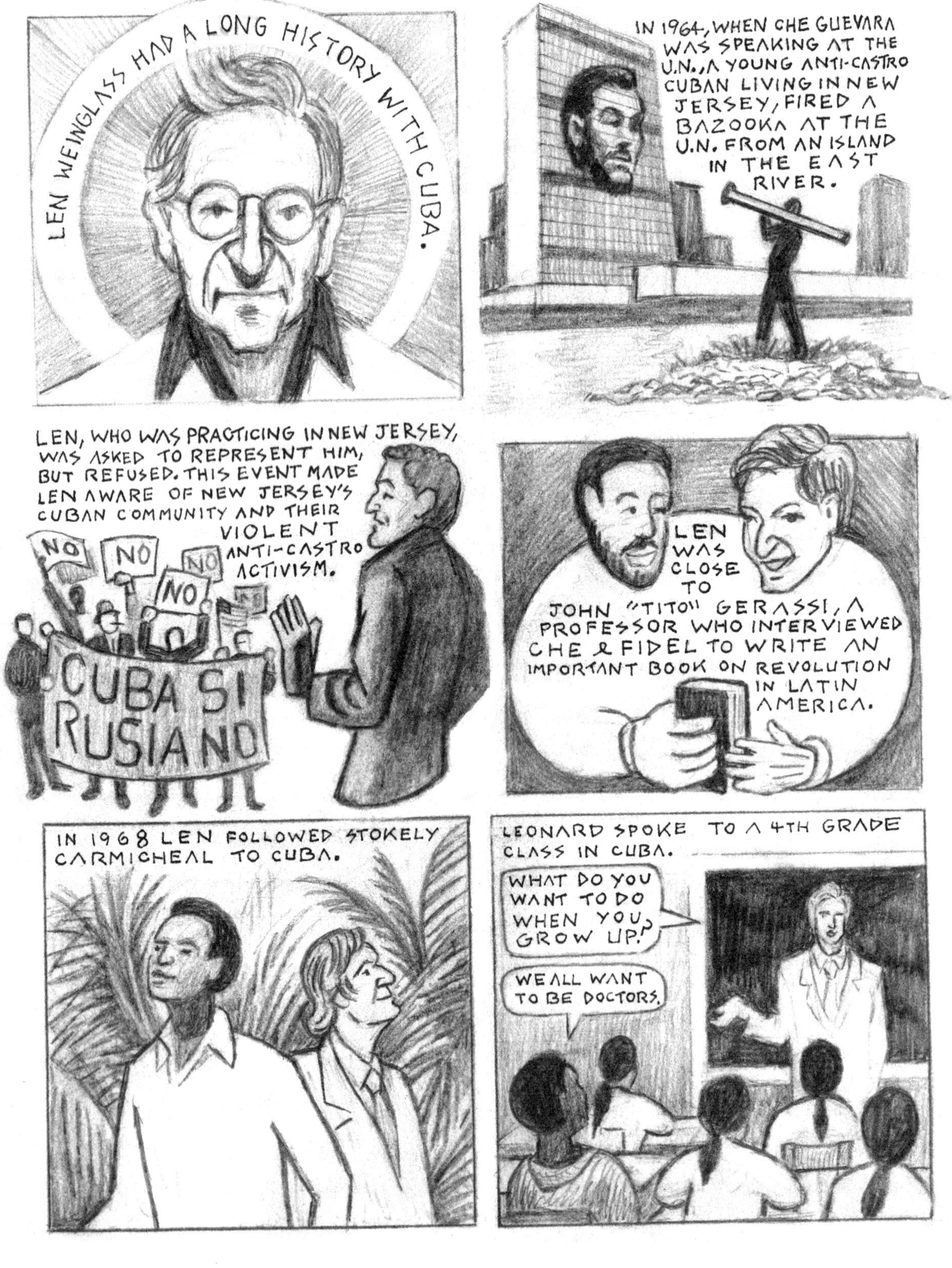
LEN WEINGLASS HAD A LONG HISTORY WITH CUBA.
IN 1964, WHEN CHE GUEVARA WAS SPEAKING AT THE U.N., A YOUNG ANTI-CASTRO CUBAN LIVING IN NEW JERSEY, FIRED A BAZOOKA AT THE U.N. FROM AN ISLAND IN THE EAST RIVER.
LEN, WHO WAS PRACTICING IN NEW JERSEY, WAS ASKED TO REPRESENT HIM, BUT REFUSED. THIS EVENT MADE LEN AWARE OF NEW JERSEY'S CUBAN COMMUNITY AND THEIR VIOLENT ANTI-CASTRO ACTIVISM.
NO
NO
NO
NO
CUBA SI RUSIA NO
LEN WAS CLOSE TO JOHN "TITO" GERASSI, A PROFESSOR WHO INTERVIEWED CHE & FIDEL TO WRITE AN IMPORTANT BOOK ON REVOLUTION IN LATIN AMERICA.
IN 1968 LEN FOLLOWED STOKELY CARMICHEAL TO CUBA.
LEONARD SPOKE TO A 4TH GRADE CLASS IN CUBA.
WHAT DO YOU WANT TO DO WHEN YOU GROW UP?
WE ALL WANT TO BE DOCTORS.

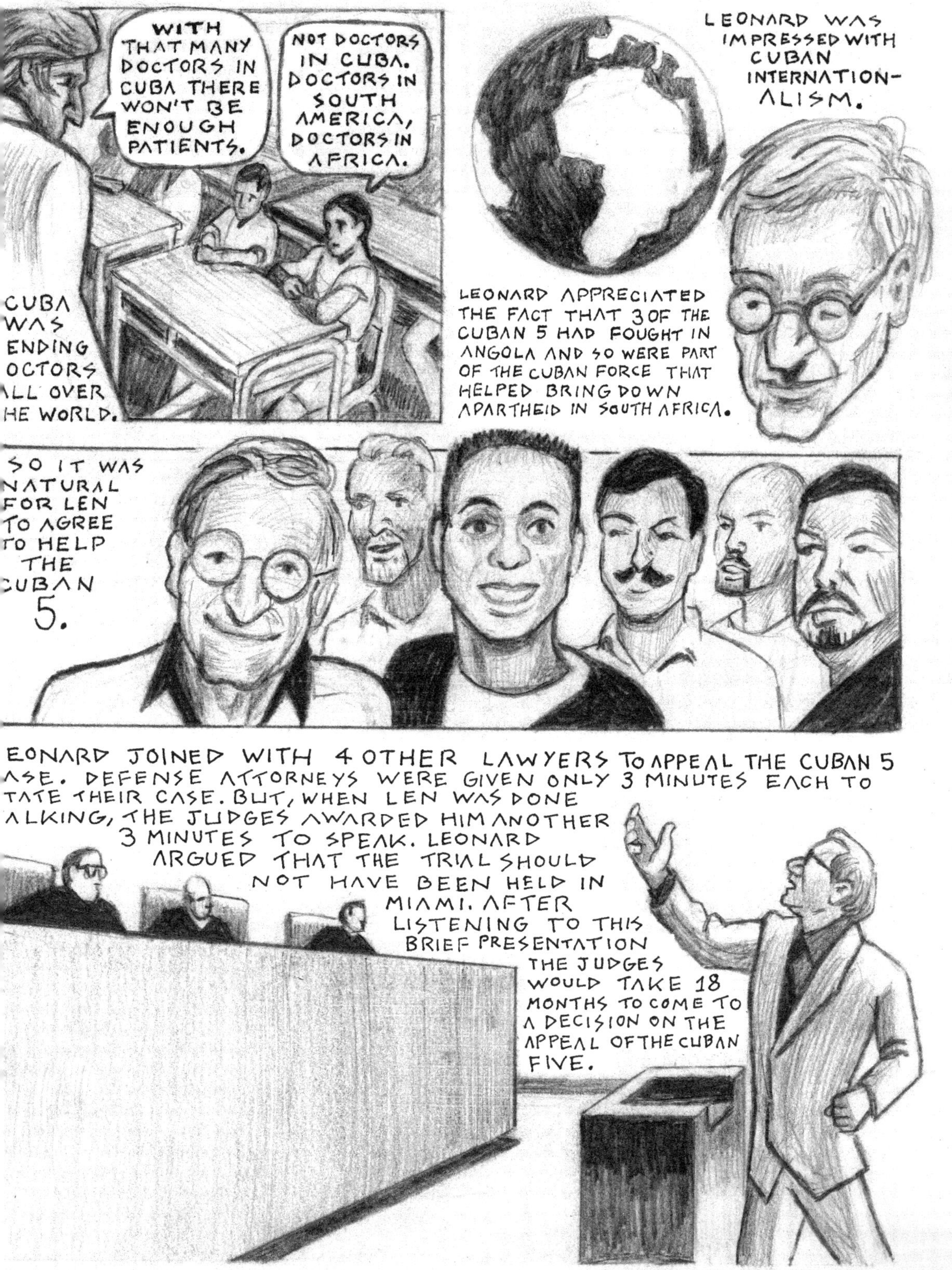
WITH THAT MANY DOCTORS IN CUBA THERE WON'T BE ENOUGH PATIENTS.
NOT DOCTORS IN CUBA. DOCTORS IN SOUTH AMERICA, DOCTORS IN AFRICA.
CUBA WAS ENDING OCTORS LL OVER HE WORLD.
LEONARD WAS IMPRESSED WITH CUBAN INTERNATION-ALISM.
LEONARD APPRECIATED THE FACT THAT 3 OF THE CUBAN 5 HAD FOUGHT IN ANGOLA AND SO WERE PART OF THE CUBAN FORCE THAT HELPED BRING DOWN APARTHEID IN SOUTH AFRICA.
SO IT WAS NATURAL FOR LEN TO AGREE TO HELP THE UBAN 5.
EONARD JOINED WITH 4 OTHER LAWYERS TO APPEAL THE CUBAN 5 ASE. DEFENSE ATTORNEYS WERE GIVEN ONLY 3 MINUTES EACH TO TATE THEIR CASE. BUT, WHEN LEN WAS DONE ALKING, THE JUDGES AWARDED HIM ANOTHER 3 MINUTES TO SPEAK. LEONARD ARGUED THAT THE TRIAL SHOULD NOT HAVE BEEN HELD IN MIAMI. AFTER LISTENING TO THIS BRIEF PRESENTATION THE JUDGES WOULD TAKE 18 MONTHS TO COME TO A DECISION ON THE APPEAL OF THE CUBAN FIVE.

THE JUDGES REVERSED ALL OF THE CHARGES AND RULED THAT THE CUBAN 5 SHOULD EITHER BE FREED OR RETRIED.

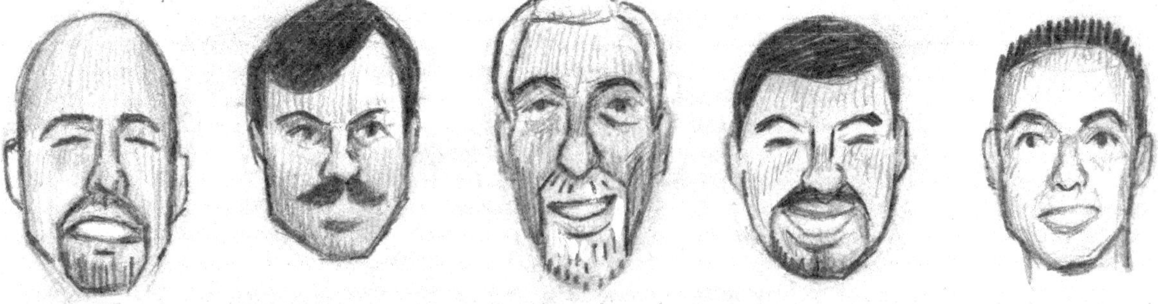

BUT PRESIDENT GEORGE W. BUSH'S ATTORNEY GENERAL, ALBERTO GONZALEZ, INTERVENED AND APPEALED THE DECISION TO THE FULL COURT OF APPEALS, A MORE BIASED BODY. THIS COURT REINSTATED ALL OF THE CONVICTIONS, ALTHOUGH THEY SHORTENED SOME OF THE SENTENCES.

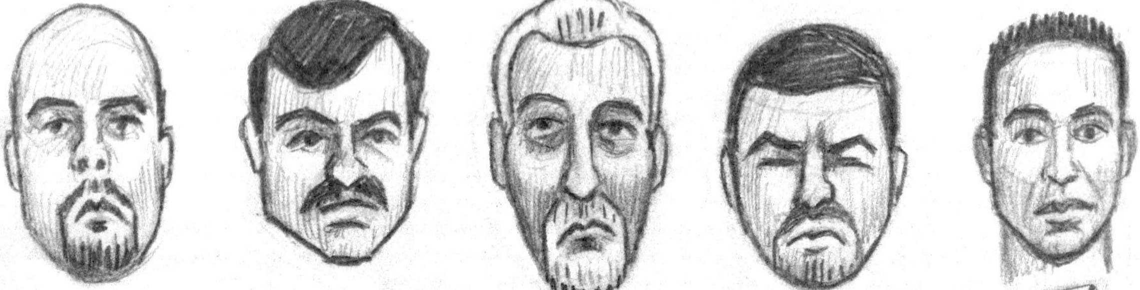

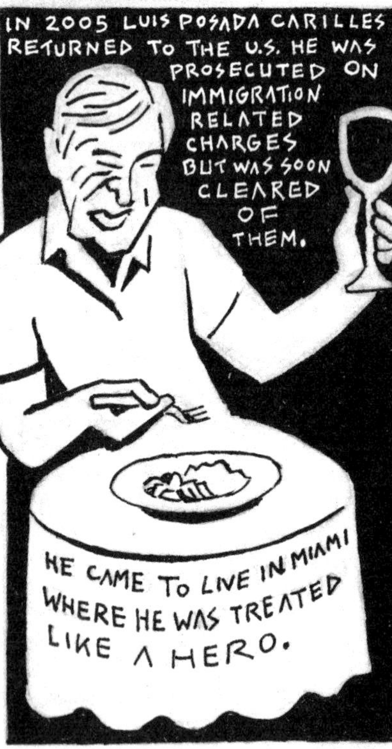
IN 2005 LUIS POSADA CARILLES RETURNED TO THE U.S. HE WAS PROSECUTED ON IMMIGRATION RELATED CHARGES BUT WAS SOON CLEARED OF THEM.
HE CAME TO LIVE IN MIAMI WHERE HE WAS TREATED LIKE A HERO.

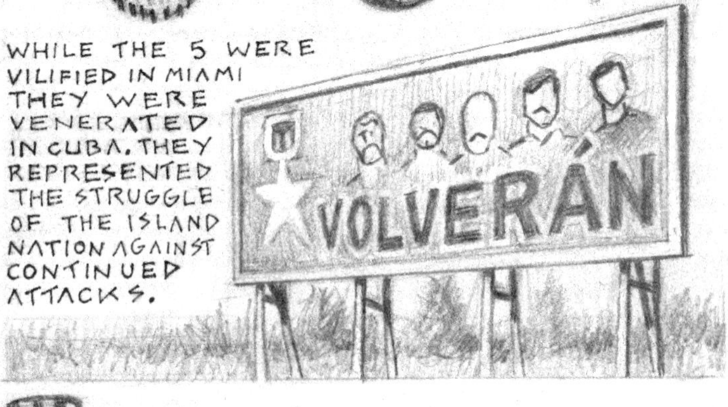
WHILE THE 5 WERE VILIFIED IN MIAMI THEY WERE VENERATED IN CUBA. THEY REPRESENTED THE STRUGGLE OF THE ISLAND NATION AGAINST CONTINUED ATTACKS.
VOLVERÁN

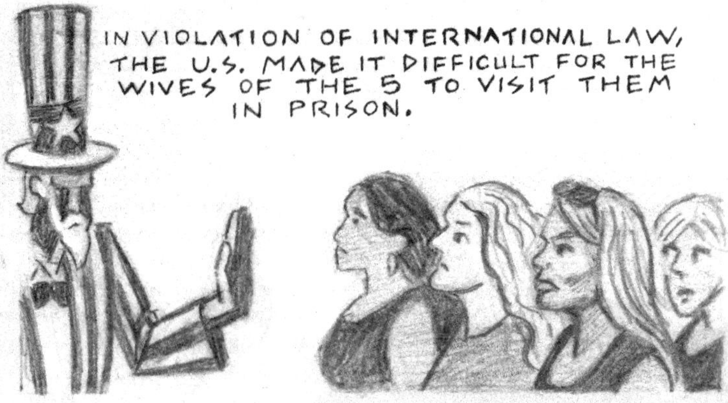
IN VIOLATION OF INTERNATIONAL LAW, THE U.S. MADE IT DIFFICULT FOR THE WIVES OF THE 5 TO VISIT THEM IN PRISON.

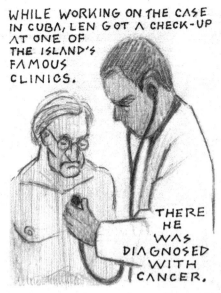

WHILE WORKING ON THE CASE IN CUBA, LEN GOT A CHECK-UP AT ONE OF THE ISLAND'S FAMOUS CLINICS.

THERE HE WAS DIAGNOSED WITH CANCER.

HE WAS SOON HOSPITALIZED IN THE BRONX. HE CONTINUED TO WORK, PROOFREADING BRIEFS FOR THE CUBAN FIVE CASE FROM HIS HOSPITAL BED.

MANY FRIENDS AND RELATIVES CAME TO SEE HIM, BUT LEONARD REMAINED RECLUSIVE, DECLINING TO SEE MOST OF THEM.

MUMIA ABU JAMAL SENT A GET-WELL VIDEO MESSAGE FROM PRISON.

TOM HAYDEN VISITED WHEN LEN WAS BRIEFLY IN A REHAB FACILITY IN GREENWICH VILLAGE.

191

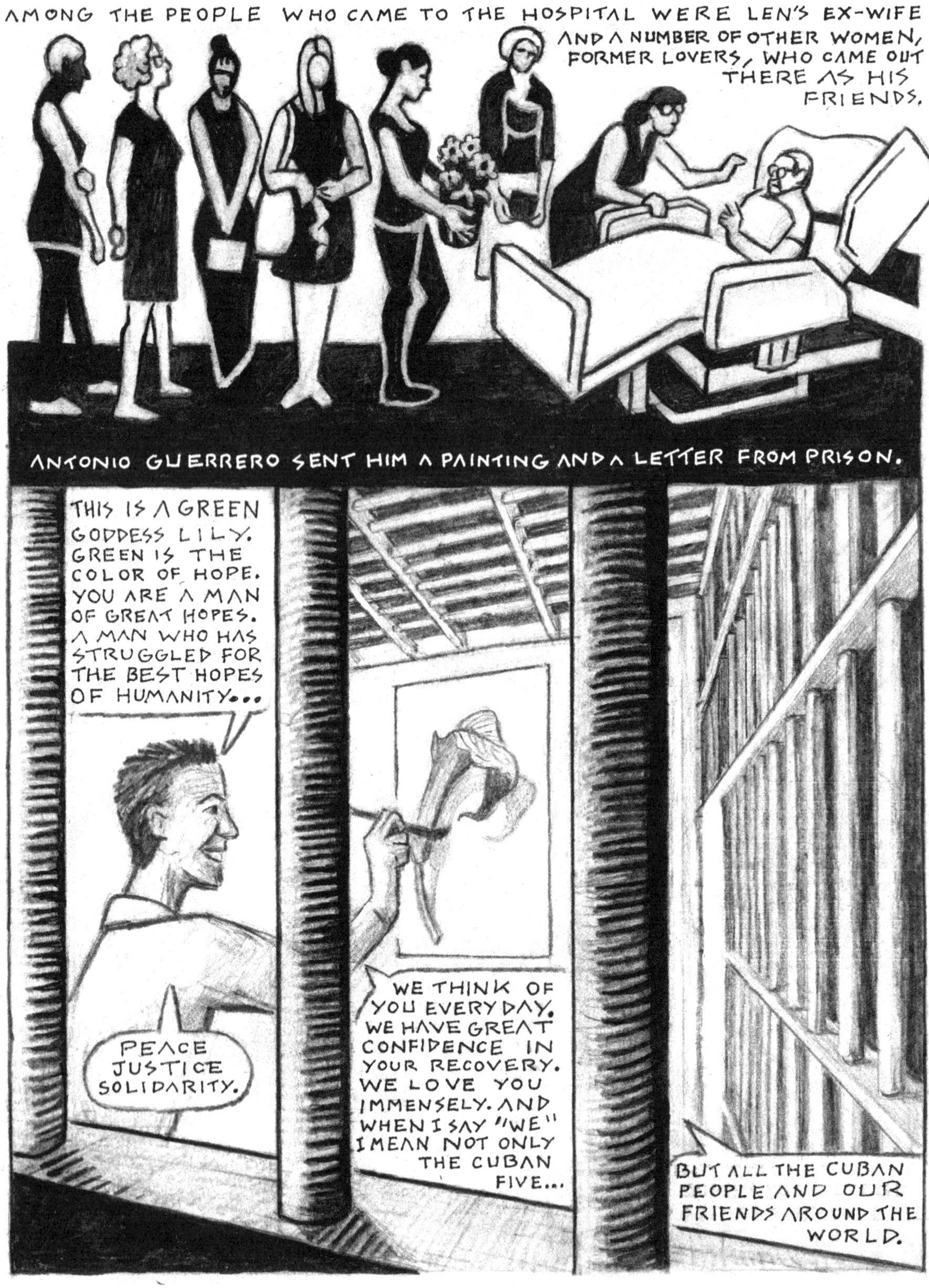
AMONG THE PEOPLE WHO CAME TO THE HOSPITAL WERE LEN'S EX-WIFE AND A NUMBER OF OTHER WOMEN, FORMER LOVERS, WHO CAME OUT THERE AS HIS FRIENDS.
ANTONIO GUERRERO SENT HIM A PAINTING AND A LETTER FROM PRISON.
THIS IS A GREEN GODDESS LILY. GREEN IS THE COLOR OF HOPE. YOU ARE A MAN OF GREAT HOPES. A MAN WHO HAS STRUGGLED FOR THE BEST HOPES OF HUMANITY...
PEACE JUSTICE SOLIDARITY.
WE THINK OF YOU EVERY DAY. WE HAVE GREAT CONFIDENCE IN YOUR RECOVERY. WE LOVE YOU IMMENSELY. AND WHEN I SAY "WE" I MEAN NOT ONLY THE CUBAN FIVE...
BUT ALL THE CUBAN PEOPLE AND OUR FRIENDS AROUND THE WORLD.

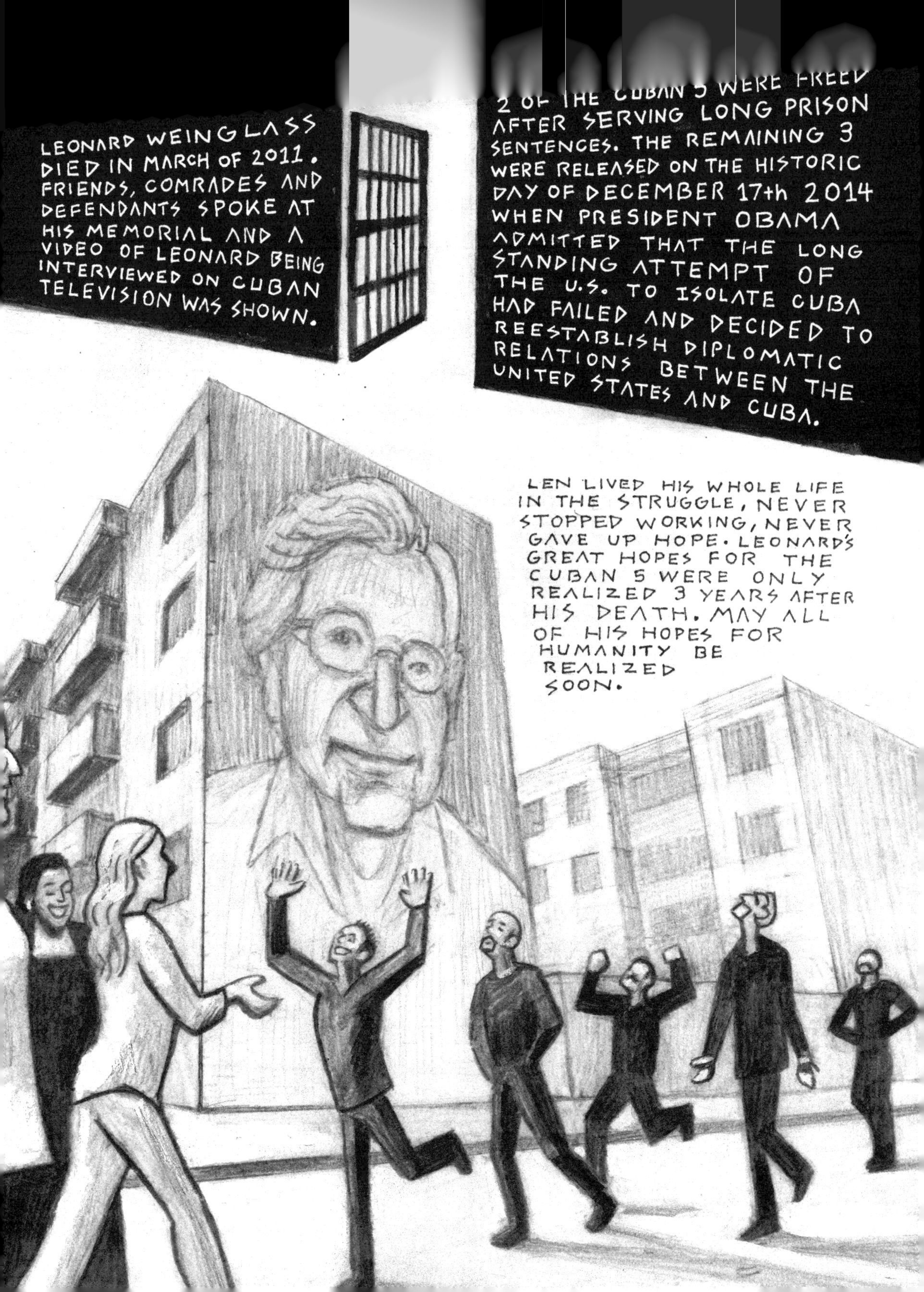

LEONARD WEINGLASS DIED IN MARCH OF 2011. FRIENDS, COMRADES AND DEFENDANTS SPOKE AT HIS MEMORIAL AND A VIDEO OF LEONARD BEING INTERVIEWED ON CUBAN TELEVISION WAS SHOWN.
2 OF THE CUBAN 5 WERE FREED AFTER SERVING LONG PRISON SENTENCES. THE REMAINING 3 WERE RELEASED ON THE HISTORIC DAY OF DECEMBER 17th 2014 WHEN PRESIDENT OBAMA ADMITTED THAT THE LONG STANDING ATTEMPT OF THE U.S. TO ISOLATE CUBA HAD FAILED AND DECIDED TO REESTABLISH DIPLOMATIC RELATIONS BETWEEN THE UNITED STATES AND CUBA.
LEN LIVED HIS WHOLE LIFE IN THE STRUGGLE, NEVER STOPPED WORKING, NEVER GAVE UP HOPE. LEONARD'S GREAT HOPES FOR THE CUBAN 5 WERE ONLY REALIZED 3 YEARS AFTER HIS DEATH. MAY ALL OF HIS HOPES FOR HUMANITY BE REALIZED SOON.

Artist's notes

I was recruited by Paul Buhle and Michael Steven Smith to produce this graphic biography of Leonard Weinglass in 2011. I did not expect it to take me five years. It turned out to be quite a bit of work to recreate the life of a man I had never met, in times I was too young to have participated in. My own experience of activism, in different places and times, guided my decisions, but could not replace the research.

Thanks to the following art models: Louisa Ashleigh, Kevin Glabeau, Britt McMurray, Tyrone Browne-Osbourne, Edwin Vasquez, Junior Lewing Koo, David Modello, Carla Cubit, Johnny McMahon, Mark Blinstrub, and Anthony Yeung.

Proofreading by: Debbie Smith and Charles Weigl.

CHAPTER 1. LEN:

This chapter is based in part on the booklet written for Leonard's memorial by Mike Smith. Mike also arranged for me to have a day interviewing Leonard's family out in New Jersey (including Len's sisters: Natalie Franzblau and Elaine Nicastro, Len's cousin: Irving Berkowitz (deceased), and others). They provided snapshots of Len at many different ages. Particularly useful were the letters he sent home from college and from the military. All of this I squared with what every conscious Jewish person knows about the American Jewish experience during the Great Depression and World War II.

CHAPTER 2. WITNESS TO NEWARK

Newark in 1967, Ferguson, and Baltimore today.

It was very helpful that Carol Glassman was kind enough to sit for an interview about her SDS days in Newark. I also spoke to Frank Askin, an ACLU lawyer who Leonard worked with on the Plainfield case.

Every American should read Tom Hayden's book *Rebellion In Newark*. It is still shocking and relevant today and it provided much of the basis for this chapter. There was also an article by Hayden for the *New York Review of Books* of that year and a chapter in his memoir, *Reunion*, that came in handy. The documentary film *Rebellion '67* was useful as was Junius Williams's important book *Unfinished Agenda: Urban Politics In The Era Of Black Power*.

The paintings of Jacob Lawrence, depicting the great migration of Blacks from the rural south to the urban north, provided profound inspiration.

CHAPTER 3. PROTEST WITHOUT PERMISSION

I doubt it would be possible for a person to watch every movie and read every book about the events that took place in Chicago during the Summer of 1968. It is virtually a genre unto itself. So much has been produced. The difficulty is in cutting through all the magnificent subjectivity of these accounts to find some truth relevant to our times.

I started with *Voices of The Chicago Eight* by Tom Hayden, Ron Sossi, and Frank Condon, and sections of Hayden's *Reunion*. Abbie Hoffman's *Revolution For The Hell Of It* and *Soon To Be A Major Motion Picture*, two books describing the same events, but written many years apart, present almost contrary views. I soon found I needed something more objective to work from.

The Tales Of Hoffman, by Levine, McNamee, and Greenberg, is based on the trial transcript. But it is highly edited. It has great courtroom drawings by Verna Sadock.

A more complete transcript is published in *The Conspiracy Trial*, by Clavir and Spitzer. This was really useful. I followed up on that by reading *Conspiracy On Appeal*, edited by Kinoy, Schwartz & Peterson. This is Leonard's appeal, which, in the end, won the day for the defendants.

I got a lot from looking at an Agitation and Propaganda Newsreel documentary that appeared to have been produced by SDS members at the time and is available on YouTube. There are actually all sorts of bits and pieces of video on Youtube by unnamed photographers, some of them quite powerful. I put off looking at the *Chicago Ten* feature film as long as I could and found it had a lot of the same footage. I owe a huge debt to the many courtroom illustrators assigned to the story.

Coming of age in the 1970s we were always told that there was some special thing that happened in "the sixties" that could never happen again. But I find the circumstances of this story to be very familiar. The contested public space, the medieval combat between police and protesters, the arcane negotiations over permits, the ambiguous role of the music industry, the undercover cops, the fragile coalitions, the lead-lined glove, the "temporary autonomous zone," even the slogan "It's our fucking park!" All things we've seen in Tompkins Square, in the anti-globalization movement, or in Occupy. The same questions come up again and again.

I had a great time drawing this chapter. I listened to the MC5 as I worked and decided they were as good as The Clash.

CHAPTER 4. TRUTH OR TREASON

We are very fortunate that in Daniel Ellsberg we have not only a brave and intelligent man but an excellent writer. His memoir, *Secrets*, gave me more information than I could use about his case. This was supplemented by the film *The Most Dangerous Man In America* and a telephone interview with Mr. Ellsberg. I found Dan to be one of the nicest people I spoke to on this project. After all he'd endured he was gracious and serene. I could tell he was happy with the decisions he had made in life.

Much of this chapter was drawn at TAJ residency in Bangalore, India.

CHAPTER 5. THEIR SECOND CHANCE

Julie Rubin put me in touch with Karen Rudolf Simmons. Of all the people who mourned Leonard's passing, Karen Rudolf is the only one I know of who did extensive and personal video interviews with him while he was alive.

Karen produced a documentary about her husband's case called *Making The River*. But most of Len's interview wound up on the cutting room floor. I was fortunate to be able to view these outtakes where Len expressed his deep feelings about the defense of Jimi Simmons. I did a phone interview with Karen that took up the better part of a day. (Melissa Jamesson transcribed the audio recording into text.) Karen loves to tell this story. And why shouldn't she? It is a Disney fairy tale for those of us too world weary to believe in Disney fairy tales. Karen has been a constant support to me in persevering with this project. Karen, you are the heart and soul of this book.

CHAPTER 6. PUTTING THE CIA ON TRIAL

Len Weinglass said this was his favorite case. But unlike some of the earlier chapters, very little has been written about it. I don't know of a single book on it. In the '80s it seemed America was determined to ignore the left. In frustration I put out a request on Facebook for anyone involved with the trial. I was contacted by Doug Calvin who did an interview and put me in touch with Steve O'Halloran. Steve ought to be the mayor of Amherst. Everyone there seems to know him. He took me around the campus, showed me where things had happened, brought me to an archive where documentation of the case and of the local Nicaragua Solidarity movement was on file. And finally turned over a complete transcript of the trial! Solid gold! I also got great interviews with Deborah Cohen, Betsy O'Connor Tomlinson, and Thomas Lesser. Much credit goes to the people of Amherst, a progressive community where they seem to be rather proud of having run the CIA out of town.

CHAPTER 7. THE PATRIOT ACT

This is based on the transcript of a lecture Leonard gave at the Left Forum in 2002, made available to me by Michael Steven Smith. Civil liberties activist Sarah Hogarth went over the text and confirmed that it is all, unfortunately, still relevant today.

CHAPTER 8. A MAN OF GREAT HOPES

I have never had strong feelings about Cuban politics although I do appreciate what they have done for Assatta Shakur. But Leonard clearly loved the Cuban Revolution from the bottom of his heart and this piece is written in that spirit. I found *What Lies Across The Water* by Stephen Kimber to be the best source of information but also had access to video and print documentation of various public presentations Leonard Weingless made about the case. Michael Steven Smith, Kathy Boudin, and Frances Goldin all provided anecdotes about Len's days in the hospital.

WHY THERE IS NOT A CHAPTER ON THE CASE OF MUMIA ABU-JAMAL IN THIS BOOK

It's a fair question.

When I told my longtime political comrade Howard Branstein that I was working on a graphic biography of Leonard Weinglass, the first words out of his mouth were "Good! We'll finally clear this up!" What he hoped I would "clear up" were the many unanswered questions as to why Mumia Abu Jamal, a great writer falsely convicted of murder, had fired his attorney, Leonard Weinglass, in 2001.

And I could see why Howard thought I was just the guy to do this. I have done three comic strips about Mumia's case. The first, a fifteen page black and white piece published in *World War 3 Illustrated* in 1993, the second a two-page color comic originally intended for *High Times* in 1999, the third a short piece about Mumia's current health situation published a number of places this year. I have also published Mumia's own art and writing regularly in *World War 3 Illustrated*.

I would love to "clear this up." The disagreement between these two giants of the American left has split the movement the way a bad divorce divides a family. Who wouldn't want to fix this?

But here's the rub:

Every piece I have done about Mumia has been shown to him before publication. I have always involved him in the process of producing these comic strips. If you saw it, he saw it first. I wanted to be sure that he was ok with what I was putting out about his case. I do this because of his uniquely vulnerable situation. For most of the last thirty years he was on death row. Today he is in general population but faces serious health problems.

Although I communicate with Mumia about other projects, he has declined to tell me about his relationship with Weinglass, and even let me know that he is not interested in looking at anything I produce on the subject. I simply wouldn't feel right about doing a piece about Mumia behind his back. So, at least for now, these questions go unanswered.

Maybe someday, when Mumia is sitting in a cafe in Paris or Berlin, enjoying the royalties from his many great books, we can add another chapter to this biography. May that day come soon.

See more of Seth's work and projects at:

sethtobocman.com

Also available from AK Press:

YOU DON'T HAVE TO
FUCK PEOPLE OVER
TO SURVIVE
BY SETH TOBOCMAN

DISASTER
AND RESISTANCE
COMICS & LANDSCAPES FOR THE TWENTY FIRST CENTURY
BY SETH TOBOCMAN

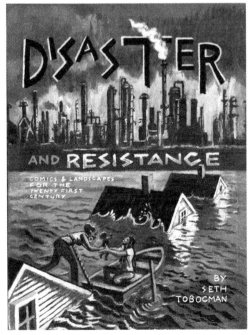

FROM PAUL BUHLE:

Marxism in the United States: A History of the American Left (Verso, third edition, 2014).

Radical Hollywwod: The Untold Story Behind America's Favorite Movies, by Paul Buhle and Dave Wagner (The New Press, 2002).

FROM MICHAEL STEVEN SMITH:

Imagine: Living in a Socialist USA, edited by Frances Goldin, Debby Smith, and Michael Steven Smith (Harper Perennial, 2014).

Who Killed Che? How the CIA Got Away With Murder, by Michael Ratner and Michael Steven Smith (O/R Books 2011).

AK Press is small, in terms of staff and resources, but we also manage to be one of the world's most productive anarchist publishing houses. We publish close to twenty books every year, and distribute thousands of other titles published by like-minded independent presses and projects from around the globe. We're entirely worker-run and democratically managed. We operate without a corporate structure—no boss, no managers, no bullshit.

The Friends of AK program is a way you can directly contribute to the continued existence of AK Press, and ensure that we're able to keep publishing books like this one! Friends pay $25 a month directly into our publishing account ($30 for Canada, $35 for international), and receive a copy of every book AK Press publishes for the duration of their membership! Friends also receive a discount on anything they order from our website or buy at a table: 50% on AK titles, and 20% on everything else. We have a Friends of AK ebook program as well: $15 a month gets you an electronic copy of every book we publish for the duration of your membership. You can even sponsor a very discounted membership for someone in prison.

Email friendsofak@akpress.org for more info, or visit the Friends of AK Press website: https://www.akpress.org/friends.html

There are always great book projects in the works—so sign up now to become a Friend of AK Press, and let the presses roll!